THIS IS A CARLTON BOOK

This edition published by Carlton Books Limited 2002

A CIP Catalogue record for this book is available from the British Library

ISBN 1 84222 835 8

PROJECT EDITOR: Tim Dedopulos
SENIOR ART EDITOR: Zoë Maggs
DESIGNER: Simon Mercer
PICTURE RESEARCH: Lorna Ainger, Richard Philpott
ADDITIONAL PICTURE RESEARCH: Catherine Costelloe
PRODUCTION: Marianna Wolf

Printed and Bound in China

20th
cars

THE COMPLETE GUIDE TO THE
CENTURY'S CLASSIC AUTOMOBILES

HILTON HOLLOWAY
& MARTIN BUCKLEY

CARLTON

Contents

Introduction

This book contains, by our reckoning, nearly 400 of the most significant cars of all time, but that doesn't mean the pages are packed with the fastest, most expensive and most outrageously-styled cars of all time. To be included on a list of the truly significant, a car needs to have been a real benchmark in motoring history. Most of those included have been admirable machines, but to put the history of the car industry in perspective we've also included cars that for various reasons failed to achieve their aims, sometimes by a massive margin.

A significant and successful car might, for example, have redefined the exploitation of interior space, stretched the performance envelope, been a landmark in the use of new materials and production processes or been the first with new under-the-skin technologies that would later filter down to everyday transport. It may have for ever changed the way the public looked at the possibilities that the car offered.

The Citroën DS – a truly innovative, visionary vehicle that was way ahead of its time.

This A-Z format has allowed a thorough view of the progress of the automobile across all the many manufacturers that have designed, developed and launched their own new models, from famous Italian tuners Abarth, through to Zil, which built limos for the Soviet communist bosses. Detailed data is included for each car – even if sometimes years of launch, production, sale and availability clash confusingly.

Cars have never simply been consumer durables. They're a huge part of everyone's everyday lives, often used for political ends and usually reflecting the culture and climate of the nation that created them. Perhaps only a nation of enthusiasts such as Italy could have created the incredible Alfa Romeo Alfasud, which is still a benchmark for responsive handling, clever use of interior space and crisp styling. But perhaps only in Italy would the Alfasud have been subject to an overwhelming political will that controlled where it was built and even the source of the raw steel used to make it.

In a similar vein, the Austin Mini Metro wasn't a ground-breaking design by any means, but it was the last desperate government-funded throw of the once-mighty British motor industry, laid low in a single decade by management incompetence and industrial unrest. The Metro went a long way to propping up the UK industry and thus qualifies as significant in the history of the car.

Renault discarded its family-only image for once and for all with the blistering Sport Spider.

Despite the development of international brands and products like Pepsi and Nike, the motor industry has never managed to successfully sell the same product around the world in the various different markets. The 'world car' is still a theory being pursued by the likes of Ford and General Motors – when it comes to the car, the different continents all have very different tastes.

This perhaps is why American cars have often failed to make a big impact outside of their home territory. The North American market is so big it's practically self-supporting, so maybe it's no surprise that the home-grown products were often out of step with the rest of the world.

Take the magnificent Buicks, Cadillacs and Chevrolets of the 1950s, a golden decade for the American industry which delivered more technology and even more extravagant styling with each new model year. Of course, these chrome-laden giants would have been highly impractical for European motorists in a continent still recovering from a war and struggling to overcome petrol rationing.

Moreover, it was the vast American roadscape that encouraged the generous dimensions, and inexpensive fuel that allowed engines with giant capacities to become commonplace.

Europe's own circumstances also closely guided car development. Higher population densities, the narrow winding lanes of ancient cities and higher fuel prices encouraged a trend towards compact and economical city cars, which crystallized with the Austin Mini in 1959. For some reason never really defined, the European staple car has effectively developed into a hatchback version of the original compact, transversely-engined Mini typified by the VW Golf and Fiat Punto. Mystifyingly, in the US the hatchback family car hasn't possessed anything like the same grip it has on the European buying market.

Glancing down the list it seems that all the cars included in this A-to-Z selection were aiming for excellence in at least one of four attributes – speed, style, utility and the use of ground-breaking technology. Vehicles that have combined as many as three of these qualities in one design – the Range Rover was a stylish, speedy, utility vehicle – can rightly be categorised as major landmarks in automotive design, destined to be much-copied. Some, however, are notable for not making it, like the AMC Pacer, an attempt at a stylish utility town car that failed dismally.

A combination of speed and style is much the most common mix, spawning long and distinguished lines of sports cars like those from Aston Martin, Porsche and Ferrari. But while Ferrari and Aston tended to stick to traditional engineering solutions,

Doing 0–60mph (96km/h) in 6.1 seconds, the Esprit Turbo finally gave makers Lotus a supercar challenger.

Porsche, with its background as a prodigious engineering consultancy, preferred to push the barriers of design and technology with cars like the 928 coupe and 959 sports car.

Utility is a much more wide-ranging attribute, and one that runs from the cost-effective engineering that produced people's cars such as the Ford Model T, VW Beetle and Citroën 2CV, to the Audi Quattro's 4x4 drivetrain that allowed supercar performance to be utilised in nearly any weather and road surface. Even the design of the foldable and removable seats in the original Renault Espace MPV was a breakthrough in automotive design, and it went on to introduce a whole new type of vehicle to the market.

The single-minded pursuit of one benchmark attribute can often lead to achieving another. Style couldn't have been further from the minds of the engineers working on the Second World War Jeep produced by Willys-Overland, but the pure functionality of this military vehicle never went out of style and was copied by all 4x4 makers from Land Rover to Suzuki. Equally, Jaguar's E-Type was styled by Malcolm Sayer using new technology in the form of aerodynamic theory, then still very much in its infancy. But the upshot was one of the most beautiful cars ever made, and one of the very few to become a permanent exhibit at the New York Museum of Modern Art.

This A-to-Z of the most significant cars of all time will give the reader a unique view of the myriad of routes that car design has taken over the last century. It might also provide a few clues as to its direction in the future...

Fiat 500

1963–1971

ENGINE: Flat-twin, air-cooled, 593cc

POWER: 38bhp

CHASSIS: Monocoque

BRAKES (F/R): Drum

TRANSMISSION: Four-speed manual

SUSPENSION: Independent

TOP SPEED: 87mph (139km/h)

ACCELERATION: 0–60mph (96km/h) in 15 seconds

Carlo Abarth established his tuning company in Turin in 1949. At the beginning he specialized in Fiats, but eventually built cars that were definitely separate models in their own right.

By the early 1960s, his firm was turning out approximately 3000 cars a year and employed more than 350 people, which put it on a similar scale to such respected and well-loved firms such as Coopers in the UK.

One of the staple products of his impressive little operation was the 1958 Fiat 500, from which he managed to produce amazing performance improvements. These were achieved by increasing the capacity of the little flat-twin, using a bigger carburettor and working on the valves.

Abarth was able to tease nearly 40bhp from the most highly tuned SS versions of the vehicles. This meant that the Abarth Fiat 500 could manage almost 90mph (144km/h). The standard, factory, 21bhp Fiat 500 could only ever hope to struggle to about 55mph (88km/h) – a figure which came via some very breathless acceleration.

The handling and braking of the Abarth were dramatically uprated to make the tiny car – bedecked with stripes and flared wheelarches – into the ultimate boy racer's giant-killer.

Production of the Abarth Fiat 500 ended in 1971, and Fiat took the company over in 1973, although the name still lives on as a high performance badge on today's smaller Fiats.

AC Ace

1953–1963

ENGINE: Straight-six (AC, Bristol and Ford), 1991cc/1971cc/2553cc

POWER: 102–170bhp

CHASSIS: Tubular ladder type

BRAKES (F/R): Drum (disc later)

TRANSMISSION: Four-speed, with optional overdrive

SUSPENSION: Independent

TOP SPEED: 117mph (187km/h) – Ace Bristol

ACCELERATION: 0–60mph (96km/h) in 11 seconds (Ace Bristol)

To replace its range of ageing 2-litre cars, AC Cars of Thames Ditton in Surrey, England, took up a design by John Tojeiro that used a ladder-type tubular frame, all-independent transverse leaf-spring suspension, and an outstandingly pretty, open two-seater alloy body – clearly inspired by the Ferrari Barchetta of the day. This car was to become the Ace, the car that made the company's reputation after the Second World War.

Early cars used AC's elderly 2-litre overhead-camshaft straight-six (first seen soon after the end of the First World War) to give a top speed of 102mph (163km/h) and 0–60mph (96km/h) in 13 seconds. It was hardly a sporting engine, however, and it was felt that something more modern and powerful was required to put the newer chassis to more effective use.

Thus, from 1956 onward there was the option of Bristol's superb 2-litre 120bhp straight-six and slick four-speed gearbox. The top speed leaped to 116mph (186km/h), with a 0–60mph (96km/h) time in the nine-second bracket, and engine response was much sweeter and in keeping with the expectations of the day. With the engine well back in the chassis, the Ace also handled well – a factor that contributed to the high levels of success it enjoyed when the car was used in competition.

From 1961 to 1963, a few Aces were built with Ford's 2.6-litre straight-six to replace the Bristol unit. These Ken Rudd-modified engines were capable of giving up to 170bhp. However, by that point, the Thames Ditton company was already gearing itself up for the production of Cobra – an altogether different kind of AC.

AC Cobra

289 and 427

1962–1968

ENGINE: 90-degree V8,
4261cc/4727cc/6997cc

POWER: 164–490bhp

CHASSIS: Alloy body, tubular frame

BRAKES (F/R): Disc

TRANSMISSION: Four-speed manual

SUSPENSION: Independent front and rear

TOP SPEED: 136–180mph
(218–288km/h)

ACCELERATION: 0–60mph (96km/h)
in 4.2 seconds

In 1961 Texan racer Carroll Shelby approached AC cars of Thames Ditton in Surrey with the idea of fitting a 4.2-litre Ford V8 engine into its handsome Ace sports car. Enter the legendary Cobra, perhaps the most famous muscle-car of them all, and certainly one of the fastest.

Using essentially the same tubular-steel chassis layout as the six-cylinder Ace, this two-seater sports car had electrifying performance thanks to the relatively light weight of the body and the high torque of the V8 engine. The first cars used a 164bhp 4.2-litre unit, but it wasn't long before a bigger 4727cc engine was slotted in, boosting power to 195bhp. Top speed of the 289 car was 138mph (221km/h), but even more impressive was the acceleration: 60mph (96km/h) came up in 5.5 seconds, and the standing quarter-mile in 13.9.

This wasn't enough for Shelby, however. In 1965 he slotted in the 6989cc engine to produce the 7-litre Cobra. With a claimed 345bhp in stock form – tuned SC cars gave 480bhp or more – its acceleration put the Cobra in the record books in 1967 as the world's fastest-accelerating production car: 0–60mph (96km/h) in 4.2 seconds.

In reality, the 7-litre was virtually an all-new Cobra, with fat arches front and rear housing huge Goodyear tyres. It shared only the doors and bonnet with the 289. More importantly, the chassis was totally redesigned and much stiffer, while the suspension now used coil rather than leaf springs.

Cobra production stopped in 1968, the 4.7- and 7-litre cars running concurrently. In the USA the cars went under the names Shelby Cobra and Ford Cobra, and were homologated as Shelby American Cobras.

AC 428

1967–1973

ENGINE: V8, 7016cc

POWER: 425bhp

CHASSIS: Tubular ladder frame

BRAKES (F/R): Disc

TRANSMISSION: Three-speed automatic

SUSPENSION: Independent

TOP SPEED: 140mph (224km/h)

ACCELERATION: 0–60mph (96km/h) in 5.9 seconds

The AC 428 was an attempt to make a civilized GT out of the Cobra 428 Mk III. It shared that car's all-independent suspension and disc brakes on all four wheels, but had a longer wheelbase and was usually fitted with the less-powerful 345bhp, 7016cc Ford Galaxie engine.

The 428 had a three-speed automatic transmission – a feature that remained constant throughout the range, even in the few 428s which were produced with more powerful Cobra engines instead of the standard Galaxie.

Frua styled – and also fitted – the car's steel bodies, which looked not unlike their body for the attractive Maserati Mistral. The two automobiles actually shared some common body panels.

The production process required to turn out a 428 was famously and ridiculously convoluted. AC had to import the running gear from across the Atlantic, from Detroit, and then send the chassis to Italy to have the bodies fitted.

Top speed and acceleration were absolutely electrifying, but the car lacked the refinement that many of its rivals were able to offer. It was also very expensive, and only a two-seater, so it wasn't really any more practical than the Cobra it had been unsuccessfully attempting to civilize.

Not surprisingly, sales for the 428 were very slow. Production finally ended in 1973 with a grand total of just 51 fastbacks and 29 convertibles having been built.

3000ME

1979–1988

ENGINE: V6, 3024cc

POWER: 138bhp

CHASSIS: Steel chassis, fibreglass body

BRAKES (F/R): Disc

TRANSMISSION: Four-speed manual

SUSPENSION: Independent

TOP SPEED: 120mph (192km/h)

ACCELERATION: 0–60mph (96km/h) in 8.5 seconds

The AC 3000ME had a complex and extremely turbulent history. It was first shown by its creators (Peter Bohanna and Robin Stables) in 1973, when it was fitted with an Austin Maxi engine/transmission.

AC – which had just finished production of the big 428 – liked the design and announced that they would make it in 1974. However, the 3000 didn't see production for five years.

In the AC version, power came from a transverse, mid-mounted, 3-litre Ford V6 engine driving through a specially made gearbox. However, the performance was surprisingly disappointing – 120mph (192km/h) top speed – and its handling rather uncertain when taken to the limit. By the time AC eventually got the 3000ME into production, the price

had shot up in a dramatic fashion and the 3000ME looked dated next to newer rivals.

Bad luck continued to dog the design. In 1984, the rights to the AC 3000ME were bought by a Scottish businessman, but his new company made only 30 examples in ten months.

In 1985 a replacement model, the Ecosse, was announced. This had a completely new body style, a 2.5-litre Alfa Romeo V6 engine, and a claimed top speed of 145mph (232km/h), but the company folded within a few weeks. As late as 1988 a new English company had taken over the design, and that year it showed the Signature, which had a 162bhp, turbocharged, double overhead camshaft, 2-litre Fiat engine. Only one example was ever built.

Alfa Romeo

Spider 'Duetto'

1966–1993

ENGINE: Four-cylinder, 1962cc

POWER: 131bhp

CHASSIS: Monocoque

BRAKES (F/R): Disc

TRANSMISSION: Five-speed manual

SUSPENSION: Independent front, live axle rear

TOP SPEED: 124mph (198km/h)

ACCELERATION: 0–60mph (96km/h) in 9.2 seconds

The Alfa Spider 'Duetto' was launched at the Turin Motor Show in 1966, and was the last complete design by Battista Pininfarina – the founder of the famous styling house who died that year.

Although sales were initially disappointing when buyers proved resistant to the rounded, boat-tail styling, the model went on to be highly successful and extremely long-lived.

The last versions of the car were produced in 1993. Bodies were built, as well as styled, by Pininfarina and were noted for their excellent hood mechanism that could be raised or lowered with one hand. The round-tail styling had been changed to square-tail as early as 1969.

All models used Alfa's classic four-cylinder twin-cam engine, at first in 1600cc form, then later as a 1750cc and 2-litre. There was also a 1300cc version. All models of the Spider 'Duetto' came with a delightful five-speed transmission.

Drivers loved the car for its responsive engine and impressively crisp handling, and with the biggest engines the cars were flexible as well as fast – offering a top speed of 124mph (198km/h). All the major mechanical components were shared with the Giulia models, which were contemporary with the Duetto in the mid-1960s.

In the '60s film *The Graduate*, Dustin Hoffman can be seen driving a red 1600 Duetto to the sounds of Simon and Garfunkel's classic soundtrack. Although the name was never used on the 'roundtails,' Alfa introduced a Spider model named 'The Graduate' in the 1980s.

Alfa Romeo

1750 GTV

1967–1977

ENGINE: In-line four-cylinder, 1779cc

POWER: 122bhp

CHASSIS: Monocoque

BRAKES (F/R): Disc

TRANSMISSION: Five-speed manual

SUSPENSION: Independent front, live axle rear

TOP SPEED: 118mph (189km/h)

ACCELERATION: 0–60mph (96km/h) in 9.5 seconds

Of all the 105-Series Alfa Romeos that came out of the 1960s and 1970s, it is the Bertone-designed 1750GTV coupe – first seen in 1967 – that is closest to drivers' hearts. When you look at the car it is easy to understand why.

Although later 2-litre versions may have been quicker, the 1750 was by far the sweetest and smoothest of Alfa's classic, double-overhead-cam, in-line four-cylinder engines.

The strength that the engine was able to offer was matched with an impressive and very slick five-speed gearbox that was a total delight to use. It was a combination that helped win the car a legion of supporters and give the 1750GTV coupe the type of character any car deserving of the much-abused term 'classic' needs to have.

Great brakes, smooth steering and a balanced chassis made the cars a superb tool on a twisty road, where it often proved more fun than many bigger, faster machines.

It was just as happy cruising at over 100mph (160km/h) on the highway – a fact not lost on its American enthusiasts – where its relative refinement made it seem like both a relaxing businessman's express and a fun-filled open road cruiser.

Bertone's shape for the coupe dated from 1963 and the first 'step-bonnet' 1600 Giulia coupes. It remained in production – with regular changes to trim and badging – for 10 years, until 1977. It crossed over briefly with the much less charismatic Alfetta coupes that were designed to replace it, but they never matched the 1750GTV coupe's appeal.

Alfa Romeo Junior Z

1970–1975

ENGINE: Four-cylinder, 1290cc/1570cc

POWER: 87–113bhp

CHASSIS: Monocoque

BRAKES (F/R): Disc

TRANSMISSION: Five-speed manual

SUSPENSION: Independent front, live axle rear

TOP SPEED: 115–118mph (184–189km/h)

ACCELERATION: 0–60mph in 11 seconds (1300cc), 9 seconds (1600cc)

The Junior Z was a beautiful and innovative aerodynamic study on the Alfa Giulia 1300 GT chassis by Zagato, first seen in 1969. Designer Ercole Spada created a glorious wedge-shaped two-seater coupe with a sharply cut-off tail that incorporated an early form of integral spoiler.

At the front the lights and grille were covered in Plexiglass, and the car enjoyed a large glass area for the cabin. It also featured a rear hatchback that could be wound open electrically for extra through-flow ventilation if required.

At first, pundits were unsure about the car's radical shape, but owners raved about the amazing straight-line speed of the Junior Z, which was good for 115mph (184km/h) on just 1300cc, thanks to its slippery profile.

What's more, its light weight helped to sharpen up the already excellent handling and brakes of the Giulia, ensuring that Junior Z owners got a thrilling drive. The extra visibility was a feature of the car which brought with it a certain feeling of invulnerability when you got behind the wheel.

The 1300 Junior was replaced by the 1600 Junior in 1972. This model had new, long-tail styling to give increased luggage accommodation and, of course, a bigger engine with improved power and torque. The extra length also introduced a touch more elegance into the already stunning design, which was further accented by a very distinctive front bumper.

The Junior Zs were expensive cars with specialist appeal. Just 1,108 1300s and 402 1600s were built. Production finished in 1975.

Montreal

1970–1976

ENGINE: V8, 2593cc

POWER: 200bhp

CHASSIS: Monocoque

BRAKES (F/R): Disc

TRANSMISSION: Five-speed manual

SUSPENSION: Independent front, live axle rear

TOP SPEED: 137mph (219km/h)

ACCELERATION: 0–60mph (96km/h) in 7.6 seconds

The Montreal was a rare excursion by Alfa Romeo into the highly competitive super-car arena, with a front-engined V8 coupe.

The shape, created by Bertone, had first been shown as a dream car at the World Fair in Montreal in 1967. However, the public were so surprisingly enthusiastic about it that Alfa Romeo decided to put it into production.

Although it was to be based on ordinary Giulia running gear, Alfa had decreed that its new flagship vehicle should come with a new engine. This was to be a road-going version of its Type 33 racing V8 with four camshafts, Spica fuel injection and an output of 200bhp from 2.6 litres.

Matched to a ZF five-speed transmission, the car was good for almost 137mph (219km/h), but many critics thought the chassis – which used a fairly primitive, live rear axle – was not worthy of the power offered by its engine. The handling was safe but somewhat uninspired. Worse, the ride was appalling jolty for what was intended to be a luxurious long-distance express – two of the most critical errors for any car in its class.

The radical look of the Montreal led to it appearing in quite a few mid-1970s films, such as *The Destructors*, where Michael Caine's Montreal chases a yellow Porsche 911.

The shape – although dramatic, with its slats and shapely glass area – seemed to date quickly. By the mid-1970s, Alfa had lost interest in the car, which was in very low-volume production anyway and never seemed destined to make much money.

Alfasud

1972–1983

[1.5 Ti] ENGINE: Flat four-cylinder, 1490cc

POWER: 95bhp

CHASSIS: Steel monocoque, three- and five-door

BRAKES (F/R): Disc/disc

TRANSMISSION: Five-speed manual

SUSPENSION: Struts front, rigid axle rear

TOP SPEED: 107mph (171km/h)

ACCELERATION: 0–60mph (96km/h) in 11.5 seconds

The 1972 Alfasud was by general consent the greatest car of the decade. Its name, though, was an indication of the insane government intervention that tragically thwarted it from becoming one of the greatest cars of all time.

The Alfasud – an Italian phrase meaning 'Alfa South' – was a complete break from the company's past engineering strategy. Alfa Romeo was directed to construct a factory in an area of high unemployment near Naples in the southern half of Italy to build the startling, all-new machine. This was the source of the uncharismatic 'Alfa South' name that the car was unfortunately destined to bear.

The design team was led by Rudolph Hruska, who had previously worked with Porsche on the VW Beetle. A characteristically masterful Giugiaro-styled bodyshell clothed a flat-four engine and – in a big break for Alfa – a front-wheel-drive chassis.

Hruska's strict engineering brief meant the Alfasud was light and wieldy, but few commentators could have ever guessed that the very ordinary, uninspiring ingredients would ultimately combine to create such a remarkable car.

The Alfasud's handling prowess remained a benchmark right into the 1980s – such was the excellence of the chassis which offered amazingly agile and razor-sharp responses. The chassis always felt worthy of more power.

Although demand was huge, the Alfasud's success was severely hampered by the appalling build quality, particularly the shocking rust problems and highly questionable electrics. It is rumoured that the Alfasud was ruined by recycled Soviet steel, which the then-left-wing Italian government bought in an effort to help support the Communist state's ailing economy.

Alfa Six

1978–1985

ENGINE: 60-degree V6, 2492cc

POWER: 158bhp

CHASSIS: Monocoque

BRAKES (F/R): Disc

TRANSMISSION: Automatic or five-speed manual

SUSPENSION: All-independent

TOP SPEED: 121mph (194km/h)

ACCELERATION: 0–60mph (96km/h) in 11.4 seconds

The Alfa Six is an interesting lesson in how not to do things in the luxury-saloon class. Designed to look discreet and dignified rather than flagrantly expensive – Alfa felt that wealthy buyers would want to avoid unwanted attention in bandit-ridden Italy – the Six looked stodgy and dated when it came to the European market in 1978.

An opulent interior somewhat made up for its external looks – not to mention the high specification, which included power windows, central locking, plush velour trim, standard ZF automatic gearbox and power steering.

Dynamically, the Six didn't shine in any particular area. The 2.5-litre V6 engine was smooth and eager, but was having to work very hard in the heavy saloon. So while its 119mph (190km/h) top speed looked reasonable, the 16mpg

(18litres/100km) fuel consumption it offered didn't – even among the amenable expense accounts of the executive class.

On the road, fairly strong understeer characterized the safe but unexceptional handling, coupled to a ride that was only averagely comfortable for the class. Faced with stiff competition from GM (Opel Senator), Audi (200 Turbo) and Rover (the SD1), the gawky big Italian gathered dust in Alfa showrooms.

Even the addition of fuel injection systems and some minor styling tweaks could do nothing to help stimulate sales. The car died quietly in 1985, having made few friends.

Alfa went on to break its big-car curse in 1988 with the 164, putting their jewel of a V6 to good use in a handsome and highly competent all-rounder.

Alfa Romeo 164 V6

1988–1997

ENGINE: V6, 2959cc

POWER: 192bhp

CHASSIS: Monocoque

BRAKES (F/R): Disc

TRANSMISSION: Five-speed manual, four-speed automatic

SUSPENSION: All-independent

TOP SPEED: 149mph (238km/h)

ACCELERATION: 0–62mph (100km/h) in 8.4 seconds

The 'Type Four' project has to go down as one of the most successful manufacturing co-operations ever experienced in the automobile industry. It is certainly the most successful of modern times and has provided a model that other companies have strived to follow.

It began as a tie-up between Saab and Lancia, but Fiat and Alfa also produced Type Four-based cars. By sharing the basic floorpan, front suspension, roof and doors, the four makers were able to slash development and production costs by incredible amounts and yet still produce some highly memorable and commercially successful vehicles.

The last of the Type Four cars to arrive was Alfa's 164, an extremely handsome executive sports saloon which, after years of drift and compromise, drove the Italian company firmly back into mass-market contention. In short, the 164 was the winner Alfa had been desperately seeking for more than a decade.

Despite the Type Four connection, the Alfa was the most individual-looking car of the group. This was mainly thanks to its own – unique – doors.

The superb wedge-shaped, nose-down styling was drawn up by Pininfarina. Alfa was said to be very angry when the remarkably similar Pininfarina-styled Peugeot 605 appeared, unsurprisingly.

Build quality was quite decent, as was the driving position. The 164's reputation as a fine driving machine was boosted by the 3.0 V6 engine, which lived up to its heritage as an Italian powerplant.

The 164 survived for ten years, its troubled successor (the 166) being delayed. The 164 was a high point for Alfa, which it failed to cap until the much needed arrival of the 156 in 1997.

Alfa Romeo SZ Zagato

1989–1993

ENGINE: V6, 2959cc

POWER: 210bhp

CHASSIS: Steel chassis, composite bodyshell

BRAKES (F/R): Disc/disc

TRANSMISSION: 5-speed manual

SUSPENSION: Struts front, de Dion axle rear

TOP SPEED: 152mph (243km/h)

ACCELERATION: 0–60mph (96km/h) in 7 seconds

The Alfa Romeo SZ was a short-run coupe intended to give Alfa's image – badly tarnished in the 1970s and 1980s – a serious boost. However, it became known as *Il Monstro* in its home country, where enthusiasts had been weaned on a diet of finely sculptured Italian sports cars.

Serious motoring writers called it the world's ugliest car, but its brutally stark lines had a real effect on the future of car styling. Like automotive punk rock, it took a stylistically complacent industry by the scruff of the neck. Also like punk rock, its reverberations can still be felt to this day in some of the top designers' best work.

The SZ was based on the rear-wheel-drive floorpan of the 75 saloon and powered by a 3.0 V6 engine, but real effort went into the car's chassis dynamics, which were extensively praised – as were the SZ's brakes and steering.

The chassis was developed from a Group A race version of the 75, which included race-ready details such as nylon-bushed rose joints. The interior was made up of a one-off carbon-fibre dashboard and beautiful cream-leather sports seats. Not surprisingly, luggage space wasn't a high priority when the design brief of the SZ was being composed and this was restricted to a small, flat deck situated behind the driver and passenger.

The car was constructed by Zagato and just 1000 – including an even more bizarre-looking convertible version – of these far-sighted supercars were built.

GTV

1995-

ENGINE: In-line, 16v four-cylinder, 1970cc

POWER: 150bhp

CHASSIS: Steel monocoque, two-door

BRAKES (F/R): Disc with ABS

TRANSMISSION: 5-speed manual/ 4-speed automatic

SUSPENSION: Struts front, multi-link with double wishbones rear

TOP SPEED: 133mph (213km/h)

ACCELERATION: 0–62.5mph (100km/h) in 8.6 seconds

Despite the encouragement provided by the arrival of the 164, Alfa's progress as a maker of fine cars spluttered badly – but somewhat predictably – with the introduction of the lacklustre mid-size 155 and the Golf-rivaling 145/6.

Once again it was left to an Alfa sports car to give the famous marque a lift. The much needed boost came in the form of the hard-top GTV and its sister cabriolet, the Spider – two startling looking cars that demanded attention, inspired the imagination and succeeded in generating a great deal of comment in both the motoring industry and the press.

However, both vehicles were based on the ubiquitous Tipo structure, which also spawned the 155, 145, Lancia Dedra and numerous others. This inevitably led to the GTV being subject to some damaging compromises for a car in its class.

Perhaps the worst fault was in the structure, which was unable to stay properly rigid without a roof. Despite this, the Spider was still an immensely desirable and attractive car, even if it was not as good to drive as its sister, the GTV.

The other compromise was the disappearance of the boot, because of the adoption of multi-link rear suspension. However, the enhanced performance of the chassis made it a worthwhile sacrifice that balanced out the loss of carrying capacity.

The well-respected 2.0-litre Twin-Spark engine was the main powerplant, but Alfa's 3.0 V6 unit soon became an option.

Dramatic styling was again the mark of a big step forward for Alfa, and this was undoubtedly one of the main reasons that the GTV earned itself so many fans. The aggressive wedge shape – broken by a deep swage running around the body – was, like its SZ predecessor, a real shock for a lot of people when the vehicle was launched.

The four-lamp nose was something of a trick, however. Behind the four holes in the bonnet were two large, squared-off headlight units.

Alfa Romeo 156

1997–

ENGINE: V6, 24 valve, 2492cc

POWER: 190bhp

CHASSIS: Steel monocoque, four-door

BRAKES (F/R): Disc with ABS

TRANSMISSION: 5-speed manual/4-speed automatic

SUSPENSION: Double wishbones front, struts rear

TOP SPEED: 138mph (221km/h)

ACCELERATION: 0–62.5mph (100km/h) in 7.5 seconds

Practically every new Alfa since the early 1970s has been billed as the 'breakthrough' car. Fierce competition in the burgeoning European 'small prestige' market in the second half of the 1990s meant that Alfa's replacement for the 155 had to be absolutely first rate – but few expected it to be.

The 156 was, in all areas, a remarkable car. The styling – completed in-house by Alfa – stayed close to the long-established low-nose, high-tail theme, but abandoned hard edges for a much more muscular, fluid style. The nose was dominated by a large chrome grille, which plunged down into the front bumper. The sides of the car were smooth and uncluttered, to the extent that the rear door-handle was hidden in the rear window surround. Alfa went to the expense of casting an old-fashioned alloy door handle for the front doors. Inside the retro theme continued, with the instruments contained in two huge binnacles moulded into the dashboard.

The really important steps forward were made in the areas of build quality and chassis. To ensure that the 156 was a truly first-class road car, Alfa Romeo abandoned the conventional front-wheel-drive chassis for a much more sophisticated and expensive solution – MacPherson struts at the back and a double-wishbone arrangement at the front. Alfa's well-known charismatic Twin Spark and V6 engines were the icing on a very desirable cake.

Allard J2X

1949–54

ENGINE: V8, 5420cc

POWER: 180bhp

CHASSIS: Separate chassis, alloy body

BRAKES (F/R): Drum

TRANSMISSION: Four-speed manual

SUSPENSION: All-independent

TOP SPEED: 130mph (208km/h)

ACCELERATION: 0–60mph (96km/h) in 8 seconds

The now legendary South London motor-trader Sydney Allard based his famous rugged sports cars on Ford V8 power. His pre-war special cut its teeth in mud-lugging trials and kicked off the successful Allard racing heritage. However, it wasn't until later, after the Second World War, that Sydney Allard decided to launch himself and his vehicle into the world of production motor cars.

The K1 and J1 of 1946–48 were sparse and primitive, but very fast – especially when fitted with the bigger 3.9-litre Mercury version of the tried-and-tested flathead Ford V8. Production blossomed with the more civilized versions such as the four-seater L Type and the Monte Carlo Rally-winning – and best-selling – P1 saloon with up to 4.4 litres of engine.

The most exciting and coveted vehicle of the breed though was the J2/J2X of 1949, a stark four-wheeled-motorbike of a car which, with the modern type of overhead-valve Cadillac V8, could accelerate faster than the Jaguar XK120.

It was Jaguar, however, that meant the beginning of the end for Allard and many other excellent cars of its ilk. The nature of the company was such that their cars were produced in very small numbers, and this meant they couldn't compete with the mass-market Jaguars on a value-for-money basis.

Sales fell sharply after 1953, and the company produced its last car, the Palm Beach, in 1958 – an unfortunately belated bid for a market then dominated by Austin Healey.

TD/TE/TF

1958–1967

ENGINE: Straight-six, 2993cc

POWER: 120–150bhp

CHASSIS: Steel body, separate chassis

BRAKES (F/R): Disc/drum

TRANSMISSION: Four and five-speed manual, or three-speed automatic

SUSPENSION: Independent front, live axle rear

TOP SPEED: 110–120mph (176–192km/h)

ACCELERATION: 0–60mph (96km/h) in 13 seconds

For Alvis of Coventry, post-war car production became something of a sideline to its more profitable armoured-vehicle interests. That isn't to say that the TD, TE and TF were not fine cars – far from it. Developed from the 'Greylady' TC21, these were mature motor cars for discerning enthusiasts – luxurious, well built and well mannered, yet with a surprising turn of speed.

The TD's shape was the work of Graber, who had licensed Willowbrooks of Loughborough to build the bodies in Britain. These cars, dating from 1956, were known as the TC108G. Quality was not all it should have been, and for the TD of 1958 Alvis commissioned Park Ward of London to build its bodywork, at the same time tidying up the rear of the roofline.

Powered by a 120bhp version of the familiar Alvis 3-litre straight-six, these cars could achieve 100mph (160km/h) with ease and looked particularly elegant in drophead form. Series II TDs had disc brakes, and – from October 1962 – a desirable ZF five-speed gearbox of the type used in the contemporary Aston Martin. The four-headlamp 1963 TE developed 130bhp, and had purchase options of automatic transmission and power steering.

Best and last of the breed was the TF of 1965, with a triple-carburettor 150bhp engine and a top speed of 120mph (192km/h) via the five-speed gearbox. By then the writing was on the wall for Alvis as a producer of passenger cars. Rover took a controlling interest, and stopped TF production in 1967.

AMC Pacer

1975–1980

ENGINE: Straight-six, 3795cc

POWER: 90bhp

CHASSIS: Steel monocoque front/ separate chassis and steel panels rear

BRAKES (F/R): Drum

TRANSMISSION: 4-speed automatic

SUSPENSION: Independent with coils front, leaf-sprung live axle rear

TOP SPEED: 104mph (166km/h)

ACCELERATION: 0–62.5mph (100km/h) in 14.3 seconds

Popular legend says the distinctive Pacer was the American Motor Corporation's answer to the fuel crisis, an attempt to offer the internal space of a traditional US car but with much more compact dimensions and reasonable economy.

In fact, a clay model of the Pacer was built in 1971 by AMC's chief stylist Richard Teague, and it was hawked around the USA the following year to be assessed by the public in the then-new 'product clinics' to establish what options buyers might want and whether any changes were necessary. Teague's US-market definition of a compact car anticipated the unforeseen circumstances of the fuel crisis.

The original engines for the Pacer were going to be either an imported Citroën Comotor rotary or one of GM's twin-rotor Wankel rotaries. However, the huge rise in fuel prices and the Wankel's reputation for thirst meant AMC fitted the Pacer with 3.8-litre and 4.2-litre straight-sixes.

Aside from a reasonable use of interior space, a big feature of the Pacer was the extensive glazing, calculated to account for 50 percent of the body area. AMC sold it as the first wide small car – which was no exaggeration, the Pacer being nearly as long as it was wide. The front half of the car was a monocoque with independent suspension and rack-and-pinion steering. The rear half used a separate chassis and leaf-sprung rear axle. The base model even had drum brakes front and rear – front discs were optional at the launch. With everything added in, the Pacer weighed 3,000lb (1364kg).

Although it was seen as something quite refreshing at first, the Pacer became known as a joke in the motor industry. It was really not helped by various idiosyncratic details such as the left door being longer than the right one for easier access into the rear, and its podgy lines dated badly. America soon forgot about costly fuel, and about the Pacer.

Amphicar

1961–1968

ENGINE: Four-cylinder, 1147cc

POWER: 38bhp

CHASSIS: Monocoque

BRAKES (F/R): Drum

TRANSMISSION: Four-speed

SUSPENSION: Independent

TOP SPEED: 65mph (104km/h)

ACCELERATION: 0–60mph in 42 seconds

There is strange and there is strange, and the Amphicar was strange indeed. It was an amphibious vehicle built in Germany – a country that is not exactly celebrated the world over for its pronounced eccentricity or its history of building quirky or frankly bizarre cars. VW and BMW could be said to epitomise the German car industry, and so it was something of a surprise to find that the eccentric Amphicar came from where it did.

The Amphicar was first built at Karlsruhe, and then later at the Berlin company Deutsch Waggon und Maschinenfabrik, where it was produced right through until 1968.

On land it looked like a rather ugly little convertible, with tail fins and too much ground clearance. It was as ungainly to drive as it looked, too, with abysmal, ponderous steering and a complete lack of notable performance from the rear-mounted 1147cc Triumph Herald engine.

The engine was woefully underpowered, and struggled with the car's considerable weight. The car's top speed, if you were brave enough to try and attempt to obtain it, was a rather unimpressive 65mph (104km/h) – completely ruling it out of any high-speed autobahn cruising

Sadly, the Amphicar didn't make a very good boat either. In fact, it was even worse when it came to proving its amphibious nature. With a top speed in the water of just 7.5 knots from its single propeller, it suffered from a pair of extremely unfortunate tendencies in a water vehicle – it rusted badly, and leaked due to sealing problems.

Apparently, amateur attempts to fit the car with a more potent Triumph Vitesse six-cylinder engine were not successful – the modified car sank. Today, the Amphicar is a much sought-after rarity. It is rarely seen for sale, as just 2,500 examples were built in its seven year production life.

Star Sapphire

1959-1960

ENGINE: Six-cylinder, 3990cc

POWER: 165bhp

CHASSIS: Separate chassis

BRAKES (F/R): Disc/drum

TRANSMISSION: Three-speed automatic

SUSPENSION: Independent front, live axle rear

TOP SPEED: 100mph (160km/h)

ACCELERATION: 0–60mph (96km/h) in 13 seconds

The Star Sapphire was easily the best car that Armstrong Siddeley of Coventry ever made, although it was only in production for one year. It is a car that has gone down in automotive history and passed into legend among car enthusiasts. It is one of those vehicles that truly deserves the label 'classic'.

Derived from the established Sapphire 346 saloons, its dignified 'six-light' styling concealed an impressive new 165bhp version of Armstrong's hemi-head straight-six powerplant.

Smooth and flexible, this engine gave the Star Sapphire sufficient straight-line muscle to challenge the big Jaguars that had taken over its market since the end of the Second World War. It also featured the latest labour-saving luxuries, such as power steering and three-speed automatic

transmission, which, while taken as standard in today's market, were the cutting edge of technology as the '50s gave way to the '60s.

Although the engineering of the Star Sapphire was highly conventional – it had a sturdy separate chassis and a beam rear axle – the car really scored with its equipment levels.

It possessed a beautifully crafted walnut and leather interior. Generously, this featured heating units for both front and rear passengers, and it boasted sumptuous seating for five.

Tragically, the Star Sapphire proved to be simply too expensive to have much appeal in the face of cheaper opposition, and the model died – along with the Armstrong marque – in 1960, with fewer than one thousand examples having been built.

DB2/DB4 and B MkIII

1950–1958

ENGINE: Straight-six, 2580-2922cc

POWER: 105–178bhp

CHASSIS: Monocoque

BRAKES (F/R): Drum and disc/drum

TRANSMISSION: Four-speed manual

SUSPENSION: Independent front, live axle rear

TOP SPEED: 100–119mph (160–190km/h)

ACCELERATION: 0–60mph (96km/h) in 9.3 seconds (Mk III)

Tractor tycoon David Brown bought the ailing sports-car maker Aston Martin in 1947, but had something of a false start with the underpowered four-cylinder Aston Martin DB1 of 1948. He more than redeemed himself, however, with the DB2 of 1950 – a car that set the pace for all subsequent Astons.

Here was a luxurious upper-crust coupe with modern performance and old-world charm. It used a smooth, powerful, six-cylinder, twin-cam 116bhp engine courtesy of its sister, the Lagonda 2.6 saloon – Brown had bought Lagonda as well in 1947.

Clothed in handsome alloy bodywork, these cars could reach more than 120mph (192km/h) in high-compression Vantage form. Underneath, the cruciform chassis blessed the cars with thoroughbred handling of the highest order. Coil sprung, the live rear axle was located by trailing links – with a

Panhard rod for the high side-loads the car was capable of generating – and damped by Armstrong lever-arms. The front suspension was unusual: a trailing-link design with the main lower locating member running across the front of the car.

For the DB2/4, the fastback shape was made more practical – but not so pretty – by the addition of rear seats and a side-hinged rear hatchback door. By the time the 3-litre MkIII had arrived, the tall DB2 grille had evolved into a mouth, and small fins had sprouted on the rear wings.

David Brown supplied the gearbox on all models. This had the option of overdrive on top gear on the 178bhp MkIII, giving 28.4mph (45.5km/h) per 1000rpm. Girling front disc brakes were another innovation added on the MkIII model. The DB MkIII was replaced by the touring-styled DB4 in 1958.

Aston Martin DB6

1965–1970

ENGINE: Straight 6, 3995cc

POWER: 282-352bhp

BRAKES (F/R): Disc

CHASSIS: Steel platform

TRANSMISSION: Five-speed manual/ 3 speed auto

SUSPENSION: Independent front, live axle rear

TOP SPEED: 148mph

ACCELERATION: 0-60 in 6.5 seconds

By 1965 the lithe and elegant Aston Martin DB4, via the more refined and faster DB5, had become the bigger heavier and more brutal DB6. It was a car that almost forced you to admire it instead of charming you with its refined elegance as its predecessor had been renowned for doing, but it was a distinctive vehicle and not one to be forgotten quickly.

Its headlights were fared-in, its chassis lengthened, and its tail chopped for better aerodynamics at high speed. Little survived of Tourings' original and much-loved 1958 shape.

Beneath the alloy skin the Superleggera method of construction was abandoned. From this point on, all Aston Martins would have aluminium outer panels on steel inner panels.

Power came from a 4-litre twin cam straight-six, and was much the same as before. It came as standard with triple SUs but the Vantage version had triple Webers and this gave it significantly better acceleration – something not lost on those who were lucky enough to enjoy the visceral pleasure provided by driving the Vantage.

Options were similar to those of the DB5 but with the addition of a limited slip differential and, after 1967, power steering. You could even order automatic transmission on your Aston Martin – and an increasing number of buyers did.

The Mk II version of 1967 had flared wheelarches and DBS-style wire wheels. Some even had Lucas fuel injection systems. There were 140 'Volante' convertibles. Some six of these were converted into shooting brakes by skilled London coachbuilder Harold Radford, making them the ultimate in high speed estate cars.

Lagonda Saloon

1976–1990

ENGINE: V8, 5340cc

POWER: 280bhp

CHASSIS: Steel platform, alloy body

BRAKES (F/R): Disc

TRANSMISSION: Three-speed automatic

SUSPENSION: Independent

TOP SPEED: 140mph (224km/h)

ACCELERATION: 0–60mph (96km/h) in 8 seconds

The Lagonda saloon, which completely dominated the 1976 Earl's Court Motor Show, could have been beamed down from another planet.

Low and razor-edged, it was a show-stopper – and just the publicity-grabber that troubled Aston Martin needed. The 170 deposits that were taken at the show pulled the company back from the brink of oblivion. Buyers weren't to know that their cars wouldn't be ready until 1979 because of problems with the high-tech electronics.

Mechanically the Lagonda was well-proven – essentially a stretched Aston Martin V8 with a meaty, four-camshaft, 5.3-litre V8 engine. The suspension came from the same source too, but with self-levelling for the de Dion rear end.

Weighing in at almost two tons (2000kg), this was the biggest and most opulent Lagonda since the war. Extras like air-conditioning and electric seats were all included in the price.

Pundits had nothing but praise for its ride and handling – superb for a large saloon – but some dared to suggest that it could have been quicker. Others raised eyebrows at the lack of rear-seat legroom in such a huge car. Aston tried to answer these criticisms with a still-born twin-turbo version, whilst specialist firm Tickford built a trio of stretched Lagondas with twin colour TVs.

By the mid-1980s, interest in the car had waned and the design seemed to age rapidly. Stylist William Towns tried to redeem his rapidly ageing super saloon with a more rounded offering in 1987, but it was too late. The dream car that had raised so many pulses back in 1976 died quietly in 1990, with a total of 645 cars having been sold.

V8 Zagato

1986–1989

ENGINE: 90-degree V8, 5340cc

POWER: 475bhp

CHASSIS: Alloy body, steel platform

BRAKES (F/R): Disc

TRANSMISSION: Five-speed manual

SUSPENSION: Independent front and rear

TOP SPEED: 186mph (298km/h)

ACCELERATION: 0–60mph (96km/h) in 4.8 seconds

An exclusive, 50-off, one-chance-only supercar, the Aston Martin V8 Zagato had its place in the sun in the mid-to-late 1980s. It made headlines as the fastest Aston ever at 186mph (298km/h), and the company's first two-seater since the DB4 GT. Even at £70,000 each, the whole production run was sold before a single car was built. With exclusivity assured, greedy investors laid Zagatos down like fine wine, putting them up for sale at anything up to half a million pounds each on the open market.

Flat-bottomed and flush-glazed, it had a sleeker appearance than the standard Aston Martin Vantage, recording an impressive 0.29Cd figure. It also weighed in 10 percent lighter, and had a more powerful 432bhp version of the quad-camshaft, 5.3-litre Vantage engine. Even today it is still in the slingshot league: a French motoring journal timed one at 186mph (298km/h), with a 0–60mph (96km/h) time of 4.8 seconds.

Not everybody liked the Zagato's shape. The double-bubble roof seemed superfluous and the grille unresolved, flanked by mean headlights behind light-diffusing glass. In profile, the awkward C-pillar dropped away to a truncated tail, where most of the length – 16in. (40.6cm) less than the standard V8 – had been cut. The boot was tiny, but space lost to the sliced-off rump was reclaimed behind the seats.

Just two a month were built between 1986 and 1988, if you don't count the prototype and a run of 25 convertibles. Orders worth £7 million were placed on the strength of just a styling sketch, and once values started to rocket, Aston wasn't above increasing the retail price to whatever the cars were realizing on the markets. When the investors' market slumped in the late-1980s, many speculators lost thousands as the value of these cars halved almost overnight. Even so, the V8 Zagato remains one of the most collectable post-war Aston Martins.

Aston Martin **Virage Vantage**

1994–1999

ENGINE: V8, 32 valve, twin superchargers, 5340cc

POWER: 550bhp

CHASSIS: Steel chassis, aluminium body panels

BRAKES (F/R): Disc with ABS

TRANSMISSION: Six-speed manual

SUSPENSION: Wishbone and coils front, triangulated radius arm rear

TOP SPEED: 186mph (298km/h)

ACCELERATION: 0–62.5mph (100km/h) in 4.7 seconds

Aston Martin finally surrendered its independence in 1987 when the giant multi-national Ford bought a controlling share of the company. Despite what some loyal followers of the firm thought would happen, this takeover actually had little noticeable impact on the often extremely chaotic nature of Aston's new car development.

Sadly, part of this was due to an under-funded and ill co-ordinated development programme. Like the Lagonda, Aston's new V8 coupe went from being 'signed off' to appearing at the 1988 Earl's Court Motor Show in just two years.

The imposing styling was completed by Royal College of Art tutors Ken Greenley and John Heffernan. However, the shaping of the Virage was controversial, as the car's tail had to be raised to reduce aerodynamic lift at speed, and Aston bosses insisted on retaining the familiar shape of the Aston radiator grille in the new model.

Although the first cars were launched with a new 32-valve V8 engine, Aston finally released the long-awaited Vantage development of the car in 1994, bolting a supercharger on each cylinder bank to create an engine good for 550bhp.

To match the pace, the Vantage wore a huge front bumper, six small, square headlights and sported massive wheels, giving it a very aggressive and highly macho overall appearance.

The Vantage was one of the most powerful road cars ever sold, with as much horsepower as some eight-seater aircraft. It was not a fundamentally great car, but this kind of sheer speed, distinctive engine noise and unmistakable British character is unlikely to be seen again.

DB7

1995–

ENGINE: In-line 24-valve supercharged straight-six, 3228cc

POWER: 335bhp

CHASSIS: steel monocoque, composite and steel panels

BRAKES (F/R): Disc with ABS

TRANSMISSION: Five-speed manual

SUSPENSION: Double wishbones front, independent wishbones rear

TOP SPEED: 165mph (263km/h)

ACCELERATION: 0–62.5mph (100km/h) in 5.9 seconds

After standing back and watching the troubled development of the Virage/Vantage, and with a recession starting to bite as the 1980s gave way to the 1990s, Ford decided to take Aston Martin under its experienced wing. Aston's new owner felt it needed a 'cheap' accessible car that would compete with top-range Mercedes models.

Despite worries by Aston die-hards that Ford would 'dilute' the essence of Aston Martin, the owner raided the parts bin of its recently acquired luxury-car maker, Jaguar. It started the DB7 project with the remnants of Project XX, a replacement for the ageing XJS. Ford decided that Aston would take over work on redeveloping the XJS running gear, and that Jaguar would start work on a completely new coupe.

The result was a remarkably beautiful, flowing car which captured everybody's ideal of what an Aston Martin should look like. The interior was similarly flowingly stylish, extensively wooded but, like the whole car, not oversized and intimidating like the Virage. Aston buyers clearly didn't care that the DB7 was riddled with borrowed components, from the Ford switches to the Mazda 323F rear lights.

The DB7 was hand-assembled at the Jaguar XJ220 facility, which was attached to an old farm in Oxfordshire, England. The car was a tremendous success for the company, and even continued to do very well after the arrival of Jaguar's XK8 – a direct competitor that was more modern from stem to stern, as well as considerably cheaper.

100S Coupe

1970–1976

ENGINE: Four-cylinder, 1871cc

POWER: 115bhp

CHASSIS: Monocoque

BRAKES (F/R): Disc/drum

TRANSMISSION: Four-speed manual

SUSPENSION: Independent front, dead axle rear

TOP SPEED: 112mph (179km/h)

ACCELERATION: 0–60mph (96km/h) in 10.6 seconds

As a refined and luxurious coupe, the Audi 100S – launched at the Geneva Motor Show in 1969 – had few peers in the 2-litre class in the early 1970s. With a top speed of 112mph (179km/h) and doing 0–60mph (96km/h) in 10 seconds, the Mercedes-designed, in-line, 113bhp, four-cylinder engine – canted over to give a lower bonnet line – packed a punch that was much heavier than its size would suggest. What's more, the front-drive handling was solidly predictable, and the brakes – vented inboard discs at the front – superb.

A svelte fast-back with space for four (this was no cramped two-plus-two) and a big boot, critics at the time loved the car's build quality and pace, praised its 30mpg (9.5litres/100km) economy and compared the styling with that of the Aston Martin DBS.

In fact, the body was identical to the sober Audi 100 saloon up to the windscreen, which was larger and more steeply raked. The wheelbase was shortened by 5in. (12.5cm), but the 100S featured the same suspension and running gear, with wishbones at the front and a beam axle on trailing arms and torsion bars at the rear.

The four-speed manual gearbox – with closer ratios than the 100 saloon – came as standard, with the option of three-speed VW automatic transmission for those that wanted it.

There were few changes made to the model during its six year production run. September 1973 brought a narrower front grille and bigger rear lights, head restraints and some computer diagnostic connections. More significantly, the rear suspension was modified to the Audi 80 type with coil springs, eliminating the torsion bars.

Late Mk2 cars – post-September 1975 – had Federal bumpers for the North American market and new negative-offset front suspension geometry, plus different wheels.

Audi 100 CD

1983–1991

ENGINE: In-line four cylinder, 1781cc

POWER: 113bhp

CHASSIS: Steel monocoque, four-door or five-door

BRAKES (F/R): Disc/drum 1980s, 1990s

TRANSMISSION: Five-speed manual or three-speed auto

SUSPENSION: Front struts and rigid rear axle

TOP SPEED: 128mph (205km/h)

ACCELERATION: 0–62mph (100km/h) in 9.7 seconds

Ferdinand Piech, Audi's chief engineer (and a member of the Porsche-owning family), was firmly of the view in the late-1970s that the way forward for Audi was an emphasis on new technology. It was this vision that helped create such important cars for the firm as the 100 CD, and fuelled the Audi's strength in the eighties and nineties.

Shortly after the pioneering Quattro model, Audi launched the slippery 100 saloon, and introduced the term 'Cd' to the car-buying public.

The Cd (drag coefficient) is a measurement of just how aerodynamic a car is. The figure of 0.30 was thought to have been an impracticable aim for a mainstream car. However, the 100 wore the achievement on its sleeve – a small 'Cd 0.30' sticker appeared in the car's rear quarter-light and could be spotted by the eagle-eyed.

Audi's engineers spent thousands of hours in the wind tunnel to lessen the drag, and the upshot was a car that was long, wide and barrel-sided. However, the 100 also benefited from some fine detail engineering, including flush-fitting windows, and this helped bolster its appeal.

The slick body and high gearing meant the 100 was a fine motorway cruiser and was capable of excellent fuel economy. Like all Audis, although the vehicle was front-wheel drive, the engine was placed lengthways in the nose.

Audi got exceptionally good value out of the basic 100 design. It spawned Quattro versions, and was the basis for the 100 Avant estate and the more upmarket 200. It eventually donated its centre section to the 1988 Audi V8, the company's top-line 4x4 executive car.

Audi **Quattro**

1983–1991

ENGINE: Turbocharged 20 valve in-line five-cylinder, 2226cc

POWER: 220bhp

CHASSIS: Steel monocoque, two-door coupe

BRAKES (F/R): Disc

TRANSMISSION: Five-speed manual

SUSPENSION: Independent front and rear

TOP SPEED: 142mph (227km/h)

ACCELERATION: 0–62mph (100km/h) in 6.1 seconds

There aren't many true landmark vehicles in the history of the car, but the Audi Quattro has a strong claim to be one of them.

It introduced four-wheel drive to road cars, and provided a way of harnessing very high levels of power to make high-performance driving possible in all weathers and on all types of road – more than enough excellent firsts to make it a real contender for landmark vehicle status.

The outcome of such innovation was a car that was both easier to drive and quicker point-to-point than a traditional supercar. It was also a huge success on the rally circuit. Not surprisingly, other manufacturers could be seen making a very hasty and undignified rush to copy the format.

The Quattro was based on the two-door coupe version of the 80 saloon, and borrowed its transmission from the VW Iltis military vehicle.

Initially it was powered by a turbocharged 2.1-litre five-cylinder engine, and divided the 200bhp on tap equally between the front and rear wheels. Inside, the driver was provided information by the then-futuristic digital instruments – adding a touch of science fiction innovation to the classically high standards of engineering and build quality that the ground-breaking Quattro represented.

The Quattro concept was refined over the best part of a decade, culminating in the 20V version. This had a new 2.3-litre turbocharged 20V engine, and the drivetrain had a 'Torsen' differential – the term is an acronym for Torque Sensing – which could automatically send more power to the wheels to provide the most grip.

It is still hailed as one of the all-time motoring greats, and its replacement – the S2 Coupe – could never deliver the Quattro's raw-edged thrills.

80/90 Series

1986–1994

[90 Series 20V Quattro] ENGINE:
20V in-line five-cylinder, 2309cc

POWER: 170bhp

CHASSIS: Galvanised steel monocoque, four-door

BRAKES (F/R): Disc with ABS

TRANSMISSION: Five-speed manual

SUSPENSION: Struts front, independent wishbone rear

TOP SPEED: 137mph (219km/h)

ACCELERATION: 0–62mph (100km/h) in 8 seconds

Audi's growing reputation for technical innovation took a back seat with the launch, in 1986, of the Audi 80 and 90. The company decided to focus on how it was pushing back the frontiers of modern styling, build quality and safety, instead of concentrating on its already established reputation for being the world leader when it came to effective utilisation of cutting edge developments in automobile technology and engineering.

The 80 (four-cylinder) and 90 (five-cylinder) were based on the floorpan of the old square-shaped 80 and 90, so it was no real surprise when the handling of the two cars came in for some very heavy criticism from certain sectors of the motoring press. Pundits were also quick to point to the lack of luggage space. For both the 80 and 90, the boot was seen as very shallow for cars in their markets.

The car's excellent build quality and production detailing (the flush-fit door handles, for instance) were supplemented by a fully-galvanised bodyshell – the first production car to be effectively rustproof.

The 80/90 also led on safety with the Pro-con Ten system, which used steel cables to pull the steering wheel away from the driver and tension the seatbelts in a head-on collision.

Both the 80 and the 90 were available with the Quattro drivetrain, but it wasn't until this was finally combined with a 170bhp 20V five-cylinder engine in the 90 that the car began to gain real credibility as a serious driving machine.

The 80 was substantially redesigned for 1992, gaining a new rear axle and a substantially reworked floorpan. Sensibly, this allowed for a bigger boot, and also featured folding seats.

These developments also allowed Audi to launch an estate version of the 80. Unfortunately, the greatly increased weight of the vehicle meant that the 80 was still marked down by road testers.

Audi **RS2**

1994–1995

ENGINE: 20V turbocharged in-line five-cylinder, 2309cc

POWER: 315bhp

CHASSIS: Steel monocoque, five-door

BRAKES (F/R): Disc with ABS

TRANSMISSION: Six-speed manual

SUSPENSION: Struts front, independent wishbone rear

TOP SPEED: 158mph (253km/h)

ACCELERATION: 0–62mph (100km/h) in 5 seconds

Nothing has ever demonstrated the inherent strength of Audi's remarkable engineering better than the Porsche-developed RS2 estate. It is one of those cars that grandly epitomizes everything that is the best in its maker.

Audi had already carried through the logic of its Quattro-driven, turbocharged S-series and developed the S2 estate. This was an exceptionally swift and sure-footed compact estate car. It would have been a rare and unnecessarily fussy breed of driver who would have dared to call for greater power than the standard 220bhp that was already on offer when they got behind the wheel.

However, Audi and Porsche combined forces to build the RS2, one of the fastest production cars of all time. The 'unburstable' reputation of the five-cylinder engine was lifted to new levels when the output was hiked from 220 to 315bhp without any increase in capacity proving necessary.

Modifications to the running gear were limited to fitting Porsche 968 Club Sport brakes, as well as specially tuned dampers. Porsche also supplied the 17-inch wheels and door mirrors.

Styling modifications included the aggressive front bumper – fitted with Porsche lighting units – and a new rear light cluster.

With room for four passengers and their luggage, and performance to beat all but the most rarefied of supercars, the RS2 demolished all the conventional stereotypes of road-car abilities.

It wasn't perfect though. It suffered horribly from tremendous turbo lag at low revs, and when the boost finally decided to kick in, the acceleration was nothing short of brutal. Then again, some drivers like a touch of brutality in their cars.

One thing is above debate – the Quattro drivetrain was undoubtedly the key to keeping the RS2 firmly planted on the road.

Audi A8

1994–2002

ENGINE: 90 degree V8, 4172cc

POWER: 300bhp

CHASSIS: Aluminium Space Frame chassis, with aluminium body panels

BRAKES (F/R): Disc with ABS and electronic brake-force distribution

TRANSMISSION: Five-speed manual or five-speed auto Tiptronic

SUSPENSION: Four-link front suspension and independent rear

TOP SPEED: 155mph (248km/h)

ACCELERATION: 0–62mph (100km/h) in 7.3 seconds

Fourteen years after the Quattro, Audi's technological onslaught resumed with the all-aluminium A8 limousine. Because aluminium is less stiff than steel, pressing a conventionally engineered body out of aluminium would have proved difficult, if not impossible. With the type of lateral thinking that has come to typify Audi's approach, the company developed a whole new way of constructing a car.

Under the sleek, aluminium-panelled skin lies a skeleton of large-section aluminium beams, which are both welded and bonded together. Not only does this result in a weight saving of over 300kg compared with a conventional steel-bodied car, but it has allowed Audi engineers to use the inherent properties of aluminium to provide class-leading safety. The separate chassis/body construction also made a significant contribution to isolating the vehicle's passengers from exterior noise.

The A8 was also the first Audi to feature the company's new four-link front suspension. This design was said to be a big step forward over previous conventional front strut suspension systems, which had been fitted to nearly every front-wheel-drive car for the previous three decades.

The range-topping 4.2 Quattro used the Porsche-designed Tiptronic automatic transmission, which also offered the driver sequential manual gear selection. Unfortunately, the A8 appeared to show every sign of being ahead of its time.

Sales were initially slow, and no other maker has followed Audi's lead into Aluminium Space Frame (ASF) construction. ASF technology, though, is being applied to the AL2, Audi's forthcoming super-economical town car – something which is sure to give the company another massive technological lead in the field of automobile engineering.

Audi A6

1997–

ENGINE: 90 degree V6, 2393cc

POWER: 165bhp

CHASSIS: Steel monocoque, four-door

BRAKES: (F/R): Disc with ABS

TRANSMISSION: Five-speed manual, or five-speed auto Tiptronic

SUSPENSION: Four-link front suspension, independent rear

TOP SPEED: 138mph (221km/h)

ACCELERATION: 0–62mph (100km/h) in 9.1 seconds

By the mid-1990s, Ferdinand Piech had bounced his way from being the chief at Audi to his position as the boss of the truly giant VW Group.

His technical genius saw him hatching a plan to build numerous VWs, Audis, Seats and Skodas – the four brands in the company portfolio – using the maximum number of shared components.

However, despite sharing these parts, the four brands still had to retain distinct identities, something that many doubted they would be able to accomplish. It wasn't long before, once again, Ferdinand Piech proved his doubters – in the VW company, the industry as a whole, and in certain sections of the motoring press – conclusively wrong.

The 1997 A6 saw the flowering not only of Piech's platform strategy, but an amazing rebirth of the genius of German industrial design – echoing and paying homage to all of its grand accomplishments earlier in the century.

Under the skin, the A6 shared much with the new VW Passat, and although the suspension systems and floorpan were near-identical, the engineering was subtle enough to allow slightly different wheelbases and tracks – sufficient flexibility to give the cars different driving characteristics.

For the average buyer, though, it's the styling – both inside and out – that gives a car its identity. The A6 was so distinctive that it was a real shock for a lot of people. Audi's stylists, led by Peter Schreyer, had rediscovered the pre-war German industrial design aesthetic typified by the revolutionary Bauhaus design school. For many people, the Bauhaus school defined the true nature of industrial design in the 20th century.

The A6's futuristic rump, with narrow lamp clusters mounted on each corner of the tail and heavily curved roof pillars, was both modern and reminiscent of art deco and ocean-liner style.

Audi TT

1998–

ENGINE: In-line turbocharged four, 1797cc

POWER: 215bhp

CHASSIS: Steel monocoque, three-door

BRAKES (F/R): Disc with ABS

TRANSMISSION: Six-speed manual

SUSPENSION: Struts front, independent wishbone rear

TOP SPEED: 140mph (224km/h)

ACCELERATION: 0–62mph (100km/h) in 6.4 seconds

The VW Group's common component strategy – that many doubted would ever work effectively – reached its pinnacle in 1998 with the stunning launch of the exceptionally powerful TT coupe.

It's almost impossible to believe that the TT was based on the humble Golf floorpan, and even more staggering to think that it incorporated the basic 1.8-litre 20V engine that was fitted to both humble Skodas and assorted Golfs.

As with the A6, Audi's design team managed to produce a very distinctive shape that fell within a style of design that is perhaps best described as a kind of machined modernism. The TT was nothing if not high-tech – its looks would not have been out of place on the set of a futuristic sci-fi film chronicling the lives of people in the year 2019.

The two-seater profile hid the fact that the TT was actually a three-door hatchback, with clever folding rear seats to maximise carrying capacity. Under the skin, the turbocharged 1.8-litre engines came in two grades of tuning, developing 185bhp and 215bhp. A transversely mounted engine meant that the 'quattro' drivetrain was not actually the real thing, but was closer in spirit to a development of the old 'part-time' VW Syncro system.

An all-new electronically controlled clutch system, however, could divert up to 100 percent of the available power to either the front or rear wheels – something that drivers of the TT notice immediately and come very quickly to appreciate, as it makes the car a really great drive.

Inside, the TT avoided the compromise of an existing dashboard design. Instead, it was given a unique styled interior that benefited from extensive aluminium detailing.

The searing performance of the 215bhp model promised to make it genuinely competitive when put up against the similarly priced Porsche Boxster.

Austin Atlantic

1948–1952

ENGINE: In-line four-cylinder, 2660cc

POWER: 88bhp

CHASSIS: Separate steel body and chassis

BRAKES (F/R): Drum

TRANSMISSION: Four-speed manual

SUSPENSION: Independent front, live rear

TOP SPEED: 91mph (146km/h)

ACCELERATION: 0–60mph (96km/h) in 16 seconds

In the context of an austerity-gripped Britain, the Austin Atlantic was a sensation in 1948 – an all-new 95mph (152km/h) British convertible car with modern, full-width styling. Incredibly, the Atlantic could be had with a powered hood and windows. Other discerning luxuries included an Ecko radio, adjustable steering wheel and a heater.

Austin had been first off the mark into post-war production in 1945, and the A90 Atlantic was Britain's first car designed specifically for the American market. The rugged internals comprised a long-stroke, overhead-valve, 2660cc four-cylinder engine giving 88bhp. More telling was the 140lb/ft of torque at just 2500rpm. There were four speeds on a very American-style steering column shift, with soft coil springs and wishbone suspension at the front and semi-elliptics to locate the solid rear axle.

The Atlantic's pace impressed the pundits. At the time, it was one of the handful of cars since the war that could top 90mph (144km/h), and 0–60mph (96km/h) in 16.6 seconds wasn't exactly hanging about in 1948.

Stateside sales never took off, despite Austin's valiant attempt to allay fears about its durability – in 1949 an Atlantic broke 63 American stock-car records at Indianapolis over seven days. Later, Len Lord was to claim that the attempt hadn't helped sell a single Atlantic in the USA.

Austin tried to sustain interest in the car with a huge $1,000 price cut in 1949 and, in 1951, by offering a fixed-head saloon. But the writing was on the wall by then. The convertible ceased production in January 1951, while the saloon struggled on until September 1952. The final production tally for the Austin Atlantic was 7,981 cars.

A40 Countryman

ENGINE: Four-cylinder, 948cc

POWER: 34bhp

CHASSIS: Monocoque

BRAKES (F/R): Drum

TRANSMISSION: Four-speed manual

SUSPENSION: Independent front, live axle rear

TOP SPEED: 72mph (115km/h)

ACCELERATION: 0–60mph (96km/h) in 35 seconds

Although hardly a revolutionary design – it shared many parts with the A35 – the 1958 Austin A40 Countryman has one claim to fame: it was the first hatchback family car. Given what has followed in the auto industry since 1958, it is an achievment that it would be foolish to overlook. It's certainly guaranteed the A40 a place in the annals of automobile history for many years to come.

There had been cars which had featured an opening 'tailgate' before, most memorably Citroën's Traction Avant and the Aston Martin DB2, but none had the A40's neat 'two-box' shape – one box for the engine and another for the passengers and luggage – which today is universal.

Apart from the Range Rover, few other cars have adopted the A40's horizontally split hatch either – with the bottom (metal) half dropping down and the upper (glass) part swinging upwards.

The A40's crisp styling, by Pininfarina, was the height of modernity in 1958. But somehow the model never captured the imagination in the same way as the similar-sized Ford Anglia and Triumph Herald managed – neither of them were as innovative or as versatile, either.

That isn't to say the A40 was unsuccessful. It has a very long and a very happy production life. In fact, there were more than 340,000 units produced in the nine years up until 1967.

Sadly, most of those have now been scrapped, but that just makes those few remaining survivors even more desirable for those enthusiasts that want to own a little piece of auto history.

Austin Healey Sprite

1958–1971

ENGINE: In-line four-cylinder, 948cc

POWER: 43bhp

CHASSIS: Monocoque

BRAKES: Drum all round

TRANSMISSION: Four-speed manual

SUSPENSION: Independent front, live axle rear

TOP SPEED: 84mph (134km/h)

ACCELERATION: 0–60mph (96km/h) in 20.5 seconds

There may have been many faster small sports cars than the 1958 Austin Healey Sprite, but it is almost certain that none of them has ever been more endearing. With its gaping grin and the pop-eyed headlights that gave it its 'Frogeye' nickname, this car captured the hearts of enthusiasts the world over. In fact, the trademark protruding lights were an afterthought when the extra cost involved ruled out Donald Healey's idea for retracting headlights.

Taking its mechanics from the well-filled British Motor Corporation (BMC) parts bin – mostly the Morris Minor and Austin A35 – the 11ft 5in. (3.48m) Sprite had a chirpy character on the road, too, with a respectable top speed of 84mph (134km/h) and up to 45mpg (6.3litres/100km) attainable.

Following on as the little brother to the big Healey 3000, the Sprite's one-piece front end lifted up to afford excellent access to the 948cc A-series engine, which gave all of 43bhp. The Sprite spawned many variants featuring increasing levels of ugliness and luxury. Partly in compensation, the drivers of the last Sprites of the early-1970s found themselves driving a car whose performance was way above that of the original Frogeye.

The Sprite was nothing if not persistent. There was even a badge-engineered MG variant which revived (and disgraced) the old Midget name. Unfortunately it lasted until the late-1970s in a totally hideous, rubber-bumpered form – about which the less said, the better.

Austin Healey 3000

1956–1967

ENGINE: Six-cylinder, 2912cc

POWER: 124–150bhp

CHASSIS: Separate chassis, steel body

BRAKES (F/R): Disc/drum

TRANSMISSION: Four-speed manual, optional overdrive

SUSPENSION: Independent front, live axle rear

TOP SPEED: 114–120mph (182–192km/h)

ACCELERATION: 0–60mph (96km/h) in 10 seconds

The original Austin Healey was the Healey 100 of 1953. Hastily adopted by the British Motor Corporation (BMC) as the Austin-Healey 100 – with the 2.6-litre, four-cylinder engine from the Austin Atlantic – its body was built by Jensen of West Bromwich, with final assembly taking place at the MG factory at Abingdon. It had a separate chassis, cam-and-peg steering and a solid rear axle sprung and located by half-elliptic leaf springs.

The six-cylinder BMC C-series engine from the Austin Westminster was shoehorned into a stretched version of the car in 1956 to make the 100/6. However, this wasn't entirely successful, as performance was down compared

with the old four-cylinder, which was a very torquey engine.

Redemption arrived in the form of the 3-litre 3000 Mkl in 1959 – outwardly the same shapely, low-slung two-seater, but featuring a sprightly 2912cc 124bhp engine. Top speed increased to 114mph (182km/h), whilst new front disc brakes improved the stopping power.

For 1961 BMC upped the power to 132bhp with triple SU carburettors for the MkII 3000, followed a year later by the MkIIa, with wind-up windows, a curved windscreen and a proper convertible

hood. From this point the cars were 2+2 only, and can be recognized by a vertical-slat front grille.

Last, and best, of the line was the 1964 MkIII with improved breathing providing 148bhp, pushing the top speed to over 120mph (192km/h). Brakes were improved by adding a servo, and inside the car had a wooden dashboard. US safety legislation – North America was always the car's largest market – finally forced the 3000 out of production in 1967. BMC replaced it with the far less successful MGC.

Princess

1975–1981

ENGINE: In-line four-cylinder, 1993cc

POWER: 92bhp

CHASSIS: Steel monocoque, four-door

BRAKES (F/R): Disc/drum

TRANSMISSION: Four-speed manual

SUSPENSION: Hydragas interconnected suspension

TOP SPEED: 110mph (176km/h)

ACCELERATION: 0–62mph (100km/h) in 12.9 seconds

The life and times of the Princess series perfectly sum up the chaos that the British motor industry found itself completely swamped by in the 1970s.

The low nose, high-tail shape penned by Harris Mann was years ahead of its time. It was incredibly space-efficient, and the original design even included a hatchback – a format unknown in this size of car at the time. Inexplicably British Leyland management insisted that the car should be launched as a saloon, wasting a major competitive advantage. It was some five years before the similarly aerodynamic and hatchbacked Sierra appeared.

The Princess arrived in 1975 as the 18-22 series, but after nine months the initial build quality was so bad – and the company had been nationalised by the government – that it was relaunched as the Princess, the new name standing in for Austin, Morris and Wolseley versions.

Under the space-age skin was equally high-tech Hydragas suspension, often praised in road tests for a superb ride quality, and, very unusually, transversely mounted in-line six-cylinder engines. Early examples of the six-cylinder installation were surprisingly poorly engineered. Four-cylinder engines sufficed for the cheaper models.

Eventually the Princess was reskinned – although it's debatable whether the looks were improved – finally given the hatchback that was always intended for it, and relaunched as the Ambassador. It only lasted two years before being phased out. It was effectively replaced by the Austin Maestro – which was a class below it in size.

Mini Metro

1980–1990

ENGINE: Four-cylinder in-line, 998cc

POWER: 63bhp

CHASSIS: Steel monocoque, three- and five-door

BRAKES (F/R): Disc/drum

TRANSMISSION: Four-speed manual

SUSPENSION: Hydragas interconnected suspension

TOP SPEED: 93mph (149km/h)

ACCELERATION: 0–62mph (100km/h) in 14.9 seconds

The Metro was probably the most-discussed new car project ever. The British motor industry was effectively saved from bankruptcy by the government in 1974, with the result that ADO 88 – a replacement for the famous Mini – was the subject of much debate in the Houses of Parliament, in the motoring and national presses and in the saloon bars of many pubs up and down the country.

ADO 88 was billed as the car to save British Leyland. However, the first attempt was a stylistic disaster and only an emergency restyling some 18 months before launch saved the project – and the British car industry – from certain failure.

Financial restrictions ruled out new running gear so the Metro – as it was eventually to be called – relied on Mini subframes, suspension and the ancient four-speed sump-mounted gearbox.

However, the old A-series engine was somewhat updated, to become the A+.

Despite the rocky road to production that it had to travel, the Metro was a surprisingly decent car and one that deserves to be remembered fondly. Its utilisation of space was second to none, and it was also the first car to feature an asymmetrically split rear seat. It handled with alacrity, and even spawned MG and MG Turbo versions.

The Metro was given a comprehensive make-over as a Rover vehicle in 1990 which, albeit briefly, put it at the top of the supermini league.

The final version of the car, badged the Rover 100, stayed in production until December 1997 – still selling at a decent rate. Although outlasted by the original Mini it was based on, it did indeed help to save the British auto industry.

Bentley Continental

1952–1955

ENGINE: Straight-six, 4566cc

POWER: Not quoted

CHASSIS: Separate chassis, alloy body

BRAKES (F/R): Drum

TRANSMISSION: Four-speed manual

SUSPENSION: Independent front, live axle rear

TOP SPEED: 124mph (198km/h)

ACCELERATION: 0–60mph (96km/h) in 13 seconds

In the early 1950s, the Bentley Continental was not only the fastest genuine four-seater car in the world – it could top 120mph (192km/h) with ease – but also one of the most beautiful. Shaped in Rolls-Royce's Hucknall wind tunnel in the East Midlands, its bold, distinctive fastback profile was influenced – although no one would admit it – by the Cadillac 62 series Coupe of 1948.

The Continental's alloy bodywork was built in London by H.J. Mulliner on a special high-performance chassis. The 4566cc engine breathed more freely thanks to a higher compression ratio and a big-bore exhaust system.

There was a weight-loss regime for this, the first sporting Bentley since the 1930s. Bumpers were made of aluminium, not steel, and inside the armchair seats of the R-Type saloon had given way to smaller sports buckets with alloy frames.

Out on the road, tall gearing gave the Continental a fantastically long stride, with 80mph (128km/h) attainable in second, 100mph (160km/h) in third and 124mph (198km/h) in top. This was all achieved in fuss-free refinement.

Inevitably, the later cars watered down the concept of the original lightweight R-Type Continental which had made the car such a classic. Fat-bottomed tycoons wanted fatter, more luxurious seats, lazy drivers with little real passion for motoring wanted automatic gearboxes, steel bumpers replaced the alloy type, and before long the Continental was just another heavy coachbuilt Bentley – albeit a superbly handsome one.

In fact, the Continental look lived on for a time on the S-Series chassis of 1955. By then, however, the Continental name was applied to all manner of coachbuilt Bentleys.

Turbo R

1985–1992

ENGINE: V8, 6750cc

POWER: Not available

CHASSIS: Monocoque

BRAKES (F/R): Disc

TRANSMISSION: Three-speed automatic

SUSPENSION: Independent

TOP SPEED: 140mph (224km/h)

ACCELERATION: 0–60mph (96km/h) in 6.7 seconds

The turbocharged Bentley four-door models that emerged in the 1980s were the first moves towards giving the marque a separate identity from Rolls-Royce – something it hadn't enjoyed since the days of the R-type Continental in the 1950s.

The original Mulsanne Turbo of 1983 slightly misjudged the mood of the market, however. With 50 percent more power and torque from the big, all-alloy pushrod V8, it was certainly fast, but Crewe's engineers had decided that the soft, under-damped suspension of the standard Mulsanne was adequate for this two-ton (2036kg) gentleman's hot rod. The result was a car that could be an ungainly handful out on the road, especially when driven in the wet.

They followed it up three years later with the Turbo R. This model, lowered and stiffened and fitted with wider tyres, showed that the Crewe company could build a car that really handled. The top speed was limited to 140mph (224km/h) – because there were no tyres available that could handle such a combination of weight and speed – but it was the car's magnificent acceleration that really impressed, with 0–60mph (96km/h) taking just seven seconds.

All the Bentley qualities of refinement and high-class appointments remained, of course, and it wasn't long before the Turbo R was out-selling its Rolls-Royce sister models. It will certainly be a classic super-saloon of the future.

Bentley Continental T

1996–2003

ENGINE: V8, 6750cc

POWER: 550bhp

CHASSIS: Monocoque

BRAKES (F/R): Disc

TRANSMISSION: Four-speed automatic

SUSPENSION: Independent

TOP SPEED: 170mph (272km/h)

ACCELERATION: 0–60mph (96km/h) in 6.5 seconds

For some enthusiasts, the 400bhp and 500lb/ft of torque developed by Bentley's elegant Continental R coupe were not enough. To help them, the company thoughtfully provided the 550bhp Continental T, launched by the marque in 1996.

This wonderfully excessive 2+2 coupe was slightly shorter than the 'R' and featured a highly flamboyant interior. This was intended to be a throwback to the impressive racing Bentleys of the 1920s, echoing the glorious history of the marque during that period.

The dashboard was finished in turned alloy in place of the usual walnut. The interior also featured drilled pedals in a laughable attempt to save weight in this 2.5-ton (2,545kg) monster.

You could spot one by its flared arches, five-spoke alloys and mesh grille. Bentley claimed 170mph (270km/h) and 0–60mph (96km/h) in 5.7 seconds, thanks to a V8 engine – still basically the same all-alloy unit introduced in 1958 – that probably had the highest torque figure of anything on the public road: 650lb/ft at just 2200rpm.

For something of its size, the stiffened Continental T handled well and had enormous grip, thanks to traction control and massive tyres. The down side was a slight loss of refinement compared with the standard car, and regrettably the ride was both fidgety and noisy.

In 1997, the price of such opulence was almost a quarter of a million pounds.

BMW 507

1956–1959

ENGINE: V8, 3168cc

POWER: 150–160bhp

CHASSIS: Separate chassis, alloy body

BRAKES (F/R): Disc/drum

TRANSMISSION: Four-speed manual

SUSPENSION: Independent front, live axle rear

TOP SPEED: 125–140mph (200–224km/h)

ACCELERATION: 0–60mph (96km/h) in 9 seconds

In search of a flagship glamour-car to boost US market sales in the mid-1950s, BMW commissioned Albrecht Goertz, a German aristocrat with an American-based industrial-design agency, to style a new super-sports-car.

Goertz – later responsible for the best-selling Datsun 240Z – sketched a slim, pinched-waist roadster that was an object lesson in elegant purity. With its long bonnet, pert tail and impeccable detailing, it was an instant classic.

Packing 150bhp from a high-compression version of BMW's fine, all-alloy V8 (with a four-speed manual gearbox), it went as impressively as it looked too, with 140mph (224km/h) available and 0–60mph (96km/h) coming up in

around nine seconds. Torsion-bar suspension front and rear provided a supple ride with confident handling – perfect for the car's role as a suave, high-speed express for the Monte Carlo set.

Beautifully crafted in alloy, the 1956 507 was aimed squarely at the Mercedes 300SL's market, but somehow it was more of a soft tourer than the complex and difficult-to-handle SL. Serious drivers never really took it to their hearts.

Production ceased in 1959, just 253 cars having gone down the line. If anything, the intended flagship glamour-car only added to BMW's shaky financial problems at the time, but almost 40 years on it rates as perhaps the most collectable of post-war BMWs.

BMW 3.0 CSL

1971–1975

ENGINE: Straight-six, 3003cc

POWER: 200bhp

CHASSIS: Monocoque

BRAKES: Disc all round

TRANSMISSION: Five-speed manual

SUSPENSION: Independent

TOP SPEED: 133mph (213km/h)

ACCELERATION: 0–60mph (96km/h) in 7 seconds

The lightweight CSL BMWs were built to homologate the big six-cylinder coupes into Group 2 European Touring Car racing. They proved spectacularly successful, and remained competitive long after the production cars had been replaced.

Based on the pillarless Karmann-built steel shell that dated back to 1965, the first road-going 3.0 CSL – announced in May 1971 – was a real stripped-out road racer. It featured thinner body panels, no front bumper (fibreglass rear bumper), racing latches on the bonnet, manual winding side windows (made from Plexiglas) and alloy-skinned opening panels – all in the name of weight reduction.

Along with a drastically cheaper interior, 400lb was paired off the coupe. Whilst the top speed was not greatly affected by this diet, acceleration was decisively improved.

The suspension was stiffened and the wheels were fat Alpina 17in. (43cm) alloys with chrome wheelarch extensions to keep them legal. Black accent stripes distinguished the CSL from the standard CS/CSi. A total of 169 examples were built, all with left-hand drive.

Originally fitted with the 2985cc carburetted version of the in-line six (giving 180bhp), a slight size increase in August 1972 gave 3003cc, which allowed the CSL to slip into 3-litre Group 2 competition. At the same time Bosch electronic fuel injection replaced the twin Zenith carburettors, and power rose to 200bhp.

The bespoiled 3.2-litre CSL was announced in August 1973. It had a bigger 3.2-litre 206bhp engine to homologate the 84mm stroke used on the 3.5-litre works racing coupe. The famous 'Batmobile' spoiler (or racing kit) was packed away in the boot on cars sold in West Germany, where such appendages were never legal. Manual steering and Bilstein gas-pressure shock absorbers meant that the 3.2-litre CSL didn't need an anti-roll bar.

Around 100 of these cars were built, but production stopped in 1975, as BMW began to prepare the way for the Six Series.

2002 Turbo

1973–1975

ENGINE: Four-cylinder, 1990cc

POWER: 170bhp

CHASSIS: Monocoque

BRAKES (F/R): Disc/drum

TRANSMISSION: Four and five-speed manual

SUSPENSION: Independent

TOP SPEED: 130mph (208km/h)

ACCELERATION: 0–60mph (96km/h) in 8 seconds

BMW's first turbocharged design was the mid-engined Turbo show car of 1972. Originally just two of these vehicles were built, but the car gave a foretaste of some of the engineering to be found on the company's first full-blown production model, the 2002 Turbo of 1973.

Its 170bhp engine was considerably detuned compared with the show car. Despite this, it was still more than enough to give the boxy little two-door saloon some serious kick.

The top speed went up to 130mph (208km/h) and the 0–60mph (96km/h) time came down to just 8 seconds – an astonishing figure for a 2-litre road car in the early 1970s.

Lowered suspension and fatter tyres gave the 2002 Turbo better grip than the standard car, but the primitive early turbocharger installation lacked the flexibility and response of modern units – the boost could come in rather viciously. Driving it quickly required a considerable amount of skill to handle the sometime brutal nature of the turbo's muscular boost.

It was to be a short-lived model, which is perhaps a shame. Unfortunately the 2002 Turbo came into being in the midst of the 1970s fuel crisis, and became another tragic casualty of the period's war on its class of car.

Company executives thought that the 2002 Turbo's aggressive stripes and spoilers were somewhat inappropriate, too. BMW withdrew the car from production in 1974, after just 1,674 examples had been built.

1979–1980

ENGINE: In-line 24-valve six-cylinder, 3453cc

POWER: 277bhp

CHASSIS: Steel spaceframe, composite bodyshell

BRAKES (F/R): Disc

TRANSMISSION: Five-speed manual

SUSPENSION: Double-wishbone front and rear

TOP SPEED: 162mph (259km/h)

ACCELERATION: 0–62.5mph (100km/h) in 5.6 seconds

Plans for BMW to enter the Group 4/5 World Championships were laid in 1975. The company, then a tiny player on the world car-making scene, thought this route would be both a more high-profile way of publicising the BMW badge than Formula One, and would give BMW a chance to compete directly with – and beat – Porsche.

The then head of BMW's Motorsport division, Jochen Neerpasch, decided that a mid-engined car would have to be created, a move that would require 400 road-going versions for homologation purposes. Unusually for a German car maker, BMW mishandled the birth of the M1, as it became known.

It set a production deadline of early 1978 by which to finish a run of 800 production M1s. Unfortunately, it was a total that couldn't be accommodated either by BMW's main production line or the specialist Motorsport division, so

the M1 project was farmed out. From there on the project went sadly awry.

While Italian stylist Giugiaro was completing the body styling, BMW decided to commission Lamborghini to build it. Lamborghini, however, looked incapable of meeting the quality standards and also seemed on the verge of closure. Other delays, including a redesign of the engine's cylinder head, meant that the car missed the Group 4

homologation deadline.

The road-going M1 was built, but it went through five different companies in Germany and Italy before being finished. And with no race series to compete in, BMW had to invent the 1979 Procar race series to give the M1 a purpose. Despite being far better conceived and more reliable than contemporary Ferraris or Lamborghinis, only 453 M1s were sold. The result is an extremely sought-after car.

BMW

Z1

1989–1991

ENGINE: In-line six-cylinder, 2494cc

POWER: 170bhp

CHASSIS: Steel backbone chassis, composite floorpan and body panels

BRAKES (F/R): Disc all round with ABS

TRANSMISSION: Five-speed manual

SUSPENSION: Struts front, multi-link rear

TOP SPEED: 141mph (226km/h)

ACCELERATION: 0–62.5mph (100km/h) in 7.9 seconds

In mid-1985 BMW decided to found a new internal division called Technik GmbH. It was to be an advanced design and engineering counterpart to the company's already proven and highly successful Motorsport division.

By late 1988 Technik's engineers had launched the Z1 roadster, the first in the wave of modern roadsters. Z stood for zukunft, the German for future. It was an appropriate name given the nature of the vehicle that was being developed. The Z1 would play an important role in shaping the future technology of other BMW vehicles.

The Z1 was masterminded by Ulrich Bez and styled by Harm Laagay; shortly after the launch, both men left for Porsche where they had earned themselves deserved reputations as innovators.

Although not revealed at the launch, the Z1 started life as a 'mule' used to develop the complex and clever rear suspension for the 1991 3-Series. Technik, however, put in a much bigger effort than simply manufacturing what at first looked like a re-bodied 325i cabriolet.

The Z1 was built on a steel backbone chassis, which gave the car all its strength. The 13 exterior bolt-on plastic panels didn't provide any strength – the Z1 could be driven without them.

It also used massive sill sections into which the side doors would slide and disappear, giving the driver a truly open driving experience. The car's actual 'floorpan' was a high-strength, foam-cored sandwich panel bolted to the metal chassis.

At its launch, the car proved to be a revelation in terms of handling and grip, and benefited enormously from the beautifully sculpted, hard-edged styling. Production capacity immediately sold out up to two years in advance.

The BMW Z1 was not only a step into the future. It was the accumulation of everything that BMW had learned over the decades up to that point about producing great roadsters.

Without the technological jumps that the development of the car helped bring about, fabulous later vehicles such as the BMW Z3 roadster would not have been conceivable.

BMW M5

1990–1996

ENGINE: In-line six-cylinder, 3535cc

POWER: 315bhp

CHASSIS: Steel monocoque, four-door

BRAKES (F/R): Disc with ABS

TRANSMISSION: Five-speed manual

SUSPENSION: Struts and lower wishbones front, semi-trailing arms rear

TOP SPEED: 155mph (248km/h), restricted

ACCELERATION: 0–62.5mph (100km/h) in 6.9 seconds

When it was launched in 1990, the M5 was the fastest saloon in the world. One motoring publication wondered whether the world had seen the launch of a four-door Ferrari.

Its heart was the classic twin-cam, straight-six unit first seen in the M1, but tuned to make it – at 315bhp – BMW's biggest and most powerful six-cylinder engine, quite an achievement.

Like all BMW engines, especially those developed by the Motorsport division, it needed to be revved very hard if you wanted to extract the best performance. Once above 4000rpm, however, the M5 shook off its low-revs lethargy and began to sprint with some serious vigour, the rev counter spinning around to 7200rpm with ease.

The standard-issue suspension was good enough not to need major re-working, but stiffer springs and dampers were utilized, as well as thicker anti-roll bars. The brakes were uprated and the M5 also had a limited-slip differential.

Like a Ferrari, the M5 was completely hand-built, aside from the bodyshell construction, but as one of the best-made mass-market cars on sale, it was no surprise that the M5's exquisite quality in every area of its construction was one of the car's biggest attractions.

Complaints that the first generation of the 1990 M5 lacked the element of sheer fun that might have been expected were dispelled with a power boost to 340bhp in 1992. Performance was further tweaked with the adoption of a six-speed gearbox and electronically controlled adaptive suspension in 1994.

5-Series

1996–2003

ENGINE: In-line 24-valve six-cylinder, 2793cc

POWER: 190bhp

CHASSIS: Steel monocoque, floorpan

BRAKES (F/R): Disc with ABS

TRANSMISSION: Five-speed manual, or automatic

SUSPENSION: Struts with double ball joints front, multi-link rear

TOP SPEED: 145mph (232km/h)

ACCELERATION: 0–62.5mph (100km/h) in 8.9 seconds

After the big advances made by the 1991 3-Series and the highly regarded 5-Series before it, much was riding on the all-new 5-Series which was launched in 1995. BMW's inherent devotion to leading-edge technology was amply demonstrated in the model. The new 5-Series shared only gear-boxes and its differential with the out-going model.

It's rare for replacement models to be completely new. Engineering a large executive car to a high standard is an incredibly complex task and also an incredibly costly one – even for a company as large as the mighty BMW.

BMW's dedication to making the 5-Series as sporting as possible and its willingness to invest serious money was not obvious when looking at the 5-Series. In fact, at the time of launch

the overly smooth styling was badly received after the chiselled edges of the 3-Series.

However, under the skin was a suspension system expensively constructed from aluminium – not just the suspension arms, but the front struts, sub-frames and brake calipers, a complex and costly move. Unsurprisingly, the BMW 5-Series proved to be an absolutely impeccable road car. It offered a remarkable combination of a very compliant ride and strong, sporting handling.

The car's build quality was unmatched by few cars available at any price. Ironically, the 5-Series' lofty talents were so evenly spread, it was sometimes marked down as lacking in character, proving that however good something is, you just can't make everyone happy all of the time.

Mini

2001–

ENGINE: 1598cc 16-valve four cylinder

POWER: 114bhp

CHASSIS: Steel monocoque

BRAKES (F/R): Disc with ABS

TRANSMISSION: Five-speed manual

SUSPENSION: Struts front, multi-link 'Z" axle rear

TOP SPEED: 125mph (200km/h)

ACCELERATION: 0-62mph 9.2secs

BMW's 1994 take-over of the British Rover Group ended six years later with vast debts and much political recrimination. BMW broke the company into three: it virtually gave away Rover and MG (which was bought out by management and dealers for £10, but given a £550m dowry and the Rover engine plant), it sold Land-Rover to Ford but it kept the Mini brand.

Development of the new Mini started in 1995 with a mass-styling competition. The winning design was by American BMW designer Frank Stephenson. His new Mini was longer, wider and taller than the original, though in the flesh it appears much bigger than it is. BMW says the up-sizing can be blamed on the need to provide top-level crash safety and the fact that the average European is 50mm taller than in 1960.

Under the skin was a very sophisticated cocktail of BMW technology, particularly the 'Z' rear axle and the electronics system. Packaging all this tech under the Mini's tightly-pulled skin was a real challenge for the Rover-based engineering team. The engine, though was based on Chrysler design and built in Brazil. BMW polished the unit sufficiently, though.

The Mini was a much higher-quality car than its £10,000 + price tag suggested and had a driving experience to match. It received universal rave reviews for its superb handling and was a runaway success when it was launched. Initially it came as the basic Mini One, the more powerful Cooper and a 163bhp supercharged (six-speed) Cooper S. A Toyota-powered diesel version was also planned as was – further into the future – a cabriolet.

BMW X5

1999–

ENGINE: 4398cc V8

POWER: 288bhp

CHASSIS: Steel monocoque

BRAKES (F/R): Disc with ABS

TRANSMISSION: Five-speed auto

SUSPENSION: Struts front, multi-link 'Z" axle rear

TOP SPEED: 125mph (200km/h)

ACCELERATION: 7.2sec 0-60mph

When BMW bought Land-Rover in 1994 plans to build its own SUV were, understandably but onto the backburner. Wolfgang Reitzle, BMW's number two had other ideas. He had toured the global motorshows and was convinced that a sports utility vehicle was something BMW had to build. After some delay, BMW re-started work on what would become the X5.

Early prototypes were based on the four wheel-drive BMW 525 iX Touring and were seen – suitably jacked up – plying the motorways between Germany and Britain. Indeed, the X5 is probably best understood as a tall estate car - or traditional station wagon - rather than having any pretence to real off-road abilities.

The X5 was launched in Atlanta in late 1999, close to the factory were the car was to be built. Journalists at unveiling drove the car both on roads and at a race circuit. BMW wasn't being overconfident – the X5 was a complete revelation. It handled like a sporting saloon car rather than a station wagon. Praise was lavished on its direct steering and agility even on winding country lanes. The X5 was also beautifully built.

For some reason BMW restricted the numbers the Spartanburg factory could build so long waiting lists for the car grew almost immediately. Three years later demand for the excellent 3.0-litre diesel X5 still well exceeded supply. The X5 also proved that BMW was right to sell Land-Rover in 2000. Shortly after launch plans for a smaller 'X3' SUV were also being hatched by BMW.

Bond **Bug**

1970–1974

ENGINE: Four-cylinder, 700cc

POWER: 29bhp

CHASSIS: Ladder frame, tubular cross members

BRAKES (F/R): Drum

TRANSMISSION: Four-speed manual

SUSPENSION: Independent

TOP SPEED: 75mph (120km /h)

ACCELERATION: 0–60mph (96km/h) in 26 seconds

The first Bond cars were curious three-wheelers built for economy-minded motorists in the late-1940s and 1950s at a factory in Preston, Lancashire.

With its Triumph-based Equipe models, the company attempted to move up-market in the mid-1960s – while keeping the economy-car associations – with its little three-wheeler, rear-engined 875.

However, Bond will always be best remembered for the Bug, which was introduced in 1970 after the company had been taken over by British manufacturers Reliant, of Tamworth.

With its uncompromising wedge shape, orange paint job and swing-up cockpit canopy, this sporty three-wheeler was a clear attempt to grab some of the affluent youth market of the 'Swinging Sixties.' However, by the time of its introduction in 1970, the great expectations of that decade had all but evaporated.

The styling was by Tom Karen of Ogle, the company responsible for the then-trendy Scimitar GTE. With Reliant's game little 700cc light-alloy engine providing the power, the Bug was good for a brave 75mph (120km/h) flat-out, with lively acceleration into the bargain. Its enthusiasts often point out that it has the acceleration of a Mini Cooper.

It had no doors, only curtains, which allegedly offered some protection. It had two seats, sitting some 8 inches above the road.

More troublesome was the handling on just three wheels, which nobody regarded as much 'fun.' The model died in 1974 after a four-year production run in which a mere 2,562 cars had been produced.

Isabella

1954–1961

ENGINE: Four-cylinder, 1493cc

POWER: 75bhp

CHASSIS: Monocoque

BRAKES (F/R): Drum

TRANSMISSION: Four-speed

SUSPENSION: Independent

TOP SPEED: 95mph (152km/h)

ACCELERATION: 0–60mph (96km/h) in 17.4 seconds

Although the name is little known today, Borgward made some excellent cars before its untimely demise in 1961. Most memorable is the Isabella range first seen in 1954.

Named after the wife of company founder Karl Borgward, these lively and well-made cars were the BMWs of their day, featuring unitary construction and all-independent suspension. The alloy-headed engine produced 75bhp in TS form, giving the car a top speed of over 90mph (around 150km/h).

There were estate and two-door-saloon versions of the Isabella, but undoubtedly the most desirable model was the coupe. This was allegedly put into construction to prevent Dr Borgward's wife from buying a VW Karmann Ghia.

Its shapely lines were much admired, but high prices made sure it was never destined to be a top seller. It deserved better.

Even more glamorous and expensive was the cabriolet version, converted by the coachbuilder Deutsch of Cologne. This must be the ultimate collector's Borgward, as only 29 of these very desirable cars were ever built.

Dr Borgward's big dream was to build a car to rival the more up-market Mercedes models. He finally managed this with the short-lived Big Six of 1959.

Sadly, the realisation of this dream included huge development costs. They were so high in fact that the dream cost Borgward his company, and the last cars were built in 1961.

Big Six

1959–1961

ENGINE: Straight six, 2238cc

POWER: 100bhp, 1950s

CHASSIS: Monocoque

BRAKES (F/R): Drum

TRANSMISSION: Four-speed manual

SUSPENSION: Independent

TOP SPEED: 100mph (160 km /h)

ACCELERATION: 0-60mph (96 k/ mh) in 14 seconds

Borgward had luxury car ambitions in the late fifties and desperately wanted a slice of the German big-car market dominated by Mercedes. Its challenger was the P100 'Big six', a faster, cheaper and better-equipped foil to Stuttgart's important new 'Fintail' 190/220 range. With its restrained tail fins and wrap-around screens front and rear, the P100 was fashionable without being flash.

The hull was all steel, unitary and a true five seater with generous legroom, opulent seating and a huge boot. Power came from the 2,240cc 6M2.3 11 TS engine, basically an Isabella unit with two extra cylinders producing 100bhp. The P100s biggest claim to fame was its 'airswing' air suspension which comprised air bag units with Bosch control and levelling valves. It was pressurised by an air pump, belt driven off the front crank pulley and feeding a reservoir mounted at the front of the engine compartment. The Big Six was the first German car to use the system.

The new P100s threat to the Fintail did not please Mercedes and, the way Borgward fans tell it, Stuttgart had more than a little to do with the downfall of the family-owned Borgward empire. It was alleged that they pulled financial strings to bring the company's creditors – component suppliers – knocking at the door at just the wrong moment.

Borgward, over-stretched by the development costs of the P100, folded in January 1961. Big Six production stood at just 1,400 cars.

There is a bizarre footnote to the Big-Six story, though. The liquidators sold the tooling to a company called Fansa, who built a further 2,500 Big Sixes at a factory near Monterey in Mexico.

Bristol 401

1951–1953

ENGINE: Straight-six, 1971cc

POWER: 85bhp

CHASSIS: Separate chassis, alloy body

BRAKES: Drum

TRANSMISSION: Four-speed manual

SUSPENSION: Independent front, live axle rear

TOP SPEED: 97mph (155km/h)

ACCELERATION: 0–60mph (96km/h) in 15.1 seconds

As you would expect of a car built by an aeroplane maker, there was no room for penny-pinching compromise in the design or construction of the Bristol 401.

Even at a Purchase-Tax-inflated £3,112 in Britain – three times the cost of an 'equivalent' 1949 Jaguar – it's unlikely that Bristol's car division, which split from the parent company in 1961, ever turned in much of a profit.

The 401's alloy body was just one example of the high-minded extravagance that permeated the design of the car. The alloy panels, wrapped around small-diameter tubes, were graded in thickness according to function – heavier on top of the wings, for instance, where mechanics leant during servicing.

The engine, a straight-six 'borrowed' from BMW after the war as part of reparations, was a gem.

It yielded almost 100mph (160km/h) from an 85bhp 2-litre engine pulling an opulently trimmed full four-seater, which was impressive, but outright speed wasn't what this car was all about. Fine handling – especially in the days before motorways – was even more important, and the 401 was well blessed with poised good manners that gained the marque many enthusiastic lifelong friends.

The memorable 'Aerodyne' body, shaped on the firm's own runway at Filton, near Bristol, was as slippery as the name suggests. In tests carried out 20 years after the 401's demise, only four modern cars were found to be more aerodynamic. The 401 became the 403, with a bit more power and better brakes, in 1953, and the company built its last six-cylinder car – the 406 – in 1961, losing the battle with increasing weight.

409/410/411

1970–1976

ENGINE: V8, 6277cc

POWER: 335bhp

CHASSIS: Separate chassis, alloy body

BRAKES (F/R): Disc

TRANSMISSION: Three-speed automatic

SUSPENSION: Independent front, live axle rear

TOP SPEED: 138mph (221km/h)

ACCELERATION: 0–60mph (96km/h) in 7.2 seconds

The V8 Bristol has outlived all its Euro-hybrid competitors. While American-engined exotica such as Jensen, Gordon Keeble, Iso and Monteverdi floundered, Bristol have ridden out every storm.

They have managed to achieve this minor miracle by keeping small and selling their cars – still alloy-bodied and separately chassised – to a discreet and discerning few.

Today's Bristol Blenheim is a direct descendant of the 407 of 1962, a radically different car for Bristol which forsook their traditional straight-six engine configuration and transverse leaf-spring front suspension for a big, all-iron Chrysler V8 and conventional wishbones and coils. Although the 407 and 408 were fast and impressive, the handling and balance suffered. The really nice V8 Bristols begin with the later 409s, which had their engines further back in the chassis for better handling. More importantly, they had power steering – a sensitive ZF set-up reckoned to be one of the best in the world.

The 410 of 1968 had subtle styling changes to give it a smoother line. The first of the 411s of 1970 had a lower ride-height with clipped fins, less brightwork, a limited-slip differential and – best of all – an even bigger 6.2-litre engine.

Series-2 411s (1970) had automatic self-levelling suspension, whilst the Series-3 (1972) models had entirely new front-end styling with twin 7in. (18cm) lights. Series-4 cars (1973) had an even bigger 6.6-litre engine, giving 330bhp. Last-of-the-line Series-5 411s (1975) had a black grille, stiffer chassis and improved cooling.

Despite their patrician looks, the bigger-engined cars could nearly touch 140mph (224km/h), and boasted dragster-like acceleration that left heavier luxury machines floundering. Such performance – combined with whispering refinement, exceptionally tasteful bespoke ambience and well-honed chassis balance – gave these cars their unique appeal. This has not dimmed over the years.

Royale

1926–

ENGINE: 12,800cc straight-eight

POWER: 200bhp

CHASSIS: steel ladder chassis

BRAKES (F/R): cable-operated drums

TRANSMISSION: three-speed manual

SUSPENSION: live axles with elliptic springs

TOP SPEED: not known

ACCELERATION: not known

Ettore Bugatti founded his company around 1909, and it soon gained a reputation for very high-class, sophisticated and even beautiful engineering. Indeed, Bugatti is often referred to as an artist-engineer.

Although many of his cars were regularly winning races, Bugatti also produced luxury models and he wanted to build the ultimate luxury machine. In the mid-1920s Bugatti worked on a 16-cylinder aero engine for the French Air Force, but a proper deal didn't emerge and he took the opportunity to use one, eight cylinder bank of the design to create a powerplant for his luxury dream car.

The prototype of the car he called 'La Royale' (it's said he wanted to sell the car to royalty) had a massive 14.7-litre engine and a huge 187in wheelbase. In production

form the engines was 12.8-litres and chassis had a 170in wheelbase. The price for the basic chassis and running gear (as was the style, customers had to have a body manufactured) was a staggering £6500 – twice the price of a Rolls-Royce Phantom II.

Six Royales were manufactured initially, although 29 engines were built in anticipation of further orders. It seems just three Royales were delivered to customers and another three remained in the hands of the Bugatti family until well after WW2. Amazingly, the remaining 23 engines – and another 163 new units – were used in a Bugatti-built French national railways railcar which were in use until the 1960s. The most famous Royale example – with a Kellner body – was sold for £5.5m in 1987.

Roadmaster

1949–1958

ENGINE: Straight-eight, 5200cc

POWER: 150bhp

CHASSIS: Separate

BRAKES (F/R): Drum

TRANSMISSION: Two-speed automatic

SUSPENSION: Independent front, beam axle rear

TOP SPEED: 100mph (160km/h)

ACCELERATION: 0–60mph (96km/h) in 17 seconds

The 1949 Buick Roadmaster was the first truly new Buick to be built after the Second World War, and it came with dramatically low styling that set the tone for the decade to come. Its shape was decisively imprinted on numerous other vehicles, and on our collective memories of that time.

The sweeping fastback design was based on GM's 'C' body family shared with the Cadillac and Oldsmobile divisions of the giant American company, and featured a 25-tooth chrome grille that became known as the 'Dollar Grin'.

All Buicks had 'Ventiports' in the front wings, but the top-of-the range Roadmaster featured four rather than three, to signify its status as the most expensive and luxurious model of them all.

Although Buick's 5.2-litre straight-eight engine was regarded as old hat compared with the new generation of overhead-valve V8s in the latest Cadillacs, there was no denying that it delivered the goods, with a top speed of 100mph (160km/h).

Buick V8s didn't arrive until 1953, but even more impressive was the two-speed Dyna-Flow fully automatic transmission that had been pioneered by Buick on its 1948 model-year cars. It was a standard feature on the Roadmaster and proved to be a big favourite with Buick owners

The Roadmaster name managed to last until 1958, but by then the passage of the the years had transformed it into just another glitzy barge, with ever-bigger tail fins.

Riviera

1963–1965

ENGINE: V8, 6572cc

POWER: 325bhp

CHASSIS: Separate chassis, steel body

BRAKES (F/R): Drum

TRANSMISSION: Two-speed automatic

SUSPENSION: Independent front, live axle rear

TOP SPEED: 130mph (208km/h)

ACCELERATION: 0–60mph (96km/h) in 8 seconds

Forsaking the chrome and glitz that were hallmarks of its contemporaries, the 1963 Buick Riviera had that rare quality – class. Swoopy in its styling, yet delightfully restrained, the vehicle had presence and gravitas where Cadillacs and Chrysler Imperials were merely big. It stood alone as an almost mythical figure – a 1960s big American car that was actually very tasteful.

Conceived as Buick's answer to the best-selling Ford Thunderbird, the Riviera was a kind of American Bentley Continental. It was blessed with some of the finest styling to come out of Detroit in the 1960s – or any other period, when it comes right down to it.

Under the bonnet was the inevitable V8 engine, initially sized at 6.5 litres, but later featuring 7.0 litres and anything up to 365bhp. Even with the obligatory two-speed automatic gearbox, this huge car – a five-seater – was good for 130mph (208km/h), although handling was strictly conventional on the separate chassis.

Unfortunately, the drum brakes were never really up to the job. They had the bad habit of quickly succumbing to serious fade at high speed.

Inside, the Riviera driver wanted for nothing, with electric windows and power steering as part of the package. The dashboard was impressive too, looking distinctly elegant by Detroit standards.

Inevitably, in a land of built-in obsolescence, Buick couldn't help but fiddle with the Riviera's classic and very appealing styling – particularly when it came to the clamshell-covered lights. After 1965, the car lost something of its unique personality and character, sharing its underpinnings and structure with the Cadillac Eldorado.

Buick

1971–1973

Riviera 'Boat Tail'

ENGINE: V8, 7459cc

POWER: 330bhp

CHASSIS: Perimeter frame

BRAKES (F/R): Disc/drum

TRANSMISSION: Three-speed automatic

SUSPENSION: Independent front, live axle rear

TOP SPEED: 125mph (200km/h)

ACCELERATION: 0–60mph (96km/h) in 8.5 seconds

Buick's flagship Riviera line, once a styling leader, had begun to lose its way in the late 1960s with slick, smooth looks that seemed much like every other big American luxury coupe of the period. It also failed to capture the unique sense of class possessed at an earlier point in its history.

Ford's Thunderbird began to overtake it in the sales charts, and it soon became clear that Buick needed something new and different if it was going to redress the balance.

The Riviera found its saviour in a new design by GM styling boss Bill Mitchell, unveiled in 1970 for the 1971 model year. Here was a much more dramatic look with an aggressive snout, curved hips and a fastback roofline that narrowed down into a pointed boat-tail. This also allowed a sporty wrap-around rear window, which clearly had its stylistic roots in the split-screen Corvette Stingrays of the early 1960s.

Mechanically, the cars were much as before. The Boat Tail was powered by a huge 7459cc V8 which, in tuned GS (Grand Sport) form, produced 330bhp and propelled this two-ton motorcar to a top speed of 125mph (200km/h).

Although controversial at the time, the Boat Tail quickly became recognized as a classic. Following its demise in 1974, successive Rivieras became uglier, smaller and more conventional – taking the same damaging path the Boat Tail had originally been designed to correct.

Cadillac Series 62

1949

ENGINE: V8, 5426cc

POWER: 162bhp

CHASSIS: Separate chassis

BRAKES (F/R): Drum

TRANSMISSION: Three-speed auto

SUSPENSION: Independent front, live axle rear

TOP SPEED: 100mph (162km/h)

ACCELERATION: 0–60mph (96km/h) in 13 seconds

The 1949 Cadillac marked the beginning of the tail-fin craze. It was a form of American styling that would not fade for a further decade.

Inspired by the Lockheed P-38 aircraft, the fins began as modest blips on the '48 car which was otherwise a fairly restrained design, even rather elegant in Sedanette form. This body, with its long sweeping tail and curved windscreen, is said to have inspired the original Bentley Continental R-Type of 1952, and there is no denying the similarity between the two.

As well as being one of the most dramatic looking cars on American roads, the '49 model Series 62 was also one of the fastest. This was thanks to a new overhead valve V8 which had been ten years on the drawing board.

The engine delivered a 162bhp punch. Quiet and smooth with its five main bearings and hydraulic valve lifters, it was good for the magic 100mph and could push the Series 62 to 60mph in 13 seconds – faster than most sportscars of the day. Naturally the Series 62 featured automatic transmission, a Cadillac feature since 1941.

Cadillac later adopted a tubular X-frame, without side rails, for later models of the Series 62. This resulted in greater structural rigidity and provided for lower body lines without loss of useable space.

New front end styling was marked by rubber bumper guard tips and dual circular parking lamps set into the lower bumper section. Side trim was revised and the tail light theme was used throughout the line. Upgrades such as these helped ensure the continuing popularity of the Series 62.

Cadillac

1957–1958

ENGINE: V8, 6384cc

POWER: 325bhp

CHASSIS: X frame

BRAKES (F/R): Drum

TRANSMISSION: Three-speed automatic

SUSPENSION: Independent front, live axle rear, air suspension

TOP SPEED: 118mph (189km/h)

ACCELERATION: 0–60mph (96km/h) in 11 seconds

Eldorado Brougham

The 1957 Eldorado Brougham was the most prestigious Cadillac since the V16 models of 17 years before. The design had started life as a dream car at the 1954 and 1955 Motorama exhibitions, its pillarless styling and knife-edge fins almost restrained for this gaudy period in American design.

Quadruple headlights, a stainless-steel roof and narrow-band whitewall tyres were industry firsts, but the Brougham was more than just a styling exercise. Under the skin there was an advanced air-suspension system, with self-levelling valves and a small engine-driven compressor.

Powered by Cadillac's big 6.3-litre V8, the Brougham was marketed as a super-exclusive model for the super-rich, and featured an amazing list of standard features that was unmatched at the time. Power steering, power brakes and automatic transmission were becoming the norm on cars of this class, but the Brougham also featured such luxuries as an automatic headlamp dipper, cruise control, electric door locks, and it even had an electric boot-lid opener.

There were magnetized drinks tumblers in the glovebox, cigarette and tissue dispensers and, for the ladies, even a special cosmetics set that included lipstick, powder puff, a mirror and comb and an Arpège atomizer with Lanvin perfume. Buyers could choose from 44 trim combinations, as well as specifying Karakil or lambskin carpeting.

Cadillac couldn't sell the Brougham for anything like the amount it cost to build, however. After two years of losses, the model was dropped.

Eldorado Biarritz

1959

ENGINE: V8, 6384cc

POWER: 345bhp

CHASSIS: Separate chassis, steel body

BRAKES (F/R): Drum

TRANSMISSION: Three-speed automatic

SUSPENSION: Independent front, live axle rear

TOP SPEED: 115mph (184km/h)

ACCELERATION: 0–60mph (96km/h) in 12 seconds

The 1959 Eldorado Biarritz has passed into popular legend, pushed beyond the cultural reference point into the realms of cliché. It has come to symbolize an era when the most powerful nation on earth was at its most confident, and its faith in the future at its most bullish and brash.

The American obsession with the tail-fin reached its zenith in 1959, and nobody did it bigger, or better, than Cadillac – Detroit's premier luxury motor-car manufacturer. An outrageous 42in. (107cm) in height, 1959 Cadillacs had the biggest fins around, their jet-age imagery accentuated by a pair of bullet-shaped turn- and stop- lights. Front-end styling was equally distinctive, with twin headlights and double-decker grilles across the board.

Twenty feet (6.1 metres) long, six feet (1.83 metres) wide and scaling two tons (2000kg) in weight, the 1959 cars came as two-door coupe De Villes, pillarless four-door hardtops or as an even bigger Fleetwood 75 formal limousine. There was a high-spec Fleetwood version of the stock four-door saloon too. All were based on a simple perimeter-frame chassis

with drum brakes all round.

Best-remembered, though, is the Eldorado Biarritz convertible, with a more powerful 345bhp version of Cadillac's famous 6.3-litre V8.

The ultimate in four-wheeled glamour, naturally the six-seater Biarritz came fully equipped with power-operated seat adjustment, electric boot opening and even automatic headlamp dipping – over and above the obligatory power steering, automatic transmission, power hood and electric windows. Air suspension was one of the few options on this $7,401 monster, the purchase price being three times that of the cheapest Chevrolet that year.

To comment on the dynamic qualities of such a cultural icon seems superfluous. It was certainly fast in a straight line at 115mph (184km/h), but the sheer weight combined with soggy springs gave the Eldorado handling qualities that could only be compared with a boat. Fuel consumption was in the 8mpg (35litres/100km) range, but then petrol economy was not an issue at a time when fuel was still so optimistically cheap.

Cadillac Seville

1975–1979

ENGINE: V8, 5700cc

POWER: 170bhp

CHASSIS: Monocoque

BRAKES (F/R): Disc/drum

TRANSMISSION: Three-speed automatic

SUSPENSION: Independent front, live axle rear

TOP SPEED: 115mph (184km/h)

ACCELERATION: 0–60mph (96km/h) in 11.5 seconds

The Seville was Cadillac's answer to the smaller, more efficient European luxury cars of the mid-1970s that were eating significantly into its market. In the midst of a fuel crisis, it signalled a move away from the dinosaurs of the past.

The Seville was notably shorter than any of its predecessors, and was styled with a deliberate restraint that gave it an almost European flavour.

Although hardly nimble, the Seville was far less ungainly than the full-size models, and with its downsized 5.7-litre V8 engine (an Oldsmobile unit) it could manage a respectable 15mpg (19litres/ 100km) and 115mph (184km/h). Later, there was even a diesel version – the first oil-burning Cadillac ever – but there were few other technical innovations.

However, the Seville drivers did not feel that they were being short-changed. The interior featured all the power operation for the seats and windows found on larger Cadillacs, plus a trip commuter for calculating fuel consumption. Leather or cloth seats were also available. The vehicle certainly offered a lot for a car of its size.

The model proved a huge success, and set the agenda for a whole raft of new, smaller Cadillacs in the 1980s. The Seville itself became the bizarre Elegente in 1979, and found itself with a razor-edged bustle-back styling strongly reminiscent of a post-war Daimler or Rolls-Royce.

The Seville name still survives today, on a new generation of front-wheel-drive Cadillacs.

Cadillac Allante

1990–1996

ENGINE: V8, 4894cc

POWER: 170bhp

CHASSIS: Monocoque

BRAKES (F/R): Disc

TRANSMISSION: Four-speed automatic

SUSPENSION: Independent

TOP SPEED: 130mph (208km/h)

ACCELERATION: 0–60mph (96km/h) in 8 seconds

The Allante was Cadillac's answer to the Mercedes SL convertibles. These cars had been powerfully dominating the luxury open two-seater market in America for the best part of 20 years.

In search of a sophisticated European image for its new flagship, Cadillac joined forces with the Italian house of Pininfarina. They were the stylist and coachbuilder to all of Europe's most prestigious marques – including Ferrari.

Not only did Pininfarina style the new car, but it built the bodywork, too, air-freighting the trimmed steel shells over from Turin to the Cadillac factory in Detroit. It was an expensive process, but then the Allante was going to be an expensive car – pitched in the same $50,000 bracket as the Mercedes machines that inspired it.

This wasn't the first time Cadillac had been associated with Pininfarina. In the 1930s the company had built a special body on a V16 Cadillac, and there had

even been a production run of Brougham Pininfarina models in the late 1950s and early 1960s, pitched as exclusive top-line models for customers who preferred something a little more discreet.

The Allante's clean lines certainly didn't look American, and it had a high-class leather interior to match, with all the latest electric labour-saving devices. Cadillac's first two-seater, the Allante was based on the front-wheel-drive Seville floorpan.

Early cars used the transversely mounted 4.1-litre pushrod V8, while later cars (from 1990) used the advanced 4.9-litre 'Northstar' with sequential injection matched to traction control.

Wieldy and refined, the Allante certainly found favour with buyers, but it never really stood a chance of getting close to the Mercedes SL's unassailable position. It didn't come as a particularly great surprise to anyone when production of the vehicle was eventually stopped in 1996.

Cadillac STS

1998–

ENGINE: 32-valve V8, 4565cc

POWER: 305bhp

CHASSIS: Steel monocoque

BRAKES (F/R): Disc with ABS

TRANSMISSION: Four-speed automatic

SUSPENSION: Struts front, multi-link rear

TOP SPEED: 152mph (243km/h)

ACCELERATION: 0–62.5mph (100km/h) in 6.9 seconds

Cadillac's quest to expand outside North America and a few eastern markets didn't die with the Allante. Once again it tried to conceive a car that would attract the professional classes of the USA's eastern and western seaboards – which are so keen on 'imports' – as well as translate overseas. Cadillac also went to the trouble of producing a right-hand-drive conversion, potentially opening up the key UK, Japanese and South African markets.

The STS was considerably shorter – around 8in. (20cm) – than the US-market car from which it was derived. Reducing the size of the Cadillac was necessary for the crowded driving conditions of Europe. The STS's styling was also more Euro-slick than any American car before it.

A desire to match Lexus extended inside for the most un-American interior design – again aimed at those tempted by the Lexus. In truth the Cadillac looked good enough inside and out to be the most serious US road-car attempt on the world market yet. Its Northstar V8 was a world-class powerplant. Alone in this class as a front-wheel-drive vehicle, the STS must have been one of the most powerful front-wheel-drive cars ever sold.

There was evidence that the STS lacked the honing required for high-speed European motoring – body control, stability at motorway speeds and quality of plastics – but its standard specification was so extensive that the STS was seen as a bargain, even at the price.

General Motors' need to see the Cadillac brand globalized was made even clearer by the creation of a satellite styling studio in Britain's automotive heartland, the West Midlands.

Caterham Seven JPE

1992–

ENGINE: Four-cylinder, 2000cc

POWER: 250bhp

CHASSIS: Steel space-frame

BRAKES (F/R): Disc

TRANSMISSION: Five-speed manual

SUSPENSION: Independent

TOP SPEED: 150mph (240km/h)

ACCELERATION: 0–60mph (96km/h)
in 3.4 seconds

The JPE was the ultimate Lotus Seven. Stripped of all unnecessary weight, it was designed to give the sensation of Formula One driving on the road. For once, cost was irrelevant, giving Caterham's engineers a chance to use the best of everything in the name of ultimate performance.

At the car's heart was a £13,000 Group Two Touring Car-specification Vauxhall 2-litre engine delivering 250bhp, which meant a power-to-weight ratio of 472bhp per ton. Power went through a Quaife straight-cut, close-ratio gearbox. To keep the weight down, carbon-fibre and Kevlar were widely used in the construction, and it even did without such niceties as windscreen wipers and a windscreen.

Fine tuning of the design was completed by ex-Formula One driver Jonathan Palmer – hence the name JPE (Jonathan Palmer Evolution) – and with its wild fluorescent-green colour scheme, the car got a lot of attention in the Press.

Naturally it was very, very fast. One magazine recorded a 0–60mph (96km/h) time of just 3.4 seconds, while another managed a 0–100–0mph (0–160–0km/h) run in just 12 seconds – three seconds faster than a Ferrari F40.

Although docile at lower speeds, the 150mph (240km/h) JPE was no car for the novice. Buyers under 25 years of age had to take a high-performance driving course before they could take delivery.

Caterham Super Sport

1996–1999

ENGINE: Four-cylinder, 1998cc

POWER: 138bhp

CHASSIS: Space-frame

BRAKES (F/R): Disc

TRANSMISSION: Five- or six-speed manual

SUSPENSION: Independent

TOP SPEED: 138mph (221km/h)

ACCELERATION: 0–60mph (96km/h) in 4 seconds

After 21 years of producing the Seven – he took the design over from Lotus in 1973 – Caterham Cars boss Graham Nearn finally decided that the company was in a position to build a new car from the ground up.

It wasn't intended as a replacement for the classic, sketchy, two-seater fun car, but as something a little more modern and forgiving, with an all-enveloping body to provide more room inside.

Physically, however, the new car would not be much bigger than the Seven, and would retain the same wheelbase and front and rear tracks. That way, the existing suspension components could be transferred straight over.

Designer Ian Robertson was contracted to create a new body. He sketched a lithe and elegant roadster inspired, perhaps, by the Lotus Eleven in its wing line. The new design had a spare and muscular feel all of its own, though.

The interior, with its stacked dials and rounded consoles, was as bold as the exterior. It helped ensure that the car was the talk of the 1994 Birmingham Motor Show.

Powered by the multi-valve Vauxhall 2-litre engine or Rover's K-series, performance was mind-blowingly strong, with 0–60mph (96km/h) coming up in four seconds from the Vauxhall unit.

Although the prototype was finished in polished aluminium, production cars – built at a rate of no more than 250 per year – used fibreglass, and were offered in fully built-up and component forms, just like the original Seven.

Checker Marathon

1956–1982

ENGINE: Straight-six, 3704cc

POWER: 145bhp

CHASSIS: Separate X frame

BRAKES (F/R): Drum

TRANSMISSION: Three-speed automatic

SUSPENSION: Independent front, live axle rear

TOP SPEED: 93mph (149km/h)

ACCELERATION: 0–60mph (96km/h) in 14 seconds

The Checker Marathon is better known as the classic yellow New York taxi cab, which first appeared in 1956 as the A8 and was offered as a passenger car for private use from 1960 to 1982.

As you would expect, the car was based around rugged – rather than advanced – engineering. After all, its designers knew the type of life a car that could be used as a New York taxi cab could expect once it left the production line.

Power came from a long-lived L-head straight-six unit, giving as little as 80bhp on 1950s models and up to 155bhp on later cars with overhead-valve Chevrolet-derived engines. There was a Chevrolet V8 option, and by the mid-1960s automatic transmission was an almost universal fitment.

Checkers could be ordered in six- or eight-seater forms, the latter being a special 129in. (328cm) wheelbase limousine called Town Custom.

There was even a Station Wagon version. There was a famous eight-door Aerobus designed for airport and hotel use, too. The dumpy styling of the Checker hardly changed at all over the years though, which was probably why its appeal as a commercial passenger car was fairly limited.

Sales dwindled in the 1960s and 1970s as even New York cabbies abandoned the durable Checker for more conventional big saloons, and today the once familar and distinctive car has disappeared from the streets of the Big Apple – though it will forever be linked with the city.

Corvette

1953–1956

ENGINE: Straight-six, 3849cc

POWER: 150bhp

CHASSIS: Separate chassis, fibreglass body

BRAKES (F/R): Drum

TRANSMISSION: Two-speed automatic

SUSPENSION: Independent front, live axle rear

TOP SPEED: 103mph (165km/h)

ACCELERATION: 0–60mph (96km/h) in 12 seconds

In the early 1950s, General Motors (GM) was trailing behind its rivals, Ford and Chrysler, in sales terms – it didn't even offer a V8 engine in its staid family Chevrolet range. So it was while searching for a more sporty image that Chevrolet launched the Corvette at 'Motorama' in 1953.

When this dazzling roadshow for General Motors' latest models opened at the Waldorf Hotel in New York in January of that year, this new sports-car took centre-stage. For the first time, chief stylist Harley Earl had created a 'dream' car that looked as if it was going to go into production. So enthusiastic was the public reaction to this bold fibreglass roadster that GM bosses gave the go-ahead right away, and the Corvette went from a clay model to the showroom in just 15 months.

Under the skin, though, enthusiasts were disappointed by the car's specification. The 'stovebolt' six-cylinder power unit barely produced 150bhp. Worse still, the two-speed Powerglide automatic transmission was rightfully derided by sports-car buffs, who wanted sporty, European-style 'stick-shifts'. What is more, the car was too expensive – its price was only a few dollars short of a Cadillac's and, with its credibility shattered, sales were poor. Only 700 were sold in 1955.

Ironically, it was the release of Ford's fashionable Thunderbird that spurred GM into making a proper sports car out of the Corvette, and for the 1956 model-year new V8 engines became available to give the car the performance it deserved. Sales took off and the Corvette – now a match for imported sports cars in a straight line, never mind the wallowy T-Bird – never looked back.

Bel Air

1957

ENGINE: V8, 4639cc

POWER: 185–285bhp

CHASSIS: Separate box-section type

BRAKES (F/R): Drum

TRANSMISSION: Three-speed manual, three-speed automatic

SUSPENSION: Independent front, live axle rear

TOP SPEED: 90–120mph (144–192km/h)

ACCELERATION: 0–60mph (96km/h) in 8–12 seconds

With the 1957 Bel Air, Chevrolet created one of the best-loved American classic cars of all – its strong, simple lines and impressive performance (from a sporty new V8 engine) appealing to a whole generation of youthful Americans.

Based on its 150 Series, the Bel Air was Chevrolet's top-of-the-range car. You could always recognise one instantly by the generous amount of extra chrome side trim it featured.

By the standards of the day, its fins were rather slim and restrained – helping to give it a touch of elegance. The clean shape was derived from the completely redesigned 1955 model cars.

As well as two and four-door six-passenger sedans, the Bel Air was available as a classy convertible, with optional power hood. A unique three-door, hard-top station-wagon version was called the Nomad.

The basic engine was a straight-six, but the Bel Air – like its lower-priced siblings – could be had with a whole range of V8s. These went from a 185bhp Turbo-Fire to a potent 285bhp fuel-injected unit as found in the contemporary Corvette.

Chevrolet claimed that the latter was the first production engine to provide one horsepower per cubic inch (283cu.in./283bhp), but Chrysler had actually beaten Chevrolet to it a few months earlier with its 300 Series. With this engine though, the Bel Air was a true 120mph (192km/h) car. At an extra cost of $500 dollars for the upgrade, there were few takers for this expensive option.

Inevitably the Bel Air became less special with every passing year after the 1957 model. By the early 1960s, it had lost most of its native character and charm, and had been reduced to just another overweight American car.

Chevrolet Corvair

1959–1969

ENGINE: Flat-six air-cooled, 2377/2684cc

POWER: 80–180bhp

CHASSIS: Monocoque

BRAKES (F/R): Drum

TRANSMISSION: Three- and four-speed manual, two-speed automatic

SUSPENSION: Independent

TOP SPEED: 87–105mph (139–168km/h)

ACCELERATION: 0–60mph (96km/h) in 12 seconds (Monza)

The Chevrolet Corvair was General Motors' response to the huge influx of low-priced European economy cars into the North American market in the late-1950s and early-1960s. With its rear-mounted, air-cooled, flat-six engine and fully independent suspension, it was far removed from the general run of American cars and particularly its 'compact' rivals from Ford and Chrysler, which were really just scaled-down large cars.

Launched in 1959 as a 1960 model, the controversy surrounding the handling of the early models inspired safety campaigner Ralph Nader to write a book called 'Unsafe at any speed'. It was a best-seller, and proved to be the herald of a new era of government regulations that continues to this day.

Enthusiasts loved the European flavour of the car, but ordinary buyers weren't anything like as convinced, and the Corvair's more conventional rivals comfortably outsold it. It took the introduction of the little Monza coupe, with its punchier engine, for the Corvair to find its niche in the market as a compact sporty car.

Its fortunes took a turn for the better again when a convertible version was launched in 1962, and there was even a turbocharged version. Sadly, the honeymoon wasn't to last. The bad publicity from Nader's book gave the car a reputation for wayward handling, and when Ford introduced the Mustang in 1964, the Corvair didn't stand a chance as buyers gravitated towards its more conventional, safer engineering and equally sporty image.

GM tried to rescue the Corvair in 1964 with a handsome restyle and improved rear suspension. But sadly the damage had been done and sales never recovered, although Chevrolet kept the Corvair in its line-up until 1969.

Impala SS

1961–1964

ENGINE: V8, 4639–6704cc

POWER: 230–360bhp

CHASSIS: Separate box-section type

BRAKES (F/R): Drum

TRANSMISSION: Three- and four-speed manual, two-speed automatic

SUSPENSION: Independent front, live axle rear

TOP SPEED: 135mph (216km/h) – 360bhp engine

ACCELERATION: 0–60mph (96km/h) in 7.8 seconds (360bhp engine)

The SS was a new package on Chevrolet's aggressive-looking Impala line for 1961. Although nobody knew it at the time, it was really one of the first 'muscle cars' produced and this has helped earn it a place in auto history.

Presenting a slimmer profile with a large glass area and virtually no rear fins, the Impala was a sub-series of the basic Biscayne and Bel Air models that formed the backbone of the Chevrolet range, yet it was a very different type of car.

The shape dated back to the 'seagull wing' 1959 design. The SS, a dealer-fitted option package, featured leather-grained vinyl upholstery, bucket seats, swirl-pattern instrument panel inserts, a silver anodized rear panel and special wheel trims.

Power came from a choice of five V8s, ranging in size from a relatively 'soft' hydraulic-lifter 283cu.in. (4639cc) unit developing 230bhp, to a wild solid-lifter 360bhp 409cu.in. (6704cc) lump.

Thus equipped, the Impala was a real brute, capable of 0–60mph (96km/h) in 7.8 seconds. SS models came with power brakes and steering, and had their suspension uprated with heavy-duty shock absorbers and springs.

The drum brakes came with sintered metallic linings in an attempt to address the problem of fade during high-speed use.

The Impala spearheaded a brief American domination of saloon-car racing in Europe where, driven by such legendary talents as Graham Hill and Dan Gurney, the Impala showed it could keep up with – and sometimes even beat – the Mk II Jaguars who had grown used to having it all their own way in European competitions.

Chevrolet

Corvette Stingray

1963–1967

ENGINE: V8, 5356–7000cc

POWER: 250–560bhp

CHASSIS: Separate chassis, fibreglass body

BRAKES (F/R): Drum and disc/drum

TRANSMISSION: Three- and four-speed manual, two-speed automatic

SUSPENSION: Independent rear

TOP SPEED: 118–145mph (189–232km/h)

ACCELERATION: 0–60mph (96km/h) in 5.6 seconds

The first of the Chevrolet Corvette sports cars was produced in 1953. Despite this, the marque did not really reach maturity until 1962, with the introduction of the Stingray.

Like its ancestors, the new car had a fibreglass body, but the styling – with its fashionable retractable lights – was all-new. Underneath, the separate chassis remained, but the Corvette was unusual for an American car in having independent rear suspension. A range of V8 'small block' 5.4-litre engines was offered, from a base model giving 250bhp, to a 300bhp unit with a bigger carburettor and the 340bhp L76 with solid tappets and a higher 11.25:1 compression ratio. The latter was available with the famous Rochester fuel-injection system, unleashing a further 20bhp. In the relatively light Corvette, performance was electrifying, with 0–60mph (96km/h) coming up in 5.6 seconds.

Each year of production brought minor cosmetic and technical changes to the vehicle. However, the big news for the 1965 model was the optional big-block 396cu.in. V8, packing a colossal 425bhp and 415lb/ft of torque at 4000rpm.

The engine went up to a full 7 litres (427cu.in.) for 1966, and could be had in 390bhp or 425bhp forms. The last year for the Stingray was 1967. It was offered with 300bhp and 350bhp small blocks and big blocks ranging in output from 390bhp to 435bhp, depending on the carburation and compression ratio.

For racers only there was the near-legendary L88 engine, giving 560bhp on 103-octane petrol. For the 1968 model year, the new 'Coke bottle' Stingray was announced – a fairly worthy successor that, somehow, never recaptured the spirit of the 1963–67 Stingrays.

Camaro

1967–1972

ENGINE: V8, 5736cc

POWER: 360bhp

CHASSIS: Monocoque

BRAKES (F/R): Disc/drum

TRANSMISSION: Four-speed manual, three-speed automatic

SUSPENSION: Independent front, live axle rear

TOP SPEED: 125mph (200km/h)

ACCELERATION: 0–60mph (96km/h) in 7.5 seconds

The original Camaro of 1967 started life as Chevrolet's answer to the top-selling Ford Mustang, a sporty two-door 'Pony car' with strong youth appeal, available in a range of options that covered everything from meek and mild economy straight-sixes to monster, tyre-shredding V8s.

Although the styling of the model – always twinned with Pontiac's Firebird in the GM stable – never lost its sense of sporty purpose in the way the Mustang did, the Camaro definitely had its good years and bad years. By the end of the 1960s, sales of the car were flagging badly, and even a complete and rather handsome restyle for 1970 didn't do much to help at first.

Bleak as things looked, this period produced perhaps the best Camaro of them all, the classic Z28. This was a special-performance option that featured a 360bhp V8, and was recognizable by its dual exhausts, stripes, rear spoiler and black-painted grille. To handle the power, Z28 models came with sports suspension, front disc brakes and a 'posi-traction' rear axle that incorporated a limited slip differential. Buyers could choose from either three-speed automatic or close-ratio, four-speed manual transmissions.

General Motors allowed the Camaro to wither on the vine in the early 1970s, denying it the significant yearly changes that kept buyers interested. The issue of its survival was forced in 1972 when thousands of bodyshells were stranded on the production lines in a strike.

By the time the dispute was over, the cars couldn't be sold under new Federal safety regulations, and they were all scrapped. They would have been followed by the Camaro model itself, had GM bosses had their way.

Chevrolet fought for the survival of the badge, however, and by the middle of the decade had turned its fortunes around. The basic shape lasted well into the 1980s.

Nova SS

1968–1972

ENGINE: V8, 5737cc

POWER: 245–375bhp

CHASSIS: Monocoque

BRAKES (F/R): Disc/drum

TRANSMISSION: Three- and four-speed manual, three-speed automatic

SUSPENSION: Independent front, live axle rear

TOP SPEED: 110–125mph (176–200km/h)

ACCELERATION: 0–60mph (96km/h) in 6–8.7 seconds

Based on Chevrolet's basic 'senior compact' sedan developed from the Chevy II line of the early 1960s, the Nova SS was a miniature muscle car built for boy racers with a restricted budget and a passion for large amounts of power. Although they were big cars by European standards, in their humble six-cylinder form the Novas provided everyday transport for thousands of Americans who regarded cars as mere domestic appliances.

With the V8 engines fitted, however, the Nova took on a new personality. It became one of the most respected off-the-shelf hot-rods around.

The SS package offered small and big-block V8s, the latter delivering up to 375bhp in solid-lifter L-38 form. These cars – available only by special order, and not always officially catalogued –

could complete a quarter-mile (400m) dash in 14 seconds and top 120mph (192km/h).

There were three- and four-speed manual and three-speed automatic transmission options. The SS package also included special decals, sports wheels and hood ornaments to let other drivers know what they were dealing with.

Other options included significantly beefed-up suspension and front disc brakes. Power steering was an option – the steering was very heavy without it – but despite this the Nova SS was well regarded for its handling.

Hot-rods like the Nova became less socially acceptable as the 1970s dawned, and after 1972 no more uprated SS versions were offered. This helped to make it a highly collectable vehicle.

Corvette Stingray '68

1968–1984

ENGINE: V8, 5.7/7.5 litre

POWER: 300–500bhp

CHASSIS: Separate box-section chassis, fibreglass body

BRAKES (F/R): Disc

TRANSMISSION: Four-speed manual, three-speed automatic

SUSPENSION: Independent

TOP SPEED: 117–170mph (187–272km/h)

ACCELERATION: 0–60mph (96km/h) in 5.7–8 seconds

The third generation of the Corvette didn't get a very good reception when it was launched in 1968. The pundits were unimpressed with the new flamboyant styling, inspired by the Mako Shark show car of 1966. With its aggressive pointed nose, flying buttresses flanking the rear window (on the coupe) and the sharply cut-off tail featuring pseudo-Ferrari round tail-lights, it seemingly failed to please.

Although Chevrolet advertised the car as 'all new all over', in fact the 1968 car was little different from its predecessors, retaining the same separate chassis and a crude – but fairly effective – form of independent rear suspension first seen in 1963. The fact that it drew so heavily from its predecessors was the main strength of the car. It certainly helped to keep it strong with the public in terms of popularity, sales and performance.

Disc brakes were at least standard across the board now. The car was also offered with a range of V8 engines that gave it the performance to live up to its aggressive looks.

The basic 5.7-litre small block was good for 300bhp and 0–60mph (96km/h) in 8.4 seconds – even with automatic transmission. If you opted for one of the big-block 427 units, you had a truly awesome machine. The Tri-Carb delivered 435bhp.

If the critics didn't like the Corvette at first, then the buyers certainly did. That was why the car became the most long-lived and successful of the marque, lasting in production until 1984. Basically, the real reason why the critics were holding back on praise for the new Corvette was because it was replacing a generation of Corvettes that had won a place in almost everyone's hearts.

Monte Carlo

1970–1972

ENGINE: V8, 5737–7442cc

POWER: 300–360bhp

CHASSIS: Perimeter frame

BRAKES (F/R): Drum

TRANSMISSION: Three-speed automatic

SUSPENSION: Independent

TOP SPEED: 115–134mph (184–214km/h)

ACCELERATION: 0–60mph (96km/h) in 7.7 seconds (7442cc version)

The Monte Carlo was Chevrolet's answer to the Ford Thunderbird. It was an urbane coupe with a sporty image in the then-popular 'personal luxury' mould.

Based on the same platform as the 1969 Pontiac Grand Prix, the handsome, clean-cut Monte Carlo significantly undercut the price of the Thunderbird, however, and outsold it handsomely. Chevrolet built 130,000 Monte Carlos in its first year, compared with just 40,000 Ford Thunderbirds.

Inside, the Monte Carlo had a walnut dashboard and all the power-operated devices you could want to make driving easy and stress-free. It was also fast – very fast for a car of its type – especially with the biggest SS 454cu.in. V8 engine option in place. This 360bhp workhorse could rocket the Monte Carlo to 60mph (96km/h) in a time of less than eight seconds, and push it to a top speed of more than 130mph (208km/h).

All but a handful of Monte Carlos had automatic transmission – as you might expect – and the car made a great long-distance cruiser, capable of maintaining 110mph (176km/h) all day long. If you had to do a long journey, it was a dream of a car.

Smooth and quiet-riding, the Monte Carlo also enjoyed some success on the stock-car tracks. It did particularly well in the hands of drivers such as Richard Petty and Bobby Allison.

Production of the original-shape Monte Carlo ended in 1972, to be replaced by an uglier, less-powerful version that continued the model's success.

Chevrolet Corvette ZR-1

1988–

ENGINE: 32-valve V8, 5727cc

POWER: 380bhp

CHASSIS: Welded steel chassis, composite body panels

BRAKES (F/R): Disc with ABS

TRANSMISSION: Six-speed manual

SUSPENSION: A-arms and coils front, multi-link with transverse leaf rear

TOP SPEED: 180mph (288km/h)

ACCELERATION: 0–62.5mph (100km/h) in 4.5 seconds

In 1987, news leaked out from General Motors (GM) that it was working on a development of the Corvette nicknamed 'king of the hill'. The key to the new car would be a very powerful engine. Codenamed LT5, GM handed development of the vehicle over to its UK subsidiary, Lotus.

The original target set for the ZR-1 was to create the fastest production car in the world, without sacrificing low-speed driveability or fuel economy. The new engine also had to fit in the engine bay – a task made more tricky because the Corvette engine was offered into the nose from underneath. The upshot

was a space between the chassis rails of 27x27in. (69x69cm). The engine capacity had to stay at 5.7 litres, a figure much revered by US Corvette fans.

Lotus's development of the engine centred on sophistication, but it ended up taking the best part of four years to get the LT5 engine into the production car. Clever features included two fuel injectors for each cylinder and a variable valve timing system, but the engine didn't quite manage 400bhp and 400lb/ft of torque, finally settling at 380bhp.

Even so, GM claimed 180mph (288km/h) for the ZR-1. GM took the ZR-1's sheer power very seriously by equipping the car with two ignition keys. One key started the car and allowed it to run at 80 percent of its maximum power using just three valves and one injector per cylinder. The second activated a power key on the centre-console to open up all 32 valves and 16 injectors. And the reason? According to GM's boss, "Some owners wouldn't want their spouses or sons in charge of the car's full potential."

Chrysler 300

1955–1962

ENGINE: V8, 5426cc

POWER: 300bhp

CHASSIS: Separate chassis, steel body

BRAKES (F/R): Drum

TRANSMISSION: Three-speed automatic, four-speed manual

SUSPENSION: Independent front, live axle rear

TOP SPEED: 125mph (200km/h)

ACCELERATION: 0–60mph (96km/h) in 8 seconds (C300)

The Chrysler 300 of 1955 was the USA's most powerful production car. It took its name from the racy 300bhp engine, which sported twin four-barrel carburettors and a full-race camshaft. With the power came handsome looks.

Chrysler's flamboyant styling chief, Virgil Exner, had taken his inspiration from the latest Italian GT cars, and married it to the impressive scale of Detroit's products to fashion one of the cleanest and most stylish hardtop coupes on the market. It was only available in black, red or white.

The 300's interior was also one of America's most luxurious, with full leather upholstery. It was hand-built, expensive and exclusive. The 300 cost $4,109 in 1955, and just 1,725 examples were made.

In 1956 came the 300B, which began a year-by-year march through the alphabet for the series ending in 1965 with the 300L – the last of what collectors now call the 'Letter' cars. The 300B broke the world passenger-car speed record at Daytona Beach, averaging 139.9mph (224km/h), and it was the first American car to top its cubic capacity (354cu.in., or 5798cc in European terms) with its power output (355bhp), which it did in 1957, for the 300C.

Exner produced a totally new style, with an aggressive, forward-leaning nose and dramatic rear fins. It was longer, lower, wider and sleeker than any other American luxury car.

The 300G, made only in 1961, was the pinnacle of the breed's evolution. It had the highest top speed – the mechanically identical 300F won the Flying Mile competition at Daytona with 145mph (232km/h). It also had the hottest engine – the largest engine produced 450bhp – and the wildest styling. Exner's fins reached their dramatic peak before his replacement, Elwood Engel, ordered them to be removed from the 1962 300H. All Chrysler 300-series cars are now very collectable.

Ghia L6.4

1960–1962

ENGINE: V8, 6279cc

POWER: 335bhp

CHASSIS: Monocoque

BRAKES (F/R): Drum

TRANSMISSION: Three-speed automatic

SUSPENSION: Independent front, live axle rear

TOP SPEED: 140mph (224km/h)

ACCELERATION: Not available

Many Italian design studies were built on American mechanics in the 1950s and 1960s, but few got beyond the stage of being a one-off prototype. One that did make it through was the Ghia L6.4 of 1960, of which 26 were built in two years.

A big coupe inspired by the Virgil Exner-designed Ghia Dart, it also bore a striking resemblance to the Fiat 2300S Coupe, another Ghia design of the period. Hand-built on Chrysler 6.4-litre V8 mechanics, the car received a lot of interest when its development was first announced.

The L6.4's $15,000 price tag meant that it was only within reach of the very rich. Its exclusivity gave it tremendous appeal to celebrities and showbusiness stars, such as Frank Sinatra and other members of the infamous 'Rat Pack'.

The L6.4 was funded not by Chrysler but by Gene Casaroll of Automobile Shippers Inc., who had initiated a similar project in the 1950s, that inspired the Dodge Firearrow. A total of 102 of these original cars were built, but the L6.4 was much less successful – just 26 found owners.

It has become the dream of many Chrysler enthusiasts to try and own one of the few remaining Ghia L6.4s. This has pushed their value on the collector's markets right up into the stratosphere.

Gas Turbine

1963

ENGINE: Gas turbine

POWER: 130bhp

CHASSIS: Monocoque

BRAKES (F/R): Drum

TRANSMISSION: Not available

SUSPENSION: Independent front, live axle rear

TOP SPEED: Not available

ACCELERATION: 0-60mph in 10 seconds

Several motor manufacturers experimented with passenger-carrying gas-turbine cars in the post-war period – most notably the British company Rover – but none got nearer to producing a genuine production car than American car giant Chrysler.

As an experiment the company built 50 gas-turbine-powered coupes in 1963. These 130bhp cars, styled by Elwood Engle, who had previously designed the Ford Thunderbird, were built by the Italian firm Ghia, and handed out to voluntary owners for a temporary trial period.

They were found to be quick enough – 0–60mph (96km/h) took ten seconds – but rather on the thirsty side, with little better than 12mpg (23.5litres/100km) possible. It was a fact that would have probably doomed them comercially if they had been produced, even without with the 1970s oil crisis looming on the horizon.

Even less encouraging news was on hand. There was a real problem with the high interior temperatures generated by the hot-running turbines.

It soon became clear that the car wasn't a commercial proposition, and Chrysler terminated the project. Forty of the prototypes were destroyed to avoid import duty on their Italian-built bodywork, while the remaining ten ended up in museums.

Talbot Sunbeam Lotus

1979–81

ENGINE: Four-cylinder, 2174cc

POWER: 150bhp

CHASSIS: Monocoque

BRAKES (F/R): Disc/drum

TRANSMISSION: Five-speed manual

SUSPENSION: Independent front, live axle rear

TOP SPEED: 121mph (194km/h)

ACCELERATION: 0–60mph (96km/h) in 7.4 seconds

To give it a presence in international rallying, Chrysler UK developed a high-performance version of its hatchback Sunbeam model in 1979. This move would eventually produce a car with plenty of character as well as speed.

A deal was struck with Lotus to supply its twin-cam four-cylinder engine, but in slightly bigger 2.2-litre form to give improved low-speed torque. This was matched to a five-speed ZF transmission and a much stronger live rear axle. The shell, too, was modified for strength and sent down from the Linwood factory in Scotland, first to Lotus at Hethel – where the mechanicals were fitted – and then it travelled across country to Coventry for checking and pre-delivery inspection.

Although announced as a Chrysler, by the time production had got into its stride all the company's European businesses had been bought by Peugeot. Thus, all Sunbeams, Horizons, Avengers and Alpines were renamed Talbots, and this low-volume homologation special became the Talbot Sunbeam Lotus.

It was a fast car, with fun handling and an aggressive personality. Top driver Henri Toivonen gave the model some well-deserved credibility, when he managed to win the World Rally Championship in a Sunbeam Lotus.

It proved too expensive to sell in large numbers, however. Only something like half of the planned 4,500 examples were built.

Voyager

1983–1996

ENGINE: V6, 3295cc

POWER: 150bhp

CHASSIS: Steel monocoque, five-door

BRAKES (F/R): Disc with ABS

TRANSMISSION: Four-speed automatic

SUSPENSION: Struts front, leaf-sprung rear

TOP SPEED: 107mph (171km/h)

ACCELERATION: 0–62.5mph (100km/h) in 13.5 seconds

When recently ousted Ford chairman Lee Iacocca took over as Chrysler's chairman in late-1978, he clearly didn't expect to find himself at the head of a company on the verge of collapse. So desperate was Chrysler's position that Iacocca had to plead for government help. The USA's resistance to state subsidy was overridden by Iacocca's claim that 600,000 jobs rested on Chrysler's existence.

Iacocca's product-based turn-around was to hinge on the new K-car line-up. These late-1980 cars would be compact, front-wheel drive, fuel-efficient and modern-looking – as well as affordable for ordinary Americans. Chrysler's brand holding meant that Iacocca also had three badges – Plymouth and Dodge were the other two – with which to penetrate the market.

The K-car platform strategy allowed the company product line to be extended quickly and cheaply, so another three Chrysler and Dodge-badged front-wheel-drive cars

appeared. It was in 1983 that Chrysler really hit the big time though, with the K-car-based Voyager minivan.

The Voyager was a revolutionary idea, and was instantly popular with the American public – so much so that the company couldn't turn enough of them off the production lines at first. Chrysler had thought laterally about the massive minivan concept and simply scaled it down, while retaining excellent interior space. The Voyager became a versatile family wagon that drove like a car and was much easier to manoeuvre in tight down-town spaces.

Chrysler stylists had also managed to make the car look so right from the outset that it survived until 1991 before it was given a facelift, and even then it amounted to little more than an aerodynamic nose and a fresh interior. It wasn't replaced until 1996, ensuring a place for the Voyager as one of the all-time great mass-produced cars.

Eagle Vision

1992–

ENGINE: 24-valve V6, 3485cc

POWER: 214bhp

CHASSIS: Steel monocoque

BRAKES: Disc all round with ABS

TRANSMISSION: Four-speed automatic

SUSPENSION: Struts front, longitudinal and transverse links rear

TOP SPEED: 134mph (214km/h)

ACCELERATION: 0–62.5mph (100km/h) in 9.5 seconds

In 1990, Chrysler boss Bob Lutz was looking at the same situation that had greeted Lee Iacocca just over a decade earlier. Even before the global slow-down kicked in, the company's sales had started to slide, and at one point Chrysler shares were almost worthless. Again the management's answer was, according to Lutz, "to launch new top-quality products in as short a time as possible."

This race to get new cars to market centred around a $16 billion investment. To try to boost confidence, Chrysler showed a number of its up-and-coming new cars – including the Vision and the replacement for the long-running Voyager – as thinly disguised concept cars. But this didn't help, with Chrysler losing another $800 million in 1991.

Chrysler must have been very relieved to see the family car codenamed LH finally appear in showrooms in mid-1992. Badged Eagle Vision in the USA, it was a large and very distinctive saloon that simply had to reel in serious profits. The Vision cost some £1.5 billion to develop, took three-and-a-quarter years from a clean sheet, and had 700 engineers working on it. Cynics in the automobile industry claimed LH was short for 'Last Hope'.

The Vision featured the cab-forward styling theme developed by design boss Tom Gale, which stretched the windscreen and its pillars much further forward from the driver. It was, perhaps, one of the first modern US styling jobs to lead the rest of the world.

One of the key aspects of the Vision – and other new generation road cars that helped to keep the Chrysler corporation alive in the 1990s – was not the raw sales figures it achieved but the sheer profit that Chrysler realised on each car sold. The company managed to keep its bottom line very low without compromising too massively on the engineering.

Viper

1992–1998

ENGINE: V10, 7997cc

POWER: 450bhp

CHASSIS: Separate chassis, GRP body panels

BRAKES (F/R): Disc

TRANSMISSION: Four-speed automatic

SUSPENSION: Independent

TOP SPEED: 180mph (290km/h)

ACCELERATION: 0–60mph (96km/h) in 4.5 seconds

At the Detroit Motor Show in 1989, Chrysler showed a concept car called the Viper, a low, wide and mean-looking two seater roadster with a hint of the AC Cobra in its hunched stance.

The public loved it. They were even more impressed – and even more keen to buy – when they discovered it had an 8 litre, 90 degree V10 engine. Chrysler were so encouraged with the response that they decided to put into production. Despite a suprisingly hefty all-in weight nobody was disappointed with the Viper's titanic strength. Its engine, reworked by Lamborghini, developed 450lb/ft of torque so the Viper didn't really care what gear it was in, delivering its power with a suprisingly benign exhaust note out of dramatic side pipes. 0-60 took four seconds and most road testers ran out of nerve

at around 170mph. So high was the gearing in sixth – 53.3mph per 1,000 revs – that the Viper was just loafing at 100mph. As a straight-line ground coverer, it was the perfect companion.

When the hype slowed down, pundits began to notice that the car's hood was useless, that the build quality had a kit-car feel to it in places and that handling, despite quick (assisted) steering and great brakes, was a little ragged and unforgiving, especially on bumpy roads. Others began to complain that the car was too wide, particularly outside of the United States, to be much use. None of that mattered. As an image-booster for Chrysler around the world, the Viper was unbeatable. It was later to spawn its very own fixed-head version, the Dodge Viper GTS.

Jeep Cherokee / Grand Cherokee

1992–1998

ENGINE: Straight-six, 3960cc

POWER: 184bhp

CHASSIS: Separate steel chassis, steel body panels

BRAKES (F/R): Disc/drum with ABS

TRANSMISSION: Four-speed manual

SUSPENSION: Beam axles with coils front and rear

TOP SPEED: 113mph (181km/h)

ACCELERATION: 0–62.5mph (100km/h) in 10.9 seconds

Between 1982 and 1991, sales of so-called Sport Utility Vehicles (SUVs) in the USA rocketed from 100,000 to 900,000 per year. Chrysler had wisely bought up the Jeep brand name and image when it took over AMC in 1987. The company suddenly found itself with possibly the world's best-known off-roading badge with which to exploit a massive booming market niche.

Two new Jeep-badged off-roaders were an integral part of Chrysler's recovery plan for the early 1990s. The smaller of the two, the Jeep Cherokee arrived just before the Range Rover-sized Grand, which was launched in early 1992. The Grand said a lot about Jeep's engineering and styling abilities – even as part of the ailing AMC empire. It was especially surprising considering that the Grand Cherokee's predecessor was an ancient mock-luxury truck.

With a new vehicle entering the luxury off-road segment, Chrysler found itself with a car that had a badge to challenge the prestige of Range Rover and a styling package that suggested a futuristic version of the classic British workhorse. Early reports on the Cherokee were sure that it was also far better built than its British-made rival.

Under the stylish shell, the Grand, like the Jeep, rode on comparatively crude (though well-located) beam axles and coil suspension. It had a very well-developed ride for its class of car, and it handled with surprising alacrity. Finely conceived and good-looking SUVs, the Cherokees were big successes in the home market, and made serious inroads into the brand-conscious European market. Although the Grand was replaced in 1998, the original was probably good enough to sell on into the new millennium.

Cisitalia

202 Coupe

1947–1952

ENGINE: In-line four-cylinder, 1089cc

POWER: 50bhp

CHASSIS: Tubular frame, alloy body

BRAKES (F/R): Drum

TRANSMISSION: Four-speed manual

SUSPENSION: Independent front, live axle rear

TOP SPEED: 105mph (168km/h)

ACCELERATION: Not Available

The 1947 Cisitalia 202 Coupe was a seminal moment in post-war styling. It featured a bonnet positioned lower than the front wings, headlights that blended into the wings – rather than being free-standing – and smooth, sweeping, simple lines.

Pininfarina explored these themes on other chassis, but it is for the Cisitalia that it is best remembered. The New York Museum of Modern Art has, since 1951, kept an example of 'sculpture in movement.' Vignale, Frua and Stabilmenti Farina, as well as Pininfarina again, produced convertible variants.

Thanks to slippery aerodynamics, the Cisitalia could achieve 102mph (163km/h) on just 50bhp from a tweaked Fiat 1100 engine. Competition-tuned variants were able to do up to 120mph (192km/h).

Cisitalia was founded in 1946 by racing-driver and businessman Piero Dusio. The company's first project was a single-seater racing car with Fiat Topolino front suspension and the four-cylinder engine from the Balilla. But as early as 1949, Cisitalia was facing bankruptcy due to over-ambitious plans for a Porsche-designed Grand Prix car.

Dusio went to live in Argentina, but the 202 continued in production until 1952. The marque survived until 1965 under the control of Dusio's creditors, but was never to achieve the fame it gained with the classic 202 coupe.

Citroën

Light 15

1934–1957

ENGINE: In-line four- and six-cylinder, 1911/2866cc

POWER: 46–80bhp

CHASSIS: Monocoque

BRAKES (F/R): Drum

TRANSMISSION: Three-speed manual

SUSPENSION: Independent

TOP SPEED: 70mph (112km/h)

ACCELERATION: 0–60mph (96km/h) in 23 seconds

The high development costs of the Light 15, or Traction Avant, sent a penniless André Citroën to an early grave and his company into the arms of Michelin, but at least the Light 15 and its many derivatives went on to be successful, selling strongly for the next 23 years.

A towering reference point in the history of the motor car, the Light 15 pioneered front-wheel drive on a mass-produced family saloon. By the standards of 1934, the road-holding capability of the car was almost unbelievably good.

Front-wheel drive wasn't the whole story, of course. Unitary construction was still a rarity in 1934, and the car was both roomy and comfortable to ride in, with torsion-bar independent suspension front and rear. Top speed with the 45bhp, 1911cc, four-cylinder engine was 70mph (112km/h). There were numerous variations on this enduring theme – cabriolets, long wheelbase models and an up-market six-cylinder version.

It was years before the opposition began to catch up with the standards set by the Light 15, and only when they had another world-beater in place – the DS of 1955 – did Citroën feel that they were able to finally let the vehicle die.

André Citroën would have been proud to know that his vision, that inspired the development of the Light 15, was to produce a car that took on the world and won, earning it – and himself – a well-deserved place in the annals of motoring history.

Citroën 2CV

1948–1990

ENGINE: Flat-twin, 375–602cc

POWER: 9–29bhp

CHASSIS: Platform

BRAKES (F/R): Drum

TRANSMISSION: Four-speed manual

SUSPENSION: Independent

TOP SPEED: 41–67mph (66–107km/h)

ACCELERATION: 0–60mph (96km/h) in 32 seconds (602cc version)

The 1948 Citroën 2CV, with its trademark corrugated-steel bodywork, was an economy car designed to put rural France on wheels after the Second World War. In all respects, the car was uncompromisingly basic, so as to keep servicing easy and running costs low. Its willing twin-cylinder, 375cc, air-cooled engine delivered an impressively economic 56mpg (5litres/100km), and could just about squeeze out 43mph (69km/h) – although that dropped to 37mph (59km/h) with four people aboard.

Still, slow as it was, the 2CV was considerably more comfortable than many bigger, faster competitors, with superbly practical hammock-type seats that could be lifted out to accommodate extra loads, and an excellent soft ride

that took rutted farm tracks in its stride. The all-independent suspension was designed to be supple enough to transport a basket of eggs across a ploughed field without breaking a single one.

Huge body roll was the inevitable result of spirited cornering in the 2CV, but front-wheel drive meant it gripped beautifully. All the body panels detached easily as well, and the fabric roof rolled back to allow very pleasant open-air motoring, or to cater for times when there was a tall load to carry.

The car was a great success and remained in production – eventually with a 602cc engine – until 1990, having spawned many derivatives on the same theme, most memorably the Dyane and the Ami. More than five million units were produced.

Citroën DS

1955–75

ENGINE: Four-cylinder,
1911/1985/2175/2347cc

POWER: 63/84/109/115/130bhp

CHASSIS: Monocoque

BRAKES (F/R): Disc/drum

TRANSMISSION: Four- and
five-speed manual, and semi-
automatic

SUSPENSION: Independent
hydropneumatic

TOP SPEED: 84–117mph
(134–187km/h)

ACCELERATION: 0–60mph (96km/h)
in 23 seconds (ID), and 10.4
seconds

The 1955 Citroën DS was a car that was a decade – or maybe two – ahead of the game, and a true showstopper. Never before has a single model embraced so many technical innovations.

Chief among these was the suspension. Moving aside from conventional springs, Citroën engineers suspended their new saloon on hydraulic, self-levelling, hydropneumatic struts, with a unique adjustable ride-height facility that meant the DS could raise itself to negotiate rough terrain.

The engine powered the hydraulic high-pressure central nervous system, and controlled the ultra-sharp power steering, the pleasantly powerful brakes – including inboard discs up front – and the clutchless hydraulic gearchange.

With front-wheel drive, its handling and stability were almost as sensational as its magic-carpet ride. Only its elderly engine let it down – a clattery 1934 design from the old

Light 15, unworthy of such an advanced machine. From the mid-1960s there was a better, more modern 2-litre four-cylinder engine, but somehow the DS never quite got the kind of smooth, unstressed motor it deserved.

The DS spawned a whole raft of derivatives during the 1950s and 1960s. Downgraded models, such as the ID19 and, later, the D Super – with fewer power-assisted systems and less horsepower – appealed to thousands of Paris taxi-drivers. The cavernous Safari Estate cars were the ultimate in family load-haulers, whilst the beautiful DS *décapotable* convertibles were expensive and exclusive.

High-specification Prestige models and the last-of-the-line 2.3-litre DS23 cars with five speeds and fuel injection further broadened the model's appeal in the face of competitions from younger rivals. The DS was replaced by the CX in 1975.

Citroën SM

1970–1975

ENGINE: V6, 2670/2965cc

POWER: 170–180bhp

CHASSIS: Monocoque

BRAKES (F/R): Disc

TRANSMISSION: Five-speed manual, three-speed automatic

SUSPENSION: Independent

TOP SPEED: 140mph (224km/h)

ACCELERATION: 0–60mph in 8 seconds

The first fruits of the marriage between Citroën and Maserati were the big Citroën SM of 1970, a prestige GT car utilizing the best from both companies. Power came from a smaller V6 version of Maserati's long-lived quad-cam V8 which, at 2.7 litres, came in just under the punitive French tax laws that penalized engines of over 2.8 litres capacity.

Like the DS, the SM possessed a front-wheel drive, with the gearbox/transaxle slung out ahead of the compact engine. The power output of 170bhp through the front wheels was handled by Citroën's predictable and well-tried hydropneumatic self-levelling suspension, interconnected with the four-wheel disc brakes (inboard up front) and ultra-quick power steering.

Fast and refined with excellent handling – once the driver had mastered a sensitive touch with the steering and brakes – the SM was an extremely impressive long-distance GT.

It was the shape, though, that captured enthusiasts' hearts. Styled inside Citroën, it was dramatic and purposeful with a broad, fully-flared-in glass nose and a tapering tail that was as slippery and aerodynamic as it looked.

Sales were initially strong, but the love affair was to be short-lived. The fuel crisis hit in 1973, making all the various big 18mpg (15.8litres/100km) super-cars somewhat unpractical.

Citroën went on to further improve the car with fuel injection, a bigger 3-litre version and an automatic option, but it was to no real avail. Production ceased in 1975, 13,000 cars down the line.

GS Birotor

1973–1975

ENGINE: Twin-rotor Wankel

POWER: 106bhp

CHASSIS: Monocoque

BRAKES (F/R): Disc

TRANSMISSION: Three-speed semi-automatic

SUSPENSION: Independent

TOP SPEED: 110mph (176km/h)

ACCELERATION: 0–60mph (96km/h) in 14 seconds

Ever forward-looking, Citroën was keen to follow NSU with a rotary-engined production saloon. Never a company to do things by halves, it built a factory dedicated to rotary-engine production and produced a pilot run of 260 experimental, rotary-engined fastback coupes based on the Ami 8.

Placed in the hands of high-mileage Citroën drivers to prove their durability in the field, they clocked up 18 million development miles, which satisfied Citroën that a fully tooled-up, mass-market version could ultimately prove to be a very commercial proposition. It was a huge misjudgment of the marketplace on their part.

Enter, in 1973, the Citroën GS Birotor. Although it looked superficially like Citroën's well-known air-cooled saloon, it was almost totally different, illustrating Citroën's commitment to the project.

Outwardly, it had flared arches to accommodate wider tyres, while under the bonnet all the pressings around the bulkhead had been changed to accommodate the twin-rotor Wankel engine.

Good for 106bhp, this smooth, lusty unit drove through a semi-automatic, clutchless, three-speed gearbox. The Birotor even had a very different interior from the stock GS, with much smarter seats and upgraded carpeting.

Pundits liked the car, which added speed and mechanical refinement to the well-known GS qualities of ride comfort and good handling. However, potential buyers were badly put off by the car's fuel consumption figures. In typical Wankel Rotary Engine fashion, this was definitely on the wrong side of 18mpg (16litres/ 100km).

The cars were difficult to sell, and such was Citroën's humiliation with the project that it offered to buy cars back from their owners and scrap them. A total of 847 of them were built, but only some 200 examples survive today.

Citroën CX

1974–1991

ENGINE: Four-cylinder, 1995–2437cc

POWER: 102–168bhp

CHASSIS: Monocoque

BRAKES (F/R): Disc

TRANSMISSION: Four and five-speed manual, three-speed automatic

SUSPENSION: Independent

TOP SPEED: 110–130mph (176–208km/h)

ACCELERATION: 0–60mph (96km/h) in 7–14 seconds

Citroën knew that replacing the DS would be a difficult job. The car had been in production for 20 years, and in certain aspects of ride and refinement it still had few peers in the big-car class. It was with some relief, then, that Citroën-fanciers greeted the new CX in 1974 – in every respect, it was a worthy successor.

Outwardly its sleek, fastback shape looked as aerodynamic as it actually was, although it was a surprise to find that it wasn't a hatchback. Under the skin, front-wheel drive was still employed, but this time the four-cylinder engines – essentially the same pushrod units found in the last of the DS models – were mounted transversely and drove through new four- and five-speed transmissions. Self-levelling hydropneumatic suspension remained – adjustable between three positions via a lever between the front seats – combining the magic carpet ride comfort with surprisingly agile handling.

Roomy and comfortable, with a futuristic interior to match the styling, the CX was an immediate success, finding much favour as a long-distance express. Later came a huge estate version – called the Familiale – with either an extra row of seats or a massive load area, whilst for those looking for the ultimate in Citroën luxury, there was always the leather-trimmed, long-wheelbase Prestige.

There were thrifty diesel and 2-litre petrol models and, perhaps best of all, the 168bhp Gti Turbo, the fastest Citroën since the demise of the SM.

More than one million CXs were built before the car was replaced in 1989 by the XM – a model which has proved much less popular and charismatic.

Cord 810/812

1937–1938

ENGINE: V8, 4730cc

POWER: 170bhp

CHASSIS: Monocoque

BRAKES (F/R): Drum

TRANSMISSION: Four-speed manual

SUSPENSION: Independent front, dead axle rear

TOP SPEED: 100mph (160km/h)

ACCELERATION: 0–60mph (96km/h) in 13 seconds

Cord was founded in 1929, and set itself apart from other American manufacturers in its use of front-wheel drive on a series of large, luxurious, straight-eight-powered machines called L29s. It is for the coffin-nosed 810/812-Series cars that the marque is best remembered, however.

Powered by a specially designed side-valve V8 engine this time, the 810/812 Series had crowd-stopping looks featuring retractable headlamps and a wrap-around grille on a long, narrow bonnet (hence the 'coffin nose' nickname). Created by Gordon Miller Buehrig, their smooth and slippery profile was truly futuristic, and they had a futuristic specification to match that included an electric gearchange and, of course, Cord's trademark front-wheel drive.

Several different variations on the original styling theme were employed. Without any doubt, however, the most beautiful and sought-after of these variants was the convertible model – particularly in the 1937 812S form, featuring an extremely impressive supercharged 170bhp engine.

Thus equipped, the Cord was a supremely powerful 100mph (160km/h) car, capable of doing 0–60mph (96km/h) in 13 seconds. In the 1930s, that was supercar performance.

Unfortunately, Cord as a company was in trouble by then, and its new owners decided to pull out of car production altogether for 1938. There would be no more big front-drive American cars until the introduction of the Oldsmobile Toronado 30 years later.

Imperial

1957–1964

ENGINE: V8, 6789cc

POWER: 350bhp

CHASSIS: Box-section

BRAKES (F/R): Drum

TRANSMISSION: Three-speed automatic

SUSPENSION: Independent front, live axle rear

TOP SPEED: 112mph (179km/h)

ACCELERATION: 0–60mph (96km/h) in 12 seconds

Imperial was originally the up-market brand name of Chrysler vehicles built to compete directly with Cadillac and Lincoln models. For much of the 1950s, its cars had rather sedate styling, with much less glitz than that of rival marques, but after 1954, when Imperial became a separate division from Chrysler, all that began to change.

Fins started to become taller and chrome embellishment more fancy. Finally, an entirely new Virgil Exner-designed body was introduced in 1957 with wrap-around screens and a set of quadruple front headlights.

The range comprised two- and four-door hardtop models, a limousine and a wonderfully extravagant convertible – all powered by a 345bhp V8 engine. Each successive year Imperial tail fins grew bigger, but so did everyone else's.

What the company needed was a gimmick that nobody else had, and they found it in their 1961 models – free-standing headlights. Hoping to evoke memories of the pre-war classic, this was the ultimate in non-functional design, which generated copy in the press but pleased few buyers. It was dropped in 1964 as the range began to feature the clean-cut styling inspired by Lincoln's Mk IV Continental. The marque became more closely aligned to its Chrysler parent – until 1975, when the Imperial was dropped as a separate line altogether.

1959–1963

ENGINE: 590cc two-cylinder OHV

POWER: 22bhp

CHASSIS: Integral body and frame

BRAKES (F/R): Drum

TRANSMISSION: Variomatic

SUSPENSION: Independent front, sprung axle rear

TOP SPEED: 56mph (90km/h)

ACCELERATION: 0-50mph (80km/h) in 33 seconds

DAF stands for Doornes Aanhanger Fabrieken (Doornes Trailer Factory) after the brothers Hubert and Wim van Doorne, who founded the company in 1928. They made their reputation as truck builders, largely for the army, but in 1958 they moved into car manufacture with a revolutionary innovation.

The car in question, the 600, was unremarkable to look at – boxy and dull – but under the skin lay the first fully automatic transmission system to be seen on a small car. Called 'variomatic' it consisted of two strong belts running round conical wheels, which moved closer together or further apart as required to adjust the travel on the

belts and give infinitely variable transmission ratios. It was to become the hallmark of DAF cars until the company was taken over by Volvo in 1975.

The DAF 600 may not have been pretty and it certainly wasn't quick – its air-cooled, two cylinder, four-stroke engine pulling it to a top speed of 59mph – but it did attract a loyal following, due to its comfort and value for money. It underwent some styling tweaks at the beginning of the 1960s – larger headlights, chrome trim around the grille – but never won the hearts of the buying public. By the end of production in 1963, just over 30,000 DAF 600s had been made.

55 Marathon

1971–1972

ENGINE: 1.1 litre, four-cylinder in-line

POWER: 63bhp

CHASSIS: Integral body and frame

BRAKES: (F/R): Drum

TRANSMISSION: Variomatic

SUSPENSION: Independent front, sprung axle rear

TOP SPEED: 91mph (146km/h)

ACCELERATION: 0-50mph (0-80km/h) in 10.5 seconds

In 1968 DAF entered the London to Sydney Marathon with two 55s. This model, launched the year before, had spelt the start of something new for the company, being their first car to have a 4 cylinder engine. The 1.1 litre in-line, water-cooled unit came from the Renault 10, but this wasn't enough to attract the buyers DAF had hoped for. The car's lines, closely resembling the 44, failed to turn heads in those style-conscious times.

The London-Sydney Marathon, however, was to provide a fillip for the 55, with both cars finishing, one making 17th place. To capitalise on the PR value of this achievement,

DAF produced an upgrade kit to bring the 55 up to Marathon spec. Alloy wheels, a rev counter, springs to improve the rear suspension and a new exhaust pipe came with an engine-modification set.

The kit went down a treat, prompting DAF to introduce a factory 55 Marathon, which sold 11,000 models in two years of production. This factory model threw in a brake-assister, wider wheels and the luxury of carpet on the floor. Performance still wasn't exactly electrifying, topping 90mph compared to the 55's 85mph and pulling to 50mph one and a half seconds quicker in 10.5.

SP250 Dart

1959–1964

ENGINE: V8, 2548cc

POWER: 140bhp

CHASSIS: Separate chassis, fibreglass (GRP) body

BRAKES: Disc all round

TRANSMISSION: Four-speed manual, three-speed automatic

SUSPENSION: Independent

TOP SPEED: 125mph (200km/h)

ACCELERATION: 0–60mph (96km/h) in 10 seconds

The decision to build the SP250 came after a change of management at Daimler in the late-1950s. The company was in trouble, and the top brass thought that a new sports car would be a fine way to woo American buyers.

Based on a chassis and suspension layout hastily copied from the Triumph TR3, Daimler took the then-radical step of using a fibreglass body. It proved to be a gawky, finned affair that found few friends.

Its major redeeming feature, however, was its engine, a 2548cc V8 producing 140bhp. Designed by Daimler's managing director Edward Turner – famed for his Triumph motorcycle engines – this smooth, torquey, free-revving engine could power the fairly light SP250 to 125mph (200km/h).

An acceleration time of 0–60mph (96km/h) in 10 seconds was not to be sniffed at either. Unfortunately, the excellence of the performance seemed somehow at odds with the amateurish, hastily designed body and chassis. Handling never earned top marks, as the steering was heavy and the chassis somewhat 'whippy' – especially when compared to other cars in its class.

The fate of the SP250 was sealed as early as 1960, when Jaguar took over the ailing Daimler concern to boost its production capacity. Jaguar boss Sir William Lyons never liked the Dart because the styling offended him. He pulled the plug on the SP250 in 1964 with no regrets and few mourned the vehicle's passsing.

Majestic Major

1959–1968

ENGINE: V8, 4561cc

POWER: 220bhp

CHASSIS: Separate chassis, steel body

BRAKES (F/R): Disc

TRANSMISSION: Three-speed automatic

SUSPENSION: Independent front, live axle rear

TOP SPEED: 122mph (195km/h)

ACCELERATION: 0–60mph (96km/h) in 9.7 seconds

The Daimler Majestic Major was one of the most impressive performance saloons of the early 1960s. By fitting a brand-new hemi-head 4.7-litre V8 into its biggest executive saloon, Daimler created a 120mph (192km/h) hot-rod limousine that was quicker than contemporary Jaguars. This was an embarrassing situation, given the Jaguar take-over of Daimler in 1960. The car also had astonishing acceleration – 0–60mph (96km/h) took just 9.7 seconds.

Despite its traditional separate chassis and tall, dignified body, the Majestic Major had good manners to match its performance. The vehicle was well reviewed in the press at the time.

At just over £3,000 it was good value for money too, with automatic transmission, power steering and disc brakes as standard. Busy managing directors could lounge in leather-lined comfort in the Majestic Major, which also featured an appropriately huge boot space.

For Daimler's carriage-trade customers, there was a limousine version of the Majestic Major called the DR450, with a stretched chassis to accommodate extra occasional seats. However, the real beauty of the Majestic was the fact that it was such a great car to drive. It wasn't a car to be chauffered in if you had a passion for driving.

Production of the Majestic Major was always designed to be very small-scale so sales were low, and the last examples were made in 1968. From then on all Daimlers were destined to be badge-engineered Jaguars.

Daimler

2.5-litre V8

1962–1969

ENGINE: V8, 2548cc

POWER: 140bhp

CHASSIS: Monocoque

BRAKES (F/R): Discs

TRANSMISSION: Three-speed automatic, four-speed manual

SUSPENSION: Independent front, live axle rear

TOP SPEED: 112mph (179km/h)

ACCELERATION: 0–60mph (96km/h) in 13 seconds

By installing Daimler's own hemi-head 145bhp V8 – an engine developed originally for the ill-starred SP250 sports car – in its compact Mk II saloon, Jaguar created the Daimler 2.5 litre V8. It was a very effective bit of niche marketing, creating a genteel car that appealed to the slightly older buyers who were looking for something that wasn't quite as brash as the Mk II. It also gained a slightly better interior than that of the Mk II – another very strong selling point in its intended market.

An incidental benefit was gained in the handling, because the little V8 weighed rather less than Jaguar's XK straight-six, yet was still good for well over 100mph (160km/h) – even with the obligatory automatic transmission. The engine note held a distinct burble that simply added to the car's already extensive charm.

The car was a strong seller from the start. It continued to live on in a slim-bumpered form after 1967 as the Daimler 250 V8. Some of these later cars had the rare option of manual transmission, which unleashed considerable extra performance — although it is hard to see any of the car's intended drivers making the most of it.

The 250 V8 was the last Mk II variant to go out of production (in 1969), and also the last Daimler to have a real Daimler engine – two additional reasons why it is remembered so fondly.

DS420

1968–1992

ENGINE: Straight-six, 4235cc

POWER: 245bhp

CHASSIS: Monocoque

BRAKES (F/R): Disc

TRANSMISSION: Three-speed automatic

SUSPENSION: Independent

TOP SPEED: 110mph (176km/h)

ACCELERATION: Not quoted

The Daimler DS420 dates from 1968. It was based on the floorpan of Jaguar's 420G flagship, but with an extra 20in. (51cm) let into the wheelbase. The driver sat on a bench seat behind a glass division, whilst rear passengers stretched out in the back in opulent comfort – the DS420's rear seat spanning over six feet (1.83m) in width.

The Daimler DS420 was bought in enthusiastic quantities by the funeral trade as mourners' cars or hearses. Countless local authorities and embassies bought the cars too, and in Hong Kong the Regent Hotel still runs a fleet of 22. Even the Queen and Queen Mother have both been Daimler Limousine owners, re-establishing the Royal patronage that Daimler lost to Rolls-Royce in the early 1950s.

Originally built at the Vanden Plas works in London, production moved to Jaguar in Coventry in 1979, where it continued until 1992. Trim levels varied from the 'base model' –

with wind-up windows – to a mobile boardroom built for Jaguar boss John Egan in 1984, complete with TV, fax, cocktail cabinet and computer. Always hand-made, the DS420 had a fascia like any other 1960s Jaguar, remaining faithful for many years to the old-fashioned steering-column selector for the automatic gearbox, push-button starter and the pencil-thin black-plastic steering-wheel.

Undercutting its nearest rival, the Rolls-Royce Phantom VI, by 50 percent or more, this big Daimler was always fine value. With its Le Mans winning twin-cam Jaguar engine – the last car to use it – the Daimler Limousine was no sluggard either, pulling an easy 110mph (176km/h) flat-out, although most examples never went above a processional 30 or 40mph (64km/h). Last of the proper carriage-trade limousines, the DS420 was a car with presence and authority. Its like will not be seen again.

DKW F5 Roadster

1935–1937

ENGINE: 690cc, two-cylinder

POWER: 18bhp

CHASSIS: Separate U-section

BRAKES (F/R): Drum

TRANSMISSION: Three-speed chain transfer

SUSPENSION: Independent

TOP SPEED: 50mph (80km/h)

ACCELERATION: Not available

When DKW linked up with Horch and Wanderer to form Auto Union in 1932, having already absorbed Audi, it was a dominant force in German motor manufacture. The initials stood for Dampf Kraft Wagen (steam powered vehicle), pointing to the company's origins.

By the 1930s, however, DKW had moved on to petrol engines and had made a name for itself with some impressive racing cars. In 1931 they broke new ground, adopting front-wheel drive, and developed a series of cars that were renowned for their excellent roadholding.

The base model was an economy four-seater. It had a fabric covered plywood body built on a double-backbone frame, with a transverse-mounted, 700cc water-cooled twin engine and a three-speed gearbox operated through the dashboard.

In 1935 DKW pushed their sporty image a step further, lowering the build and restyling the bodyshape with sleeker lines. The result was a nippy two-seater cabriolet, the F5, with the excellent roadholding bestowed by front-wheel drive and sprightly performance low down, thanks to its lightweight bodywork and two-stroke punch.

The F5 Roadster was a symbol of DKW's prowess during a strong era for the company in the mid-1930s but it was only produced for three years.

Datsun Fairlady

1965–1970

ENGINE: Four-cylinder, 1595cc

POWER: 90bhp

CHASSIS: Ladder frame

BRAKES (F/R): Disc/drum

TRANSMISSION: Four-speed

SUSPENSION: Independent front, live axle rear

TOP SPEED: 105mph (168km/h)

ACCELERATION: 0–60mph (96km/h) in 13 seconds

The Fairlady was Datsun's answer to the British sports cars that dominated the lucrative North American market in the 1960s. Its trim lines showed a strong European influence, and its similarity to the MGB of the time had to have been more than a coincidence. Even the hood looked the same. Inside, early versions had a traditional painted-metal dashboard, but this was later changed to a padded, Federal type that was much less attractive.

Launched with a twin-carburettor, 90bhp 1500cc engine in 1965, the Fairlady improved steadily over the years, bowing out of production in 1970 with a 2-litre twin-cam engine. This allowed it to develop 145bhp, and a five-speed gearbox helped to get the maximum performance. A top speed of 125mph (200km/h) was claimed for these cars, and they did pleasingly well in American club racing.

Fairlady chassis engineering was rudimentary, with a separate ladder frame and a beam rear axle sprung and located by semi-elliptic leaf springs. Sports car drivers were coming to expect rack-and-pinion steering, but the Fairlady made do with a steering box – which inevitably meant that handling wasn't one of its strong points.

Datsun sold 40,000 Fairlady convertibles, never coming near the total domination of British marques in that sector of the market. The Fairlady was just a taste of things to come, however. Its successor, the 240Z, would eventually manage to become the world's best-selling sports car.

Datsun 240Z

1969–1974

ENGINE: Straight-six, 2393cc

POWER: 151bhp

CHASSIS: Monocoque

BRAKES (F/R): Disc/drum

TRANSMISSION: Five-speed manual

SUSPENSION: Independent all round

TOP SPEED: 125mph (200km/h)

ACCELERATION: 0–60mph (96km/h) in 8 seconds

Launched in 1969, few people would have guessed that the Datsun 240Z was destined to become the best-selling sports car of the 1970s. What the marque lacked in romance and cachet, the 240Z more than made up with its well-balanced, muscular lines, penned by Albrecht Goertz, the father of the beautiful BMW 507.

With its long bonnet, recessed lights and those flowing, tense rear haunches, the Z clearly took its styling cues from the E-Type Jaguar fixed-head. Despite that, it was pure and elegant enough to have an appeal of its own.

A well-equipped two-seater with a rear hatchback, there were few surprises under the skin, yet the 240Z lacked for nothing. The engine was a smooth and punchy straight-six, and it could develop a raunchy 151bhp from 2393cc.

Power went through a five-speed gearbox to a well-sorted strut-and-wishbone rear end. There were struts at the front too, and precise rack-and-pinion steering. The car handled superbly, even if it did so rather traditionally, and it went like the wind, topping 125mph (200km/h) with ease.

Sales took off and Datsun never looked back, selling 150,076 units before the 260Z took over in 1975. In search of more refinement, Datsun made the 260 a softer, less aggressive car and, inevitably, it was a heavier, slower one.

Vallelunga

1962–1965

ENGINE: Four-cylinder, 1498cc

POWER: 102bhp

CHASSIS: Backbone

BRAKES (F/R): Disc

TRANSMISSION: Four-speed manual

SUSPENSION: Independent

TOP SPEED: 130mph (208km/h)

ACCELERATION: Not Available

Alexandro de Tomaso initially made his name building racing cars, but dreamed of producing a high-performance road car. The Pantera and Mangusta are his most famous efforts, but before those big V8 machines came the delicate little Vallelunga of 1962.

One of the pioneers of the mid-engined layout in a road car, its Ford-supplied 1600 engine and Hewland gearbox were structural members in the rear half of the car, bolted to a U-shaped spine chassis that help give it good handling.

Triumph Herald uprights could be found at the front, but there were few other proprietary components in the Vallelunga, which was named after a Rome racing track that de Tomaso used for testing its sports cars.

The prototype had an open two-seater body, but production cars were coupes, styled by Fissore. Early cars were built in aluminium, but those built by Ghia have fibreglass bodywork.

Noisy, fast and supremely agile, the Vallelunga was a car that pointed the way forward in sports-car design, although it was destined never to be very popular. Just 50 were built before it gave way to the Mangusta on the production lines.

De Tomaso Mangusta

1966–1972

ENGINE: V8, 4727cc

POWER: 305bhp

CHASSIS: Backbone

BRAKES (F/R): Disc

TRANSMISSION: Five-speed manual

SUSPENSION: Independent

TOP SPEED: 155mph (248km/h)

ACCELERATION: Not Available

Hot on the heels of the Lamborghini Miura, Alexandro de Tomaso introduced his own mid-engined super-car, the Mangusta, in 1967. Styled by Ghia – de Tomaso owned the company – it was a low-slung, muscular two-seater powered by a 4.7-litre Ford V8 mounted amidships. This could be viewed through either of the engine covers, which were hinged down a central spine. There was a box-section pressed-steel backbone chassis to carry the engine and ZF transmission. The car was neatly suspended on a coil-spring and wishbone suspension system that promised impeccable handling.

Sadly, it was in this regard that the Mangusta let itself down. There was too much rear weight bias, making the car difficult to control in some high-speed situations. It acquired a reputation for being a bit of a handful and – perhaps even worse – it was not really a practical long-distance machine, with minimal luggage space and too much engine noise.

Still, it was fast – 155mph (248km/h) was claimed – and it proved to be a highly exciting machine for those skilled enough to drive it properly. After 401 examples had been constructed, it gave way to the much more practical Pantera.

Pantera

1970–1993

ENGINE: V8, 5763cc

POWER: 330bhp

CHASSIS: Monocoque

BRAKES (F/R): Disc

TRANSMISSION: Five-speed manual

SUSPENSION: Independent

TOP SPEED: 160mph (256km/h)

ACCELERATION: 0–60mph (96km/h) in 5.9 seconds

Alessandro de Tomaso, an Argentinian tycoon who had settled in Italy, built his first car, the Vallelunga, in 1962. Despite good looks and impressive mid-engined handling it flopped, and whilst his second effort – the V8-engined Mangusta – was really rather beautiful, it acquired a reputation for being difficult to control at high speeds.

With the 1970 Pantera, de Tomaso was determined to get it right. He struck a deal with Ford of North America whereby they got his Ghia coachbuilding firm – hence the Ghia badge on today's Escorts and Fiestas – if it agreed to sell his new car, powered by a 5.8-litre Ford V8

engine, through its dealers in the USA. A total of 4,000 Panteras were sold in the USA before Ford shut the door on imports in 1974, tired of complaints about build quality – not that the Pantera was a bad car to drive. It was fast in a straight line, reaching a blistering 160mph (256km/h), and with that mid-mounted engine the handling proved to be excellent.

Also, because the engine was an ordinary Ford unit, it was strong and reliable – and cheap to fix if it did go wrong. The model lasted until 1993, by which point its once proud image had been cheapened by boy-racer-like spoilers and stickers, and ever-fatter tyres.

Deauville

1971–1988

ENGINE: V8, 5763cc

POWER: 330bhp

CHASSIS: Monocoque

BRAKES (F/R): Disc

TRANSMISSION: Three-speed manual

SUSPENSION: Independent

TOP SPEED: 140mph (224km/h)

ACCELERATION: 0–60mph (96km/h) in 8 seconds

De Tomaso's most famous car was the Pantera, a mid-engined slingshot that looked set for widespread American success until it was dropped unceremoniously by its sponsor, Ford.

As well as the Pantera, De Tomaso built the Deauville, a large four-door saloon that was the company's challenge to the Jaguar XJ6. In fact, it looked so much like a Jaguar XJ6, that you can hardly help wondering how they ever avoided a lawsuit.

Designed by an American working for the Ghia design studio, called Tom Tjaarda, it used Ford Mustang engines – although the

prototype had a special overhead-cam Ford V8 – and many other components. Early Deauvilles, while sumptuously trimmed in soft Italian leathers and suedes, sported hideous plasticky steering wheels straight from a 1970s Ford gas-guzzler.

Only a few hundred Deauvilles were made during their long-lived proudction, which ran between 1970 and 1988. They were very quick cars with strong, effective handling. However, they never attained the levels of sophistication – in terms of build quality and refinement – that were expected of their mass-produced rivals.

Longchamp

1972–1990

ENGINE: V8, 5769cc

POWER: 330bhp

CHASSIS: Monocoque

BRAKES (F/R): Disc

TRANSMISSION: Five-speed manual, three-speed automatic

SUSPENSION: Independent

TOP SPEED: 147mph (235km/h)

ACCELERATION: 0–60mph (96km/h) in 7.5 seconds

The De Tomaso Longchamp was basically a two-door version of the Deauville, although the bodywork – by Tom Tjaarda of Ghia – was different and built on a slightly shorter wheelbase, giving the car a very different and distinctive look.

Among many proprietary components to be found on the car were Fiat 130 Coupe tail-lights. The coil-spring and wishbone suspension and power-assisted rack-and-pinion steering were shared with the Deauville, along with the mass-production 5.7-litre Ford V8.

Those with the wallets equipped to buy and maintain a Longchamp could choose between a ZF five-speed manual gearbox or a Ford automatic gearbox – though most wanted the manual.

The handsome, square-cut styling of the Longchamp suited the times perfectly and proved quite enduring, lasting in production until 1990. Like the Deauville, they were pleasingly quick cars and had very good handling.

Later additions to the Longchamp range of vehicles included a rare – and highly desirable – convertible and a more powerful, if somewhat less tasteful, GTS version.

A Maserati version of the Longchamp was offered from 1976. Fitted with the four-camshaft Maserati V8, this car was badged Kyalami. Its styling was gently retouched by Pietro Frua, although only an expert could ever have hoped to be able to tell the two cars apart at a glance.

Charger R/T

1968–1970

ENGINE: V8, 7206cc

POWER: 375bhp

CHASSIS: Monocoque

BRAKES (F/R): Disc/drum

TRANSMISSION: Three-speed automatic, four-speed manual

SUSPENSION: Independent front, live axle rear

TOP SPEED: 150mph (240km/h)

ACCELERATION: 0–60mph (96km/h) in 6 seconds

A classic American 'muscle car,' the Dodge Charger was a full-size fastback coupe. With its buttressed rear pillars and tastefully simple front – the twin headlights were mounted behind electric flaps – it was a far cry from the chintzy gin-palace American cars of the 1950s.

The first car to bear the Charger name – a bold, but somehow bland, fastback that was announced in 1965 – had lasted just a couple of seasons.

The 1968 shell however, was to last – with minimal changes – until 1970. Myriad options meant that the Charger could be tailored to customer requirements – some had quite mild 5.2-litre V8 engines – but for those in the know it was the 1968 R/T (Road and Track) model that was the one to have or the one to dream about having.

Under the bonnet was a 7.2-litre engine, giving 375bhp and an abundance of tyre-smoking torque. Off the line, the Charger could out-pace most Italian exotica with a 0–60mph (96km/h) time of six seconds, steaming up to 100mph (160km/h) in 13 seconds with wheel-spin in every gear. If you mashed your foot to the floor, it would eventually wind up to 150mph (240km/h).

By bolting the heavy-duty suspension down rock hard and fitting scaffolding-sized anti-roll bars, Dodge actually made the Charger R/T handle, too. Like most American cars, the Charger came as a three-speed automatic, but for serious drivers there was also a heavy-duty Hurst manual gearbox.

The Charger model line lasted until 1978, but its credibility as a performance car progressively faded away as the American industry moved its emphasis from performance to luxury and safety.

Diplomat

1977–1989

ENGINE: V8, 3180cc

POWER: 140bhp

CHASSIS: Monocoque

BRAKES: Discs

TRANSMISSION: Three-speed automatic, four-speed manual

SUSPENSION: Independent front, live axle rear

TOP SPEED: 114mph (183km/h)

ACCELERATION: 0–60mph (96km/h) in 13-14 seconds

Embodying the whole spirit of "Dependable Dodge," the Diplomat was highly reliable, a real workhorse that endeared itself to police forces and taxi companies across the US. Its immediate design predecessor was probably the Dodge Aspen, but it also shared design characteristics with many other vehicles of the time. It shared its production line too, with its "M"-body 'twins,' the Chrysler LeBaron and the Plymouth Caravelle.

The Diplomat was an immediate hit, and after six months it was Dodge's second best-selling car. Originally provided as a sedan, coupe and wagon versions were available for a brief spell, from '78 until '81. Somehow, the sedan body captured the spirit of the model in a way that other shapes did not. During the energy-conscious early 80s, it was marketed as economical – if you had a slant six 225 engine and manual transmission, you could get an efficient 28mpg on the highways.

The 318 V8 engine was more commonly found on the road, alongside a Torqueflite 3-speed automatic transmission.

Like most Dodge products of the time, the "M"-body exterior was distinguishable from its twins only through the trim and nameplates, although the up-market LeBaron had several distinguishing features bolted on. Throughout the later 80s, the Diplomat was sold as Chrysler's baseline "large car," although really, it was closer to midsize.

Performance was reliable rather than stunning, but it was the machine's ability to soak up punishment that really made it stand out. Its sheer hardiness was the deciding factor for many fleet buyers. Although the police fleet models featured several performance enhancements, the true core of the Diplomat remained unchanged – its stubborn, unrelenting endurance.

Dodge Viper GTS

1995–1996

ENGINE: V10, 7997cc

POWER: 450bhp

CHASSIS: Separate

BRAKES (F/R): Disc

TRANSMISSION: Five-speed manual

SUSPENSION: Independent

TOP SPEED: 146mph (233km/h)

ACCELERATION: 0–60mph (96km/h) in 4.6 secs

The Dodge Viper GTS wasn't just a Viper with an impressive roof. About 90 percent of the car was all-new. Inspired by the 60s Cobra Daytona Coupe racers, the GTS sweeping double-bubble roofline gave a much better drag factor too, helping to push the top speed up to over 180mph.

There was a bigger front spoiler with NACA intake, and louvers to stop air pressure building up. Inside the facia was all new, with the speedo and rev-counter closer together and the inevitable air bag where the glove compartment was on the open-topped version.

However, what you lost in the glove box you more than gained in the boot. For the first time the Viper had a luggage compartment - now accessed through a glass rear panel – and what's more, it was big enough to hold two or three large cases.

Best of all, the GTS had an improved, lighter V10 engine with an extra 35bhp and 10 extra lb/ft of torque thanks to reworked heads and block. All this was slotted into a car that was actually lighter than the roadster by 27Kg, despite the added weight of glass and the roof.

Though still a challenging drive, improvements to the suspension had produced a car that was just that little bit more forgiving in the hands of a novice, though the razor sharp steering and strong brakes remained. Never a car for the shrinking violet, the Viper driver could at least now pose in all weathers in a car that was much more usable day-to-day.

Ram V10 Pick-Up

1998–

ENGINE: V10, 7997cc

POWER: 300bhp

CHASSIS: Separate

BRAKES (F/R): Disc/drum

TRANSMISSION: Three-speed automatic

SUSPENSION: independent front, live axle rear

TOP SPEED: 113mph

ACCELERATION: 0–60mph (96km/h) 8.5 seconds

One of the largest and quickest-growing segments of the American new car market in the last half of the nineties was the full-size pick-up truck. Huge and brutish, these vehicles sold on their macho image rather than their utility – massive carrying capacity and the ability to tow enormous weight were merely side issues to the all important business of looking tough on the quiet roads of suburbia.

These vehicles were not about subtly, economy practicality or discreet charm. The pick-up trucks were huge, throbbing powerhouses of industrial engineering which screamed for attention.

None of them ever looked tougher than the bull-nosed Dodge ram. Some 20 feet long and 2573kg unladen it was available with a range of options that made the mind boggle. There were 200 possible drive train combinations – two- or four-wheel drive was just the beginning. It also featured all kinds of labour-saving additions to make the driver think he was driving a luxury saloon.

However, it was in the engine department that the Ram truly made the other trucks that were supposed to be its comnpetition look puny. The basic power plant was a V6 but, for just a few hundred dollars more, buyers could upgrade to an 8 litre V10. This meant Golf GTi-type acceleration and a top speed electronically limited to 113mph. For thriftier motorists, there was always the V8.

Duesenberg SJ

1932–1937

ENGINE: Straight-eight, 6882cc

POWER: 320bhp

CHASSIS: Separate

BRAKES (F/R): Drum

TRANSMISSION: Three-speed manual

SUSPENSION: Beam axles, leaf springs front and rear

TOP SPEED: 130mph (208km/h)

ACCELERATION: 0–60mph (96km/h) 10 seconds

Although European enthusiasts often deride post-war American cars, the Duesenberg SJ model is proof that, before the Second World War, the Americans could produce a car as good as any in the world. As well as being the basis for some spectacular coachwork, the SJ was more than just a pretty face.

In supercharged form, its twin-camshaft, four-valves-per-cylinder Lycoming straight-eight engine produced 320bhp, and could push the monstrous 50cwt (2545kg) car up to a more than respectable speed of 130mph (208km/h).

With its hemispherical combustion chambers and fully balanced, five-bearing, nickel-plated crankshaft, this long-stroke design could rev safely to 5000rpm. There were servo-assisted hydraulic brakes to do the stopping, and the chassis was a massive affair with six tubular cross members.

In chassis form alone, the car was more expensive than a Rolls-Royce. Ownership was strictly the preserve of millionaires, celebrities and film stars – Clark Gable, Gary Cooper, Greta Garbo and William Randolph Hurst all owned SJs.

Founded in 1920 by Fred and August Duesenberg, the company was best known for its racing cars, but poor sales led to a take-over by E.L. Cord and the Auburn firm at the end of the decade. Cord provided the brothers with the money to build an ultimate car from the ground up – the J and SJ being the result. Only 26 SJs were built between 1932 and the end of production in 1937.

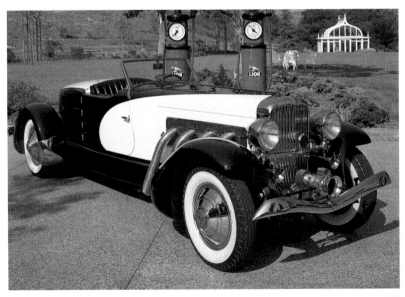

Edsel

1958–1960

ENGINE: Straight-six and V8, 3655–6719cc

POWER: 147–350bhp

CHASSIS: Monocoque

BRAKES (F/R): Drum

TRANSMISSION: Three-speed manual, three-speed automatic

SUSPENSION: Independent front, live axle rear

TOP SPEED: 90–108mph (144–173km/h)

ACCELERATION: 0–60mph (96km/h) in 12 seconds (V8 version)

The Edsel has passed into popular modern mythology as the ultimate in corporate blunders. It was a marque pitched by Ford at the lower-medium market sector, between the much bigger Fords and the budget Mercury models.

By the time it was launched, the market was in a slump, buyers were looking for smaller cars and the Edsel – the wrong car at the wrong time – became an unfortunate victim of its own massive hype.

Forecasting 200,000 sales in the first year, Ford claimed that the new car – named after the dead son of Henry Ford – had cost $250 million to develop.

When only 62,000 buyers were tempted, critics blamed the styling, with its unusual vertical grille. In fact, the Edsel was reasonably restrained by the excessive standards of the period, its fins well clipped with a clean side profile.

Spanning 15 separate models, the Edsel was actually something of a separate Ford division, with saloon, convertible and station-wagon bodies on the same ultra-conventional basic floorpan.

As usual with Ford at the time, there were six-cylinder and V8 engine options – ranging in output from 145bhp to 345bhp – with three-speed manual and automatic transmission versions.

There was a mild restyle for 1959, when Ford bosses tried to arrest dramatically falling sales. A totally new shell in a much-reduced line-up followed for the 1960 model year.

In fact, the Edsel line was dead by the end of 1960 – cancelled due to lack of interest. The ill-omened name came to represent just how badly motor manufacturers could misjudge the marketplace and a car's appeal to the public.

Facel Vega HK500

1958–1961

ENGINE: V8, 6268cc

POWER: 360bhp

CHASSIS: Tubular

BRAKES (F/R): Drum (disc from 1960)

TRANSMISSION: 4-speed (manual/auto)

SUSPENSION: Independent

TOP SPEED: 130mph (208km/h)

ACCELERATION: 0–60mph (96km/h) in 8.4 seconds

Jean Daninos, founder of Facel Vega, made his name producing special bodywork for Panhard, Simca and Ford. However, he had long cherished the ambitious dream of building his own high-performance car, and he went on to finally achieve his ambition in 1954 with the Facel Vega FVS.

The Vega FVS was a glamorous, close-coupled four-seater using an American Chrysler engine. This set a trend for the use of Detroit power in up-market European chassis, and in the 1960s Jensen, Gordon Keeble and Bristol would all follow in the wheel-tracks of the dramatic FVS.

Beautiful and fast, the FVS was followed in 1959 by the uprated HK500 which boasted a bigger engine and standard power steering, if automatic transmission was specified. Most HK500s had disc brakes, too – a feature that was very much a necessity on these rapid, heavy cars. They were good for a top speed of 130mph (208km/h) or – if you were the courageous type – even more.

Handling wasn't the car's strongest point, adding a certain something to high speeds, but that didn't stop the HK500 from being much favoured as a long-distance express, and it was driven by many famous personalities and racing drivers of the day.

Sold alongside the HK500 was the even more dramatic Excellence, a four-door, pillarless, luxury saloon on an extended wheelbase.

Facellia

1959–1963

ENGINE: Four-cylinder 1648cc

POWER: 115bhp

CHASSIS: Tubular

BRAKES (F/R): Disc

TRANSMISSION: Four-speed manual

SUSPENSION: Independent front, live axle rear

TOP SPEED: 114mph (188kmh)

ACCELERATION: 0-60mph (96kmh) in 8.2 seconds

Although the big V8 engined Facels had proved very successful, company founder Jean Daninos still had a longing to build an all French sportscar pitched at a lower price. It was a vision that, given Daninos' track record of turning his ideas into reality, should have worked. However, the result of his hopes for a lower-priced French sportscar was the Facellia of 1960, a pretty two-seater – its lines designed to reflect those of the larger models – on which the company pinned its hopes for the future.

Sadly the Facellia was to prove to be the car which led to the undoing of Facel Vega. The problem lay with the car's bespoke twin-cam engine, which tended to burn holes in its pistons and suffered nastily from prodigious oil leaks.

Even an improved F2S version couldn't rescue the car's reputation in time, and warranty costs soon buried the company. It was a shame, because the Facellia was otherwise a very pleasant little car with a lot to offer. It could boast truly handsome lines, very swish appointments and interior, and some good handling.

There were a couple of last-ditch attempts to save the model by using a different engine – the Facel III used a Volvo 1800 unit, and the Facel Six a sleeved-down Austin Healey straight six. Neither of these did much for the cars handling but they did offer reliability. Another reason to remember the Facellia, and a more pleasant one, is that it was also the only Facel ever offered as a convertible.

Facel ll

1962–1964

ENGINE: V8, 6286cc

POWER: 360bhp

CHASSIS: Tubular

BRAKES (F/R): Disc

TRANSMISSION: Four-speed manual/three-speed automatic

SUSPENSION: Independent front, live axle rear

TOP SPEED: 135mph (216kmh)

ACCELERATION: 0-60mph (96kmh) in 8 seconds

Aware that his HK500 was beginning to look slightly dated – the shape originated in 1954 – Facel Boss Jean Daninos decided to have a new body created for the car in 1962. Lower and more angular, following the dominant early 1960s idiom, the Facel II had Mercedes-style headlamps flanking a scaled-down version of the Facel grille.

If the HK500 had seemed to be influenced by American design in its looks, then the Facel II was definitely much more European, with less wrap-around to its screens and generally less glitz.

Mechanically the car was much as before, and it was offered with the same choice of twin or single carb Chrysler engines, linked either to four-speed manual transmission or a three-speed Chrysler automatic transmission for customers who wanted the option.

Unlike the HK500, which used TV-style push-button selection for the automatic transmission, the Facel II made use of a conventional floor shift. Dunlop disc brakes were used all round, and power steering, leather seats and electric windows were all standard. This was a very expensive car, and it cost the equivalent of two E-types and a Lotus Elan on the British market. In the final analysis, just 184 Facel IIs were built before the company closed its doors for the last time in 1964.

275GTB

1964–1968

ENGINE: V12, 3286cc

POWER: 280–300bhp

CHASSIS: Tubular frame, alloy body

BRAKES (F/R): Disc

TRANSMISSION: Five-speed manual

SUSPENSION: Independent

TOP SPEED: 150–165mph (240–264km/h)

ACCELERATION: 0–60mph (96km/h) in 6.9 seconds

The 275GTB of 1964 was the first Ferrari road car with truly sophisticated suspension, answering demands for a car that could be driven quickly in comfort. For good weight distribution and traction, the five-speed transmission was separated from the engine, in unit with the final drive casing. On early cars it was connected by a slim prop-shaft, but this was later replaced by a torque tube to provide better rigidity.

Double-wishbone rear suspension replaced the usual solid axle with leaf springs that were found on the 250GT series, and the obligatory four-wheel Dunlop-type disc brakes were fitted all round. Up front was Ferrari's famous all-alloy 3.3-litre 60-degree V12, producing 280bhp in single-overhead-camshaft form. The 275

nomenclature was taken from the capacity, expressed in cubic centimetres, of each of the engine's cylinders.

Clothing all this was a two-seater coupe body styled by Pininfarina and built in steel by Scaglieti just up the road from Ferrari's Modena factory. The frame was of the traditional multi-tubular type.

From 1965 there was a Series II car with a longer nose and a smaller air intake, and from 1966 the four-cam 275 GTB/4 with six carburettors and dry-sump lubrication. Top speed soared from around 150mph (240km/h) to 165mph (264km/h), with 0–60mph (96km/h) coming up in under seven seconds.

The 275 was finally replaced in 1968 by the 365 GTB/4 Daytona. It was undoubtedly faster, but perhaps not so well balanced.

Ferrari Daytona

1967–1973

ENGINE: V12, 4390cc

POWER: 352bhp

CHASSIS: Tubular frame

BRAKES (F/R): Disc

TRANSMISSION: Five-speed manual

SUSPENSION: Independent

TOP SPEED: 174mph (278km/h)

ACCELERATION: 0-60mph (96kmh) in 5.4 seconds

While Lamborghini were forging ahead with their range of impressive mid-engined flagship supercars, the Ferrari solution for the late '60s and early '70s came in the desirable form of a front engined V12 Coupe, the 365 GTB/4 Daytona.

Launched in 1968, the car was named Daytona in honour of Ferrari victory in the American 24 hour race of the same name. Not surprisingly, it wasn't to be their last success at the legendary Daytona and in many ways the car that bore its name was a real winner. The 365 denoted the capacity of each of its 12 cylinders, and '4' gave the number of camshafts. The maximum power output was 352bhp.

Pundits at the time had to admit that they were a little disappointed that the car had a conventional layout. Despite that, almost all of them were quick to appreciate the car's bold and muscular styling, which came from the pen of Pininfarina.

Similarly, few could have been disappointed with the car's straight-line performance. Top speed worked out at 174mph, with 0-60 developing in 5.4 seconds. These figures easily put the Daytona's performance beyond that of the Miura.

At low speeds, the Daytona felt heavy and ponderous, and it only really sparkled out on the open road where the steering shed its weight and the hard suspension – classic double wishbones all round – smoothed out.

The car proved extremely popular by Ferrari's exclusive standards, and was built until 1973 alongside a rare Spider version. It is now one of the most collectable of all road going Ferrari models.

The Daytona also happens to be one Ferrari that non-enthusiasts are able to recognise instantly, thanks to its regular slot as Sonny Crockett's car in the hit 1980s cop show *Miami Vice*.

Dino 206/246

1967–1973

ENGINE: V6, 1987/2418cc

POWER: 180/190bhp

CHASSIS: Multi-tubular

BRAKES (F/R): Disc

TRANSMISSION: Five-speed manual

SUSPENSION: Independent

TOP SPEED: 140/148mph (224/237km/h)

ACCELERATION: 0–60mph (96km/h) in 7 seconds

Although the 206/246 Dino was never to wear a Ferrari badge, it was in every respect – other than the number of cylinders – a 'proper' Ferrari and deserved to wear the badge. Capable of turning out 140mph (224km/h), it was a car with superb handling and a stunningly beautiful shape – one of styling-house Pininfarina's finest moments. It was, for many drivers, the first step on the ladder of fabulous dreams that needs to be climbed before one finally becomes a Ferrari owner.

The alloy-bodied 2-litre Dino 206 arrived in 1968 boasting 180bhp, and was powered by the same 65-degree V6 engine as in the Fiat Dino. However, the big difference was that it was turned through 90 degrees and mounted transversely behind the two-seat passenger cell, incorporating a five-speed gearbox and transaxle.

It handled as well as it looked, but it soon became apparent that, in the face of faster opposition from Porsche, the 206 was under-powered. The 246 was Ferrari's answer, with 195bhp from a 2418cc iron-blocked version of the V6, and more torque produced lower down the rev range. It was definitely not under-powered.

Made as a fixed-head GT and GTS open targa (from 1971), its body was now made from steel. Bolt-on alloy wheels, rather than the more attractive centre-locking hubs found on the 206, were another immediate recognition point.

Just over 4,000 206/246s were built between 1968 and 1973, before the introduction of the much less attractive 2+2 Dino 308GT4. The passage of time has done nothing to dampen the desirability of owning a Dino 246.

Ferrari Boxer

1971–1985

ENGINE: Flat 12, 4390–4942cc

POWER: 344–360bhp

CHASSIS: Tubular chassis, alloy body

BRAKES (F/R): Disc

TRANSMISSION: Five-speed manual

SUSPENSION: Independent

TOP SPEED: 171mph (274km/h)

ACCELERATION: 0–60mph (96km/h) in 6.2 seconds

You could trace the history of Ferrari's first flagship mid-engined car, the Boxer, back to the 250LM Road Berlinetta, a fanciful road version of the 250LM. Alternatively, you could perhaps cite the weird three-seater, central-steering 365P show car of 1966 as its true spiritual father. But it wasn't until 1968, with the beautiful P6 show car, that Ferrari's favoured stylist really began to think aloud about the swoopy wedge profile of Maranello's super-car of the 1970s. Pininfarina's stylists progressed from a 'big Dino' look, and flirted with the radical wedge influence of the 512 Modulo and futuristic 512S special Berlinetta, until finally settling on the elegant simplicity of the production car, which was announced – prematurely – at Turin in 1971. Production didn't actually begin until 1973.

Under the big alloy engine cover was a new alloy 4.4-litre flat-12, descended from the 1500cc 512 Formula One car of 1960 and the 312B. To save space, the five-speed transaxle snuggled up under the engine, alongside the sump. Although the flat 'boxer' configuration had the advantage of a low centre of gravity and low height for better aerodynamics, the Boxer had a definite rear weight bias, with 56 percent of its total weight at the rear. Boxers were quick – among the quickest cars in the world – but could never quite match the outlandish Lamborghini Countach. The earliest cars were fastest, with a top speed of 171mph (274km/h).

The 5-litre 512BB took over in 1976. Its bigger-bore engine – now with dry-sump lubrication – produced no extra power but it did yield 10 percent more torque. You can spot a 512 by its front spoiler, wider rear tyres, side air vents to cool the rear brakes, differently vented engine lid and a four- rather than six-tail-light rear end.

308 GTB/GTS

1975–1989

ENGINE: V8, 2926cc

POWER: 250bhp

CHASSIS: Tubular steel, fibreglass body

BRAKES (F/R): Disc

TRANSMISSION: Five-speed manual

SUSPENSION: Independent

TOP SPEED: 155mph (248km/h)

ACCELERATION: 0–60mph (96km/h) in 6.9 seconds

Almost 20,000 308GTB and GTS models were built between 1975 and 1989, making it one of Ferrari's most successful models ever. Compared with a Porsche, however, these cars were rare – something which has constantly helped keep the price of these beautiful vehicles high. Ferrari took 15 years to build as many cars as Porsche – at its intensive peak of production – could churn out in four or five months.

The first GTBs, with their mid-mounted V8 engines, had fibreglass bodywork, but by the time the GTS appeared in 1977, the factory had reverted back to steel panels. The change in construction was noticeable as it made the car much heavier and significantly less rust-resistant.

Nobody cared though, and the American market lapped up the GTS, which consistently out-stripped sales of the hardtop car by a huge margin. This was not particularly surprising, given America's longstanding love affair with soft tops.

Fuel injection replaced carburettors in 1980, making the V8-engined 308 easier to live with, but somewhat slower. Again sales did not falter, and in any case the GTB/GTS was short-lived. It was supplanted in 1982 by the Quattrovalvole with its four-valves-per-cylinder heads.

All the performance returned, with a top speed of over 150mph (240km/h) available in appropriate conditions. Better news was the fact that the handling was as sensational as ever. You could tell what car you were driving with your eyes shut – if you were lucky enough to be behind the wheel of one.

Last and best of the line was the 328, with sharpened-up handling and better build quality. Drivers of the 328 were able to enter motoring nirvana with a drive unparalled in its quality, character and sheer thrill factor. The formula of a smaller, second-division model has been a winning one for Ferrari, and continues today with the F355.

400i

1979–1989

ENGINE: V12, 4390–4942cc

POWER: 320–340bhp

CHASSIS: Monocoque

BRAKES (F/R): Disc

TRANSMISSION: Five-speed manual, three-speed automatic

SUSPENSION: Independent

TOP SPEED: 156mph (250km/h)

ACCELERATION: 0–60mph (96km/h) in 8 seconds (400i)

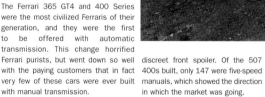

The Ferrari 365 GT4 and 400 Series were the most civilized Ferraris of their generation, and they were the first to be offered with automatic transmission. This change horrified Ferrari purists, but went down so well with the paying customers that in fact very few of these cars were ever built with manual transmission.

The crisp, chisel-edged Pininfarina shape began life at the Paris Show in 1972 with a four camshaft, 4.4-litre V12 engine and a five-speed manual gearbox only. A 150mph (240km/h) four-seater, the 365 proved a short-lived variant, replaced by the 400GT in 1976. This car's bigger 4.9-litre engine gave more torque, thanks to modified camshafts and valve timing, but from the outside there were few differences compared with the outgoing model – apart from a

discreet front spoiler. Of the 507 400s built, only 147 were five-speed manuals, which showed the direction in which the market was going.

With the 400i of 1979 came Bosch fuel injection, which improved the car's driveability but robbed the V12 of 30bhp – although minor improvements later in the production run reclaimed that loss to some extent. Again, most of the 800 cars built were fitted with the smooth GM400 automatic gearbox.

Last, and best, of the 400 line was the 412 of 1985. Its bigger 5-

litre V12, with redesigned combustion chambers and new Marelli injection, gave 340bhp and 9.5 percent more torque, whilst anti-lock brakes and bigger tyres improved the dynamic performance of these large, hefty cars. Outwardly Pininfarina had discreetly modified the styling, with a raised rear deck, body-colour bumpers and flush alloy wheels.

Production of the 412 ended in 1989. It was the last traditional front-engined Ferrari in production until the release of the 456GT in 1992.

Ferrari F40

1987–1992

ENGINE: V8, 2936cc

POWER: 478bhp

CHASSIS: Tubular

BRAKES (F/R): Disc

TRANSMISSION: Five-speed manual

SUSPENSION: Independent

TOP SPEED: 201mph (322km/h)

ACCELERATION: 0–60mph (96km/h) in 4.5 seconds

The F40 was built to mark Enzo Ferrari's 40th year as a car manufacturer in 1988. However, it was also intended, from its inception, to represent the super-car in its ultimate form. It was a great way to celebrate Enzo's birthday, and an even greater way to celebrate the supercar.

Outwardly the shape owed something to the contemporary 328GTB. The F40 was much wider and more aggressive though, with a rear hoop spoiler and an uncompromisingly chopped tail. It was nothing if not a head-turner.

Based on the floorpan of the 288GTO and retaining the classic tubular-steel frame chassis, it made extensive use of weight-saving composite materials. It also featured all the latest Formula One

turbocharging technology, applied to a special, short-stroke 3-litre V8 engine. Twin IHI turbochargers were used to obtain an output of 478bhp, and Ferrari claimed a top speed of 201mph (322km/h).

Not only was this car sensationally fast, but it was also incredibly noisy. The cabin, bereft of carpets, acted just like a sound-box. The stripped-out, rather austere interior further hammered home the fact that when you got down to it, the F40 was really a racing car for the road – although ironically the cars were never raced in anger.

Many, in fact, were bought as investments. Such was the demand for the car that Ferrari more than doubled the original intended production run to 1,200 cars. Production lasted until 1992.

Ferrari 456GT

1992–

ENGINE: V12, 5474cc

POWER: 442bhp

CHASSIS: Monocoque

BRAKES (F/R): Disc

TRANSMISSION: Six-speed manual

SUSPENSION: Independent

TOP SPEED: 193mph (309km/h)

ACCELERATION: 0–60mph (96km/h) in 5.1 seconds

The introduction of the 456GT in 1992 marked the return of the classic front-engined V12 layout to Ferrari's ultimate road car. It was also exactly what most people dreamed a Ferrari should be – very beautiful, fast, amazingly sharp-handling, and dauntingly expensive for all but the extremely rich.

Not since the demise of the Daytona in 1973 had the fastest Ferrari had a front engine. In some senses the 456, with its 2+2 seating, was also an overdue replacement for the old 412 coupe, Maranello's famous last V12 model.

Pininfarina was commissioned to do the styling for the 456, and clearly took inspiration from the chunky, elegant, tapering profile of the Daytona. Looking at the rear view especially, there were strong echoes of the old car.

Under the 456's bonnet was a new four-camshaft V12, delivering its power to a rear-mounted, six-speed transaxle for perfect weight distribution. Classic double-wishbone suspension was matched to advanced electronic damping and power steering, so the 456 combined thoroughbred cornering poise with a deliciously supple ride.

As you would expect, the 456GT also had a beautifully crafted interior, combining soft, boldly coloured leather with high-quality detail – the big chrome-topped gear-lever was a powerful evocation of 1950s Ferrari Grand Tourers. It was a design that skillfully echoed the whole glorious heritage of Ferrari and yet was at the same time unobtrusively but very stylishly modern.

The 456 was joined in 1996 by the front-engined 550 Maranello. This move confirmed Ferrari's commitment to producing front-engined layouts for its fastest cars, making them much easier to drive and much easier to live with.

Ferrari **F355**

1994–1999

ENGINE: V8, 3496cc

POWER: 380bhp

CHASSIS: Monocoque

BRAKES: Disc

TRANSMISSION: Six-speed manual

SUSPENSION: Independent

TOP SPEED: 173mph (277km/h)

ACCELERATION: 0–60mph (96km/h) in 4.6 seconds

The 1994 F355 was the latest in a very long line of smaller 'entry level' mid-engined Ferraris. These dated back to the absolutely classic 206 Dino, which was launched upon a Ferrari loving market as long ago as 1967.

The F355's predecessor, the 348, had always been rather disappointing in terms of driver appeal. The new car represented a huge improvement across a whole swathe of fields. The F355 used a virtually all-new, 90-degree V8 mounted longitudinally behind the seats and driving the rear wheels. With five valves per cylinder, it now made all the right noises and delivered superb punch through six closely stacked gears.

The chassis, too, was much improved – thanks to advanced adaptive damping that sensed any excessive wallows that were beginning to build when cornering. It also allowed for the type of supple, comfortable ride that you'd expect from this type of car.

The sheet metal of the chassis itself was much stiffer than before, and the result of this was a car that handled sensationally well, yet was also much easier to drive and much more comfortable. Unlike the 348, the F355 was an absolute

pleasure for any driver to get his or her hands on.

And, of course, there was a new body – as usual, it was the work of Ferrari's favourite stylist, Pininfarina. Perfectly proportioned, typically beautiful, it had more curves and much more presence than the out-going 348. The F355 also enjoyed a much more inviting interior.

Good for 173mph (277km/h), many pundits reckoned the F355 was the best road-going Ferrari for ages – better, even, than the big 512TR.

Ferrari F50

1995–1996

ENGINE: V12, 4698cc

POWER: 520bhp

CHASSIS: Carbon fibre

BRAKES (F/R): Disc

TRANSMISSION: Six-speed manual

SUSPENSION: Independent all round

TOP SPEED: 202mph (323km/h)

ACCELERATION: 0–60mph (96km/h) in 3 seconds

When the time came to build a new flagship, the brief for Ferrari's engineers was simple and uncompromising – take the 1990 Formula One racing car, the 641/2, and transform it into a street-legal 200mph (320km/h) road car. With this as the masterplan, Ferrari simply couldn't fail.

Enter then, in March 1995, the F50 – a two-seater, V12, carbon-fibre, 200mph, mid-engined sports car. Clothed in a Pininfarina body that recalled Ferrari's sports racers of the early 1970s, it was easily the wildest road car Ferrari ever made.

Ferrari decreed that only 349 examples should be built, compared with 1,311 F40s, which was Ferrari's previous ultimate road car. This strategy has ensured extremely high values for the car ever since the day they were first announced.

With 520bhp from the F1-derived V12, the F50 would do 64mph (102km/h) in first gear, 74mph (142km/h) in second, 112mph (179km/h) in third, 138mph (221km/h) in fourth, 160mph (256km/h) in fifth and 202mph (323km/h) in sixth.

The handling was more forgiving than that of the F40, despite the extra speed, but with the engine rigidly mounted to the chassis the noise was incredible, both in volume and quality. It wasn't just the fabulous look of the car that turned heads.

Fiat 8V

1952–1953

ENGINE: V8, 1996cc

POWER: 105bhp

CHASSIS: Multi-tubular

BRAKES (F/R): Drum

TRANSMISSION: Four-speed manual

SUSPENSION: Independent all round

TOP SPEED: 120mph (192km/h)

ACCELERATION: 0–60mph (96km/h) in 13 seconds

Fiat first mooted a flagship V8 model in the late-1940s, but the big saloon prototype proved to be too heavy and slothful. Fiat's top brass were not impressed, and the project lost momentum. That left a 70-degree 2-litre V8 engine going begging, so why not fit it to a sportscar? Enter the Otto Vu – Italian for Eight Vee – launched at the Geneva Show in 1952.

The shape may have been an in-house Fiat design, but it vied with the best efforts of the local coachbuilders for elegant purity. Designed in the Turin Polytechnic wind tunnel, the 8V was as smooth as its appearance promised. Chief Fiat test-driver Carlo Salomano managed to record a two-way maximum of 207km/h (129mph) on the Turin–Milan autostrada – highly impressive for the time.

Design boss Dante Giacosa raided Fiat's parts bin to produce an exceptionally accomplished chassis using Fiat 1100 independent suspension at both the front and rear. The 8V bodies were built at Lingotto by Fiat in its experimental coachwork department, with local specialist Siata contracted to produce the mechanical elements.

Fiat built just 114 Otto Vu chassis, but not all had the standard Fiat body – Vignale, Bertone, Ghia and Pininfarina all clothed the 8V with their own designs, and Fiat even built a special plastic-bodied version of the standard car as a Motor Show one-off. One of the fastest catalogued 2-litre cars of the 1950s, the 8V turned out to be the only production V8-engined car that Fiat ever made.

Multipla

1955–1966

ENGINE: In-line four-cylinder 633/767cc

POWER: 24–29bhp

CHASSIS: Monocoque

BRAKES (F/R): Drum

TRANSMISSION: Four-speed manual

SUSPENSION: Independent all round

TOP SPEED: 55–60mph (88–96km/h)

ACCELERATION: 0–50mph (80km/h) in 30 seconds plus

Although Renault may claim to have invented the space-efficient 'people carrier' with the Espace in the 1980s, it was Fiat who actually got there first with the Multipla – albeit 30 years too early. That is surely enough to earn the vehicle a place in the automobile history books, given the way that the 'people carrier' market has boomed in the late-1980s and throughout the 1990s.

Launched in 1955, this teardrop-shaped little minibus – with its extremely bouncy ride and vague gearchange – was based on the mechanicals of the Fiat 600. This latter vehicle was a best-selling rear-engined family saloon that the company was producing during that period of the 1950s.

Thanks to a 'forward control' driving position, the Multipla could accommodate anything up to six people on three rows of bench seats in its 139in. long and 62in. wide body. On the production lines for 11 years, it found much favour with Italian taxi drivers, and many were also used as delivery vans as well as people carriers. To this day, there are still quite a few Multiplas seeing active service in the vehicle's native country.

Early versions had a 633cc version of Fiat's little overhead-valve four-cylinder engine, whilst later versions were fitted with a 30bhp, 767cc engine that pushed the top speed up from 55mph (88km/h) to 60mph (96km/h).

Fiat 500

1957–1975

ENGINE: Two-cylinder, 499cc

POWER: 18bhp

CHASSIS: Monocoque

BRAKES (F/R): Drum/drum

TRANSMISSION: Four-speed manual

SUSPENSION: Independent all round

TOP SPEED: 60mph (96km/h)

ACCELERATION: 0–50mph (80km/h) in 30 seconds plus

Designed as utilitarian transport for the masses, the Fiat 500 was the vehicle that put Italy on wheels during the 1960s. More than four million examples were built in a 20-year production run and they truly became the 'people's car'. It's long history has not only been marked by huge production numbers, but also the production of a large number of variants.

A minimalist four-seater with kart-like handling, the original car was powered by a 479cc, flat twin, air-cooled engine mounted in the rear. This was later boosted to 499cc to give a heady 18bhp. Speed was not why the 500 was created.

The 500 could cruise at 55mph, and boasted Scrooge-like economy, with over 53mpg (5.4 litres/100km) possible. Early cars had rear-hinged 'suicide' doors and a full-length sunroof, whereas post-1965 500F models had conventional front hinges. However, the 500 kept its drum brakes and crude 'crash' non-synchromeshed gearbox right through to the end. The 1968 500L version gave buyers an alternative to the stark, basic version that they were used to whilst the run-out 500R model used the engine and floorpan from the 126 – making it a very different type of 500.

From 1960 there was an estate version called Giardiniera, which had a surprisingly useful load area that many other cars of the time would be jealous of. Latterly badged as an Autobianchi, this model outlived the standard version by a couple of years. It retained its rear-hinged doors to the end.

Fiat **850C**

1965–1972

ENGINE: Four-cylinder, 843/903cc

POWER: 45–52bhp

CHASSIS: Monocoque

BRAKES (F/R): Disc/drum

TRANSMISSION: Four-speed manual

SUSPENSION: Independent

TOP SPEED: 91mph (146km/h)

ACCELERATION: 0–60mph (96km/h) in 18 seconds

It didn't take long for sports variants of Fiat's bread-and-butter 850 saloon to appear to fill a large gap in a very hungry market. In 1965 Bertone announced a pretty two-seater Spider version, while Fiat's own styling department got on with the business of producing a neat fastback, four-seater coupe.

When it came right down to it, the rear seats were near-useless and the luggage space in the nose was modest to say the least, but this didn't stop people from buying the little 850 Coupe and Spider in large numbers.

The top speed – with a little more power than the stock saloon – was 90mph and, despite the overhanging rear position of the willing little water-cooled pushrod engine, the handling was excellent.

The 850 featured light, positive steering, lots of grip and responsive brakes, with discs at the front. Fuel consumption of 40mpg (7.1 litres/ 100km) was another attraction.

The Geneva Show of 1968 saw the introduction of a revised coupe with a bigger 903cc engine that pushed the top speed towards 100mph (160km/h). There were minor styling revisions too, and the car carried on in this form until 1971, by which time 380,000 850 Coupes had been produced.

The Spider continued in production until 1974, due to its popularity in the USA. Even to this day, the number of American Spider clubs and committed enthusiasts is totally bewildering. No one can deny that the 850C is one Fiat that made a big impact.

Fiat 124 Spider

1966–1985

ENGINE: In-line four-cylinder, 1438/1608/1756/1995cc

POWER: 90–135bhp

CHASSIS: Monocoque

BRAKES (F/R): Disc

TRANSMISSION: Four- or five-speed manual, three-speed auto option

SUSPENSION: Independent front, live axle rear

TOP SPEED: 102–120mph (163–192km/h)

ACCELERATION: Not Available

The Fiat 124 Spider is the most commercially successful Italian sports car ever. It was popular when it was launched, it was popular throughout its prodction life, and even today the car has a staggering amount of committed enthusiasts who are proud of their little piece of Italian motoring genius.

With a belt-drive, twin-cam engine under the bonnet, it was a spirited and sweet performer, whilst well-located coil-sprung rear suspension and four-wheel disc brakes gave it wonderful dynamic performance and refinement that was way beyond its British competitors. These factors have helped ensure that no one who ever drives one will forget its unique, chirpy character.

The handsome body was styled by none other than Pininfarina and had enduring appeal – even when ugly federal-style bumpers were hung on it in the mid-1970s to comply with safety regulations in North America, always the model's biggest market. Five gears were initially optional, then later a standard fitment, and there was even an automatic version in later years.

Engine capacity grew over the years, too – first to 1608cc in 1969, then to 1756cc in 1972, with a new 1592cc 1600 base model being added. A 2-litre engine became standard across the range from 1979, as Fiat tried to counter increasing power-sapping emissions regulations.

Fuel injection was introduced in 1980. The ultimate version was the supercharged VX, which came equipped with a thundering 135bhp powerplant. Production ceased in 1985, with the later variants being marketed as Pininfarinas rather than straight Fiat Spiders.

Fiat Dino

1967–1973

ENGINE: V6, 1987–2418cc

POWER: 160–180bhp

CHASSIS: Monocoque

BRAKES (F/R): Disc

TRANSMISSION: Five-speed manual

SUSPENSION: Independent front, live axle rear (all independent on the 2.4-litre model)

TOP SPEED: 127–130mph (203–208km/h)

ACCELERATION: 0–60mph (96km/h) in 8.1–8.7 seconds

In the mid-1960s, Ferrari needed a large company to build its Formula Two V6 engine in quantity, while Fiat wanted to produce an up-market sports car with real credibility. The result of the liaison was an instant classic – the Fiat Dino, Spider and coupe.

The original quad-camshaft, all-alloy, 65-degree V6 found in the 2-litre models could trace its history back to the 1950s and Vittorio Jano. It was made into a viable production road-car engine by Aurelio Lampredi – who had an established pedigree as a one-time Ferrari employee.

To comply with Formula Two homologation rules – Enzo Ferrari's whole motivation for the venture – it had to be produced in numbers of no fewer than 500 a year. That was where Fiat came into picture, beginning a courtship between the two companies that led to Fiat's take-over of Ferrari in 1969. That was the same year in which the

engine gained its iron block and extra capacity – 2419cc – pushing power up to 180bhp at 6600rpm.

Much of the hardware found in the Pininfarina Dino Spider and its Bertone Coupe sibling was stock Fiat. The floorpan and rear suspension on the 2-litre model were shared with the old 2300S Coupe, and the coil-spring-and-wishbone front suspension with the 124 Spider (although suitably uprated). The gearbox was the four-speed unit from the 2300, with a separate casing bolted on the back for a higher-geared fifth gear.

The floorpan was supplied to Pininfarina, who then sent the shell back to Fiat to have the mechanicals fitted. It was a convoluted but successful production process. The 2.4-litre cars, announced in 1969, had the sophisticated strut-and-trailing-arm rear suspension from Fiat's up-market 130 saloon. Production of both models ended in 1973.

RLJ 976R

Fiat 130 Coupe

1971–1977

ENGINE: V6, 3235cc

POWER: 165bhp

CHASSIS: Monocoque

BRAKES (F/R): Disc

TRANSMISSION: Three-speed
automatic, five-speed manual

SUSPENSION: Independent all round

TOP SPEED: 115–118mph
(184–189km/h)

ACCELERATION: 0–60mph (96km/h)
in 10 seconds

Fiat's resoundingly unloved, unlovely 130 saloon of the late 1960s rather surprisingly spawned one of the best-looking cars of the 1970s, the Pininfarina-styled 130 coupe of 1971. Perfectly proportioned and superbly elegant from any angle, it stood apart from many luxury coupes of its day in having ample room inside for four passengers. To put it simply, it was beautiful – a car to fall in love with at first sight.

Few coupes were as sumptuous either, with rich velour upholstery on the seats, veneer door cappings and high equipment levels – electric windows, twin-tone 'town and country horns' and an electric aerial were all standard.

Mechanically it was identical to the saloon, the smooth free-revving V6 having recently been uprated from 2.8 litres to 3.2 litres to answer gripes about a lack of performance. Power was a still-modest 165bhp,

but the torque went up dramatically. Most examples were fitted with automatic transmission – by Borg Warner – although there was a five-speed manual option. With sophisticated independent suspension – shared at the rear with the Fiat Dino – the 130 Coupe had fine balance too, not to mention a supple ride worthy of a world-class luxury car. Power steering was standard.

In the end it was the Fiat name that killed off the 130 Coupe before its time. The sheer fact that it was badged as a Fiat meant its prestige pulling power was always going to be severely limited in a class dominated by the likes of the high class Germans such as BMW and Mercedes.

Unfortunately, production ceased in 1977. The coupe just about managed to hold on a for a year longer than the saloon.

Fiat X1/9

1972–1989

ENGINE: In-line four-cylinder, 1290/1499cc

POWER (1290cc version): 75bhp

CHASSIS: Monocoque

BRAKES (F/R): Disc/drum

TRANSMISSION: Four- and five-speed manual

SUSPENSION: Independent

TOP SPEED (1290cc version): 100mph (160km/h)

ACCELERATION: 0–60mph (96km/h) in 13 seconds

The Fiat X1/9 brought mid-engined handling sophistication of a sort that had previously been reserved for the exclusive owners of cars like of Lamborghinis and Ferraris to a mass audience. It was a daring move, and it paid off beautifully.

Launched to a rapturous reception from the world's motoring press in 1972, Bertone's razor-edged styling was highly praised. His design was innovative and accessible, incorporating a nifty, removable Targa roof panel stored in the front 'boot' when not in use, and pop-up headlights. The fine mid-engined road manners meant that the car was virtually assured success all over the world, and it wasn't until the mid-1980s that it had a serious competitor in the shape of Toyota's MR2.

Fitted with a 1290cc four-cylinder 85bhp single-overhead-camshaft engine and four-speed gearbox, the original car was adequately brisk. It would comfortably reach 100mph

(160km/h) at top speed, and could manage a 0–60mph (96km/h) time of around 13 seconds, but it was hardly quick enough to get the maximum benefit out of the sensational grip and razor-sharp handling.

Even so, novices and seasoned drivers alike took the X1/9 to their hearts, because it was so easy to drive. Extra performance was obtained for the vehicle in 1978, in the form of the 1500cc engine from the Ritmo/Strada hatchbacks. A good X1/9 1500 would touch 110mph (176km/h), break 60mph (96km/h) in under 10 seconds, and cruise at 100mph (160km/h) all day.

The 1500 now featured a five-speed gearbox, but big impact bumpers had by then spoiled its once-crisp good looks, unfortunately. In 1982, production of the model was taken over by the styling house Bertone. They gamely continued to manufacture and market the car, calling it the Bertone X1/9, until its inevitable demise in 1989.

Panda

1980–1995

ENGINE: In-line four-cylinder, 903cc

POWER: 45bhp

CHASSIS: Steel monocoque, three-door

BRAKES (F/R): Disc/drum

TRANSMISSION: Five-speed manual

SUSPENSION: Struts front, live axle rear

TOP SPEED: 88mph (141km/h)

ACCELERATION: 0–62.5mph (100km/h) in 16.9 seconds

It was typical of Fiat's design bravery to build a 'people's car' that harked back to the simplicity of the Citroën 2CV. It wanted to appeal to drivers who wanted ultra-simplicity and a low price tag. The truth was that Fiat really needed to build lots of small cars very cheaply to try and stay in the black.

Once again, Giugiaro was responsible for a car that was ground-breaking in its approach. Back-to-basics design parameters meant the Panda had completely flat glass, including the windscreen.

The body was also very simple in its construction, with flat body sides, a clam-shell bonnet, simple nose slots for cooling and a single wiper. The lower half of the body was clad in impact-resistant plastic. It was basic, but effective.

Inside, the clever design work was even more pronounced. The dashboard was substituted for a long tray that ran across the interior. The face-level air vents – one at each bottom corner of the windscreen – ran to the outside straight through the bodywork. All the instruments were grouped in a simple box around the steering wheel. The rear seat was simply a hammock on a frame.

Very simple running gear meant cart-spring suspension at the rear, although the Panda was eventually updated with a more modern chassis. Fiat even produced a simple 4x4 version of the Panda. Production of this exemplary utilitarian vehicle ended in 1994, although Seat built its own version, the Marbella, until late 1997.

Fiat Tipo

1988–1995

ENGINE: In-line four-cylinder, 1580cc

POWER: 90bhp

CHASSIS: Steel monocoque, three- and five-door

BRAKES (F/R): Disc

TRANSMISSION: Five-speed manual

SUSPENSION: Struts front, trailing arms rear

TOP SPEED: 107mph (171km/h)

ACCELERATION: 0–62.5mph (100km/h) in 11.9 seconds

Plenty of publicity surrounded the launch of Fiat's mainstream hatchback in 1978. The Strada was said to have been 'built by robots,' and the unusually avant garde styling seemed to confirm that the car was a high-tech production. Typically, it became known more for unreliability and rampant rust.

Fiat's replacement for the Strada stuck to the theme of design bravery, but attempted finally to give Fiat a trustworthy gloss. The Tipo was one of the most space-efficient family hatchbacks ever produced. The 100in. (254cm) wheelbase gave it exceptional legroom, and the wide body made it possible to mould the rear seat into individual spaces for three passengers. In a final move to rid Fiat of its reputation for producing cars that rusted in short order, the exterior body panels were galvanized. The basic Tipo structure was to be very important for Fiat, as it was the basis for numerous Fiats, Alfas and Lancias.

The exterior styling was completed by IDEA of Turin, and reflected the uncompromising nature of the Tipo as a space-efficient vehicle, with a large glass area and a wide windscreen. The car was very popular with design-conscious buyers, but white Tipos were nicknamed refrigerators, thanks to the unremitting squareness of the body.

However, being typically Fiat, the Tipo suffered at least one unnecessarily wacky feature. DGT-model Tipos were fitted with an unusual digital dashboard, divided into narrow strips running across the fascia. That aside, few family cars have ever matched the Tipo's space utilization.

Coupe Turbo

1993–2000

ENGINE: In-line 20-valve five-cylinder, 1998cc

POWER: 220bhp

CHASSIS: Steel monocoque, two-door

BRAKES (F/R): Disc with ABS

TRANSMISSION: Five-speed manual

SUSPENSION: Struts front, trailing arms rear

TOP SPEED: 151mph (242km/h)

ACCELERATION: 0–62.5mph (100km/h) in 5.7 seconds

Scared off by the financial consequences of extreme design, and more concerned with putting its mainstream car business on the right track, Fiat wasn't really interested in the 'surprise and delight' market as the 1980s turned into the 1990s.

This simply wasn't good enough for Fiat's new boss, however. Paulo Canterella was a passionate car enthusiast, who thought that the company should have more passion and be building enthusiasts' cars. The first result of this was the extraordinary Fiat Coupe, styled by Chris Bangle. Although the chassis of the Alfa 155 saloon lurked under the body, it was impossible to guess it. It looked like no other car before – from the giant 'slash' marks that creased the bonnet opening and tops of the rear arches, the Coupe was brutal and uncontrolled in

its details. The headlamps bulged upwards from under clear covers, and the alloy fuel filler cap was perched on the corner of the rear wing.

The rear view was a plain, flat expanse punctured by four large, round light units sunk into the tail. The coach-building firm Pininfarina designed the interior, which was equally radical, using a strip of body-matching metal across the dashboard to house the instruments – designed to recall racing cars of decades gone by.

Fiat went to great lengths to ensure the car's chassis was first rate – as it needed to be with an extremely powerful turbo engine in the top model. After a couple of years, the Fiat got new five-cylinder engines for even greater pace. It stayed at the top of the coupe tree for many years.

Punto

1993–1999

ENGINE: In-line four-cylinder, 1242cc

POWER: 75bhp

CHASSIS: Steel monocoque, three- and five-door

BRAKES (F/R): Disc/drum

TRANSMISSION: Five-speed manual

SUSPENSION: Struts front, trailing arms rear

TOP SPEED: 93mph (149km/h)

ACCELERATION: 0–62.5mph (100km/h) in 12.3 seconds

What was left of Fiat's reputation as a car maker at the beginning of the 1980s was rescued by an all-new super-mini that dominated the decade in terms of production, massively outselling even the ever-popular Peugeot 205. The Fiat Uno was in production for 11 years and shifted over 6 million units. Its success was partly due to the fact that the Giugiaro-penned body was more modern and versatile than that of the competition, being tall, roomy and airy.

When Fiat came to replace the Uno, it needed another success in the same mould. It stuck to the essence of the Uno formula by producing another super-mini that was comfortable, versatile and more modern in layout than those of the opposition.

The Punto was launched in 1993 and was a surprisingly radical-looking machine, almost aping the 'one-box' layout of the typical MPV.

The Punto interior was developed under the chairmanship of Paolo Canterella, a self-confessed car enthusiast. He insisted that the Punto's tail-lights be moved up on to the roof pillars, a feature which became the car's most identifiable feature. Giugiaro admitted later that Canterella had been absolutely right to insist on the design changes.

Fiat also sought to banish its long-term problem of designing a driving position suitable for a wide range of driver types. Ergonomic advice and the design of the front seats were handled successfully by Loughborough University in the UK.

Fiat's hope that the new Punto – launched in 1999 – would continue the success of the original model wasn't fulfilled. Fiat ran into serious financial trouble in 2001 shortly after a deal with GM saw 20 per cent of the company sold to the Americans.

Ford **Model T**

1908–1927

ENGINE: Four-cylinder, 2898cc

POWER: Not available

CHASSIS: Separate

BRAKES: Drum

TRANSMISSION: Two-speed epicyclic

SUSPENSION: Beam axles

TOP SPEED: 40mph (64km/h)

ACCELERATION: Not available

The Ford Model T of 1908 brought cheap, reliable transport within the reach of millions of Americans who never dreamed they could have owned a car. New mass-production techniques meant that large numbers of cars could be built cheaply, and by 1913 one Model T was coming off the production lines every ten seconds at Ford's new High Land Park factory. Over 15 million units were built, and for a time more than half of all the cars on the road in the entire world were Model Ts.

Long-lasting, strong and light, its hard-working four-cylinder engine had lots of torque, and featured a one-piece cylinder block and removable cylinder head for easy maintenance – innovative at the time.

It was also easy to drive, with a pedal-operated planetary transmission that anybody could use: one pedal to go forward, another for reverse. However, it could give problems – when the driver cranked the engine over at the front, it could allow the car to run him over! The model T's suspension, which was supple yet no more complex than the average hay wagon, was perfect for the mostly rough and rugged conditions of America's roads – many of which were still unmade tracks at that time.

From the beginning the car was a huge success, and such was its universal appeal that Henry Ford set up factories in other parts of the world. From 1911 Britain had its own Model T factory at Trafford Park, Manchester. Model T production ended in 1927.

V8 Pilot

1947–1951

ENGINE: V8, 3622cc

POWER: 85bhp

CHASSIS: Separate

BRAKES: Drum

TRANSMISSION: Three-speed manual

SUSPENSION: Beam axles front and rear

TOP SPEED: 85mph (136km/h)

ACCELERATION: 0–60mph (96km/h) in 20 seconds

The first British-built Ford V8s date from the early 1930s. Good for up to 80mph (128km/h), these were among the most accelerative cars on the road, with excellent torque from the smooth 'flathead' V8. They developed throughout the 1930s into a range of saloons, convertibles and estate cars that – more or less – shadowed the changes being wrought to its American equivalent on the other side of the Atlantic.

After the Second World War production started up again, but this time the car was known by a name rather than a number – the Pilot. It retained the hydro-mechanical brakes and column-change gearbox of its predecessor, but had a new, more-upright radiator grille and the seemingly retrograde fitment of free-standing headlights – previously these had been streamlined into the wings. There were no dropheads this time, but some extremely good-looking 'woody' estate cars were built on this rugged chassis, one of which was used by the British Royal Family.

Rather than being a clear cut 'good guy' car like the Dodge Diplomat, the Pilot was in a more grey area. It was very occassionally possible to see a Pilot vs. Pilot chase as discerning drivers on both sides of the law attempted to outdo each other.

Some 22,000 V8 pilots were built before the model was effectively replaced by the new monocoque-bodied Zephyrs. However, that number was more than enough to ensure that it's legend lives on in the hearts and minds of its many committed enthusiasts.

Consul/Zephyr/ Zodiac Mk 1 & 2

1950–1962

ENGINES: In-line four- and six-cylinder: 1508, 1703, 2262 and 2553cc

POWER: 48–87bhp

CHASSIS: Monocoque

BRAKES (F/R): Drum/drum

TRANSMISSION: Three- or four-speed manual, three-speed automatic

SUSPENSION: Independent front, live axle rear

TOP SPEED: 75–90mph (120–144km/h)

ACCELERATION: 0–60mph (96km/h) in 27 seconds (Consul), 0–60mph (96km/h) in 17 seconds (Zodiac II)

The 1950 Consul, replacing the V8 Pilot, was the first of the modern post-war cars from Ford's Dagenham plant, incorporating a whole raft of new technology that brought the big Fords bang up to date.

Unitary construction featured for the first time, making for a lighter, stiffer structure. Front suspension was by Macpherson struts, replacing the beam axle found on the Pilot, whilst the brakes were fully hydraulic at last. Overhead valves for the 1508cc four-cylinder engine meant more power, although it wasn't until 1951 that the big Ford got some much-needed performance in the form of the 2262cc six-cylinder Zephyr.

There was a power-top convertible version by Carbodies, an Abbott-bodied estate and, from 1954, a top-of-the-range Zodiac identifiable by its fashionable two-tone paint, white-wall tyres and fog lamps.

The cars were well received and sold well, but Ford was not a company to rest on its laurels: the Mk II Consul, Zephyr and Zodiac range arrived in 1956 with new, bigger styling and larger four- and six-cylinder engines of 1703cc and 2553cc, respectively. The Zephyr/Zodiac could now top 90mph (144km/h), and the Consul around 80mph (128km/h).

Again, there was a Carbodies-built convertible – very flash, and now much sought-after – and a rare Abbott estate car. From 1959 there was a sleeker version of the Mk II with a lower roofline. Options included front disc brakes – from 1960 – overdrive and Borg Warner automatic transmission.

The introduction of the Mk III in 1962 marked the end of the classic 1950s-style Consuls, Zephyrs and Zodiacs, which were among the best-loved British family saloons of their era.

Ford Popular 100E

1954–1959

ENGINE: Four-cylinder, 1172cc

POWER: 30bhp

CHASSIS: Separate box-section

BRAKES: Drum

TRANSMISSION: Three-speed manual

SUSPENSION: Beam axles front and rear

TOP SPEED: 60mph (96km/h)

ACCELERATION: Not available

The Ford Popular 100E was one of the cheapest and most basic cars you could buy in the UK in the 1950s. Derived from the pre- and immediately post-war Anglias, it sported tiny headlamps and an ultra-down-market specification that included only a single windscreen wiper, the most rudimentary of dashboards and a fabric roof that didn't open, in order to save on steel. There were no indicators or rear lights, and the buyer even had little colour choice. Most Populars were painted either grey or black, as if to reflect the austere, post-war ration-book mood.

Nor had such basics as independent front suspension caught up with the Popular, which had beam axles front and rear for an uncomfortable ride and unsporting handling. Stirring it along through a three-speed transmission, the Popular driver might have achieved 60mph (96km/h), but the 30bhp side-valve engine (pre-war in origin) didn't encourage hard use, and it wasn't even especially thrifty for its size. All in all, it wasn't designed to be a spectacular, comfortable or even efficient driving machine – just one that was within the rather modest financial range of the general public at the time.

There were few joys in store for the Popular driver of 1954, yet the model still engenders a great deal of affection in the minds of thousands of drivers for whom it was their first car. In the 1970s, it became a favourite with hot-rod builders.

Thunderbird

1955–1957

ENGINE: V8, 4785–5113cc

POWER: 225bhp

CHASSIS: Steel body, separate chassis

BRAKES (F/R): Drum/drum

TRANSMISSION: Three-speed manual, three-speed automatic

SUSPENSION: Independent front, live axle rear

TOP SPEED: 110–120mph (176–192km/h)

ACCELERATION: 0–60mph (96km/h) in 10.2 seconds

Standing aside from the wallowing barges that ruled the roads of the USA in the 1950s, the Ford Thunderbird was created as a two-seater, sporty 'personal car' with simple, elegant lines. Its fins were modest, its bumpers restrained, and the brightwork was minimal.

It wasn't a sports car in the true European sense – more of a brisk, luxury tourer – but the image was right. The car scored over the contemporary Chevrolet Corvette – which it outsold handsomely – in having a V8 engine under the bonnet. With 200bhp from a Mercury-sourced 4.8-litre V8, the Thunderbird would steam up to 114mph (182km/h) and whisk you up to 60mph (96km/h) in under 10 seconds. Around corners, though, it was a different story, with its soft springs and low-geared steering,

but compared with the average Detroit barge it was actually reasonably nimble.

There were automatic and three-speed manual versions, with optional overdrive transmission available. There was also a powered soft top and an optional hardtop, and 1956 Thunderbirds also had the 'Continental' spare wheel.

It wasn't to last, of course. The grille and fins grew more gawky for 1957, and for 1958 Ford introduced a completely new Thunderbird – a bigger, flabbier device with ugly squared-up styling and a grille like a mouth organ. In the early 1960s the 'bird regained some of its youthful good looks, if not its sports-car pretensions. Today the 1955–57 cars have almost passed into legend, and deservedly, they are highly collectable.

Fairlane 500 Skyliner

1956–1959

ENGINE: V8, 5769cc

POWER: 300bhp

CHASSIS: Separate box-section

BRAKES: Drum

TRANSMISSION: Three-speed automatic, three-speed manual

SUSPENSION: Independent front, live axle rear

TOP SPEED: 105mph (168km/h)

ACCELERATION: 0–60mph (96km/h) in 10 seconds

The Ford Skyliner's retractable 'hide-away hardtop' was one of the most audacious and memorable engineering gimmicks ever to find its way on to an American car. A switch on the steering column started three motors that opened up the car's rear deck, while another motor unlocked the top and another lifted the steel roof and sent it back into the boot space. The whole process took about a minute, but had to be done with the automatic transmission in 'Park' and the engine running.

Developed at a cost of $18 million, it was a traffic-stopping party-trick that required 610ft (186m) of electrical wiring and three separate motors yet, remarkably, proved reliable in service. It had its drawbacks, however – with the roof retracted there was little luggage space, and the complex mechanisms also cut into the Skyliner's rear legroom. Many admired the Skyliner but few could afford to buy it, and it was dropped from Ford's price-lists after three seasons.

Other than its roof, the Skyliner was a fairly stock Ford vehicle of fashionably vast dimensions, available with a host of V8 engines ranging up to the 300bhp 5.7-litre unit from the Thunderbird. A total of 12,915 examples were built, and survivors are highly prized collectors' cars today.

Lotus Cortina

1963–1970

ENGINE: In-line four-cylinder, 1558cc

POWER: 105bhp

CHASSIS: Monocoque, two-door

BRAKES (F/R): Disc/drum

TRANSMISSION: Four-speed manual

SUSPENSION: Independent front, live axle rear

TOP SPEED: 105mph (168km/h)

ACCELERATION: 0–60mph (96km/h) in 13.9 seconds

In 1963 Ford and Lotus got together to produce the classic, race-winning Lotus Cortina. Ford supplied the basic two-door Cortina shell – with front suspension – to the Lotus factory at Cheshunt. Here Lotus installed its own 105bhp twin-cam engine, close-ratio four-speed gearbox and special rear suspension comprising coil springs, radius arms and an A-bracket for maxiumum effect.

Sitting lower on wider wheels and fitted with front disc brakes, all Mk I Lotus Cortinas were painted cream with a green flash down their flanks, and featured split front bumpers and a matt-black front grille, making them instantly identifiable.

Light and powerful, the Lotus Cortina was an instant winner in saloon-car racing and was particularly memorable in the hands of Grand Prix ace Jim Clark. Its rallying prowess was initially held back by its unreliable A-frame rear suspension, but this reverted to semi-elliptics in 1966. Just 3,301 examples of the car were built.

The Mk I was replaced by the Mk II in 1967 with all-new bodywork but basically similar underpinnings. Power went up slightly to 109bhp, and a limited slip differential and an oil cooler found their way on to the options list. The cream with green flash livery was no longer obligatory, which pleased many people, but dismayed purists.

The Mk II was slightly quicker than the Mk I version, but has not proved to be as sought-after in classic-car terms.

Mustang

1964–1969

ENGINE: Straight-six and V8, 2788–6997cc

POWER: 101–271bhp

CHASSIS: Monocoque

BRAKES: Drum and disc/drum

TRANSMISSION: Three- and four-speed manual, three-speed automatic

SUSPENSION: Independent front, live axle rear

TOP SPEED: 90–130mph (144–208km/h)

ACCELERATION: 0–60mph (96km/h) in 8.2 seconds (V8 version)

Brainchild of hotshot Ford executive Lee Lacocca, the sporty Mustang was based on the floorpan of the budget-priced Falcon range. Its crisp, pseudo-European styling came in notchback, fastback and convertible forms, and could be ordered with a vast range of options that allowed buyers to tailor the car to their own requirements. Poseurs could opt for the weakling straight-six, and enthusiasts for a whole raft of V8s, escalating in power from 195bhp to 390bhp. There were lazy automatics, 'stick-shift' manuals, sports handling packages and front disc brakes, as well as those countless trim options.

As a marketing package it was perfect, and when it was launched in 1964 the Mustang quickly entered the history books as one of the fastest-selling cars of all time – 418,000 units in the first year, topping a million by 1966.

The attractively basic, pretty shape continued pleasingly unmolested into 1968 as rivals hurriedly prepared their own 'Pony' cars. Longer, paunchier 1969 Mustangs marked the start of the rot though, and the Mustang reached its nadir with the 1973 model Mustang II, a meek-and-mild little economy car launched in the wake of the oil crisis.

Nobody was fooled into thinking that this later, weaker version was anything like the car that it's grandfather had been, but it sold well, notching up more than a million sales, partly from long-lasting affection and perhaps partly from the relatively weak competition at the time. However, unlike the 1964 car, it will never be a classic.

Ford **GT40**

1966–1968

ENGINE: V8, 4727cc

POWER: 335bhp

CHASSIS: Monocoque

BRAKES (F/R): Disc/disc

TRANSMISSION: Five-speed manual

SUSPENSION: Independent all round

TOP SPEED: 164mph (262km/h)

ACCELERATION: 0–60mph (96km/h) in 6 seconds

Determined to beat Enzo Ferrari at his own game after its offer to buy the company was rejected in 1964, Ford turned to English racing-car firm Lola to build it a mid-engined GT car using a Ford V8 engine.

Lola founder Eric Broadley wasn't given an entirely free hand, however; Ford wanted the 'GT40' (so-called because it was just 40in. high) to be a road sports car. Detroit bosses also decreed that it had to have a cheaper mild-steel monocoque rather than the lighter aluminium 'tub' preferred by Broadley.

At first, results on the track were patchy, but the turning point came in 1966 with wins in the 24-hour Daytona and Le Mans races, and also in the tough Spa 1000km race. From a publicity point of view,

Le Mans was most important to Ford and its new 'total performance' image, and GT40s took four straight wins, from 1966 to 1969. Ferrari was nowhere to be seen, and Ford had proved its point.

Ford America withdrew from racing after 1967 but in 1968 JW Automotive, a tiny British firm licensed by Ford to make and maintain GT40s, took the World Manufacturers' Championship title away from Porsche with a privately entered GT40 – another snub towards the famous marque.

The GT40 Mk III was solely for road use. It cost £6,450 and had a detuned (330bhp) engine, road exhaust system and comfortable trim. A total of 107 GT40s were produced, of which 31 were road cars.

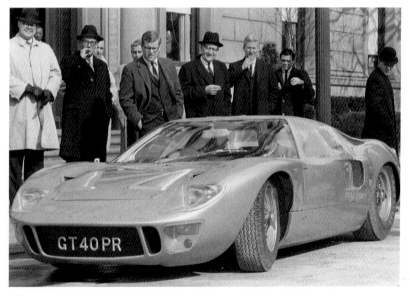

Cortina 1600E

1968–1970

ENGINE: Four-cylinder, 1599cc

POWER: 88bhp

CHASSIS: Monocoque

BRAKES (F/R): Disc/drum

TRANSMISSION: Four-speed manual

SUSPENSION: Independent front, live axle rear

TOP SPEED: 98mph (157km/h)

ACCELERATION: 0–60mph (96km/h) in 13 seconds

For such a short-lived model the Cortina 1600E made a big impact, and is fondly remembered by misty-eyed former owners as a Cortina with real character. The 'E' stood for Executive, an up-market branding already applied to the Ford Corsair and the big Zodiac V6 which, later, would find a home on the Escort.

Outside, 'E' meant stylish wide-rim Ro-Style sports wheels and a trendy matt-black grille and tail panel (on later cars), plus a reversing lamp and extra driving lights. Inside there were sports seats up front, a wooden fascia and door trims, and a sporty leather-trimmed steering wheel. All of these helped give it the feel of a much more expensive car. But the

1600E, based on the good-looking second-generation Cortina four-door shell, was more than just a tart-up. It handled really well, for a start, on lowered Lotus Cortina-style suspension, and with the later 88bhp cross-flow 1600GT engine it was a very game performer – if not exactly a road burning monster.

It was a great – though not surprising – success for Ford, which built 55,000 of them in just two short years. It was very much missed when production stopped in 1970. The 'Coke-bottle' Mk III Cortina GXL that was destined to replace it somehow never had the same appeal or touch of magic that the Cortina 1600E was endowed with.

Ford Escort RS2000

1974–1980

ENGINE: Four-cylinder, 1993cc

POWER: 100bhp

CHASSIS: Monocoque, two-door

BRAKES (F/R): Disc/drum

TRANSMISSION: Four-speed manual

SUSPENSION: Independent front, live axle rear

TOP SPEED: 108mph (173km/h)

ACCELERATION: 0–60mph (96km/h) in 9.0 seconds

Putting aside the exotic Lotus and Twin-Cam cars, the mass-market hot Escort generation really began with the Mexico (named after Ford's London-to-Mexico Rally win) and RS2000 models of 1970 and 1973, respectively – punchy, raucous cars with knock-about rear-drive handling and distinctive trim. With their quarter-bumpers and broad body striping, these machines appealed to boy-racers everywhere.

The Mk II Escort-based RS2000 of 1974 was the vehicle that took the concept a stage further. Its instantly recognizable shovel-nosed styling – the 'droopsnoot' was a tacked-on piece of polyurethane said to reduce drag by 16 percent – and the pleasingly up-market interior setting it apart from both the lesser family-car Escorts and the original Mk I RS cars.

Not that the car had gone soft – with 110bhp, the RS2000 was quicker than ever, and just as much fun to drive on a twisty road. Order books were soon bulging, its British profile undoubtedly raised by regular appearances in the TV series 'The Professionals.' Ford boosted its profit margins even more with X-Pack options for boy-racers who wanted to go that bit faster.

The Mk II Escorts were replaced by front-driven cars in 1980, the sporty flagship role taken over by the XR3. Totally different in style and engineering might have been, but in many ways the appeal – pure-bred boy-racer – was identical.

Capri

1974–1987

ENGINE: V6 OHV, 2792cc

POWER: 160bhp

CHASSIS: Steel monocoque hatchback

BRAKES (F/R): Disc

TRANSMISSION: Five-speed manual

SUSPENSION: Struts front, beam axle rear

TOP SPEED: 127mph (203km/h)

ACCELERATION: 0–62mph (100km/h) in 8.2 seconds

The Capri was famously summed up by Ford's advertising line of, 'the car you always promised yourself'. It rang true because nearly two million buyers were clearly in agreement. Influenced by the success of the Ford Mustang in the USA, the Capri offered European motorists some long-bonneted glamour, with the promise of Ford reliability and running costs. The Capri was probably the first sexy coupe based on humdrum mechanicals – a simple formula that has been extensively used ever since.

It was remarkably sharply styled for a Ford of the late-1960s and a real break from their expected output. It was available with engines ranging from an anaemic 61bhp 1300cc unit up to a 3.0-litre V6. The Capri also introduced Ford's image-building RS sports versions, including the ultra-rare RS2600 and impressively swift RS3100.

A complete restyle for 1974 was even more successful than the original, and the bodyshell now included a hatchback, making the Capri an even more practical proposition for the family man. Four years later the Capri's styling was modified again.

Despite the age of the concept, the Capri remained popular until it was phased out in 1987 with the much-admired special-edition 280, powered by a 2.8-litre V6. Surprisingly, when it left production Ford failed to replace the car directly and, ironically, missed the coupe boom of the late-1980s, led by the ultra-modern Vauxhall Calibra.

Ford Sierra

1982–1992

ENGINE: In-line four-cylinder, 1993cc

POWER: 105bhp

CHASSIS: Steel monocoque, three-, four- and five-door

BRAKES (F/R): Disc/disc

TRANSMISSION: Five-speed manual

SUSPENSION: Struts front, semi-trailing arms rear

TOP SPEED: 114mph (182km/h)

ACCELERATION: 0–62mph (100km/h) in 9.6 seconds

The late 1970s saw much discussion and experimentation with aerodynamics in the automotive industry – partly because of the fuel crisis, which put fuel economy at the top of the agenda. But 'Cortina man' wasn't prepared for the shock of the Sierra in late-1982. The square-cut Cortina saloon was replaced with an amorphously styled hatchback that soon gained itself the popular – if derisory – nickname of 'the jelly mould'.

Sales of the Sierra were notoriously slow to take off, and allowed Vauxhall to gain a sales foothold with the Cavalier that was launched a year earlier. Ironically, the first Sierras suffered from instability in cross-winds (which was soon cured) but it eventually spawned a very wide range of variants – all of which were well respected.

1983 saw the launch of the V6-engined XR4i, marked by the stylish triple-pillared side-view and large 'bi-plane' rear wing. This proved popular with a lot of drivers, particularly the older, more affluent, "not quite boy" racers, including certain more aggressive types of salesman. Two years later the rapid four-wheel-drive XR4x4 arrived, and both were developed into much more potent cars.

The crude details of the early car were eliminated with the first facelift in 1987, which featured a smooth nose and larger headlamps. This carried the Sierra through until 1992, when the car still looked modern and handsome, holding off the attentions of the fresh-faced 1988 Cavalier. Ford's design bravery had paid off in the end, but the early shock induced a decade of conservatism with Ford bosses.

Ford

Sierra RS Cosworth

1985–1987

ENGINE: In-line twin-cam turbocharged four, 1993cc

POWER: 204bhp

CHASSIS: Steel monocoque, three-door

BRAKES (F/R): Disc/disc

TRANSMISSION: Five-speed manual

SUSPENSION: Struts front, semi-trailing arm rear

TOP SPEED: 145mph (232km/h)

ACCELERATION: 0–62mph (100km/h) in 6.5 seconds

Success with the RS-badged Capris and Escorts encouraged Ford to give the Sierra a massive image boost by creating the Sierra RS Cosworth in 1985. Based around the three-door body shell, engineers slotted a turbocharged 2.0-litre twin-cam unit under the vented bonnet and uprated the suspension and brakes. The result was an unmissable main-street supercar that became the first of a legendary line of Cosworth-badged Fords.

Originally conceived for Group A saloon car racing championship, just 5000 production examples needed to be built by Ford. Ford's Dunton Special Vehicle Engineering division took the Cosworth from the drawing board to the road in just 14 months, although responsibility for designing a super-

powerful engine around the standard Sierra engine block was entirely handed over to Cosworth.

Like all sporting Fords before it, the RS Cosworth put pace before refinement and was something of a brutal machine to drive and required high levels of skill to extract the best from the car. Like the Sierra XR4i before it, the RS Cosworth attracted a fanatical near-cult following.

The RS only lasted a year in production (although Ford ended up making over 6,000 units) before it was followed by a limited run (just 500) of the even more brutal 150mph RS500s which had power boosted to 224bhp. The short run and high mortality rate of the RS500 will make it a sure-fire future classic.

Thunderbird

1988–

ENGINE: Supercharged V6, 3791cc

POWER: 210bhp

CHASSIS: Steel monocoque, two-door

BRAKES (F/R): disc with ABS

TRANSMISSION: Five-speed manual

SUSPENSION: Independent front and rear

TOP SPEED: 141mph (226km/h)

ACCELERATION: 0–62.5mph (100km/h) in 7.7 seconds

US-market presumptions about Ford's dull range and old-fashioned engineering were dealt another serious blow with the arrival of the new 1988 Thunderbird coupe. It had more than a hint of European coupe thinking in its make-up. Under Ford's corporate, but nevertheless handsome, wind-tunnel styling (which was clearly influenced by BMW's 6-Series coupe) was a rear-drive chassis. In the race to shift to front-wheel-drive technology in the early 1980s, Ford's rivals had nothing like it.

Ford's engineers spared no expense in re-designing the outgoing 1983-vintage Thunderbird, to the point where there was nothing left of the old model. To increase internal space, the wheelbase was extended by a massive 9in. (23cm). The desire to lower the base of the windscreen and give the car an aggressively sloping nose meant the expense of an all-new – and unusual – front suspension system. Ford also threw out the live axle at the rear in favour of a new independent layout.

Top-of-the-range versions of the old Thunderbird relied on a turbocharged, 2.3-litre, four-cylinder engine. The new 'Super Coupe' used the much more unusual approach of a supercharged V6. Although 210bhp doesn't sound a lot, the amazing 315lb/ft of torque more than made amends. Although big and weighing in at nearly two tonnes, the Thunderbird had an excellent chassis and was perfectly suited to long, fast days at the wheel, rather like its more expensive German counterparts.

Ford Contour

1993–1999

ENGINE: 24-valve V6, 2544cc

POWER: 170bhp

CHASSIS: Steel monocoque, four-door

BRAKES: Disc all round with ABS

TRANSMISSION: Five-speed manual

SUSPENSION: Struts front, Quadralink and struts rear

TOP SPEED: 138mph (221km/h)

ACCELERATION: 0–62.5mph (100km/h) in 8.1 seconds

When Ford came to replace the mid-range Sierra after a decade in production, product planners wanted to produce an all-new car that was packed with the latest safety features and advanced mechanical and electrical systems. The Sierra replacement was to be a massive leap forward for the 'Blue Oval' badge of Ford Motors.

The only way to make sense of a multi-billion dollar investment was to design the Mondeo as a 'world car'. By building it and selling it on both major car-buying continents (the USA and Europe), Ford had a much better chance of making a decent profit on the car. At the time Ford must have been convinced that US and European tastes in styling and packaging had already – or were about to – converge.

Launched in early 1993, the European Mondeo and the North American Contour and Mercury Mystique were essentially exactly the same car built at two different factories: Genk in Belgium and Kansas City in the USA. The car's components were drawn from suppliers world-wide.

Despite the excellent efforts under the skin, Ford's stylists produced a modern, slick – but ultimately anonymous – bodyshell. The car was highly praised in both markets for the excellence of its chassis and the depth of its all-round competence. But while the Mondeo was clearly optimized for its European market segment, the Contour was regarded in the USA as lacking in rear seat space, although the American market saw it as fun to drive.

The lack-lustre sales of the Contour and its Mercury sister perhaps again proved that US and European automotive tastes are highly unlikely to converge on anything apart from specialist niche and prestige vehicles. Nevertheless, Ford invested further into the world car plan with the 1998 Focus – a European Escort replacement, which would also be sold in the USA.

Ford Ka

1996–

ENGINE: In-line pushrod four-cylinder, 1299cc

POWER: 59bhp

CHASSIS: Steel monocoque, three-door

BRAKES (F/R): Disc/drum

TRANSMISSION: Five-speed manual

SUSPENSION: Struts front, trailing arms and torsion bar

TOP SPEED: 96mph (154km/h)

ACCELERATION: 0–62.5mph (100km/h) in 13.9 seconds

Ford's corporate machine was locked into a no-risk loop when it developed the Mk 4 Escort. The no-risk approach hit the buffers when press reaction to the car was so bad that, according to the industry story, Ford bosses ordered the car to undergo a significant facelift within days of the first press reports.

Within a couple of years aspirational engineers had taken control of the Ford machine, promising that fresh-looking cars that were good to drive would bring long-term profitability. No longer, it was claimed, could the European public be palmed off with stodgy, unadventurous transport.

The first Ford to be completely conceived under the new regime was the Ka, which was both adventurously named and styled,

and one of the best-driving cars on sale at any price when it was launched. Dubbed 'Edge Design', the highly unusual styling was borne out of contemporary softly rounded shapes, but with hard edges pressed into the overall whole. Simple join-line gaps between the panels also made the Ka easier to build.

The design was led by two young Ford stylists, and it was as adventurous inside as it was out. The Ka was also one of the first sub-B cars on to the market, aimed at the young and second-car owners who wanted adventurous design and Mini-like driving dynamics. It was the latter that amazed even more than the design. The Fiesta-based Ka offered a smooth ride and kart-like handling, and motorway refinement was also exemplary.

Ford Puma

1997–2001

ENGINE: In-line variably timed four-cylinder, 1679cc

POWER: 123bhp

CHASSIS: Steel monocoque, three-door

BRAKES (F/R): Disc/disc with ABS

TRANSMISSION: Five-speed manual

SUSPENSION: Struts front, torsion beam rear

TOP SPEED: 124mph (198km/h)

ACCELERATION: 0–62mph (100km/h) in 8.9 seconds

In 1997 Ford finally returned to the successful formula that had produced the Capri: building an inexpensive coupe on the running gear of a mainstream car. The big difference – some 28 years later – was the sophistication of Ford's engines and chassis.

The Puma was based on the 1996 Fiesta, widely held to be a revelation in terms of handling, ride and refinement – a giant leap forward for the company, masterminded by engineering boss Richard Parry-Jones. Equally revolutionary was the styling, which Ford said was developed by designers entirely on the computer screen, before being modelled in clay in full size, again by computer.

Under the bonnet was a 125bhp 1.7-litre version of the Zetec engine that was co-developed with Yamaha. The result was a superbly styled and competitively priced mini-coupe that could out-handle most cars on sale in the late-1990s. Parry-Jones's engineers had improved upon the Fiesta chassis to provide extra-sharp handling that was easy to exploit – thanks to the beefy torque delivery of the engine.

The Puma became extremely popular as, unlike its rivals, it was beyond serious criticism. It also moved ahead of its mass-market rivals for pure driving appeal and forward-looking design – essential in a European market that was turning toward 'niche' cars. The Puma's position looked solid but was phased out in 2001 with no direct replacement car in works. But Ford shifted its hopes to the Ka-based StreetKa convertible.

Frazer Nash · Le Mans Replica

1949–1952

ENGINE: Six-cylinder, 1971cc

POWER: 125bhp

CHASSIS: Separate box-section

BRAKES: Drum

TRANSMISSION: Four-speed manual

SUSPENSION: Not available

TOP SPEED: 115mph (184km/h)

ACCELERATION: 0–60mph (96km/h) in 8.8 seconds

Before the Second World War, the Aldington brothers of AFN had marketed 328 BMWs alongside their own Frazer Nash chain-drive sports cars. After the war, the company gained the rights to this brilliant German design as part of reparations, and with the help of the Bristol Aeroplane Company (which built the engines) it intended to produce a new post-war Frazer Nash fashioned around BMW 328 components.

The result was the lithe and handsome cycle-winged High Speed model, a 115mph (184km/h) two-seater with fine handling and the right pedigree that provided all that the discerning – and rich – enthusiast could want. Under the bonnet, BMW's fantastic, free-breathing straight-six – with its unique cross pushrod cylinder-head design – gave 120bhp, thanks to

triple carburettors and bigger valves and ports. The live rear axle was located and sprung firmly by torsion bars and a central A-arm.

One owner took his new car to Le Mans in 1949 and came an incredible third. So delighted was Frazer Nash by this that, henceforth, the model was known as the Le Mans Replica, of which only 34 would ever be built. The model further enhanced its giant-killing reputation when it came first in the 1951 Targa Florio in the hands of Franco Cortese.

This victory was marked by a new car with a full-width body called Targa in 1952 but these cars were expensive compared with faster opposition. The marque bowed out in 1958, but it will always be remembered best for the Le Mans Replica.

 # Syclone

1991

ENGINE: Turbocharged V6, 4315cc

POWER: 280bhp

CHASSIS: Monocoque

BRAKES (F/R): Disc with ABS

TRANSMISSION: Four-speed automatic

SUSPENSION: Wishbones/torsion beams front, live axle/leaf springs rear

TOP SPEED: 130mph (208km/h)

ACCELERATION: 0–62.5mph (100km/h) in 5.0 seconds

Truck culture is big. Indeed, each year the best-selling vehicle in America is usually a pick-up, outselling the best ordinary cars by some margin. General Motors (GM) decided at the beginning of the 1990s that it would build the fastest and most technically complex truck ever made – just, perhaps, because it could.

The Syclone was based on a standard-issue GM four-wheel-drive truck, chosen because the drivetrain was essential for the power that GM had

planned. Under the bonnet was a 4.3-litre V6 pushrod engine that was further boosted by a turbocharger and intercooler. The engine's torque figure was a remarkable 350lb/ft – more pulling strength than a Porsche 928 could muster, even.

This road-ripping power was fed into the 4x4 drivetrain, which had rear differential. This modernity was

in contrast to the less advanced suspension. GM had lowered and stiffened the chassis, though. Stylists then clad the Syclone in a sexy, aggressive body kit, with very wide wheels and low-profile tyres. The Syclone was an extreme, impressive and unusual machine, but it didn't sell well – it cost more than a Ford Taurus SHO.

Impact EV-1

1993–2000

ENGINE: Two electric motors

POWER: 32 lead-acid batteries

CHASSIS: Steel frame, composite body panels

BRAKES: Regenerative braking and conventional discs

TRANSMISSION: Four-speed automatic

SUSPENSION: Independent front and rear

TOP SPEED: 100mph (160km/h)

ACCELERATION: 0–62.5mph (100km/h) in 8.2 seconds

Environmental concerns really began to hit home with the motor industry at the end of the 1980s, as the public mood world-wide began to take on board at least part of the 'green' agenda. General Motors was ahead of the shift in the ecological zeitgeist, as it was already working on a radical electrically powered road car that could be considered as a viable proposition for the average motorist.

The Impact electric vehicle was something of a future shock machine: the overwhelming importance of having a slick aerodynamic shell to slide through the air meant the Impact's styling was both functional and high-tech. Making the car very lightweight was even more important, because an electric car relies on heavy batteries, so the Impact's body was made from composite materials.

The Impact was built around a pack of 32 batteries, which were mounted longitudinally down the centre of the car in what looked like a massive transmission tunnel. A clever box of electronics mounted in the nose converted DC current into AC with minimal power losses, powering two electric motors – one mounted on each front wheel.

The Impact had a top speed of 100mph (160km/h) and could sprint to 60mph (96km/h) faster than a VW Golf GTi. It was also well equipped, with a very modern interior featuring digital instruments and air-conditioning. What conspired against the viability of the Impact was the cost of the batteries and the need to re-charge the car for six hours, or overnight.

It took more than six years for the Impact to appear as a production car. Renamed the EV-1, the car's main market was California. But production was only running into the hundreds of cars – although it was popular with ostentatious environmentalists, and was regarded as a fine car with a handy turn of speed. Although the EV-1 was ignored by most motorists, Californian legislation ruled that manufacturers had to sell a certain percentage of electric vehicles. However, it proved unpopular and California's plans for electric car sales were abandoned.

Gordon Keeble GK1

1964–1966

ENGINE: V8, 5395cc

POWER: 300bhp

CHASSIS: GRP body, space-frame chassis

BRAKES: Disc all round

TRANSMISSION: Four-speed manual

SUSPENSION: Independent all round

TOP SPEED: 135mph (216km/h)

ACCELERATION: 0–60mph (96km/h) in 7.5 seconds

First seen in 1960 as the prototype Gordon GT (and inspired by the Corvette-powered Peerless created by Jim Keeble and John Gordon), the Gordon Keeble didn't go into faltering production until 1964, being renamed the GK1. It sounded like an ideal recipe for commercial success: cheap American V8 muscle, Italian styling and British chassis knowhow and expertise.

With a 300bhp engine from the Chevrolet Corvette and a fibreglass body, the Gordon Keeble was devastatingly quick – good for 70mph (112km/h) in first gear and nearly 140mph (224km/h) in top gear. Handling was good, too, with a de Dion axle at the rear and a complex space-frame chassis of square section providing grip, balance and a good ride – although the unassisted steering suffered from too much kickback. The simple, restrained four-seater coupe shape, with its elegantly slanted twin lamps, was the work of a 21-year-old Giugiaro, then chief stylist at Bertone.

By 1965 only 80 cars had been built, as the fledgling company battled with component supply problems and under-capitalization. Had the factory – based at Eastleigh, Southampton on the site of the local airport – been able to build the cars quickly enough, there was no doubt the GK would have been a success, if only because it was under-priced. A further 19 examples were built under new management in 1966, but despite all efforts to keep it open, the company closed its doors in that year.

Harrington Alpine

1961–1963

ENGINE: Four-cylinder, 1592cc

POWER: 102bhp

CHASSIS: Monocoque

BRAKES (F/R): Disc/drum

TRANSMISSION: Four-speed manual

SUSPENSION: Independent front, live axle rear

TOP SPEED: 100mph (160km/h)

ACCELERATION: 0–60mph (96km/h) in 13 seconds

The Harrington Alpine was a special coupe based on the Sunbeam Alpine convertible. Launched in 1961, the car was a brave attempt by Thomas Harrington to expand its traditional coach-body building activities. Between 400 and 450 Harrington Alpines and Harrington Le Mans coupes were built, before internal politics put an end to the venture in 1963.

Each car took 14 days to build at Harrington's Brighton factory and, to avoid purchase tax on the conversion, the cars were first 'bought' by the dealer. One state of tune was settled on for the engine, a 104bhp unit fitted with an oil cooler.

On the Le Mans model of 1961 a rear hatch replaced the stunted bootlid on the original Type A, with the rear seat folding down to form a reasonable 46in. load area. The cars were marketed through Rootes

dealers in North America, and sold especially well there, although the 1,000 cars forecast by the American ads were not to be; when production of the Harrington Le Mans ceased in late 1962, just 250 cars had been built.

But this wasn't the end of the Harrington Alpine story. A simplified 'Type C' car was unveiled at the Earl's Court Show in 1962, retaining the opening rear hatch of the Le Mans but with the now smaller fins of the standard Alpine still in place.

The C- and D-Type Harringtons, with very minor alterations, were basically short-lived versions and, realistically, the model wouldn't have survived much longer anyway. It forecast a trend, but was set to be out-classed and undercut by much cheaper, mass-produced coupe opposition from home and abroad, the likes of MG's BGT being a classic case in point.

2.4 Litre

1945–1950

ENGINE: Four-cylinder, 2443cc

POWER: 100bhp

CHASSIS: Separate chassis, alloy body

BRAKES (F/R): Drum

TRANSMISSION: Four-speed manual

SUSPENSION: Independent front, live axle rear

TOP SPEED: 105mph (168km/h)

ACCELERATION: 0–60mph (96km/h) in 12.3 seconds

When news came through that Donald Healey's new 2.4-litre sports car had recorded a best of 111mph (178km/h) on the Jabbeke Highway in Belgium that year, it came as a breath of fresh air to post-war motoring enthusiasts. Here was something that Britain could really be proud of – her first post-war 100mph production car.

Healey – a successful pre-war rally driver and technical director at Triumph – had schemed a light, but rigid, cruciform-braced chassis with expensively made front trailing-link suspension which had been inspired by pre-war racing-car designs. It was powered by the excellent 100bhp Riley 2.5-litre four-cylinder engine. Initially, there were two models: the open-top Westland, and the closed Eliot – both with hallmark kite-shaped grilles and bodies built in 'Birmabright' aluminium over ash-wood frames.

Even better was the 1949

Silverstone, a stark short-chassis open two-seater whose sketchy body – still in alloy – was far easier (and thus cheaper) to build. With cycle wings, stiffer springs and fold-down screen, this was the club racer's dream – a fast, no-nonsense performer cast in the mould of the pre-war BMW 328.

Also new for 1949, replacing the Westland, was the bizarrely slab-sided Sportsmobile. Sales were slow and production didn't see the year out.

With the rather different Nash–Healey waiting in the wings, Healey dropped the Eliot and the Silverstone in 1950 (after just 104 cars), and began to lose interest in the expensive Riley-engined cars after he struck up a deal with the British Motor Corporation (BMC) in 1952 to build the Austin Healey.

Healey effectively died as an independent marque in 1954 with the last of the 2.4-litre cars, as the firm was absorbed into BMC.

Hillman Imp

1963–1976

ENGINE: Rear-mounted four-cylinder, 875cc

POWER: 38bhp

CHASSIS: Monocoque

BRAKES (F/R): Drum

TRANSMISSION: Four-speed manual

SUSPENSION: Independent all round

TOP SPEED: 80mph (128km/h)

ACCELERATION: 0–60mph (96km/h) in 21.1 seconds

The 1963 Hillman Imp was Rootes' answer to the BMC Mini. But, beset with problems early in its life, the car never quite grabbed the motoring public's imagination in the same way. Enthusiasts, however, have always appreciated its novel engineering.

Technically, the Hillman Imp was indeed full of interest. The 875cc engine was a light-alloy overhead-camshaft unit derived from a Coventry Climax racing engine. That made it nippy and versatile, and tuned Imps were very successful on the racetrack. Rootes offered its own tuned 50bhp engine in versions called the Sunbeam Imp Sport and, with a fastback roof, the Sunbeam Stiletto.

But while the rival Mini was proving that front-wheel drive was the way ahead for small cars, Rootes had turned instead to the VW-Beetle-like ruse of putting the engine in the back. That certainly allowed decent cabin space, but also made for tail-heavy weight distribution.

Rootes wanted to build the Imp at its Coventry factory, but government planners had other ideas: they agreed to lend money to the company only if a new factory was erected in economically depressed Scotland. A production plant was therefore constructed at Linwood, near Glasgow.

Sadly, the Imp gained a reputation for unreliability. Its pneumatic throttle was troublesome and was quickly changed. Imps also suffered from water leaks, gasket failures and overheating. The Imp never sold well, and it lost its makers (and the British government) money. Production lasted until 1976.

Honda S800

1965–1970

ENGINE: In-line four-cylinder, 791cc

POWER: 70bhp

CHASSIS: Separate chassis

BRAKES (F/R): Disc/drum

TRANSMISSION: Four-speed manual

SUSPENSION: Independent front, beam axle rear

TOP SPEED: 95mph (152km/h)

ACCELERATION: 0–60mph (96km/h) in 13.4 seconds

Honda made its fortune building motorcycles, so it came as no surprise that its first car, the tiny S500, was heavily influenced by everything that the company had learned through its many years of motorcycle engineering.

Available as a convertible and a hardtop, its double-overhead-camshaft, hemi-head 531cc engine had a roller-bearing crankshaft and four carburettors. Maximum power – 44bhp – came at a screaming 8000rpm, which was virtually unheard-of in a road car. The S500 also had chain-drive to its independently sprung rear wheels, again following motorcycle practice. Disc brakes on the front wheels hinted at the S500's 'cost-no-object' specification, although the separate chassis was somewhat backward – even for the mid-1960s.

The S500 became the 606cc S600 in 1964 and finally the 1965 S800, the best-known and the most popular variant. When the S800 became available in Britain in 1967, it had conventional drive to the rear wheels and an ordinary live axle located by trailing arms and a Panhard rod.

It was good value for money, undercutting both the Mini Cooper and Triumph Spitfire. It was praised for having remarkable acceleration for its engine size, a very slick gear change and excellent 30mpg (9.5litres/100km) economy. the handling was predictable, although the ride was on the firm side.

S800 production continued until 1970, by when Honda was making serious in-roads into the economy-car market with the N360 and N600. It was Honda's last sports car for many years.

LUA 578F

Honda Civic

1972–

ENGINE: Four-cylinder, 1169–1488cc

POWER: 60–80bhp

CHASSIS: Monocoque

BRAKES (F/R): Disc/drum

TRANSMISSION: Four-speed manual, three-speed automatic

SUSPENSION: Independent

TOP SPEED: 88–94mph (141–150km/h)

ACCELERATION: 0–60mph (96km/h) in 13–14 seconds

Volume car making for Honda began in 1962 with the S500 sports car and, later, the little air-cooled, twin-cylinder N360 and N600.

All these cars had their merits, but proved too idiosyncratic to make significant in-roads into markets outside Japan. What the company needed was a mainstream economy car with universal appeal – cast in the mould of the Mini, but more refined and comfortable.

Honda's breakthrough came in 1972 with the Civic, a neat front-wheel-drive hatchback (and saloon) that brought new levels of comfort and quietness to the shopping car.

Honda might not have known it at the time, but the Civic was the building block of their mass-market position in both Europe and the USA. The Civic was also destined to set benchmarks that other cars in its class would have to look to beat.

The light-alloy engine was a smooth and brisk performer, and the car combined light, refined controls with good all-independent suspension. There hadn't been a Japanese car like this before, and overnight Honda became a force to be reckoned with.

In the USA and Europe the car got rave reviews and sold by the shipload. Bigger engines and longer wheelbases followed, and the Civic gave rise to more up-market Hondas such as the Accord and Prelude. Its descendants remained in production in the late-1990s, by which time the true historic impact of the car on the company was clear for everyone to see.

Honda NSX

1990–

ENGINE: Variable valve-timed quad-cam V6, 2977cc

POWER: 274bhp

CHASSIS: Aluminium monocoque, two-door, optional targa roof

BRAKES (F/R): Disc/disc with ABS

TRANSMISSION: Five-speed manual or finger-tip sequential

SUSPENSION: Aluminium double wishbone front and rear

TOP SPEED: 164mph (262km/h)

ACCELERATION: 0–62mph (100km/h) in 5.9 seconds

Throughout the 1980s the high-technology content of Honda's mainstream cars began to increase noticeably – perhaps to be expected from a race-oriented manufacturer. Few observers expected the mid-engined NSX supercar to push so many technological boundaries at once. It was obviously a calculated attempt to challenge Ferrari and Porsche on their home territory, and logic says it should have succeeded.

Firstly, the NSX was built entirely of aluminium: under the aluminium skin was an aluminium monocoque chassis. Honda even went to the extent of casting alloy sub-frames and building the suspension wishbones from aluminium. Under the glass canopy behind the cockpit Honda had fitted its very latest engine, a 3.0-litre, quad-cam V6 which was fitted with the V-TEC system which managed to combine variable valve timing and variable valve lift – something

beyond every other engine maker – so their engine gave good pulling power low down, yet could spin racer-like to 8000rpm.

Honda's careful approach to creating a supercar included styling that industry rumours reckoned was overwhelmingly influenced by the 1986 MG EX-E concept car – which was also an aluminium-bodied V6 mid-engined supercar. Likewise, the interior was carefully crafted, and the driving position highly praised.

Sadly, the NSX failed to capture the enthusiasm of supercar buyers around the world. It was arguably a better car than contemporary Ferraris and the Porsche 911, but it lacked their character in terms of styling, design and driver sensations. And not least because it was usually described as being as easy to drive as a Honda Civic supermini. Honda miscalculated by deciding that the supercar breed needed the flaws removing, but with the flaws goes the character.

Integra Type-R

1997–2000

ENGINE: In-line V-TEC four, 1797cc

POWER: 187bhp

CHASSIS: Steel monocoque, three-door

BRAKES (F/R): Disc with ABS

TRANSMISSION: Five-speed manual

SUSPENSION: Double wishbone front and rear

TOP SPEED: 145mph (232km/h)

ACCELERATION: 0–62mph (100km/h) in 6.9 seconds

In preparation for its fiftieth anniversary, Honda decided that the time had come to launch a line of stripped-out high-performance versions of ordinary road cars. In a similar vein to BMW's M-Series and Audi's S-types, Honda's new range would be dubbed Type-R. The result, in the form of the Integra, was one of the finest mainstream performance cars ever sold, and one that was little more expensive than a high-spec family car.

Starting with the basic three-door coupe bodyshell, Honda beefed up certain areas by using thicker panels, but saved weight by removing the soundproofing and fitting a thinner windscreen.

The chassis got beefier wishbones, strut braces in both the bonnet and the boot, and a limited slip differential, but the real detail effort went into the engine. The 1.8-litre V-TEC unit boasted hand-finished ports in the cylinder head, lightweight pistons, inlet valves and flywheel. Even the valve springs were made of special oval-section wire. Inside, the cabin got bright-red Recaro racing seats, aluminium pedals and a titanium gear knob.

The result was an exhilarating and beautifully built car that didn't have a hint of slack in the chassis, and a searing drivetrain that would rev to 8900rpm. It also had that rare quality – charisma – by the spadeful.

In a decade that failed to produce an abundance of classic cars, Honda's Integra had the potential to contend for that label. The best in engineering is matched with character, making it a great way for Honda to celebrate its anniversary.

Mini

1974–1982

ENGINE: Four-cylinder, 998–1275cc

POWER: 49–77bhp

CHASSIS: Monocoque

BRAKES (F/R): Disc/drum

TRANSMISSION: Four-speed manual

SUSPENSION: Independent

TOP SPEED: 87–99mph (139–158km/h)

ACCELERATION: 0–60mph (96km/h) in 13–19 seconds

The manufacturer of the Lambretta, Innocenti, began building Austin A40s under licence in Italy in 1960, and followed up with its own versions of the Austin Healey Sprite, the Austin/ Morris 1100 and, of course, the Mini, which it began producing in 1965.

These were built to a better specification than the English versions – with opening quarter-windows, lever-pull door handles and a generally a much more inviting interior. Innocenti took the idea a stage further in 1974 with a special Bertone-designed hatchback model with folding seats. It had a much more modern, squared-up body in the fashionable super-mini idiom of the day, and many pundits in the motoring press believed it was the car that British Leyland itself should have been building.

It was a typical move of the Italians to add a touch of class to an already classic and hard to improve upon design and the Innocenti Mini's definitely had a very distinctive Italian feel and character. Mechanically, the Innocenti was identical to the Mini and came with either 998cc or detuned 1275cc Cooper engines, giving a top speed of almost 100mph (160km/h).

De Tomaso took over Innocenti in 1976, which resulted in higher-specification luxury models. After 1982 the cars were fitted with Daihatsu engines, so were no longer really Minis.

Isetta
'Bubble Car'

1955–1962

ENGINE: Single-cylinder, 247–297cc

POWER: 12–13bhp

CHASSIS: Separate

BRAKES (F/R): Drum

TRANSMISSION: Four-speed manual

SUSPENSION: Independent front, live axle rear

TOP SPEED: 50–51mph (80–82km/h)

ACCELERATION: N/A

Finding its big six- and eight-cylinder luxury cars difficult to sell in the mid-1950s, BMW was looking to build something at the other end of the scale that had more mass appeal. It took up a licence with the firm of Iso in Italy to build its tiny Isetta 'bubble' cars in 1955. Often considered extremely bizarre in the '80s and early '90s, the bubble car was originally seen as quite futuristic, although it was a moot point as to how seriously it was taken in many areas. Interestingly, as the roads get increasingly crowded, the ideas that shaped the bubble car seem to be coming back into fashion with the general public at large. Extremely small and compact no longer seems quite so silly.

In Italy, the concept of a tiny motorcycle-engined two-seater had found little favour, but in Germany the vehicle was a popular choice, and competed head-on with the Heinkel and Messerschmitt 'bubble cars'. In its original form the car had a folding roof, a wrap-around rear window and small rectangular front side windows, but on all versions the driver and passenger entered through a front-opening door that brought the steering wheel with it as it opened.

For the home market all Isettas had four wheels, but some export versions were three-wheelers to take advantage of lower tax rates. BMW's own single-cylinder engine provided the power in either 247cc or 297cc form, neither of which could quite take the Isetta up to 60mph (96km/h). Built until 1962, the Isetta inspired more grown-up BMW mini-cars such as the four-seater 600 and the handsome little 700.

Grifo

1963–1974

ENGINE: V8, 5359–6998cc

POWER: 300–390bhp

CHASSIS: Integral steel box-section

BRAKES: Discs all round

TRANSMISSION: Four- and five-speed manual, three-speed automatic

SUSPENSION: Independent all round

TOP SPEED: 150–170mph (240–272km/h)

ACCELERATION: 0–60mph (96km/h) in 6 seconds (7.0-litre version)

Iso of Italy began its car-manufacturing career in the mid-1950s producing the Isetta bubble-cars – also built under licence by BMW – but in 1962 it decided to enter the high-class GT car market with the Rivolta. A cleanly styled (by Bertone) four-seater coupe with a box-section frame and de Dion rear suspension, it was powered by the V8 engine from the Chevrolet Corvette. Performance was abundant – up to 140mph (224km/h) was on offer with the manual gearbox.

The Rivolta was well received, but it wasn't until the debut of the Grifo a year later that the fledgling supercar-builder really made its mark. By shortening the Rivolta and clothing it in a sensational coupe body – again by Bertone – Iso now had a car with which to challenge Ferrari.

The original 5.4-litre V8 came in two states of tune – 300bhp and 365bhp – with a top speed of up to 160mph (256km/h) in its most potent form. Buyers could opt for four- or five-speed gearboxes, and even an automatic. Naturally four-wheel disc brakes were necessary for a car of such weight and power, and in the right hands these well-engineered cars were as quick as anything else on the road.

The ultimate version was the 390bhp 7-litre, built from 1968 to challenge the Ferrari Daytona and Maserati Ghibli. Iso claimed 170mph (272km/h) for this flagship coupe. For the last two years of production, Iso used Ford 'Cleveland' V8s rather than Corvette engines. However, by then it was on the rocks financially, and died in the midst of the fuel crisis in 1974.

Jaguar **XK 120**

1948–1961

ENGINE: Straight-six, 3442–3781cc

POWER: 160–265bhp

CHASSIS: Separate steel chassis

BRAKES (F/R): Disc (after 1959)

TRANSMISSION: Four-speed manual, three-speed automatic

SUSPENSION: Independent front, live axle rear

TOP SPEED: 120–135mph (192–216km/h)

ACCELERATION: 0–60mph (96km/h) in 7.8–10 seconds

As a package the Jaguar XK120 looked unbeatable in 1948. Jaguar boss William Lyons shaped a flowing two-seater roadster body that was a model of elegant purity: on looks alone it would have sold handsomely. But there was more – under the bonnet was a brand-new twin-cam straight-six engine, the classic 3.4-litre XK unit that was to survive well into the 1990s and power everything from Le Mans winners to tanks and fire engines. Pumping out a smooth 160bhp, it made sure the '120' tag was no idle boast – in fact, the 120mph (192km/h) XK was for a time the world's fastest standard production car.

Priced at under £1,000, Jaguar was unprepared for the demand for the XK, and production remained small-scale in 1949 as Jaguar tooled up for the big-volume steel-bodied version that came on stream in 1950.

From then on there was no looking back. An elegant fixed-head version was announced in 1951, and a roomier drop-head coupe in 1953. The XK140 of 1954 gained bigger bumpers and – best of all – rack and pinion steering, whilst retaining all three body options.

Last of the XK line was the 1957 150, basically built on the same chassis but with all new body panels, as Jaguar attempted to string out the model's appeal until the E-Type arrived in 1961.

An earlier braking problem was finally addressed by Dunlop discs on all four wheels, and in triple-carburettor 3.8-litre 'S' form (from 1959) power soared to 265bhp, with a top speed of 135mph (216km/h). Like all XKs, it was great value – half the price of the contemporary Aston DB4 and Mercedes 300SL. It was getting old though, and Jaguar had something more exciting waiting in the wings – the E-Type.

Mk VII/VIII/IX

1950–1961

ENGINE: Straight-six, 3442/2781cc

POWER: 160–220bhp

CHASSIS: Separate chassis/steel body

BRAKES (F/R): Drums and discs

TRANSMISSION: Four-speed manual, three-speed automatic

SUSPENSION: Independent front, live axle rear

TOP SPEED: 100–117mph (160–187km/h)

ACCELERATION: 0–60mph (96km/h) in 11 seconds

In 1950, 100mph twin-cam luxury saloons were pretty thin on the ground. Still fewer were pitched under the £1,000 barrier. No surprise, then, that the Jaguar plant at Brown's Lane in the Midlands could hardly keep up with the orders when they announced the flagship Mk VII.

Although the identically engined XK120 sports car tended to grab the limelight, it was the Mk VII and its siblings that filled Jaguar's coffers and positioned the company for a virtual takeover of the English luxury-car market in the decade to follow. Total production was 46,000 units.

The MKVII/VIII/IX differs from later saloons in its use of a separate chassis – derived from the Mk V – with a servo for the big drum brakes and torsion-bar front suspension, the rear end being handled by semi-elliptics. Styling, too, was descended from the pre- and immediately post-war saloons, but was more voluminous and 'well-fed'.

If it looked good on the outside, then the cabin was even better. It had more room than its predecessors, wide armchair seats and polished walnut veneer on the dash, cantrails and door cappings. In this 'gentleman's club' ambience, the Mk VII driver could dominate the road like few others: third gear alone was enough to dispose of most sports-car pretenders, whilst top gear could ease the Mk VII to 101mph (162km/h). It was, in every sense of the word, impressive.

The 1954 Mk VIIM brought detail improvements to trim and a bit more power, whilst on the 1956 Mk VIII the emphasis was shifted to tycoon luxury and extra chrome glitz. Last – and many think of it as the best – of the line was the 1958 Mk IX with a neat 223bhp 3.8-litre engine, power steering and Dunlop discs on all four wheels. The Mk IX died in 1961 to make way for the unitary, all-independent-suspension Mk X.

Jaguar C-Type

1951–1954

ENGINE: Six-cylinder, 3442cc

POWER: 220bhp

CHASSIS: Tubular space-frame

BRAKES (F/R): Drum (disc later)

TRANSMISSION: Four-speed manual

SUSPENSION: Independent front, live axle rear

TOP SPEED: 144–150mph (230–240km/h)

ACCELERATION: 0–60mph (96km/h) in 7 seconds

The C-Type was the sports car that twice won the Le Mans 24-hour race for Jaguar (1951 and 1953), and is forever associated with those two magical moments of racing glory. Based on the XK120, it capitalised on all of its elder sister's character and strengths, whilst finding plenty of ways to carve out a niche in Jaguar history for itself.

Malcolm Sayers' shapely bodywork was both beautiful and aerodynamic and, on the straight, the C-Type could manage 144mph (230km/h) – powered by a tuned, triple-carburettor, 204bhp version of the XK twin-cam engine.

A space-frame chassis and aluminium bodywork meant that the C-Type was much lighter than the XK, and also had superior handling – thanks to rack-and-pinion steering and Panhard-rod location for its transverse torsion-bar-sprung rear axle.

Later cars had the innovative disc brakes that contributed very strongly to the C-Type's victory at Le Mans in 1953. First used on aircraft, these brakes were much more resistant to fade than conventional drum brakes.

For those lucky enough to be able to afford the £2,300 asking price (about double the cost of a typical XK), Jaguar was prepared to sell cars to private customers, although its racing origins were still very much on display.

A total of 54 C-Types were built, and if you could live without much in the way of creature comforts or cockpit room, it made a sensationally quick road car that gave you a taste of what it felt like to drive a world beating race car.

Jaguar **XKSS**

1957

ENGINE: Straight-six, 3442cc

POWER: 250bhp

CHASSIS: Monocoque

BRAKES (F/R): Disc

TRANSMISSION: Four-speed manual

SUSPENSION: Independent front, live axle rear

TOP SPEED: 150mph (240km/h)

ACCELERATION: 0–60mph (96km/h) in 5.7 seconds

The XKSS, one of the most exciting road-going Jaguars of all time, was devised when 25 of the original batch of 67 production D-Types remained unsold after the factory's temporary retirement from racing in 1956.

However, the ulterior motive for creating the XKSS was to make the D-Type acceptable to the Sports Car Club of America (SCCA) as a road machine – the SCCA had decreed that 50 of these revised road-going models had to be built if the sports racing Jaguar was to be eligible.

Thus, by removing the fairing for the driver's head and the central division between the driver and passenger, adding an extra door, a full-width framed windscreen and rudimentary hood with side screen and an exhaust cowling, the D-Type became the XKSS. Whatever the reasons for its creation, it was a fabulous car.

The aluminium body was protected on all four corners by slim bumpers cut down from saloon-car pressings. Like the D-Type that spawned it, the 150mph (240km/h) XKSS was so flexible and tractable you could use it for going to the shops, and on its tall, 16in. (41cm) Dunlop tyres it had all the poise and balance of its racing-car sibling. With 250bhp and triple 45 SCOE Weber carburettors, the XK engine was in full dry-sumped D-Type tune.

Jaguar planned an initial run of 21 XKSSs, but only 16 had been built when the remaining five D-Type shells – along with the tooling – perished in the infamous factory fire of February 1957.

Of these 16 (all right-hand-drive versions), 12 went to the USA, two to Canada and one to Hong Kong. Only one stayed in the UK, although a couple of D-Types were subsequently converted to XKSS specification.

Jaguar MkII

1959–1967

ENGINE: Straight-six, 2483/3442/3781cc

POWER: 120–220bhp

CHASSIS: Monocoque

BRAKES (F/R): Disc

TRANSMISSION: Four-speed manual, three-speed automatic

SUSPENSION: Independent front, live axle rear

TOP SPEED: 125mph (200km/h) – 3.8-litre model

ACCELERATION: 0–60mph (96km/h) in 8.5 seconds (3.8-litre version)

For the ten years from 1959 to 1969, the MkII was the bread and butter of Brown's Lane – a compact Jaguar, and the last proper sports saloon that the company ever made.

A quiet, comfortable and classy businessman's express for the 'stockbroker belt' of Southern England, the MkII also made a fine name for itself on the track as a saloon-car racer. Industry personalities like the racing driver Graham Hill and Lotus-owner Colin Chapman gave the MkII the stamp of approval by using them off-duty, too.

Technically the MkII wasn't vintage Jaguar – it retained old-fashioned leaf-sprung rear suspension – but its beautifully balanced shape had the classic William Lyons touch, as did the interior with its leather seats and wooden dash and door cappings, the fascia packed with dials and switches.

Born in the year in which Britain's first motorway was opened, the MkII owner could do a legal 125mph (200km/h) in the all-singing, all-dancing 3.8-litre manual overdrive car, or 120mph (192km/h) in the 3.4-litre model.

The leisurely 2.4-litre, on the other hand, couldn't even manage the magic 'ton', which was probably why Jaguar's press department decided to never allow one out to be tested by a member of the motoring press.

More than 80,000 MkIIs were sold, and the model inspired a whole raft of more expensive variations on the same theme – the S-type, the 420 and even a Daimler with its own special V8 engine. As a classic, though, it is the pure, original MkII that has won the hearts of the public hooked on 1960s nostalgia.

Jaguar E-Type

1961–1975

ENGINE: Straight-six 3781cc, straight-six 4235cc, V12 5343cc

POWER: 265bhp

CHASSIS: Monocoque

BRAKES (F/R): Discs

TRANSMISSION: Four-speed manual, three-speed automatic

SUSPENSION: Independent all round

TOP SPEED: 150mph (240km/h)

ACCELERATION: 0–60mph (96km/h) in 7.1 seconds

The Jaguar E-Type was an instant classic, an exercise in cool aerodynamic theory and unashamed showmanship that produced probably the most beautiful sports car of the 1960s.

It had the ability to live up to the looks too. The 150mph that Jaguar claimed for the E-Type was devastatingly quick in 1961, making the new Jag Britain's fastest production car. And at a price of £2,097 for the roadster, it was probably Britain's greatest motoring bargain too, undercutting its nearest rival – the Aston Martin DB4 – by a third.

That curvy shell, inspired by the Le Mans-winning D-Type racer, was immensely stiff and thus all the more able to take advantage of its new wishbone and coil-sprung independent rear suspension. Providing the power was the 3.8-litre XK engine – already 13 years old but still a stormer, and well worthy of the new chassis.

Jaguar had a hit on its hands, and was caught napping by the strength of demand for it. Pop stars, racing drivers and Royalty jostled for position in an ever-lengthening waiting list. Lew Grade wanted to borrow one for his new TV Series, 'The Saint', but Jaguar turned him down because it didn't want the publicity – it could sell every car it could make.

Despite the great demand, development continued on the E-Type. The bigger 4.2-litre engine installed from 1964 onwards was more torquey, and came with a much better gearbox and brakes. The seats and trim improved, as did the electrics, making the 4.2-litre Series 1 E-Types the best of the bunch.

Appeals for a roomier car were answered with a 2+2 version in 1966, and there was even an automatic model as Jaguar tried to reconcile the E's performance image with a need to increase sales in the United States of America.

The rot was beginning to set in and, from the launch of the Series 2 in 1968, middle age seemed to creep up unawares on the E-Type; the final V12 Series 3 cars completed the sanitization process. Smooth and fast – but somehow less soulful – the smooth shape was ruined on the longer, fatter V12 by fashionable fat arches and a cheap chrome grille. The once-legendary sex symbol was a flabby, spent force, living on old glories – not to mention borrowed time.

It's amazing to think that Jaguar, gearing up for the E-Type's successor, the XJS, had trouble getting rid of the last few cars in 1975.

Mk X

1961–1970

ENGINE: Straight-six, 3781/4235cc

POWER: 265bhp

CHASSIS: Monocoque

BRAKES: Disc

TRANSMISSION: Three-speed automatic, four-speed manual

SUSPENSION: Independent

TOP SPEED: 120–122mph (192–195km/h)

ACCELERATION: 0–60mph (96km/h) in 9.9 seconds

The Mk X was easily the most sophisticated Jaguar saloon yet. It had the triple-carburettor 3.8-litre XK engine from the E-Type, power steering as standard and fully independent suspension – the quadruple-damper rear end also fitted to Jaguar's new sports car.

Smooth and rotund in styling with a girth of 6ft 4in. (1.93m), it was the widest British car you could buy. Its new monocoque shell was as well appointed inside as luxury saloons costing twice the price, featuring walnut trim, leather seats and even picnic tables.

As desirable as it seemed, the Mk X was the first Jaguar to get a less-than-warm reception from the Press. Many thought it was simply too big to be practical in the UK, while others criticized its power

steering, uncertain brakes and shapeless seats that allowed their occupants to slide around too much on corners. This gave a false impression of the Mk X, which actually handled well for its size. Certainly its ride was excellent.

The 4.2-litre version that came along in 1964 had more torque for better acceleration, and much improved power steering.

The automatic gearbox was more responsive, too, and for the few drivers who ordered the manual version there was now synchromesh on all the gears. The 420G of 1966 had only very minor detail styling changes.

Lengthened and rebodied, the Mk X/420G became the chassis for the big Daimler DS420 limousines that lasted into the 1990s.

Jaguar XJ220

1993–1996

ENGINE: 24-valve twin-turbo V6, 3495cc

POWER: 542bhp

CHASSIS: Bonded aluminium chassis, aluminium body panels

BRAKES (F/R) Disc

TRANSMISSION: Five-speed manual

SUSPENSION: Aluminium double wishbones front and rear

TOP SPEED: 217mph (347km/h)

ACCELERATION: 0–62.5mph (100km/h) in 3.9 seconds

The Jaguar XJ220 was by far the most outlandish of the late-1980s super-cars, a flood of which were born on the back of the world-wide economic boom. It began life as nothing more than a Christmas-holiday doodle by Jaguar's engineering boss, Jim Randle, and progressed as 'The Saturday Club', with employees volunteering weekend time to develop further the idea of the ultimate super-car.

Eventually, the XJ220 (the name reflecting the aimed-for top speed) took on a life of its own as a semi-official project, and other suppliers got involved. When the car was unveiled to open-mouthed crowds at the 1988 Birmingham Motor Show in the UK, it was a giant two-door car made completely from aluminium and powered by a 48-valve V12 engine driving all four wheels.

Such was the dramatic beauty of the car and the enthusiastic public reception, that Jaguar was given the nod just over a year later by its owner, Ford, to put the XJ220 into production. Deposits were taken – many from get-rich-quick speculators. The XJ220 had changed considerably when it finally arrived in mid-1992. It was 10in. (25.5cm) shorter, had lost the four-wheel-drive system, and the V12 had been swapped for a twin-turbo V6.

Sadly, the XJ220 project ended up turning sour. Speculators didn't want the car when the market crashed and Jaguar couldn't sell all the cars (around 350) that it had built. Although amazingly beautiful, the sheer bulk of the 220 and the restricted visibility from the cabin meant it was difficult to drive on public roads.

Jaguar XJ6

1993-2003

ENGINE: 24-valve V8, 3248cc

POWER: 240bhp

CHASSIS: Steel monocoque

BRAKES: Disc all round with ABS

TRANSMISSION: Five-speed automatic

SUSPENSION: Double wishbones front and rear

TOP SPEED: 140mph (224km/h)

ACCELERATION: 0–60mph (96km/h) in 8.5 seconds

Those who thought that Ford's ownership of Jaguar would lead to the production of elegantly styled – but Ford-based, run-of-the-mill – cars were proved very wrong by the launch of the new XJ6 in September 1994.

Codenamed X300, it was the first new Jaguar model produced under Ford ownership, and looked more like the classic XJ of the late-1960s than an executive car for the end of the millennium. The retro-style nose was sculpted around four round headlamps, with the bonnet still long and gently fluted. Because the X300 was based on the core of the outgoing XJ40, the X300 was satisfyingly old-fashioned in its interior layout, with a low roof and narrow windscreen through which the driver peered down the elegant prow.

What Ford had achieved was a giant leap forward in terms of detail quality and fit and finish, in a final attempt to rid the British company of its status as a maker of desirable, but flawed, cars. Under the bonnet was the classic straight-six engine, which could trace its lineage back over 40 years.

The X300 was a great sales success, and was further improved in 1997 when the six-cylinder unit was swapped for an all-new V8 engine of Jaguar's own design, which would power the company into the new millennium. Despite the obvious competence of German executive rivals, none could match the character of the Jaguar so ably reared by Ford.

Jaguar XK8/R

1996–

ENGINE: 32-valve supercharged V8, 3996cc

POWER: 363bhp

CHASSIS: Steel monocoque

BRAKES (F/R): Disc with ABS

TRANSMISSION: Five-speed automatic

SUSPENSION: Double wishbones front, lower wishbones rear

TOP SPEED: 155mph (248km/h), restricted

ACCELERATION: 0–62.5mph (100km/h) in 5.5 seconds

After the extensive debate over the ill-fated 'F-Type' project – which was to replace the ageing XJS – Ford cancelled the extraordinary four-wheel-drive, twin-turbo machine and decided to start from scratch on an all-new coupe.

The car had to be successful in the all-important US market. It was in many ways a make or break point for the whole of the marque.

The result was the XK8, launched in October 1996. It was everything a Jaguar coupe should be: lithe, elegant, mechanically slick and super-quick. A few, however, thought the XK8 was perhaps everything a US-bound Jaguar should be – the XK8 had more than a little Stateside influence about it. The overlong rear overhang was said to have resulted from the need to accommodate two golf bags in the boot – a pre-requisite consideration in the American market for its class.

Even so, Ford helped Jaguar to do a fine job. The XK8 felt like a real Jaguar, benefiting enormously from the superb V8 and the astonishing seamlessly shifting five-speed box. The chassis was so able that the XJ8 felt as if it could handle considerably more power – which is what it got in the spring of 1998.

Jaguar engineers took the familiar supercharging route and boosted power from 290bhp to 363bhp and the torque to a massive 387lb/ft, a move that necessitated installing a Mercedes automatic gearbox to take the strain.

The result was the XKR, which contemporary road testers decided was as good as, or even better than, the new Porsche 911.

Jensen 541

1953–1963

ENGINE: Straight-six, 3993cc

POWER: 130–150bhp

CHASSIS: Fibreglass body, steel platform chassis

BRAKES (F/R): Drum (541), disc (541 Deluxe onwards)

TRANSMISSION: Four-speed manual, three-speed automatic

SUSPENSION: Independent front, live axle rear

TOP SPEED: 116–124mph (186–198km/h)

ACCELERATION: 0–60mph (96km/h) in 10.6 seconds (541R)

What Jensen 541s might lack in pedigree, they more than make up for in character and under-stressed, post-vintage charm. Fast and long-legged, they made an excellent – and cheaper – alternative to an Aston Martin and the appeal hasn't waned a bit for their many loving enthusiasts.

The fibreglass 541 was announced in 1953, its aerodynamic body moulded in three big sections and covering a new platform chassis. Suspension was from a modified Austin A70 with a live axle at the back. The familiar Austin 4-litre straight-six engine was used, but for a lower bonnet line and added punch Jensen fitted triple SU carburettors.

The result was a 25 percent leap in output to 117bhp. A high-compression head on the 1956 541 Deluxe took the power up yet again to around 130bhp, however, the really big news was the brakes – discs all round for the first time on a British production car.

The R model of 1957 had the DS7 version of the Sheerline 4-litre engine with twin carburettors, power going up to a respectable 150bhp. The wide-bodied 541S took over in 1960, and the Austin-engined Jensens made way for the new Chrysler V8-engined CV8 in 1963.

It was a beautifully designed car in every way. Great engineering was combined with elegant styling, impressive handling matched with very attractive interior specifications. If it had been produced by another maker, it wouldn't just be Jensen owners and enthusiasts who heap deserved praise on this classic British car.

Jensen CV8

1963–1965

ENGINE: V8, 5916/6276cc

POWER: 305–330bhp

CHASSIS: Platform chassis, fibreglass body

BRAKES (F/R): Discs

TRANSMISSION: Three-speed automatic and manual

SUSPENSION: Independent front, live axle rear

TOP SPEED: 130mph (208km/h)

ACCELERATION: 0–60mph (96km/h) in 6.7 seconds

The 1963 Jensen CV8, famous for its controversial slant-eyed styling, was one of the fastest-accelerating four-seater cars of the 1960s. Using Chrysler's 5916cc 305bhp V8 (with Torqueflite three-speed automatic transmission), it easily under-cut all the big-gun opposition on price, and could reach 120mph (192km/h) from rest in less than half a minute. Although following established Jensen concepts – steel pressings and a box section to carry the suspension – the CV8's chassis was new and, like many high-class British manufacturers, Jensen went about plundering the parts bins of lowly mass-market firms for brakes and suspension. Still, the interior struck the right 'gentleman's club' tone, with leather, wood and Wilton carpet everywhere.

The model was progressively improved over just four years of production. The MkII came along in 1964 with its bigger 330bhp 6.3-litre engine, but the last and best-looking of the line was the MkIII of 1965, with its lower scuttle, equal-size lights and lack of chrome around the headlight apertures.

By this time the Interceptor was well on the way, its beautiful touring-style steel body bestowing some much-needed glamour on the ageing CV8 chassis, which was used virtually unchanged. It was heavier, though – by about 220lb (100kg) – and no Interceptor ever quite matched the ferocity of the earlier, fibreglass-bodied car through the gears, although better aerodynamics meant a higher top speed. The CV8 is a much rarer car than its successor. Only 461 examples were built compared with almost 6,000 Interceptors.

Jensen FF

1966–1971

ENGINE: V8, 6276cc

POWER: 330bhp

CHASSIS: Platform chassis integral with body

BRAKES (F/R): Disc

TRANSMISSION: Three-speed automatic

SUSPENSION: Independent front, live axle rear

TOP SPEED: 130mph (208km/h)

ACCELERATION: 0–60mph (96km/h) in 8.2 seconds

Of all the cars Jensen ever made, the FF was easily the best. FF stood for Ferguson Formula, the four-wheel-drive system developed by Harry Ferguson. Unlike the systems found on off-road vehicles, this new mechanism split the torque unequally between the front and rear to give the car unreal handling qualities for a big GT.

Combined with Dunlop Maxeret anti-lock braking – another first – critics called the FF the world's safest car. At first glance the FF, with its distinctive Vignale shape, looked identical to the much more conventional Interceptor, and indeed they had much in common. Under the bonnet was a 6.3-litre 325bhp V8, driving through a three-speed automatic transmission to a live rear axle. A closer look revealed a four-inch (10cm) longer

wheelbase, but the most instant recognition point was the extra vent on each front wing.

Underneath, the chassis was almost totally different, with the propeller shaft passing along the left of the engine and gearbox and, at the front, a differential taking the drive to the front wheels. Extra weight slightly blunted the performance of the FF compared with the two-wheel-drive Interceptor, but it was still good for 130mph (208km/h) with 0–60mph (96km/h) coming up in 8 seconds.

A Series II version was introduced in 1969 with a tidied-up interior and front-end styling, but sales were slow compared with the cheaper two-wheel-drive Interceptor, and Jensen discontinued the FF in 1971. In the end a dissapointing number – only 320 – FFs were built.

Jensen-Healey

1972–1976

ENGINE: Four-cylinder, 1973cc

POWER: 144bhp

CHASSIS: Monocoque

BRAKES (F/R): Disc/drum

TRANSMISSION: Four- and five-speed manual

SUSPENSION: Independent front, live axle rear

TOP SPEED: 119mph (190km/h)

ACCELERATION: 0–60mph (96km/h) in 8.7 seconds

By the late 1960s, Jensen needed a new, cheaper car to see it through the decade to come, and Donald Healey – whose contract with the British Motor Corporation (BMC) had run its course – was looking for a new partner.

A marriage was arranged, and its first and only fruit was the Jensen-Healey, one of the most uninspiring sports cars of the 1970s. Bland styling was its first major problem. Compared with the old Healey 3000, it looked unexciting and contrived.

The chassis – which used Vauxhall Viva suspension and steering – was no more than competent. If it was at least fast (120mph (192km/h) top speed and a 0–60mph (96km/h) time of 7.8 seconds), that was tempered by the spectre of unreliability that hung over its double-overhead-camshaft, four-valves-per-cylinder, 1973cc Lotus engine.

Over 10,000 Jensen-Healeys were sold, but with the fuel crisis affecting sales of its thirsty Interceptor models, the company went into liquidation in 1975. The Jensen GT (a sporting estate) was a last-ditch attempt to keep the model alive, and in happier times it probably would have done well – the engine was sorted, and all cars featured a five-speed Getrag gearbox.

Power windows and optional air conditioning added a touch of luxury, but the car was too expensive, and it faded away quietly and relatively unmissed with the inevitable, but unfortunate, demise of Jensen in 1976.

Javelin

1947–1954

ENGINE: Four-cylinder, 1486cc

POWER: 50bhp

CHASSIS: Monocoque

BRAKES: Drum all round

TRANSMISSION: Four-speed manual

SUSPENSION: Independent front, live axle rear

TOP SPEED: 80mph (128km/h)

ACCELERATION: 0–60mph (96km/h) in 22 seconds

Yorkshire brothers Benjamin and William Jowett initially built only engines but, after years of experimentation, they decided to introduce their own cars in 1913. These vehicles were a series of simple twin-cylinder units with a reputation for toughness.

It was the Javelin however, revealed to the public in 1946, that really served to turn the company's image around. One of the few all-new cars to appear on the market immediately after the Second World War, it featured unitary body/chassis construction, torsion-bar suspension all round, rack-and-pinion steering, and a body shape as up-to-date as anything from Europe. Later on, there was a sports-car version of the Javelin, the Jupiter, which had a distinguished career on race tracks and rally circuits, especially at Le Mans.

Light, aerodynamic and high-geared, the Javelin could fly along at around 80mph (130km/h). It was able to provide excellent acceleration courtesy of its flat-four engine, which was allied to a column-change four-speed transmission. Unfortunately, it was this very engine that was to prove the downfall of the model – and of the company – when serious durability problems ruined the model's reputation. Somewhat ironically, later versions were much improved over the older ones, and they effectively solved the majority of the earlier problems. Jowett closed down, bankrupt, in 1954.

Lada 1200

1969–

ENGINE: 1.2-litre, four-cylinder OHC

POWER: 62bhp

CHASSIS: Monocoque

BRAKES: (F/R): Drum

TRANSMISSION: Four-speed manual

SUSPENSION: Independent coil spring and wishbone front, coil spring rear

TOP SPEED: 87mph (140km/h)

ACCELERATION: 0-60mph (0-96km/h) in 20 seconds

In the mid-1960s the Russian government approached Fiat for help in setting up a car factory at Togliattigrad, named after the then chairman of the Italian Communist Party. Fiat's involvement resulted in a modified 124 being the first car off the production line.

Fitted with a somewhat rough 1.2-litre engine with overhead camshaft driving the rear wheels through a four-speed gearbox, the Vaz2101 as it was known in Russia, quickly became the most popular car in its native country, purely and simply because it was so cheap. Exported as the Lada 1200, it didn't turn any heads in terms of looks or performance, but did attract buyers looking for value for money. For an incredibly low price, it offered features such as fully reclining seats, two-speed windscreen wipers and a comprehensive toolkit which would have been regarded as luxury specifications in other makes.

It may not have been exciting but it was economical. And despite poor build quality and a rough ride, it survived in the face of far greater refinement by virtue of its unbeatable price. Between them, the Russians and the Italians had come up with a model that would run and run, and today, that simple, unassuming body shape can almost be regarded as a classic.

Lagonda 3.0

1953–1958

ENGINE: Straight-six, 2580–2922cc

POWER: 105–140bhp

CHASSIS: Separate box-section

BRAKES (F/R): Drum

TRANSMISSION: Four-speed manual

SUSPENSION: Independent

**TOP SPEED: 85–100mph
(136–160km/h)**

**ACCELERATION: 0–60mph (96km/h)
in 12–17 seconds**

The 3-litre Lagonda was a direct development of the 2.6-litre model, which was one of the first all-new British luxury cars to appear after the hostilities of the Second World War. Lagonda had enjoyed an excellent reputation before the war, and this was further enhanced when it employed the services of W.O. Bentley, whose own Bentley Motors had by then fallen into the hands of old rivals Rolls-Royce.

Lagonda showed an attractive and brave face to the world when it unveiled its all-new 2.6, which had W.O. Bentley's excellent twin-cam-shaft straight-six engine, rack-and-pinion steering, in-board rear brakes and all-independent suspension.

Gearbox tycoon David Brown liked the car and bought the ailing company in 1947. He owned Aston Martin, too, which is why the DB2 ended up with the Lagonda's engine – but that as they say, is another story for another day. Saloon and drophead coupe versions of this refined car were built, but high prices – and the fact that it was, perhaps, a little on the slow side – kept sales down.

The 3-litre was an attempt to give the car a bit more power and a more modern, slab-sided look, but in the face of cheaper, faster opposition, success still eluded the big Lagondas.

The Duke of Edinburgh's ownership of a Tickford Drophead version increased its charisma a little, but in 1958 David Brown dropped the Lagonda marque, and there were no more new Lagondas produced until the 1961 Rapide.

Lagonda Rapide

1961–1964

ENGINE: Straight-six, 3995cc

POWER: 236bhp

CHASSIS: Steel tubular

BRAKES (F/R): Disc

TRANSMISSION: Three-speed automatic, four-speed manual

SUSPENSION: Independent

TOP SPEED: 125mph (200km/h)

ACCELERATION: Not available

Despite the failure of the 2.6-Litre and 3.0-Litre models, Sir David Brown was still very eager to produce a Lagonda as a four-door companion model to his Aston Martins. He was going after the Rolls-Royce market, but he also wanted to produce a car that would appeal to the type of people who occasionally enjoyed driving themselves instead of thinking of it as an annoying chore best left to a suited, booted and cap wearing member of the staff.

The Rapide appeared at Motor Show time in 1961, and had two important features yet to be seen on production Aston Martins: a 4-litre version of the straight-six engine – for more torque at low speeds – and a de Dion rear axle, which theoretically gave a better ride and took up less luggage space underneath the car.

The in-house styling was wrought in alloy, and proved controversial due to its horse-shoe grille and fussy, twin headlights with an angled brow above them. It was a shame, because from the back the Rapide was an elegant car. What's more, it went impressively well, being capable of 125mph (200km/h) even with the automatic gearbox, not the manual which was the usual fitment.

However, at the princely price of more than £5,000 there were better luxury saloons, and few potential buyers could get on with the radical nature styling. In the end, a total of 55 Rapides were sold, many to Sir David Brown's rich friends, meaning that very few people have ever enjoyed the pleasure of driving one of these wonderfully luxurious and refined – if not totally elegant – beasts.

350GT / 400GT

1964–1967

ENGINE: V12, 3929cc

POWER: 320bhp

CHASSIS: Steel body, tubular frame

BRAKES (F/R): Disc

TRANSMISSION: Five-speed manual

SUSPENSION: Independent

TOP SPEED: 160mph (256km/h)

ACCELERATION: 0–60mph (96km/h) in 7 seconds

The early Lamborghinis were in many ways the best cars the company ever built. Class beating dream cars, the 350GT of 1964 was faster, quieter, easier to drive and more carefully made than the equivalent Ferrari, yet surprisingly they were no more expensive. In fact, Ferrucio Lamborghini lost almost $1,000 on every 350 he sold in 1964.

Under the skin there was proper race-car suspension, the best disc brakes money could buy, five speeds where a Ferrari had only four and, best of all, the world's finest engine – a delightful, four-camshaft, 3.5-litre V12 that could push the car to 160mph (256km/h). All it ever lacked was great looks: somehow the Touring's shape – though elegant in some ways – was never a classic.

The initial 350GT was the lightest and fastest of these early front-engined Lamborghinis. Later 400GT and GT 2+2s were steel bodied (the boot-lid and bonnet were

still of alloy) with more torque and horsepower to try to counteract the added weight – now a corpulent 2862lb (1300kg).

By stretching the bore to 82mm, the V12 was now a 4-litre unit – 50bhp stronger than its predecessor at 320bhp, with a useful 276lb/ft of torque. It was a car where that type of extra power didn't go to waste when you were driving it.

Although the styling was identical at a glance, and the same wheelbase was retained, the 2+2 had all-new body panels, with a taller roof-line to squeeze in rear passengers. Most 400s, and all the 2+2s, had Lamborghini's own transmission, a five-speed unit with synchromesh on reverse gear.

The 400 died in 1968. The Islero, the car that replaced the 400, was a simplified, boxy and less-glamorous development of the old car that was nothing like as well built.

Miura

1966–1972

ENGINE: V12, 3929cc

POWER: 350–385bhp

CHASSIS: Monocoque

BRAKES (F/R): Disc

TRANSMISSION: Five-speed manual

SUSPENSION: Independent

TOP SPEED: 170mph (170km/h)

ACCELERATION: 0–60mph (96km/h) in 6.7 seconds

The Lamborghini Miura was the first V12 super-car with a mid-mounted engine, borrowing design principles from the latest crop of Formula One cars and sports racers, the Ferrari 250LM and Ford GT40. It lifted Lamborghini from promising newcomer to serious contender, eclipsing Ferrari in some people's eyes as a maker of advanced road cars.

Chassis designer Giampaolo Dallara sketched a unitary steel hull comfortably big enough for two occupants. To keep the length down, the 4-litre, 350bhp, V12 engine was mounted transversely behind the cockpit. To get the drive to the rear wheels Lamborghini designed a special transaxle, mounted at the rear of the engine in unit with the light-alloy crankcase – not unlike the BMC Mini in concept, but revolutionary on a car with such high performance. Suspending the whole chassis on coil springs and wishbones, he displayed the ensemble – still without a body – at the Turin Show in 1965.

The orders soon started rolling in, and with a stack of deposits on the table Ferrucio Lamborghini felt able to commission Bertone to clothe the naked car. Nuccio Bertone put his best man on the job: Marcello Gandini. Just 25 years old at the time, he schemed a bold, sensual car that has lost none of its head-turning appeal in the subsequent decades.

Designated the P400, it was a year after its 1966 Geneva Show introduction that the car went into full production, hitting the headlines with a 170mph (272km/h) top speed. Sheer performance was only half the story, though: the balance, traction and sheer cornering power conferred by the mid-engined location put the Miura in another dimension. A faster, improved 'S' version appeared in 1969, followed by an even better, faster SV in 1971, with even more power and much improved suspension. The SV lasted just a year, bowing out in late-1972 as the LP400 Countach started to come on stream.

Lamborghini Espada

1968–1978

ENGINE: V12, 3929cc

POWER: 325–365bhp

CHASSIS: Monocoque

BRAKES (F/R): Disc

TRANSMISSION: Five-speed manual, three-speed automatic

SUSPENSION: Independent

TOP SPEED: 150–155mph (240–248km/h)

ACCELERATION: 0–60mph (96km/h) in 7.8 seconds

As a V12 express, the dramatically styled Lamborghini Espada was unique in its ability to carry four adults comfortably.

It was certainly the fastest four-seater car in the world when it was introduced in 1968. Top speed was an impressive 150mph (240km/h), with up to 155mph (248km/h) possible on the later versions. Power crept up from 325bhp to 350bhp on the 1970 Series 2, then to 365bhp for the 1972 Series 3. It was the new definition of four-seater fast and the benchmark that the few other in the class had to look towards beating.

Inspired by the Marzal show car, Bertone designed a big, high-waist coupe with a sweeping window line and a sharply cut-off tail.

The glazed rear panel above the tail-lights was unique, and improved rear vision. Up front, under a huge alloy bonnet with NACA ducts, was Lamborghini's classic quad-camshaft 4-litre V12 driving through a purpose-built and very drive friendly five-speed gearbox.

Wishbone suspension all round gave the big four-seater a superbly supple ride, but not at the expense of handling – the car's stability and lack of roll were in a different league from most big four-seaters. The type of drive was another good reason why the Lamborghini Espada was a dream car. Early cars had to make do without the luxury of power steering, while on later versions there was the option of an automatic gearbox.

In production from 1968 to 1978, the Espada remains one of the best-selling Lamborghinis ever and a true landmark when it comes to four-seater speed and style.

Lamborghini Countach

1973–1991

ENGINE: V12, 3929/5167cc

POWER: 375bhp

CHASSIS: Alloy body, tubular frame

BRAKES (F/R): Disc

TRANSMISSION: Five-speed manual

SUSPENSION: Independent

TOP SPEED: 186mph (298km/h) – 4-litre version

ACCELERATION: 0–60mph (96km/h) in 4.8 seconds

Whereas its predecessor, the Miura, was sensual and muscular, the Lamborghini Countach was a futuristic razor-edged wedge, that at the time of its launch, you could believe had just roared out of the hyperactive imagination of a sci-fi writer with a particular obsession for automotive speed and excellence.

Like the Miura, its V12 engine was mid-mounted, but it was a much better developed car – not to mention much easier to live with (despite the show-off lift-up doors) – and a lot more forgiving in its handling, as well.

It was also even faster than the Miura, with Lamborghini claiming a top speed of 186mph (298km/h). Countach, incidentally, is a Piedmontese expletive meaning 'Wow!' – or something stronger, depending on how it is pronounced.

The first Countachs went to their owners in 1974, and the model got progressively more tasteless in its styling as the years went by – especially once the bespoilered 5-litre model appeared in 1982.

The car began to put on as much flab as muscle, yet it remained popular, and kept the troubled Lamborghini – long since out of its founder's control – afloat through the dark abyss of the 1970s and 1980s.

The last QV – Quattrovalvole, four-valves-per-cylinder – cars were built in 1991, with talk of a top speed of 200mph (320km/h). In its later years the Lamborghini Countach became a kind of parody of itself, a car for anyone with too much money and not enough taste. Yet how many other 25-year-old super-cars can any child recognize at a glance?

Silhouette and Jalpa

1976–1991

ENGINE: V8, 3485cc

POWER: 255bhp

CHASSIS: Monocoque

BRAKES (F/R): Disc

TRANSMISSION: Five-speed manual

SUSPENSION: Independent

TOP SPEED: 148mph (237km/h)

ACCELERATION: 0–60mph (96km/h) in 5.8 seconds

The Silhouette and Jalpa were conceived by Lamborghini's new mid-1970s owners to tackle the big-selling Ferrari 308GTS head-on. They weren't new cars, instead they borrowed from the Urraco – Lamborghini's baby super-car of the early 1970s.

But where the Urraco was simple and elegant, the Silhouette was muscular and aggressive, a Targa-roofed two-seater that was pure machismo. Those squared-off arches concealed fat Pirelli P7 rubber on flamboyant five-hole telephone-dial alloy wheels. The fastback of the Urraco was now a 'tunnel back', with filled-in buttresses housing matt-black air scoops to provide fussy visual relief where there had once been glass. Lamborghini rehashed the interior in a mixture of Alcantara, towelling and hide, with the usual hotch-potch of cheap switchgear, poorly placed.

The engine and transmission were carried over from the Urraco – a 3-litre, four-camshaft, all-alloy V8 mounted sideways ahead of the rear wheels, with the five-speed gearbox mounted to the left of the engine in line with the crank. Yielding 250bhp, it was 30bhp up on the simpler single-cam-per-bank P250 engine in the original troubled 2.5-litre Urraco.

The Silhouette was revived from the grave as the more powerful 3.5-litre Jalpa in 1981. Its engine was reworked to give 255bhp and the vehicles had a much improved interior.

Like its predecessors, it was a fine driver's car with strong performance and impressive agility, but troubles at the factory never gave it a chance to succeed, despite a ten-year production run. Just 192 were built, compared with 12,000 Ferrari 308s over the same period.

Lamborghini Diablo

1990–2001

ENGINE: V12, 5729cc

POWER: 492-525bhp

CHASSIS: Square section tubes

BRAKES (F/R): Disc

TRANSMISSION: Five-speed

SUSPENSION: Double wishbone

TOP SPEED: 207mph (331km/h)

ACCELERATION: 0–60mph (96km/h) in 3.9 seconds

To create a successor for the legendary Countach was a tough job for Lamborghini. It would have to be faster, more practical and comply with tougher safety and emission regulations. Yet the basics of the car – launched in 1990 – remained much the same. The engine was still a quad-cam V12 but all-new and bigger now, its capacity increased from 5167 to 5729cc for an excellent output of 492bhp.

Like before it was laid out longitudinally, with the gearbox in the front and the cooling radiators in the back. Double wishbone suspension was used all round, again classic supercar hardware.

The hardest part was designing the bodywork, which had to out-wow the wildest looking car of them all. Marcello Gandini, the man who had styled the Miura and the Countach, was hired again for the new car and created a cleaner, longer shape,

though perhaps it was not such a memorable one as the Countach had been in 1971.

Where it did score over the Countach was in aerodynamics. The combination of a low drag factor and more power pushed the top speed over the impressive 200mph mark.

Acceleration was equally stunning – despite the inevitable increase in weight – and the chassis came up to the same standard, although the unassisted steering was a little on the weighty side. A four wheel drive Diablo called VT brought even higher levels of traction and, later, there were ever more powerful and lighter versions like the SE 30 and the SV, with over 500bhp. For poseurs there was always the VT Roadster. Looking set to survive into the next century, the Diablo was perhaps the last of the traditional mid-engined supercars.

Aprilia

1936–1949

ENGINE: V4, 1352–1486cc

POWER: 47bhp

CHASSIS: Monocoque

BRAKES (F/R): Drum

TRANSMISSION: Four-speed manual

SUSPENSION: Independent

TOP SPEED: 80mph (128km/h)

ACCELERATION: 0–60mph (96km/h) in 25 seconds

The Aprilia was one of Lancia's finest achievements and a contender for the title of a landmark car. It was an outstandingly advanced saloon that had features not universally found on other marques for another 20 years or more.

Lancia had already shown the way with V4 engines and unitary construction on the Lambda a generation earlier, but the Aprilia consolidated that already strong technical lead.

Its rounded shape was both aerodynamic and astonishingly roomy, and on just 1400cc the Aprilia could cruise at 70mph (112km/h) and touch 80mph (128km/h). Sweet and responsive, the V4 was matched to an equally delightful four-speed crash gearbox that made for a great drive.

Its best feature, however, was its handling. On sliding pillars at the front and torsion bars at the back, the Aprilia had the poise and agility to eclipse the majority of contemporary sports cars, never mind saloons – most of which would have fallen over had they attempted to follow it through a fast bend. At the time it was revolutionary beyond belief and truly awe inspiring.

Beautifully made in the Lancia tradition, the Aprilia gained many admirers, and was the favoured transport of many racing drivers – in some cases, long after production had finished.

In fact, the car was current until 1949, when it was eventually replaced by the Aurelia – another ground-breaking classic.

Aurelia B24 Spider

1951–1956

ENGINE: V6 2451cc

POWER: 120bhp

CHASSIS: Monocoque

BRAKES (F/R): Drums

TRANSMISSION: Four-speed manual

SUSPENSION: independent

TOP SPEED: 112mph (179km/h)

ACCELERATION: 0–60mph (96km/h) 12 seconds

Open cars don't get any more glamorous than Pininfarina styled Lancias B24 Spider. Its shape, incorporating low-slung wrap-around screen, cut-away doors and cute corner bumpers, was aimed directly at the American market and that is exactly where many B24s went – as the US has always had a thing for cars whose design just can't help screaming at you to drive them.

Under the Pininfarina bodywork was the thoroughbred running gear of the classic B20 Aurelia Coupe. There was also a lightweight 2.5 litre V6 up-front, the gearbox mounted in unit with the transaxle, located behind the front seats.

On just 120bhp the B24 was no dragster but it cornered better than almost anything on the road in the mid-50s. This was including the contemporary Ferrari models, which were technically very crude by comparison to the Aurelia B24.

Advanced DeDion rear suspension kept the rear wheels upright at all times while the brakes were generously dimensioned drums, in-board at the rear – making for a great drive.

The original wrap-around screen spider was a surprisingly short-lived model. The American market may have loved the look, but they also wanted a better, less leaky, hood and proper glass side windows – and what the American market wanted, it got. The B24 convertible with a boring up-right screen, wind-up glass windows and a more substantial soft-top supplanted the Spider in 1956.

Flavia Sport

1963–1965

ENGINE: Flat-four, 1500/1800cc

POWER: 100bhp

CHASSIS: Alloy body, tubular frame

BRAKES: Disc all round

TRANSMISSION: Four-speed manual

SUSPENSION: Independent front, dead axle rear

TOP SPEED: 112mph (179km/h)

ACCELERATION: 0–60mph (96km/h) in 12 seconds

Launched at the beginning of 1963, the Flavia Sport was the last in a trio of special-bodied sporting Flavias based on a shorter 8ft 1in. (246cm) platform than the factory saloon. With its body crafted in alloy and hung on a slender steel frame, it was around 300lbs (136kg) lighter than the off-the-peg Berlina. It sliced through the air more easily too, thanks to clean, smooth, compound curves that were probably more a product of gut feeling and experience than of scientific aerodynamic theory.

Production Flavia Sports models differed slightly from the prototypes, losing the moulded swage line that swept up to partly cover the rear wheels. Outwardly it shared little with other Flavias, except the steel disc wheels and the 'D' shaped Marelli tail-lights.

A perfectly balanced and beautifully built all-alloy, flat-four engine powered the Sport, which was tweaked – like the coupe and convertible – to give a nervous 90bhp on twin carburettors. With a top speed of 111mph (178km/h), it was one of the fastest 1500cc cars you could buy, and inherited the fine front-drive handling – and much of the refinement – of the saloon on which it was based. Like the elegant Pininfarina Flavia Coupe, the Zagato was a nominal four-seater with a roomy boot.

It remained exclusive. Only 98 were built with the original 1500cc engine, then a further 626 starting late in 1963 with the 100bhp 1800cc engine (32 of them with Kugelfischer injection) before the plug was pulled in 1965. By that time Lancia was in full swing with the Fulvia Zagato, a far less arresting design that had much more mainstream appeal.

1.6HF Coupe

1965–1976

ENGINE: V4, 1216–1584cc

POWER: 80–130bhp

CHASSIS: Monocoque

BRAKES (F/R): Disc

TRANSMISSION: Four- and five-speed manual

SUSPENSION: Independent front, dead axle rear

TOP SPEED: 100–115mph (160–184km/h)

ACCELERATION: 0–60mph (96km/h) in 9 seconds (1.6-litre), 0–60mph (96km/h) in 14 seconds (1.2-litre)

The last of the real Lancias designed prior to the Fiat take-over, the elegant little Coupe was a car with youthful driver appeal and all the engineering individuality and refinement that singled out Lancia from the rest. If they had to pick out a car to bow out on, the original Lancia team couldn't have done much better than come up with the delightful 1.6HF coupe. It epitomized exactly what Lancia were about – the creation of cars with outstanding character, grace and a whole lot of style.

Launched in 1965 as a sister car to the boxy Fulvia saloon, the in-house styling of the coupe seemed just as fresh 11 years later – classy and simple, it changed very little. When something is close to perfect, it makes good sense to not change it about that much. Early cars with just 1200cc were underpowered, but the fine front-drive handling

made the Fulvia – with its curious, but smooth, narrow-angle V4 engine – a natural for rallying.

As a stripped-for-action 1600HF, the coupe was a force to be reckoned with, making Lancia world rally champions twice over in the early 1970s.

The man behind the Fulvia, and all the 1960s Lancias, was Professor Antonio Fessia – a brilliant, but strong-willed, engineer not unlike Mini-designer Alec Issigonis in terms of the single-minded pursuit of his engineering ideals. He had no truck with corner-cutting, and whilst he left a legacy of superb cars he probably contributed as much as anyone to the company's downfall.

Lancia lost money on everything it built in the 1960s, and with debts mounting, the owner (and cement tycoon) Carlo Pesenti, sold out to Fiat for the tiny nominal sum of £6.

Stratos

1973–1975

ENGINE: V6, 2418cc

POWER: 190bhp

CHASSIS: Monocoque

BRAKES: Disc

TRANSMISSION: Five-speed manual

SUSPENSION: Independent

TOP SPEED: 143mph (229km/h)

ACCELERATION: 0–60mph (96km/h) in 6.8 seconds

The first Stratos was a wild 'dream car' built by Bertone for the 1970 Turin Motor Show and based on the Fulvia 1600HF. Once seen it would never be forgotten because it had the type of automobile magic that inspires the imagination.

Knee-high and centrally steered, it certainly inspired Lancia's competitions manager – another wild dreamer called Cesare Fiorio, to develop a purpose-built rally car. The production Stratos looked entirely different – it was a short-wheelbase wedge designed by Marcello Gandini, the talent behind the impressive and much-loved Lamborghini Countach.

It used a 190bhp Ferrari Dino mid-mounted V6, and there were plans for a cheaper version with the Fiat twin-cam engine. However, these much more simple dreams were never built in series.

Production began in 1973, and the Stratos was passed for homologation in October 1974. It is anybody's guess as to how many of these cars were actually built – some say as many as 1,000, while others reckon fewer than 500. Either way, they were slow sellers because although production ended in 1975, it was still possible to buy a new Stratos in 1980. The works rally cars were twice world-championship winners, and a privately entered Stratos won the Monte Carlo Rally in 1979.

The car was a favourite with spectators, who loved its exotic noise and flamboyant shape. For drivers it made an uncompromising, but fast, road car with sometimes tricky handling on the limit.

Some have accused the Stratos of being a prime example of 'style over content', but to fall into that trap is to deny the monumental success that it enjoyed as a rally car. If nothing else, the Stratos was exactly what Cesare Fiorio dreamed it would be – a superb purpose-built rally car.

Beta Monte Carlo

1975–1980

ENGINE: Four-cylinder, 1995cc

POWER: 120bhp

CHASSIS: Monocoque

BRAKES (F/R): Disc

TRANSMISSION: Five-speed manual

SUSPENSION: Independent

TOP SPEED: 122mph (195km/h)

ACCELERATION: 0–60mph (96km/h) in 9.2 seconds

The Monte Carlo was designed by Fiat in conjunction with Pininfarina as a big-brother companion model to the little X1/9. The decision to market the car as a Lancia was taken in 1973 in the midst of the fuel crisis, when it was felt the car wouldn't sell in sufficient volume to make it a viable Fiat model.

Launched in 1975, the Monte Carlo was the first car to use the new Beta 2-litre twin-camshaft powerplant, mounted transversely and positioned slightly ahead of the rear axle line.

Low-slung and chunky, the first Beta Monte Carlos had solid fins enclosing the rear engine lid. On later cars these incorporated a glass panel. The bodywork was built, as well as styled, by Pininfarina.

The car got good reviews, although many felt it deserved more power, because the handling and road-holding were so good. In the USA, the car was marketed as a Scorpion.

A question-mark over the brakes dogged the Monte Carlo throughout its short life. With servo assistance on the lightly laden front end only, there was a tendency for the front wheels to lock up too early in the wet. Talk like this couldn't have helped sales, which were so slow that Fiat felt compelled to withdraw the car from production in 1978. It reappeared again in 1980 with some minor trim revisions and better brakes, but by then Lancia had lost heart. They pulled the plug again just a year later.

Gamma Coupe

1976–1985

ENGINE: Flat-four, 2500cc

POWER: 140bhp

CHASSIS: Monocoque

BRAKES (F/R): Disc

TRANSMISSION: Five-speed manual, four-speed automatic

SUSPENSION: Independent all round

TOP SPEED: 120mph (192km/h)

ACCELERATION: 0–60mph (96km/h) in 9.5 seconds

The Pininfarina-styled Gamma saloon and coupe announced at the Geneva Show in 1976 displayed all the idiosyncrasies associated with the Lancia marque, not least the adoption of a big 2.5-litre flat-four engine in an executive class more used to six cylinders at the very least. Torquey and smooth at high revs, the flat-four proved a difficult one for buyers to accept – not only because it was rather throbby and unrefined at tick-over, but because it rapidly acquired a reputation for disastrous reliability.

It was a shame the car was so under-developed, because the Gamma was a great driving machine, with superb balance and the best power steering around. Being behind the wheel of one was a real delight. The Gamma gave you the type of drive that others in its class would find themselves very hard-pressed to match. The saloon was handsome in its way, but the Coupe was an elegant classic, perfectly proportioned.

Series 2 models with fuel injection, a four-speed automatic option and other detail modifications to make the engine more reliable came too late for the car, and in 1984 Gamma production ended. Had the Gamma survived, it would probably have been given 16-valve technology, and there were 180bhp Federalized turbo Gammas running as prototypes. In fact, a V6 would probably have served the Gamma better as a commercial proposition, and drawings existed for a wide-angle unit. It's a real shame that they only exist as drawings.

Delta HF Integrale

1986–1990

ENGINE: Four-cylinder, 1995cc

POWER: 185–215bhp

CHASSIS: Monocoque

BRAKES (F/R): Disc

TRANSMISSION: Five-speed manual

SUSPENSION: Independent

TOP SPEED: 128–140mph (205–224km/h)

ACCELERATION: 0–60mph (96km/h) in 5.5–7 seconds

In 1986 the regulations for the World Rally Championship were changed, effectively restricting it to Group A cars – of which 5,000 had to be produced within a 12-month period. Lancia's Delta HF 4WD looked to have potential within these new rules, and so it proved. It won the manufacturers' World Championship in its first year of competition – more than living up to it's designer's dream's of success.

In the quest for more power, Lancia developed an uprated version of the HF 4WD called the Integrale, which could be identified by its flared wheel-arches to accommodate a wider track and fatter tyres.

Developing 185bhp from its 8-valve engine, this car stunned drivers with its uncanny grip and handling, and was in such demand that many more than the 5,000 cars required for homologation were built.

A 16-valve version – identified by its bonnet bulge – upped the stakes even further, giving 200bhp and pushing the car's straight-line speed into the realms of the super-car. It boasted an impressively fast 6.0 second 0–60mph (96km/h) time and a top speed of 135mph (216km/h).

The permanent four-wheel-drive system split the torque 47/53 front-to-rear and, as before, featured a Ferguson central differential and a Torsen differential in the rear axle. There was a final run of 'Evoluzione' I and II Integrales with 210bhp and finally 215bhp, with yet bigger wheels and various skirts and spoilers to help reduce drag.

Perhaps the ultimate in 'hot hatchbacks', the Integrale will be remembered as one of the greatest driver's cars of all time.

Thema 8.32

1986–1990

ENGINE: V8, 2926cc

POWER: 215bhp

CHASSIS: Monocoque

BRAKES (F/R): Disc

TRANSMISSION: Five-speed

SUSPENSION: Independent

TOP SPEED: 139mph (222km/h)

ACCELERATION: 0–60mph (96km/h) in 6.8 seconds

In search of a 'glamour car' to bring some much needed excitement to its Thema range, Lancia conceived a Ferrari V8-engined version called the 8.32 – 8 cylinders, 32 valves. The engine was the same one as that used in the 308 Quattrovalvole, but adapted to the requirements of a luxurious saloon. It was certainly a powerful enough monster.

A two-plane crankshaft made it run more smoothly at low speeds, and it was de-tuned from 240bhp to 215bhp, although it retained impressive torque – 209lb/ft at 4500rpm. All 8.32s had a beefed-up five-speed manual transmission and, of course, front-wheel drive, which presented traction problems when having to deal with the type of power on offer.

In fact, without recourse to a limited slip differential or traction control, the Thema 8.32 was actually a very well-mannered car and a reasonably fast one, although it was not much quicker overall than

the much cheaper Thema Turbo.

There were other attractions, however. Inside, the 8.32 had a rich interior using the best woods and leathers. Air conditioning was standard, and the car even had a rear wing that extended automatically above 80mph (128km/h).

Outside you could spot an 8.32 by its more vertical grille and chunky five-spoke alloy wheels. It may not have been the most beautiful beast on the road, but at least it was a distinctive one and Lancia had wanted a car that was capable of standing out from the crowded market.

Built to special order at a rate of no more than six or seven per day, the 8.32 was not a great success commercially, but should prove collectable in years to come. There are already signs that earlier neglect of the Thema 8.32's values is being redeemed and it has a growing following.

Land Rover Series 1

1948–1954

ENGINE: Four-cylinder, 1595/1997cc

POWER: 50bhp

CHASSIS: Separate chassis, alloy body

BRAKES (F/R): Drum

TRANSMISSION: Four-speed manual

SUSPENSION: Leaf springs, beam axles

TOP SPEED: 56mph (90km/h)

ACCELERATION: Not available

Announced in 1948, the Land Rover was devised by the Rover Car Company as a low-volume workhorse for rural use – a multipurpose, four-wheel-drive vehicle cast in the mould of the wartime Jeep. Rover thought they might sell 50 a week, yet, within a year, they were making more Land Rovers than Rover cars, with 70 percent of the output going abroad.

The first 'Land Rover' prototype was a cross between a car and a tractor, with its single, central seat and no roof. The Rover board, sensing a winner, gave it the go-ahead in September 1947 and, within a year, pilot production models had been built; it was formally launched at the 1948 Amsterdam Motor Show, priced at £450.

Power came from a four-cylinder 1.6-litre engine from the Rover 60 car, and the bodywork of the Land Rover was made almost entirely from aluminium. This was more rust-resistant and also somewhat easier to obtain than steel.

At first the Land Rover had a curious four-wheel-drive system with no central differential and a freewheeling device in the front section of the drive to reduce tyre scrub. This was fine for going up hills, but not so good for coming down, where the wheels were turning at different speeds. In 1950 a cure was provided by a dogleg clutch, giving the driver two- or four-wheel drive.

Putting the Land Rover into production required little investment because it used so many off-the-shelf parts. The only major Land Rover item for which Rover had to 'tool up' was the power transfer box. By 1954, 100,000 examples had been built.

Land Rover ■ Range Rover

1970–1996

ENGINE: V8, 3528cc

POWER: 135bhp

CHASSIS: Steel ladder-frame chassis, aluminium and steel body panels, three-door

BRAKES (F/R): Disc

TRANSMISSION: Four-speed manual

SUSPENSION: Independent long-travel with coil springs front and rear

TOP SPEED: 101mph (162km/h)

ACCELERATION: 0–62.5mph (100km/h) in 11.7 seconds

Some ground-breaking ideas have to bide their time before being launched. Plans for a 'Road-Rover' had been kicked around at Land Rover since the end of the 1940s. They progressed from putting a station-wagon body on early Land Rovers to a custom-designed three-door estate. But in the early 1960s, a Land Rover market researcher in the USA uncovered a developing market for 4x4 leisure vehicles.

In 1966 the project known as the '100in. Station Wagon' got under way. A number of coincidences directed its development into a unique vehicle, including its arrival in time to take advantage of Rover's powerful new GM-derived V8 engine. This meant the car had to have permanent four-wheel drive (unlike standard Land Rovers) to divide the power between the front and rear axles, a move which helped to create its unique driving characteristics.

The remarkable styling also came about by near-accident. Engineering chief Spen King created his own razor-edged prototype, which Rover stylist David Bache then 'cleaned-up' with some very subtle surface treatments. The result was a timelessly classic shape. The Range Rover was launched in 1970 and soon became a status symbol, as well as a ruggedly useful tool. More than anything, drivers loved the elevated driving position.

Development was slow, Land Rover taking many years to develop a five-door model, and the crude dashboard was only replaced in the last two years of the car's life. But it also became more and more luxurious as it established itself as a rival to executive cars, and it became very popular in the USA and the Middle East. However, it was plagued by unreliability, a result of under-investment in the basic concept.

Land Rover Discovery

1990–

ENGINE: V8, 3528cc

POWER: 145bhp

CHASSIS: Steel ladder-frame chassis, aluminium body panels, steel roof

BRAKES (F/R): Disc

TRANSMISSION: Five-speed manual

SUSPENSION: Long-travel coil sprung, front and rear

TOP SPEED: 102mph (163km/h)

ACCELERATION: 0–62.5mph (100km/h) in 12.9 seconds

With the Range Rover moving upmarket – both socially and fiscally – at one end of the product range, and the Land Rover/Defender remaining uncompromisingly in the farmyard at the other, the British manufacturer had a serious problem on its hands. A wave of Japanese off-roaders – such as the Mitsubishi Shogun, Nissan Patrol, Toyota Landcruiser, Isuzu Trooper and the smaller Daihatsus – was occupying an expanding middle-market. These more- civilized cars were being bought by drivers who never ventured off-road, but enjoyed their distinctiveness and high driving position. Sales of off-roaders quadrupled in the second half of the 1980s.

Land Rover needed to enter the market, but was short of cash – rumoured to be because its substantial profits were being used to prop up the Rover car division – so it used the Range Rover parts bin to create a new car, which was civilized enough to rival the Ford Granada Ghia it matched in price.

The Discovery was clever. It used the Range Rover's 100in. (254cm) chassis and suspension, and numerous under-skin parts. It even used the Range Rover's windscreen. Like the original Range Rover, it was launched as a three-door and used the trusty V8. A diesel engine was optional.

The styling was criticized by some, but buyers loved it and the Discovery became the UK's best-selling off-roader. Clever interior design, using advice from mainstream design houses, was much praised. The image of the Discovery was damaged later in its life by increasing unreliability – said to be caused by over-rapid expansion of production – and its falling behind when rivals were becoming more car-like in their ride and handling.

The Discovery was completely revamped and given an innovative suspension system, although visually little changed, under the watchful gaze of the Rover Group's owner, BMW, in 1998.

Land Rover

Defender

1990–

ENGINE: V8, 3528cc

POWER: 134bhp

CHASSIS: Steel ladder-frame chassis, aluminium body panels

BRAKES (F/R): Disc

TRANSMISSION: Five-speed manual

SUSPENSION: Coil-sprung independent, front and rear

TOP SPEED: 87mph (139km/h)

ACCELERATION: 0–62.5mph (100km/h) in 15.7 seconds

First seen at the Amsterdam Motor Show in 1948, the Land Rover was definitive in its simplicity and, unsurprisingly, it was barely changed until the early 1970s, when the Series III gained a rather slicker all-synchromesh gearbox and slightly more civilized dashboard fittings.

However, by the early 1980s Land Rover – then a two-model manufacturer – was feeling the heat from rival Japanese 4x4s, which were less uncompromisingly rugged and more suitable as all-round multi-purpose vehicles. Land Rover bosses also recognized that typical buyers kept their vehicles for 10–20 years. A decisively new model would encourage loyal fans to trade up or stay away from the opposition.

The County station-wagon was launched in 1982, and threw off its military garb for trendy graphics. Inside it got proper seats and some attempt at sound-proofing, but it still rode on 'cart springs'. In 1983 the Land Rover got coil-sprung suspension.

Even so, the Defender hadn't strayed far from its roots, and remained a pretty uncompromising machine. By the time Land Rover launched a recreational off-roader in 1990, the car with no name became the Defender.

And defend its territory it did, remaining true to its origins. A V8-engined, sporty, short-wheelbase Defender was launched for the USA in the mid-1990s, becoming an instant fashion hit. A lack of airbags meant the Defender had to be withdrawn from the USA in 1998. BMW-owned Land Rover countered by simultaneously announcing that work had started on the Defender's replacement, scheduled for 2002. It is confident that it can successfully replace one of the greatest icons of transport after 54 years…

Land Rover Freelander

1997–

ENGINE: In-line four-cylinder, 1796cc

POWER: 108bhp

CHASSIS: Steel monocoque, convertible three-door and five-door

BRAKES (F/R): Disc with ABS and auto descent control

TRANSMISSION: Five-speed manual

SUSPENSION: Struts front, independent trailing arms rear

TOP SPEED: 103mph (165km/h)

ACCELERATION: 0–62.5mph (100km/h) in 10.9 seconds

Once again, despite building up a brand image bettered by few consumer-durable companies – 'The Best 4x4xFar' was the advertising slogan adopted by the company to very good effect – Land Rover found the 4x4 market changing rapidly and, once again, it was the Japanese at the root of it. Despite the off-road genre moving towards car-like convenience, the vehicles were still crudely engineered and based on truck technology.

Drivers loved the chunky styling and commanding driving position of the 4x4, but became disillusioned by the poor – compared with a car – handling, economy and performance. In 1994 Toyota was the first manufacturer to launch a car-based 4x4, the RAV-4. It was light, nippy, handled well and economical. It was also a huge success, especially in the lucrative US market. Land Rover had to compete, and revived similar work that was started in 1989, but later cancelled. The new car was codenamed CB40 – after Canley Building, Room 40, where the project started – and, like the RAV-4, was based on a conventional monocoque steel body, and used car-derived engines and transmissions.

Land Rover had long declared that it wouldn't build a small car unless it was also a superb off-roader, but the car-based CB40 had limited ground clearance – an inevitable consequence of the low-slung engine and road-derived suspension.

Land Rover had become adept at making the most from limited funds, and managed to spin off both a five-door station-wagon and convertible three-door, which was available with both a hardback and convertible softback. In the battle of the 4x4 lightweights, Land Rover managed to go straight to the top with the Freelander. With no BMW involvement, it was the last purely British Land Rover.

Range Rover Mk 3

2001–

ENGINE: 4.4-litre BMW V8

POWER: 282bhp

CHASSIS: Steel monocoque

BRAKES (F/R): Disc ABS

TRANSMISSION: Five-speed automatic

SUSPENSION: Struts front, double wishbones rear with air-springs

TOP SPEED: 130mph (208km/h)

ACCELERATION: 0-60mph (96km/h) in 9.2secs

The gestation of the third-generation Range Rover was a long and winding road. Work started in late 1996, some two and half years after BMW had taken over the British Rover Group. The initial idea was to make the Range Rover and the BMW X5 SUV sisters cars: but Land-Rover argued strongly that the Range-Rover had to be the supreme off-road vehicle.

The result was a unique and complex vehicle engineered to very high standards – it was rumoured to have cost BMW an unheard-off $1 billion to develop. Unlike most hard-core off-roaders, the Range Rover 3 was built around a steel monocoque chassis and was fitted with independent suspension supported by air-springs which allowed the car to jack itself up off-road. Its size and weight underlined the fact that it was aimed at the lucrative American market.

Land-Rover's British-based design team won the styling competition (against BMW's design centre in Munich) to shape the Range Rover – and the result was both high-tech and inspired by the original model. The car's luxurious interior came in for much praise as it was unlike anything else on the market. Most of the Range Rover's engineering was completed in Germany which, if nothing else, ensured that the car was as thoroughly thought-out as anything on the market. It was also powered by BMW's own engines.

BMW had to sell-off Land-Rover in spring 2000 as part of the break-up of the debt-laden Rover Group. New owners Ford oversaw the Range Rover's launch in late 2001. Although a very long way from the spartan original, the new car was a huge success in its first year on sale and lived up to its promise to offer luxury-car comfort in a vehicle that could cross mountain ranges.

LS400

1991–

ENGINE: V8, 3969cc

POWER: 241-260bhp

CHASSIS: Monocoque

BRAKES (F/R): Disc

TRANSMISSION: Four-speed auto

SUSPENSION: Independent

TOP SPEED: 147-155mph

ACCELERATION: 0–60mph (96km/h) in 8.3-8.5 secs

Traditionally Japanese attempts to produce an up-market luxury car in the Jaguar/Mercedes class had not met with much success in Europe. With the Lexus LS400, owners Toyota were hoping to make a break from the past and change all that.

In fact this model was marketed entirely separately from Toyota, which is an indication of how seriously the project was taken. The car was entirely new but conventionally engineered, with a 250bhp multi valve V8 driving the rear wheels.

It was a fast car but, more to the point, a very very refined one that could match the best Europe had to offer. The engine was virtually silent, the four speed automatic transmission seamless, and road noise never intruded.

Inside executives could lounge on soft leathers enjoying the best of everything: there were no options for the Lexus, just one specification that its makers considered complete. Not only did the car ride beautifully, but it also handled well, feeling much smaller than it was.

All it lacked was character. The shape was admirably aerodynamic but rather bland which, to be fair, was always the makers intention. It was marketed from the start as a car in which the wealthy would be able to keep a low profile.

The Lexus made friends instantly, despite being a completely unknown quantity. It was beautifully built and remarkably reliable, topping America's important J.D. Power Customer Satisfaction Index for several years.

Continental II

1956–1957

ENGINE: V8, 7047cc

POWER: 300bhp

CHASSIS: Separate box section

BRAKES (F/R): Drum, mid-1950s

TRANSMISSION: Four-speed

SUSPENSION: independent front, live axle rear

Top SPEED: 115mph (184km/h)

ACCELERATION: 0–60mph (96km/h) in 12 secs

The Continental II was Lincolns' attempt to move even further up-market by developing a kind of ultimate luxury car.

Stepping aside from the vulgarity of most of Detroit's products the Continental II had almost European styling and elegant, simple detailing, although it was built on the same massive scale as all of its contemporaries – its measurements coming in at 218 inches in length.

Quality was another theme of the Continental II. Each car was virtually hand built with endless layers of paint. Engines were specially dynometer tested and everything was torqued down to aircraft standards. Each Continental, built at a rate of just 13 per day, was shipped in a special fleece-lined canvas to ensure that the car arrived in pristine condition.

To protect the car's image specially selected dealers were expected to sell the Continental to the right kind of customer. They were under very strict instructions not to sell any to gangsters or other undesirables.

Even at $10,000, buyers jostled for position in the waiting list and some cars were sold for as much as $1,000 over list price. It was a position that didn't last too long though.

The Mark II was a money-loser for Ford (who owned Lincoln) and there simply were not enough buyers with requisite cash. Rolls Royces came cheaper and had a better pedigree. Thus the classy Continental II lasted just a couple of seasons and was dropped to make way for a much more expensive failure – the Edsel.

Continental

1958–1960

ENGINE: V8, 7047cc

POWER: 350bhp

CHASSIS: Monocoque

BRAKES (F/R): Drum

TRANSMISSION: Three-speed auto

SUSPENSION: Independent front, live axle rear

TOP SPEED: 116mph (186km/h)

ACCELERATION: 0–60mph (96km/h) in 8.7 secs

The 1958 to 1960 Lincolns were the biggest American cars of the post-war years. Built to out-glitz Cadillac they appeared at a time when Detroit was being criticised for the first time about the ever increasing size of its products. They were never well liked – neither the canted fins, the overly sculptured bumpers or the reverse-rake rear screen pillar sat very happily. It was a long way from the classic styling of the recently deceased Continental MkII but then the '58 Continental was a much less special (and much cheaper) car, sharing its body and mechanics with lesser Premier and Capri models. There were Sedan, four- and two-door hardtops and convertible versions.

To haul its massive weight, Lincoln specified its biggest 7.5 litre V8 engine developing a claimed 375bhp, so if nothing else, at least the Continental was pretty quick.

Technically there was even more good news, because Lincoln had switched to monocoque construction, the only car in its class to have it at the time. Coil springs had replaced leaf springs for the rear suspension too, so the Continental handled a lot better than it looked.

The car continued with minor changes until 1960. Despite this Lincoln sales continued to slip away until the introduction of the new, cleanly styled 1961 Continental.

Continental

1961–1969

ENGINE: V8, 7045/7565cc

POWER: 300–365bhp

CHASSIS: Monocoque

BRAKES (F/R): Drum

TRANSMISSION: Three-speed automatic

SUSPENSION: Independent front, live axle rear

TOP SPEED: 125mph (200km/h)

ACCELERATION: 0–60mph (96km/h) in 10 seconds

The 1961 Lincoln Continental – the 'clap door' – is a landmark in American styling. It is rightly renowned as a classic in automobile styling. Forsaking the fins and chrome then still popular on most 'domestic' cars, Lincoln (an up-market division of Ford) launched a car with clean, unadorned lines – very much American in scale, but very European in feel.

The rear-hinged rear door gave it the 'clap-door' nick-name, and chrome was applied sparingly to its crisp-edged flanks. It became the 'in' car with the rich and famous in the USA, and was even endorsed by an occupant of the White House – President Kennedy chose to drive a 'clap door' as his own off-duty form of transport. More than any other car of its class from that era, it sums up a heady mix of glamour, money and power.

There was a power-top four-door convertible version alongside the saloon from the beginning, and

a hardtop coupe joined the line-up in 1966. The Continental always had the biggest V8 engine (up to 7.5 litres), automatic transmission, and every conceivable labour-saving device.

Packing up to 365bhp, the 5215lb (2370kg) Continental was a fast car, capable of up to 125mph (200km/h) – not that such things mattered to the car's buyers. They liked it for factors such as its snob appeal and its reliability. The Continental changed little during its nine-year production run – some new chrome here, a new grille there, and every year a longer wheelbase, but essentially it retained the same clean shape all the way through.

Unfortunately for the marque, the Continental was destined to be the last good-looking Lincoln for quite a long time. However, the Mk III Continental, a two-door personal luxury car, ushered in a new era of chintzy styling.

Continental
Mark III

1968–1971

ENGINE: V8, 7538cc

POWER: 360bhp

CHASSIS: Monocoque

BRAKES (F/R): Drum

TRANSMISSION: Three-speed automatic

SUSPENSION: Independent front, live axle rear

TOP SPEED: 123mph (196km/h)

ACCELERATION: 0–60mph (96km/h) in 9 secs

The Mark III Lincoln Continental of 1968 (which is not to be confused with the controversial 1958 MkIII) was built to fill a niche nobody realised was there before – the fully equipped 'Personal luxury' car. When its initial success became apparent, Lincoln wasn't the only American car maker wondering why it hadn't thought of trying to fill the gap in the market before.

With its long bonnet and short boot, its two door styling was an evocation of the MkII of 1956, but where that car had achieved good taste – on some levels – the new car missed the mark by a mile.

The fake neo-classic grille was intended to give the car some up-market gravitas, but it only succeeded in looking totally crass, while the retractable headlights and 'continental' spare wheel hump were pure gimmickry.

Yet the buyers loved it, and bought 30,000 Continental Mark IIIs in the first year of production. Lincoln knew they were on to a good thing and followed it up with the Continental MkIV in 1972, which had more of everything except horsepower – emission controls were beginning to take their toll on Detroit's big V8s.

Lotus

1957–1973

ENGINE: Four-cylinder, 997–1599cc

POWER: 37–115bhp

CHASSIS: Space-frame, alloy body

BRAKES (F/R) Disc

TRANSMISSION: Four-speed manual

SUSPENSION: Independent front, live axle rear

TOP SPEED: 80–108mph (128–173km/h)

ACCELERATION: 0–60mph (96km/h) in 7.2 seconds (S3)

Seven and Super Seven

The now-legendary Lotus Seven of 1957 put Colin Chapman's fledgling company on the road to success. This extremely basic two-seater had a cleverly designed multi-tubular space-frame chassis with a stressed aluminium body. There were no doors – just cut-away sides – and if the hood was up, it was nearly impossible to get into the car. Minimalist mudguards covered the front wheels, and the headlights were free-standing.

There was coil-sprung independent front suspension, and a well-located live rear axle with radius arms and coil spring/damper units for superb handling. Although straight-line performance depended on the engine fitted by the owner, most went the Ford route with a side-valve unit from the Ford 100E. The space-frame was simplified on the S2 of 1962, which could also be recognized by its clamshell wings.

The Super Seven, available from 1961, came with its own series of progressively more powerful engines, from a Cosworth-enhanced 1340cc Ford Classic unit to (later) a bigger 1498cc Cortina GT or Cosworth 1599cc engine. Disc brakes appeared on the front for the first time. The S3 car used a Cortina 1600 engine, although 15 cars had a Lotus twin-cam engine of the type fitted to the company's Elan.

Attempting to bring the concept up to date, the Seven S4 of 1970 had a chunkier-looking fibreglass body bonded on to a modified chassis with Europa-type front suspension.

With the arrival of value-added tax (VAT) in the UK, the kit-car market died overnight, and in 1973 Lotus sold the rights to the design to Caterham Cars, who were still building the car in S3 form in the late-1990s very successfully.

Lotus Elite

1957–1963

ENGINE: Four-cylinder, 1216cc

POWER: 71–105bhp

CHASSIS: Fibreglass monocoque

BRAKES (F/R): Disc/drum

TRANSMISSION: Four and five-speed

SUSPENSION: Independent

TOP SPEED: 110–130mph (176–208km/h)

ACCELERATION: 0–60mph (96km/h) in 11 seconds

The Lotus Elite was a sophisticated little GT blessed with superb handling and memorable looks. It is still remembered with a lot of fondness and well-deserved, enthusiastic passion.

Launched in 1958, it was the first car to have a fibreglass monocoque made up of floor, body and structural centre-section, with the outer opening panels bolted into place afterwards.

Power came from an overhead-camshaft 1216cc Coventry Climax engine, first with 71bhp in single-carburettor form, but later with 83bhp in twin-carburettor form giving a top speed of 118mph.

The high top speed was attributable to the low-drag shape, with its amazing 0.29Cd figure. Fuel consumption of 35mpg (8.1litre/100km) was also well within reach. What made the Elite really special was its nimble handling. With coil-spring damper units at the front and modified MacPherson struts (Chapman struts) at the rear, it cornered like a go-kart, yet not at the expense of ride comfort.

Steering was rack-and-pinion, with disc brakes at the front and drums at the rear. This proved to be a very effective combination. Good as it was, the Elite was beset with problems. The monocoque shell promoted lots of drumming and vibration, whilst the cabin was very poorly ventilated – the profile of the door glass meant it was impossible to wind the windows down. Even worse, quality looked poor in the face of cheaper opposition.

From 1960 there was revised rear suspension and improved interior trim. The SE model had 85bhp and a close-ratio five-speed ZF gearbox, rather than the standard BMC-derived unit.

Further 95bhp, 100bhp and 105bhp versions were offered, before Lotus eventually pulled the plug on its prodigy in 1963 in favour of the Elan.

Elan Sprint

1970–1973

ENGINE: 4 cylinder, 1499-1588cc

POWER: 100-126bhp

CHASSIS: Backbone

BRAKES (F/R): Disc

TRANSMISSION: Four and five-speed manual

SUSPENSION: Independent

PERFORMANCE: 123mph (196km/h)

ACCELERATION: 0–60mph (96km/h) in 8.7-6.7 secs

Good as the Elite was it had proved too specialised a car to build, and was plagued with too many problems for a company the size of Lotus to produce and develop. They needed something simpler, less ambitious – easier to own but just as good to drive. Enter, in 1962, the Elan, still glassfibre but supported now by a backbone chassis and sprung on ingenious 'Chapman struts' that combined ride comfort with incredible agility.

There would be no more Coventry Climax engines. Lotus had its own twin-cam engine, a 1558cc unit based on a Ford iron block and delivering 106bhp, which in the lightweight Elan meant impressive performance on the roads.

It was on this car that Lotus built their reputation in the 60s. If wasn't perfect – quality was always suspect – then most people forgave it because the handling was so good. On the S2 of 1964 centre-lock wheels replaced the previous discs. The S3 (1966) had a high final drive ratio together with a close ratio gearbox option.

The SE (Special Equipment) version had 115bhp, close-ratio gears and servo-assisted brakes. The S4 of 1968 was an S3 SE with wider wheelarches to accommodate low-profile tyres. Power increased to 126bhp in 1970 with the big-valve Sprint some of which had five speed gearboxes.

The Elan also spawned the Elan +2, a 2+2 version for Lotus owners with families. Production of all Elans ended to clear the way for the new Elite, a move up-market that, as history has shown, wasn't entirely successful.

Europa
Twin Cam and Special

1971–1975

ENGINE: Four-cylinder, 1558cc

POWER: 105-126bhp

CHASSIS: Backbone

BRAKES (F/R): Disc/drum

TRANSMISSION: 4/5 speed

SUSPENSION: Independent

TOP SPEED: 121mph (193km/h)

ACCELERATION: 0–60mph (96km/h) in 7.7-7.0 secs

Despite early problems, the Lotus Europa was the world's first practical mid-engined road car.

First seen in 1966, it used a Renault 16 1470cc front-drive power train, turned through 180 degrees in an Elan type backbone chassis, but with the rear suspension by lower wishbones and transverse top links, similar to contemporary racing car practice.

It sounded good in theory, very good, but the car had its limitations, poor performance and claustrophobic cockpit being the two most obvious snags to its success. Its one saving grace was its handling, but Lotus knew they had to make some improvements if interest was to be maintained.

The 1969 Europa S2 had some welcome updates, but it wasn't until 1971 that the Europa received the 105bhp 'Twin-Cam' engine it deserved.

It was a much needed move that succeeded in totally transforming the car for the better. The engine replacement also came with the added bonus of much better looks thanks to a cut-down rear deck, and alloy wheels. However, even better was yet to come. The moment of triumph eventually came with the wonderful 1972 Special. It had the 126bhp 'big valve' engine and an optional five-speed gearbox. This was the car that many in the motoring press and the car buying public had wanted Lotus to make from the outset.

Elite/Eclat

1975–1985

ENGINE: Four-cylinder, 1973cc

POWER: 160bhp

CHASSIS: Steel backbone, fibreglass body

BRAKES (F/R): Disc/drum

TRANSMISSION: Five-speed manual

SUSPENSION: Independent

TOP SPEED: 125mph (200km/h)

ACCELERATION: 0–60mph (96km/h) in 7.8 seconds

The dramatic, wedge-shaped Lotus Elite of 1974 was Colin Chapman's big move up-market. Sweeping aside the old order of Elans and Europas, its backbone chassis and coil-spring suspension were pure Lotus in design and execution, and conferred fine handling and a good ride on this luxurious four-seater sports car. The new 160bhp twin-cam engine lacked torque, but could still take the car up to 125mph (200km/h).

The Eclat sister model was identical in all but its sloping rear roofline, which blended into a conventional bootlid. A bigger 2.2-litre engine in the S2 Elite/ Eclat of 1980 improved the torque, which was boosted from 140lb/ft to 160b/ft. With it came a stronger Getrag gearbox and a more up-market interior.

By this time the Elite's wedge-shaped styling was looking dated, and the model dropped out of sight

in 1982 – at which point the Eclat became the Eclat Excel, benefitting from the company's new association with Toyota. The shape was much as before – simply a bit rounded off at the edges, with a new side-window profile and more headroom in the back. The five-speed gearbox now came from the Toyota Supra – along with several other components – and the chassis was also galvanized.

Amazingly, thanks to the tie-up with Toyota, Lotus was able to cut the car's purchase price by more than £1,000. The Eclat gained power steering as standard in October 1984, and a year later the Eclat name was dropped to become simply the Excel. For 1986 there was a more-powerful Excel SE model, with 180bhp from a higher-compression version of the 2.2-litre twin-cam engine, nudging the top speed to over 130mph (208km/h).

Esprit Turbo

1980–1987

ENGINE: In-line four-cylinder, 2174cc

POWER: 210bhp

CHASSIS: Steel backbone

BRAKES (F/R): Disc

TRANSMISSION: Five-speed manual

SUSPENSION: Independent

TOP SPEED: 148mph (237km/h)

ACCELERATION: 0–60mph (96km/h) in 6.1 seconds

With the 1980 Esprit Turbo, Lotus entered the super-car arena with a 148mph (237km/h) challenger that was a best-seller for the Hethel-based (Norfolk) manufacturer during the difficult 1980s.

To banish the 'lag' often associated with turbocharged engines, Lotus engineers used a Garrett T3 turbocharger running at 8psi (lb/in^2), bolted to a specially cast exhaust manifold. It was carefully set up to use the minimum gas flow for the required maximum output – an impressive 210bhp at 6000rpm from just 2174cc.

The twin-cam engine was thoroughly reworked with different pistons to lower the compression ratio, and given dry-sump lubrication. It was matched to a Citroën SM/Maserati Merak five-speed transaxle – a very effective combination.

Now the Esprit had the power to exploit its superb chassis, but Lotus also took the precaution of strengthening the chassis around the engine bay and fitting uprated suspension, steering and brakes. This only added to the car's excellent handling.

Dating from the original Esprit of 1975, Ital Design's 'chiselled' styling still looked crisp and modern in 1981. Spoilers, NACA ducts in the bonnet and chunky side-skirting differentiated it from the conventionally aspirated Esprit S3.

The HC Turbo Esprit of 1986 boasted more torque and power from its slightly higher-compression engine – 215bhp and 220lb/ft – for improved mid- and upper-range punch. Its interior now had more useful adjustable backrests for the seats, and the exterior was mildly reworked with a new front spoiler and side decals.

The restyled X180 Esprit replaced the HC in 1988, and continued in the Lotus price lists into the late-1990s as the Sport 300.

Lotus Esprit V8

1995–

ENGINE: Four-cylinder, 3506cc

POWER: 353bhp at 6500rpm

CHASSIS: Backbone

BRAKES (F/R): Disc

TRANSMISSION: Five-speed manual

SUSPENSION: Independent

TOP SPEED: 175mph (280km/h)

ACCELERATION: 0–60mph (96km/h) in 4.8 secs

If the Lotus Esprit had a problem it was that it never had the right number of cylinders. Eight or twelve are the requisite number in any supercar worthy of the title yet Lotus felt four were enough. In turbocharged form they probably were – going on the basis of mere figures – but in terms of delivery and smoothness buyers were beginning to expect something a bit more grown-up, a bit less marginal.

The Esprit V8 of 1995 to some extent answered these criticisms. This new 32 valve, four-cam unit, fitted with two Garrett T25 Turbochargers was the first of a new family of modular engines Lotus planned to sell to other manufacturers.

It delivered 353bhp, could take the Esprit to 175mph yet took up less space in the engine bay than the old in-line four. It also had huge torque and impressive smoothness but somehow, however impossible it seemed, Lotus had contrived to make it sound no more exciting than the old four, which stayed in production as the GT3.

The real problem was that it was allied to a poor gearchange, that made the car difficult to drive smoothly. To add yet another snag, Lotus expected buyers to have to put up with the same old interior, which had lost any charm and was beginning to look very dated. Lotus took the problems to heart and at the end 1997 came up with a much improved V8 with a racing clutch and improved linkage for the Renault van derived gearbox.

Now it was possible to fully access the V8s fantastic performance and enjoy its handling, which was still right at the top of the class.

Lotus **Elise**

1996–

ENGINE: In-line four-cylinder, 1796cc

POWER: 118bhp

CHASSIS: Aluminium extrusions, bonded and riveted, fibreglass panels

BRAKES (F/R): Disc

TRANSMISSION: Five-speed manual

SUSPENSION: Wishbones front and rear

TOP SPEED: 125mph (200km/h)

ACCELERATION: 0–60mph (100km/h) in 5.9 seconds

Lotus made its name in road cars with the raw-handling Seven kit car in 1957, following that up with the small, light and fine-handling Elan in 1962. Despite the famous maxim of founder Colin Chapman – "For better performance, add lightness" – Lotus's road-car programme lurched through the 1970s based around powerful supercars and coupes. Developing and building such cars to increasingly stringent mass-market standards was a constant struggle. The commercial failure of the early 1990s Elan convertible was the catalyst for a whole new approach.

The Elise went back to Lotus's first principles. It was a very simple, very light and very innovative roadster, designed to deliver a supercar-style driving experience at a much more affordable price.

Based around an incredible all-aluminium chassis, made of large box-section extrusions, the Elise was remarkable for its chassis rigidity, incredibly compliant ride and super-sensitive steering.

It was around 30 percent lighter than the MGF, with which it shared its 118bhp engine, so while it was very quick, the Elise also managed to be very economical. The chassis was skinned with fibreglass panel work influenced by chief designer Julian Thomson's Ferrari Dino, and the interior was left in bare aluminium with some beautiful 'engineered' details. It was a revelation.

The Elise was one of the most innovative cars ever produced. It did the impossible by offering 95 percent of the supercar experience for a mere 20 percent of the price.

Marcos 1800

1963–1964

ENGINE: Four-cylinder, 1778cc

POWER: 114bhp

CHASSIS: Wooden frame, fibreglass body

BRAKES (F/R): Disc/drum

TRANSMISSION: Four-speed manual

SUSPENSION: Independent

TOP SPEED: 124mph (198km/h)

ACCELERATION: 0–60mph (96km/h) in 8.3 seconds

The 1964 Volvo-engined 1800 was the first Marcos designed to sell to non-racing customers. Designed by Dennis Adams, it cost more than an E-type Jaguar, and sales barely broke the one-hundred mark before Marcos moved to cheaper Ford power.

Later Marcos models became less specialized, but the 1800 used its own glass, specially cast alloy wheels and had a properly styled interior. The wooden chassis was unique to the car, of course, as was the de Dion rear end – dropped after the first 32 cars because it was so expensive to produce. Cost-cutting on later Ford-engined cars killed off its classy-looking dash too, as well as the handsome wooden-rimmed steering wheel with its heavily dished alloy spokes. Other casualties of the financial restraints were the delicate steel bumpers that protected each corner

– moulded in fibreglass on later cars – and the 'Adams' badges on the C-pillars.

The rugged pushrod Volvo engine, mounted well behind the front-axle line for 50:50 weight distribution, was in unit with the usual all-synchromesh gearbox (with overdrive). Worked through the gears, the 1800 sprinted to 60mph (96km/h) in 8.3 seconds, and managed an impressive 124mph (198km/h) top speed. However, the Marcos 1800 was short-lived; in 1965, after only 108 sales, cheaper Ford-engined cars took over.

Marcos needed to cut costs and win buyers, but the purity of the concept was allowed to melt away with each succeeding year. The delicacy of the early cars gave way to the 'butch' character of 3-litre models of the later 1960s and early 1970s.

Mantis

1970–1971

ENGINE: straight 6, 2498cc

POWER: 150bhp

CHASSIS: Tubular steel

BRAKES (F/R): Disc/drum

TRANSMISSION: Four-speed manual

SUSPENSION: Independent, live axle rear

TOP SPEED: 125mph (202km/h)

ACCELERATION: no figures

Like Lotus with their +2 S, Jem Marsh of Marcos saw a market for a four seater sportscar to sell alongside his 3 litre, 2 seater models. Stylist Dennis Adams, who had designed the Marcos 1800, was hired to shape the car, which became known as the Mantis. It is best remembered for its curious styling, an unhappy combination of thick curved windscreen pillars and a bug eyed nose that can't have appealed to many.

However, the looks, which didn't emerge as Adams had intended due to changes beyond his control, tend to obscure the fact the Mantis was an impressive car in many ways.

For a start it was a genuine four seater – unlike many of its rivals – with real legroom in the back. The chassis comprised a multi-tubular affair using square section tubes while the body was moulded in two halves – top and bottom – which was a method copied by Lotus for its Elite. The original intention had been to use a Ford V6 engine, but with his eye on the American market Marsh specified the Triumph 2.5 straight six, which in carburettor form was cleared for use in the States.

The front suspension was from the Triumph parts bin while the rear end was developed by Marcos themselves. The 125mph Mantis was quite well reviewed but only 32 were built before the company went into liquidation.

Quattroporte

1963–1970

ENGINE: V8, 4136/4719cc

POWER: 260-290bhp

CHASSIS: Monocoque

BRAKES (F/R): Disc

TRANSMISSION: Five-speed manual/ three-speed auto

SUSPENSION: Independent front, live rear axle

TOP SPEED: 140mph (226km/h)

ACCELERATION: 0–60mph (96km/h) in 8.3 seconds

The Maserati Quattroporte was Italy's answer to the big Jaguars of the day and represented the ultimate in speed and luxury in the saloon class.

The shape was the work of Frua and looked assertive and dignified if not quite beautiful. There was beauty to be found under the bonnet, however, in the form of Maseratis four-camshaft 4.2-litre V8 engine, possessed of great smoothness and torque.

In manual form the Quattroporte (four-door in Italian) could touch 140mph with the ZF 5 speed manual transmission which made it the world's fastest saloon car.

The original cars, pre 1965, had square headlamps and a deDion rear axle but later versions had four headlamps and a beam axle. Interiors were more luxurious on later cars too but all came with such luxuries as electric windows and many had air conditioning. A few were built which incorporated the bigger 4.7 litre V8 engine.

679 Quattroportes were built but after production stopped in 1970, the name disappeared from the Maserati price lists until 1978 and the introduction of the Quattroporte II. Based on a stretch Khyalami chassis, this model was to prove more popular and long-lived.

With ingredients such as design by Frua, large amounts of smooth power and more than a little luxury, it is easy to understand why these cultured saloons built up – and are able to still maintain – a following among certain enthusiasts.

Ghibli

1967–1973

ENGINE: V8, 4719/4930cc

POWER: 330–335bhp

CHASSIS: Monocoque

BRAKES: (F/R) Disc

TRANSMISSION: Five-speed manual, three-speed automatic

SUSPENSION: Independent front, live axle rear

TOP SPEED: 165mph (264km/h)

ACCELERATION: 0–60mph (96km/h) in 7 seconds

The Maserati Ghibli of 1967 might not have been as technically advanced as its rivals from Ferrari (the 275 GTB/4) and Lamborghini (the 350GT), but it was at least as beautiful. Indeed its lean, low shape – drawn by the talented young designer Giorgetto Giugiaro, then working for Ghia – is reckoned by many to be the best-looking of the trio.

Even though Maserati made no attempt to keep weight down with this luxurious, steel-bodied car, the Ghibli was still quick. With the earlier type of 4.7-litre V8 – a four-cam design closely related to one that originated in the 300S racer in the 1950s – the Ghibli was a 150mph (240km/h) car. With the later 4.9-litre SS engine, the top speed went up to 165mph (264km/h), although the powerplant produced only 5bhp more. Smooth and tractable,

these engines majored on torque rather than on ultimate power, and had a fairly modest rev limit. Maserati made the very traditional suspension work beautifully, and the brakes – big, four-wheel discs, of course – were well up to the job of stopping the portly Ghibli.

To increase its appeal, especially on the American market, a Spider version was launched in 1969, and is now one of the most collectable post-war Maserati road cars. Ghibli production faded away in 1973, as the Citroën-influenced Bora and Khamsin began to come on stream as Maserati's flagship super-cars.

Although it is hard to imagine an undesirable Maserati, the Ghibli is particularly sought after in some sections for its excellent mix of controlled power and seductive beauty.

Bora

1971–1980

ENGINE: V8, 4719/4943cc

POWER: 310–320bhp

CHASSIS: Monocoque

BRAKES (F/R): Disc

TRANSMISSION: Five-speed manual

SUSPENSION: Independent

TOP SPEED: 160mph (280km/h)

ACCELERATION: 0–60mph (96km/h) in 6.5 seconds

The Bora of 1971 was Maserati's answer to the Lamborghini Miura. Styling – as on the Ghibli – was by Giugiaro, who by this time had left Ghia and was running his own studio, Ital Design.

His shape (first mooted in 1969) was elegant, but lacked the sheer animal beauty of Maserati's own Ghibli and the Miura. That the Bora was fast almost goes without saying: the 4.7-litre V8, punching out 310bhp, could push the slippery Bora up to 175mph (280km/h), with 80mph (128km/h) coming up in second gear. The Bora was also a refined car, with conversation with the passenger being possible at anything up to 150mph (240km/h).

With Citroën now Maserati's owner, it came as no surprise that a few complex hydraulics entered the picture, with super-sharp brakes and powered adjustment for the pedals, seats and steering-column rake. Handling was the last word in stability, and a major advance on the front-engined Ghibli, although the stiff ride remained.

The Bora changed little in its nine-year production run, gaining only the larger 4.9-litre engine in 1976, before it bowed out in 1980. It remains perhaps the most perfect example of the best that Maserati can offer – from its wonderful styling to its raw power and impressive ride.

Khamsin

1972–1983

ENGINE: V8, 4930cc

POWER: 320bhp

CHASSIS: Monocoque

BRAKES (F/R): Disc

TRANSMISSION: Five-speed manual, three-speed automatic

SUSPENSION: Independent

TOP SPEED: 153mph (245km/h)

ACCELERATION: 0–60mph (96km/h) in 8.1 seconds (automatic)

The Khamsin was the last traditional front-engined Maserati. Styled by Bertone, the shape dated from 1972, and resulted in an angular and dart-like coupe with an abruptly sawn-off tail. An unusual feature was its glazed rear panel, with the tail-lights held in suspension by the glass.

Inside, the chunky dashboard lacked both the symmetry and restraint of more tasteful 1960s Maseratis, but air conditioning was standard, and there was an adjustable steering column and hydraulic seat-height adjustment for the driver.

All Khamsins – named after an Egyptian wind – came with the classic Maserati four-cam V8, mounted well back against the bulkhead so that, with the 20-gallon (91 litres) fuel-tank filled, weight distribution was an ideal 50/50. The Khamsin came only as a 4.9 litre, and red-lined at 5500rpm to make a full-bodied 320bhp. Torque, though, was its forte, a colossal 354lb/ft being available at 4000rpm. Needless to say, the Khamsin had massive low-speed lugging ability, so thickly spread was this torque across the 800–5500rpm power band.

Conceived as a successor to the Indy and Ghibli, the Khamsin differed from its 1960s front-engined predecessors in having proper double-wishbone rear suspension rather than an outdated, if well located, live axle. It also used Citroën hydraulics for its steering, brakes, clutch and even the pop-up headlights and driver's seat adjustment.

It was the last Maserati to feel the technical influence of Citroën's controlling power – by the time Khamsin production was getting into its stride in 1975, Citroën had pulled out. The car remained in production until 1983.

M530

1967-1973

Engine: V4, 1699cc

Power: 73bhp

Chassis: Monocoque

Brakes (F/R): Disc

Transmission: Four-speed manual

Suspension: Independent

Top speed: 95mph (154km/h)

Acceleration: 0–60mph (96km/h) in 15.6 secs

Matra was a big missile and armament manufacturer who had taken up production of the Rene Bonnet's Djet, one of the first truly mid-engined sportscars, in the early 1960s. By 1967 they felt they were ready to introduce a car of their own design, the M530.

If the Djet had been rather pretty, then the M530 had a somewhat awkward look. It had a high quality glassfibre body which was a curious mixture of a smooth, slippery nose and a chopped-off back. It was glassy and modern at least, and quite practical. There were small rear seats and a detachable targa roof panel.

Like the Djet it was mid-engined

but this time power came from Ford of Germany's Taunus V4 powerplant and transaxle. The problem was this engine couldn't really deliver the performance the M530 needed to have credibility as a sportscar which was a shame as the handling and comfort of the car were excellent. The fact that it was also rather expensive cannot have helped its cause and production stopped to make way for the Bagheera in 1973.

Although its inability to deliver the power it deserved meant that the M530 hadn't got what it took to make it a truly great sports car, Matra's flawed first outing isn't without its fans, and it is still able to offer its owner a great drive.

Bagheera

1973–1980

ENGINE: Four-cylinder, 1294/1442cc

POWER: 84bhp

TRANSMISSION: Four-speed manual

CHASSIS: Separate steel chassis, fibreglass body

SUSPENSION: Independent

BRAKES: Disc all round

TOP SPEED: 100–110mph (160–176km/h)

ACCELERATION: 0–60mph (96km/h) in 12 seconds

Matra's main line of business was rocket launchers, anti-submarine weapons and satellites, but the company decided to supplement its income with sports cars from 1964 – first with the pretty Djet and the gawky M530 and then with the Bagheera, a higher-volume model announced in 1973.

If the Bagheera had one claim to fame, it was for its three-abreast seating. A wide track gave room for an extra seat in the front for a grown-up passenger – a more credible solution, reckoned Matra, than trying to squeeze in a couple of meaningless child-sized seats behind the driver and passenger.

What's more, because the Bagheera – named after the much-loved and fondly remembered black Panther in Rudyard Kipling's famous children's story *The Jungle Book* –

was a mid-engined car, there was no gearbox tunnel to clutter the floor either.

The fibreglass-bodied, steel-chassised Bagheera was the result of a liaison between Matra and Chrysler France (Simca). Its anaemic 1300cc urge was more than made up for by its sweet handling, excellent ride and very good brakes. The restyled, uprated Murena answered cries for more performance in 1980, but it was to be a short-lived successor.

Parent company Peugeot – who bought Simca from Chrysler in 1978 – sold its 45 percent shareholding in Matra to Renault, along with a project for a one-box seven-seater that became the Espace. Renault needed space to build its new people-carrier, so the Matra had to go. The last car was built in 1984.

Rancho

1977–1984

ENGINE: Four–cylinder, 1442cc

POWER: 80bhp

CHASSIS: Monocoque

BRAKES (F/R): Disc/drum

TRANSMISSION: Four-speed manual

SUSPENSION: Independent

TOP SPEED: 91mph (249km/h)

ACCELERATION: 0–60mph (96km/h) in 14.9 secs

Chrysler marketed the Matra Rancho as a 'multi-purpose leisure vehicle' and certainly its rugged Range Roverish looks suggested off-road capability.

However, the reality was that the Rancho was a clever marketing man's wheeze which, for a while, was quite the thing to be seen in if you were cruising down London's fashionable Kings Road.

Based on the Simca 1100, it only ever came with front-wheel drive and had no more off-road talent than the average family saloon. It had no high-low gear ranges, no extra ground clearance. It was all to do with image as it had no ability to be anything other than a suburban people carrier.

From the Chrysler Alpine came the 1442cc engine and front-drive power back, fitted to a lengthened

and strengthened Simca 1100 floorpan with steel front end panels and a high, chunky glassfibre rear end – built around a steel frame – not unlike the Land Rover Discovery of many years later. There were extra lights in the grille and on the front wings, plus nudge bars and body mouldings down the side to add to its macho image.

Actually the Rancho wasn't a bad car to drive on the road. It had a very sprightly performance – it was only a very little slower than the heavy, thirsty Range Rover – and reasonable ride and handling. There was also the fact that it had a huge load area in its favour too. Production finished in 1984 when all production capacity at the Matra factory was given over to the Renault Espace.

Murena

1980–1984

ENGINE: Four-cylinder, 2155cc

POWER: 118bhp

CHASSIS: Steel base unit, grp body

BRAKES (F/R): Disc

TRANSMISSION: Five-speed manual

SUSPENSION: Independent

TOP SPEED: 121mph (193km/h)

ACCELERATION: 0–60mph (96km/h) in 9.2 secs

The Bagheera had been a moderately successful car for Matra, so for the 1980s a successor was planned along the same lines, a mid-engined three-a-breast-seater with a glassfibre body.

It emerged in 1980 as the Talbot Matra Murena and featured many worthwhile improvements. It was available with a much bigger 2156cc unit (from the new Tagora saloon) alongside the basic 1592cc engine sourced from the Solara, and made very good use of a Citroen CX five-speed transmission. In designing the new body much attention had been paid to the aerodynamics of the vehicle, and for several years the Murena had the lowest Cd figure of any mid-engined production car.

The chassis was much as before with sweet steering and fine balance. The Murena was a suprisingly refined little car too, with remarkably little engine noise and a good ride.

Everything was in its favour and it looked as if the Murena was going to have a promising future. Sadly this intriguing car became a victim of the tangled web of company politics.

Peugeot sold its share holding Matra to Renault and production stopped to make way for the radical new Renault Espace 'people carrier' – although not before Matra had used up the remaining Murena bodyshells by building a high-performance 142bhp 'S' model. The last Murena was built in 1984.

Cosmo 110S

1966–1972

ENGINE: Twin rotor wankel, 2000cc

POWER: 110bhp

CHASSIS: Monocoque

BRAKES (F/R): Disc/drum

TRANSMISSION: Five-speed manual

SUSPENSION: Independent

TOP SPEED: 115mph (184km/h)

ACCELERATION: 0–60mph (96km/h) in 10.2 secondss

With the futuristic looking 1967 Cosmo 110S Mazda beat NSU into production with a twin-rotary Wankel powered production car by just a few weeks. It had been a very close race. Like the Ro80 the Cosmo was designed from the ground up to take the new engine, taking advantage of its compact dimensions and good power to weight ratio of this new type of engine. Capacity was equivalent to about 2 litres with an output of 110bhp at 7000rpm.

Rather than using peripheral ports for maximum power Mazda had its inlet ports in the casing in the name of increased low-down torque, idling smoothness and low-speed fuel consumption.

In most other respects the 110S was a conventional luxury sports coupe that handled well and was fairly quick. Top speed was a very respectable 116mph with 0-60 in about 10 seconds, revving to 7000rpm in the usual smooth, vibration-free Wankel fashion. Built until 1972, the Cosmo changed little, gaining a closer-ratio five-speed gearbox, a longer wheelbase and a little more power – 128bhp – on the 1968 'B' model.

The Cosmo name lived on in a series of rather more conventional looking saloon-based coupes and survives right up to this day as Mazda's high-tech luxury flagship vehicle.

Mazda RX3

1971–1978

ENGINE: Wankel, 1964cc

POWER: 100-110bhp

CHASSIS: Monocoque

BRAKES (F/R): Disc/drum

TRANSMISSION: Four-speed manual

SUSPENSION: Independent front, live axle rear

TOP SPEED: 102mph (165km/h)

ACCELERATION: 0–60mph (96km/h) in 10 secs

In terms of rotary engines Mazda is best known for its RX7 sportscars but for a period in the 1970s, rotary versions of all its saloons, coupes and even pick-up trucks were available with the attraction of Wankel rotary power.

No company was more committed to the design, even in the wake of NSU's fatal miscalculations with Ro80, but Mazda reckoned they had got the Wankel right and pursued all possibilities.

The RX3 was simply Mazda's lower mid-range saloon and coupe fitted with a 100bhp – or in some markets a 120bhp – in a super-smooth form thanks to the twin rotary wankel engine.

Unlike the Ro80 these Mazdas were entirely conventional, typically Japanese cars in all other respects with rear wheel drive and beam axles at the back. It had a 10mph top speed advantage over its piston engined counterpart, the 818, and had much quicker acceleration through the gears.

The trade-off was in fuel consumption. RX3 drivers would have to be very careful to get 20mpg out of their cars, which was hardly what one would have expected out of what was essentially a cheap family saloon.

There were the inevitable engine problems, of course, and Mazda's love affair with the Wankel engine had to end when the fuel crisis began to take its toll as the '70s rolled on. It left the RX7 sportscar as the lonely champion of this fascinating design.

Mazda RX7

1978–1985

ENGINE: Twin-rotor Wankel, 2292cc

POWER: 115bhp

CHASSIS: Monocoque

BRAKES (F/R): Disc/drum

TRANSMISSION: Five-speed manual

SUSPENSION: Independent front, live axle rear

TOP SPEED: 117mph (187km/h)

ACCELERATION: 0–60mph (96km/h) in 9.9 seconds

Mazda had been the lonely, but worthy, champion of the rotary internal-combustion engine for some time, with the upmarket Cosmo coupe and the RX7 sports car of 1978. By taming the reliability problems – if not the thirst – of the rotary engine, Mazda retrieved its image and made the RX into a big seller: 570,500 were sold up to the end of Mk I production in 1985. The model was replaced by the Porsche 944 look-a-like model in 1986.

The 12A rotary engine – good for 100,000 miles – was equivalent to 2292cc, and was rated at 115bhp, giving a swift 120mph (192km/h) top speed. No one could deny that these were fairly impressive figures.

The svelte, two-plus-two body,

with its lifting glass hatchback, clothed otherwise conventional hardware, consisting of rear-wheel drive and a live axle.

But buyers got a five-speed gearbox, four-wheel disc brakes and labour-saving equipment such as electric windows and mirrors as part of the standard package. The RX7 was a great success, particularly in the USA, but later models proved more difficult to sell in the face of opposition from Porsche.

In the late 1990s, unable to make the silky rotary engine truly economical – something of a crime in these ecologically minded times – Mazda was on the point of returning entirely to conventional piston engines.

Mazda MX5

1988–

ENGINE: Four-cylinder, 1598cc

POWER: 114bhp

CHASSIS: Monocoque

BRAKES (F/R): Disc

TRANSMISSION: Five-speed manual

SUSPENSION: Independent

TOP SPEED: 114mph (182km/h)

ACCELERATION: 0–60mph (96km/h) in 9.5 seconds

With the MX5, Mazda proved to the other big car manufacturers of the world that small, relatively cheap sportscars could be built in large numbers again profitably. Not for the first time, the company had an important and worthwhile lesson to teach the rest of the industry.

Five or six years after its introduction MG, Fiat, Alfa Romeo, BMW, Porsche and even Mercedes were back in the running with small, reasonably affordable roadsters inspired by the success of the little Mazda. No one can deny that the MX5 has had a huge impact on the market and a development of the new range of affordable sportscars.

Its designers looked to the Lotus Elan for inspiration when creating the 1989 MX5, although it was always intended to be a much more durable machine than the fragile Lotus. This was a sportscar for people who were used to the comforts of modern saloons – a car with a proper heater, impeccable weather protection and a comfortable ride.

Yet it retained all the desirable aspects of sportscar driving, like a raspy exhaust note and truly excellent responsive handling that hasn't been significantly bettered by the younger and often faster opposition. The MX5 was re-skinned for 1998 – losing its pop-up headlights in the process – but the car remained essentially unchanged. It is difficult to improve a car that is already just about ideal.

McLaren F1

1994–1998

ENGINE: V12, 6064cc

POWER: 627bhp

CHASSIS: Monocoque

BRAKES (F/R): Disc

TRANSMISSION: Six-speed manual

SUSPENSION: Independent

TOP SPEED: 231mph (370km/h)

ACCELERATION: 0–60mph (96km/h) in 3.2 seconds

As an ultimate road car, there is still little to challenge the McLaren F1. Designer Gordon Murray, the man behind McLaren's Formula One cars, had a long-held ambition to build a road car – the fastest and most exciting yet – that was also docile enough to drive in town. His vision called for a dramatic, mid-engined three-seater, with the driver sitting in the middle, and a very low weight of 1000kg (2200lb). Lotus Elan stylist Peter Stevens was commissioned to create the car's shape, whilst BMW Motorsport agreed to design an all-new 627bhp, 6064cc, four-cam V12 engine from scratch.

The result was a 231mph (370km/h) projectile capable of 0–60mph (96km/h) in 3.2 seconds and 0–100mph (160km/h) in 6.3 seconds. Priced at £635,000, it was a hugely man-hour-intensive car to produce, and featured many space-age materials in its construction – not to mention gold leaf! Even at that price, however, it was probably uneconomical to make. Not surprisingly, the F1 was almost invincible on the track. The F1 GTR came first in every GT Endurance race for which it was entered except for two, while the F1 was triumphant at the Le Mans 24hrs in 1995.

Only 100 F1s were built, a third of the originally projected number, as many of the buyers who had originally put their names down for the car had melted away. Production ended in late 1997.

Mercedes 300SL

1954–1963

ENGINE: In-line six-cylinder, 2996cc

POWER: 240bhp

CHASSIS: Tubular space-frame

BRAKES (F/R): Drum (Gullwing)

TRANSMISSION: Four-speed manual

SUSPENSION: Independent

TOP SPEED: 130–150mph (208–240km/h)

ACCELERATION: 0–60mph (96km/h) in 8.8 seconds

One of the most sensational sports cars of the 1950s was the original 155mph (248km/h) Mercedes 300SL 'Gullwing' coupe. It was startling and rightly famous for with its unique roof-hinged door. It was launched in February 1954, although the Le Mans-winning prototypes had already been given a sneak preview in 1952.

The body – built in steel with alloy panels – was supported by a complex space-frame of tubes not seen before or since on a road car. Under the bonnet was an advanced, fuel-injected, overhead-cam, 240bhp, 3-litre engine which was canted over so as to keep the bonnet-line low.

This engine was derived from the straight-six unit used in the big 300 saloons. However, it was the first engine to pioneer the today standard use of fuel injection in road-going cars.

The 300SL had its problems, however. Suspect swing-axle rear suspension needed an expert to tame it if the SL was to be driven to the limit of its capabilities. Perhaps more significantly, the body was prone to leaks, and the space-frame construction was difficult to repair, making the car unpopular with Mercedes dealers.

Thus the Gullwing coupe was replaced, after 1,400 units had been produced, by the 1957 roadster – a successful attempt to make the 300SL easier to live with. Low-pivot swing axles made the roadholding far more predictable, whilst the light-alloy 3-litre engine was tuned to give more torque.

The roadster proved even more popular than the Gullwing. Some 1,858 examples found rich owners by the time production finished in 1963 to make way for the far-less-specialized 230SL.

Mercedes 220SE Fintail

1958–68

ENGINE: Six-cylinder, 2195

POWER: 110bhp

CHASSIS: Monocoque

BRAKES (F/R): Disc/drum

TRANSMISSION: Four-speed manual/auto

SUSPENSION: Independent

TOP SPEED: 105mph (168 km/h)

ACCELERATION: 0-60mph (96km/h) in 13 seconds

The 'fintails' were a whole range of midrange saloons built by Mercedes between 1959 and 1968. They comprised everything from plodding Diesel Taxi cabs to wonderfully swift and luxurious 300 SELs with air suspension.

Somewhere in the middle came the 220SE, which in many ways was the best fintail of the lot. Its injected 2195cc looked like it had a lot of work to do in these big cars, yet it was such a willing performer that the 220SE always felt as if it was a fairly quick machine.

The bodyshape seemed to age quickly, probably because of the fins which had almost gone out of fashion by the time the car was announced. Yet it had a certain charm, and it was one of the first cars to feature crumple zones or any kind of serious attention to crash protection.

Mercedes were very much in love with swing axles when the 220 was born but like all Fintails it had the low pivot type which managed to keep the handling in check nicely. The handsome W111 coupes and cabriolets were based on the Fintail floorpan and a few Universal Estates were also built by a company in Belgium.

The Fintail survival rate is quite high. This only goes to prove the excellent durability of the design. Not surprisingly given modern trends, the cars are now very collectable.

230-250-280 SL

1963–71

ENGINE: Straight six, 2306-2778cc

POWER: 150-170bhp

CHASSIS: Monocoque

BRAKES (F/R): Disc/drum, later all disc

TRANSMISSION: Four/five-speed manual, four-speed auto

SUSPENSION: Independent

TOP SPEED: 120-127mph (192-203km/h)

ACCELERATION: 0-60mph (96km/h) in 9.9 seconds

Few other classic '60s convertibles have had the enduring appeal of the SL Mercedes. Somehow its styling seems timelessly elegant, undating. You don't have to look at one of these cars very long to appreciate the excellence of the build quality.

Swift and very comfortable, the SL was a sportscar without the pain. This fact alone makes it something of a rare breed, both for cars in its time and for recently produced vehicles.

Its hood was water tight, its well-styled hardtop as solid as a fixed roof when in position. It had a proper heater, an automatic gearbox – the manual was optional – and a soft, comfortable ride. SL stood for 'Super Light' but all these SLs were heavy cars, built to last a long time.

The bodyshape hardly changed at all during the production run. However, mechanically the car was gently massaged at regular intervals, just to keep it up-to-date with the little refinements that are always trickling through the automobile industry.

The original 230SL became the 250SL in 1966 with more torque, all-round disc brakes and power steering as standard. Best of the lot was the 280SL of 1968 with a 170bhp engine with seven main bearings. The top speed had risen from 120mph to 127mph, but surprisingly it is the earlier cars that have a sportier feel. Given its all-round quality and strength, the SL has a well-deserved and enduring reputation for being the type of apsirational car typical of the best of Mercedes.

Mercedes 600

1963–1981

ENGINE: V8, 6332cc

POWER: 250bhp

CHASSIS: Monocoque

BRAKES (F/R): Disc

TRANSMISSION: Four-speed automatic

SUSPENSION: Independent

TOP SPEED: 123mph (197km/h)

ACCELERATION: 0–60mph (96km/h) in 9.7 seconds

The Mercedes 600 was the world's greatest saloon in the 1960s. It wasn't just technically accomplished and superbly comfortable, but it was fun to drive as well. The car came in two forms. There was a standard-wheelbase (126in., 320cm) four-door. However, for heads of state or those who acted as if they were heads of state, there was the Pullman, its wheelbase stretched to 153in. (389cm), and available with the option of six doors, extra occasional seats and a glass division between the front and rear compartments. Both mere mortal and world leader versions used a 6.3-litre, fuel-injected V8 producing 300bhp, driving through a four-speed automatic transmission.

The suspension used air bags on all four wheels instead of steel springs. This was powered by an under-bonnet pump, for a firm, but comfortable ride. Seat adjustment, steering power assistance and the door locks were connected to a central hydraulic system.

Despite its enormous weight – 5500lb (2500kg) for the saloon, 5850lb (2659kg) for the eight-seater Pullman – the 600 was no barge – it would top 120mph (192km/h) and storm its way up to 60mph (96km/h) in not much more than 10 seconds, although the penalty was dreadful fuel consumption. Handling, too, was surprisingly nimble, with good power steering, plenty of grip and brakes (large four-wheel discs) that were beyond reproach. Hugely expensive and hand-built in tiny numbers, the 600 stayed on the Mercedes price lists until 1981, and had no effective replacement.

300SEL 6.3

1968–1972

ENGINE: V8, 6332cc

POWER: 250bhp

CHASSIS: Monocoque

BRAKES (F/R): Discs

TRANSMISSION: Four-speed auto

SUSPENSION: Independent

TOP SPEED: 135mph (216km/h)

ACCELERATION: 0-60mph (96km/h) in 6.8 seconds

By shoe-horning its biggest and most powerful engine into its second biggest saloon bodyshell Mercedes created a hot-rod saloon with no equals in the late '60s – the 300SEL 6.3. The V8 engine came from the big 600 Grosser limousine which was no slouch itself with this hugely torquey engine. However, in a much lighter, more wieldy S-Class body the results of this union were electrifying.

This was especially true in terms of acceleration. The 300SEL 6.3 driver could turn-in sub-seven second 0-60 times – better than an E-Type Jaguar, not to mention several Ferraris – simply by slipping its automatic gearbox selector in drive and pressing the accelerator. No fuss, no drama.

The top speed was somewhere near 140mph but what mattered more was its huge mid-range punch and high speed refinement, its supple ride and its typically immaculate Mercedes fit and finish. The 300SEL body meant you got the longest S-Class shell with MBs well proven air suspension for a great ride, although the car as whole was never as silken as, say, a V12 Jaguar.

Perhaps the car's only real drawback was its fuel consumption, which could become frightening when the V8 was used in anger. Which was why, in the midst of the fuel crisis, Mercedes didn't create an immediate equivalent to the 6.3 in the new S-Class range of 1973 – despite all of the points so strongly in its favour. One can only wonder what shape that vehicle would have taken.

280SE Cabriolet

1969–1971

ENGINE: V8, 3499cc

POWER: 200bhp

CHASSIS: Monocoque

BRAKES (F/R): Disc

TRANSMISSION: Four-speed manual

SUSPENSION: Independent

TOP SPEED: 127mph (203km/h)

ACCELERATION: 0-60mph (96km/h) in 9.0 seconds

The 280SE Cabriolet was the last big Mercedes Convertible for many years. It was also the last of a long line of W111/W112 series dropheads models. This was a line that date all the way back to back to the early 1960s.

The 280SE is a much rarer car than most people realise in fact. It comes as something of a shock to learn it was only built for two years and just a couple of thousand were produced. They were very expensive cars and much hand finishing was required in their production.

This was the first car to get M-B's new overhead camshaft fuel injected V8, a flexible and smooth engine that made a perfect match with the standard automatic transmission. It made the cabriolet a fast 127mph car, and thus one of the fastest open four seaters – proper four seaters – around.

Although dated by the turn of the '60s its lines still looked graceful and well balanced and featured a slightly lower, squatter grille than the earlier six-cylinder versions. Air suspension was a feature of the 300SE cabriolet, but this was rejected for the 3.5-litre 280SE which had conventional steel springs for its suspension.

So rare and desirable was the 280SE that in real terms, as a mere secondhand car, it has never really depreciated. This means the survival rate is good and prices remain strong.

Mercedes 450SEL 6.9

1975–1980

ENGINE: V8, 6834cc

POWER: 286bhp

CHASSIS: Monocoque

BRAKES (F/R: Disc

TRANSMISSION: Three-speed automatic

SUSPENSION: Independent

TOP SPEED: 140mph (224km/h)

ACCELERATION: 0–60mph (96km/h) in 7.3 seconds

In the best Mercedes tradition, little betrayed the increased power of this ultimate Benz to the outside world. There was just a discreet 6.9 badge in the corner of the bootlid, slightly fatter alloy wheels and a bigger-bore exhaust.

Yet the 450SEL 6.9 was probably the finest and fastest saloon you could buy in the late-1970s, combining the latest S-Class long-wheelbase shell with a beefed-up version of Merc's biggest 6.3-litre V8 engine originally from the 600 limousine. Bored out to give 6834cc, power soared up to 286bhp and torque to a huge 405lb ft at 3000rpm.

This substantial power went through a three-speed automatic transmission, and with zero-offset geometry at the front and semi trailing arms at the back, the 6.9 handled superbly, aided by direct, well-weighted power steering and vented disc brakes.

Hauling more weight and with a higher-ratio top gear than the old 300SEL 6.3, the 450SEL wasn't as violently quick off the mark (0–60mph (96km/h) in 7.4 seconds, against the 6.3's 6.9 seconds). However, it managed an increased top speed of 140mph (224km/h) with an even stronger pull above the magic ton. Relaxed 130mph (208km/h) cruising was a reality in the 450SEL.

Although it was typically gimmick-free inside, 450SEL owners wanted for nothing. Air conditioning, power windows, headlamp wash/wipe and central locking were all standard. If you wanted, you could opt for leather to replace velour cloth on the firmly upholstered seats. Production ended in 1980 with output standing at 7,380 units.

Mercedes | 500SEC

1981–1991

ENGINE: V8, 4973cc

POWER: 240bhp

CHASSIS: Steel monocoque, two-door

BRAKES (F/R): Disc

TRANSMISSION: Four-speed automatic

SUSPENSION: Springs and wishbones front, independent rear

TOP SPEED: 140mph (224km/h)

ACCELERATION: 0-60mph (96km/h) in 7.6 seconds

Mercedes' high standards of engineering have been admired since before the Second World War, but they reached something of a peak during the 1980s. Its top-line S-class car of that era had a feeling of imperturbability that can only have come from the highest-quality materials engineered into the highest-quality overall whole.

In 1981, Mercedes launched the coupe-bodied SEC, which was based on the running gear of the S-class limousine that had been launched the year before. The SEC was an exceptionally attractive car, and decisively more modern than the outgoing coupe. The elegant, pillarless body survived unchanged for ten years, and proved a great inspiration to other car stylists. Mercedes' use of expansive, but gently curved, bodywork sections and very wide-radius corners gave the car a feeling of great solidity and integral quality. The approach was much copied.

Less easy to copy was Mercedes' engineering. The 5.0-litre V8 in the 500 would, even now, be regarded as a world-class powerplant. Never more than a distant thrum, even at high autobahn speeds, it simultaneously felt unburstable and unobtrusive.

Where many manufacturers were driving the engines of their executives through the relative crudity of a three-speed automatic gearbox, Mercedes had a four-speed unit with the option of both 'economy' and 'sport' modes of operation. The shift quality was unmatched for smoothness and responsiveness.

The chassis was also a gem – taut handling at all speeds, and still comfortable. Like all Mercedes, the interior layout was exceptional – clear, verging on the over-simple. There are few, if any, cars that will wear a decade of ageing and a six-figure mileage as well as the SEC.

190 Series

1982–1993

ENGINE: 16-valve in-line four-cylinder, 2299cc

POWER: 185bhp

CHASSIS: Steel monocoque, four-door

BRAKES (F/R): Disc with ABS

TRANSMISSION: Five-speed manual

SUSPENSION: Springs and wishbones front, five-link independent rear

TOP SPEED: 144mph (230km/h)

ACCELERATION: 0–62.5mph (100km/h) in 8.3 seconds

It seems extraordinary now, but there was much fuss and resistance from Mercedes-Benz die-hards when news began to leak out about the imminent arrival of the 'baby Benz' – a baby that was actually only 1in. (2.5cm) shorter than a Ford Sierra.

The Mercedes 190 was revealed in late-1982, bringing with it a remarkable level of advanced engineering. On offer were a very crashworthy body, ABS brakes, airbags, anti-submarining seats and advanced five-link rear suspension. It would be ten years before Ford launched a similarly sized car – the Mondeo – with the same array of features.

Despite scaling down, Mercedes didn't skimp on the 190's level of quality and engineering integrity. Even better, the much-admired Mercedes method of styling a body surface in clean, long-radius sections was taken further.

The early 190 range was modestly powered by 2.0-litre petrol and 2.5-litre diesel engines. By mid-1985 Mercedes had taken the courageous decision to design an outright sporting saloon. To develop sufficient power, Mercedes commissioned UK race-engine specialists Cosworth to design and manufacture a 16-valve cylinder head for the 2.3-litre four-cylinder engine.

A bigger shock for the conservative Mercedes buyer was the 190 2.3-16's body kit, which consisted of cladding on the doors, sill covers, much deeper bumpers and a pronounced boot spoiler. The suspension was lowered moderately, and a manual gearbox with a dog-leg first gear fitted.

Although peaky in its torque delivery, the Cosworth was much admired for its excellent chassis and very sweet-revving engine – as well as for the restrained, yet expressive, body kit. There are few better candidates for future classic status.

Mercedes 500SL

1989–2001

ENGINE: 32-valve V8, 4973cc

POWER: 326bhp

CHASSIS: Steel monocoque, two-seat convertible

BRAKES (F/R): Disc with ABS

TRANSMISSION: Four-speed automatic

SUSPENSION: Spring strut front, five-link independent rear

TOP SPEED: 161mph (258km/h)

ACCELERATION: 0–60mph (96km/h) in 6.3 seconds

Combine the ground-breaking leap in technology of the 190 and the build quality and timeless styling of the SEC coupes, and you would still not have the measure of the impact that Mercedes' all-new SL made at its launch in 1989.

The styling was extremely simple, yet subtle touches (especially around the shovel-nosed front end) gave the SL a remarkable stance and road presence. Mercedes' chief stylist said that the SL was greatly influenced by wind-tunnel work, and that the shape was changed many times during development.

Inside, Mercedes' standard dashboard simplicity was enhanced by lavishing some fine industrial design on the switchgear and trim. Looking at the car more than a decade after it was launched, it seems almost impossible that the SL project started out in 1981.

Safety has to be a major concern with a cabriolet, and Mercedes moved the goalposts with the SL's innovative active safety package. The car had a substantial roll-bar, which would flip up into position within 0.3 seconds of an impact, or when the wheels became airborne. Also designed to protect occupants were the massive seat structures (including integral seatbelts and headrests) – cast in one piece from magnesium, and part of the body's structural integrity. The hood was electric and could be raised and lowered in 30 seconds.

A wide range of engines – six-, eight- and 12-cylinder units – did little to make the SL a sports car of mass appeal. It was too expensive, but promised an exceptionally long life of outstanding driving pleasure. SLs were often the choice personal transport of the world's greatest professional racing drivers.

500E

1990–1996

ENGINE: V8, 4973cc

POWER: 326bhp

CHASSIS: Steel monocoque, four-door

BRAKES (F/R): Disc with ABS

TRANSMISSION: Four-speed automatic

SUSPENSION: Springs and wishbone front, five-link independent rear

TOP SPEED: 155mph (248km/h), limited

ACCELERATION: 0–62.5mph (100km/h) in 5.9 seconds

The high-performance 'family' car frenzy of the early 1990s was so pronounced that Britain's *CAR* magazine followed the report on its first drive of the 377bhp Lotus Carlton with two pages on the Mercedes equivalent, the 326bhp V8-engined E-class saloon. Like the Lotus Carlton, the 500E required some serious surgery under the standard-issue body and, like General Motors, Mercedes farmed the project out – in this case to Porsche.

Rather than spend time radically modifying the engine to fit in an ex-factory car, Mercedes fitted an ex-factory engine into a heavily modified bodyshell. The entire front section of the car had to be redesigned in order to accommodate the V8 powerplant, and heavier-gauge steel was used for better crash performance. Outwardly, the only clue was the flared wheelarches, which allowed for a wider front track. Two massive catalytic converters under the floor meant that the 500E's transmission tunnel had to be widened – the upshot was that the car had to be homologated as a four-seater.

The suspension and braking systems were pretty much carried over from the SL sports car, with some modifications including ASR – one of the first sophisticated traction-control systems. Thanks to the massive competence of the chassis, and help from ASR, the 500E was described at the time as a 'can do no wrong' car. It was extremely fast, rode surprisingly well, had exceptional roadholding, but was remarkably easy to drive flat out. Unfortunately, this limited the beautifully built 500E's non-autobahn repertoire to the role of 'king of the overtaking manoeuvre'.

Mercedes SLK

1994–

ENGINE: Supercharged in-line four-cylinder, 2295cc

POWER: 193bhp

CHASSIS: Steel monocoque

BRAKES: Disc with ABS

TRANSMISSION: Five-speed manual or automatic

SUSPENSION: Double wishbones front, independent multi-link rear

TOP SPEED: 142mph (227km/h)

ACCELERATION: 0–62.5mph (100km/h) in 7.9 seconds

The launch of the SL proved that Mercedes' grip of leading-edge technology was close to unrivalled – but then so was the Mercedes price list. The decision was made by the company that it could no longer indulge in 'cost-no-object' engineering. Mercedes also decided that it would have to diversify its model range dramatically.

The first evidence of the company's new approach was the SLK roadster concept at the Turin Show in the spring of 1994. Sport, Licht, Klein – sporting, light and small – the SLK had to carve a tricky path: that of providing traditional Mercedes innovation with high standards of build quality at a more affordable price.

There were no half-measures in the innovation department. Mercedes developed a hard-top that could fold away electrically into the boot. In action, it was a show-stopping feat of technical genius. It

also meant the SLK had the security and refinement that a hard-top brings, until it was converted into an open-top roadster.

The SLK was a pretty car – clearly a Mercedes, but somehow much more modern. It had a wonderfully compact and muscular look with its roof raised. Inside, the dashboard and switchgear seemed to have lost nothing over those in the much more costly SL.

It was never over-praised as a driving machine. Even in 193bhp supercharged Kompressor form, it felt a little stolid and unexciting – especially in the UK, where it was only available with automatic transmission. The droning engine note of the Kompressor engine wasn't inspirational either. Not that these small downsides mattered. The waiting list for the car was lengthy, and its desirability unchallenged.

A-class

1997–

ENGINE: In-line four-cylinder, 1595cc

POWER: 102bhp

CHASSIS: Steel monocoque, five-door

BRAKES: Disc with ABS

TRANSMISSION: Five-speed manual

SUSPENSION: Struts front, independent rear

TOP SPEED: 111mph (178km/h)

ACCELERATION: 0–60mph (96km/h) in 9.9 seconds

Mercedes' decision to apply its engineering genius to totally new formats – rather than the further refinement of established designs – saw its ultimate realization with the A-class. The supermini segment is the largest in the European market, and the old, premium-priced Mercedes wasn't remotely involved.

So when Mercedes decided to build a congestion-friendly mini-car, it had to overcome two fundamental problems before the car could wear the three-pointed star: first, it had to be very safe; second, it had to be properly spacious. Designing a supermini that is as safe as a compact executive car and just as roomy seems an impossible contradiction. Mercedes, though, came up with a format that can truly be called revolutionary.

One of the biggest problems in a head-on crash is the damage caused by the engine being driven into the cabin. To get around this,

Mercedes designed a double-decker floorpan and mounted the engine block at 45 degrees. In an accident, the engine and transmission are forced under the passengers' feet. The extraordinary roominess of the A-class comes from a subtle working of the flat floor, upright seating and the ability to place the front passengers nearer the nose.

But Mercedes' massive feat was shattered mid-launch by news that a motoring magazine had rolled an A-class during a test. After bluffing for a week or two, the mighty Benz succumbed, admitted there was a problem, and redesigned the rear suspension.

But the fundamentals remained. The A-class was – like the Austin Mini when it was launched in the 1950s – the shape of future European motoring, and one of the most significant cars ever made.

M-class

1997–

ENGINE: 18-valve V6, 3199cc

POWER: 215bhp

CHASSIS: Steel monocoque, front and rear sub-frames, five-door

BRAKES (F/R): Disc with ABS

TRANSMISSION: Five-speed automatic

SUSPENSION: Wishbones and torsion bars front, wishbones and coils rear

TOP SPEED: 112mph (179km/h), limited

ACCELERATION: 0–60mph (96km/h) in 9.3 seconds

Mercedes watched the boom in the 4x4 market – especially in the USA, where some three million sport utility vehicles (SUVs) were being sold annually by the late-1990s. The company did build an off-roader, but the low-run G-Wagen was an uncompromising semi-military vehicle in the mould of the Land Rover Defender.

The M-class, another part of Mercedes' dash for diversification, was designed to enter the booming sector and to succeed by addressing the problems inherent in the majority of 4x4 designs. Because most were tall vehicles based on old-fashioned separate chassis technology, they handled poorly, could be unrefined and in some circumstances less safe in a crash than conventional monocoque-bodied vehicles.

The M-class steered a middle course through the contradictions of the 4x4 genre (they were designed for excellence off-road, but used

exclusively on-road) by being lower and having a longer wheelbase than the norm. And although it hadn't dispensed completely with a separate chassis (the M-class used giant sub-frames front and rear), Mercedes made sure the crash performance was up to scratch. Space-efficient design meant room for a third row of fold-down seats – something the opposition couldn't manage at the time.

Built in Mercedes' factory in Alabama in the USA, the M-class was a huge hit right from the launch. The Benz badge helped, but it was also a class above rivals in that it combined the looks, utility and ruggedness of a 4x4 with near-carlike levels of handling. Even more surprising was the Mercedes' pricing, which managed to undercut (with a few quality compromises) the opposition – massively in the case of the Range Rover, previously the unchallenged king of the off-road scene.

Mercedes Smart

1998–

ENGINE: Turbocharged in-line three-cylinder, 600cc

POWER: 55bhp

CHASSIS: Steel monocoque, composite body panels, three-door

BRAKES (F/R): Disc with ABS

TRANSMISSION: Six-speed sequential shift

SUSPENSION: Transverse leaf and wishbones front, multi-link and de Dion rear

TOP SPEED: 84mph (134km/h)

ACCELERATION: 0–62.5mph (100km/h) in 17.9 seconds

Mercedes' diversification didn't stop at the re-definition of the supermini. In conjunction with Swiss watchmaker Swatch, the company attempted to invent a car that would be ideal for congested inner-city commuting, making sense of the fact that the majority of motorists drive solo.

The Smart car project was a huge risk, and one into which Mercedes invested over £1 billion. A completely new factory was built at Hambach in France, using a radical new method of construction: suppliers created large 'sub-assemblies', which underwent final assembly at the factory.

Like the A-class, the Smart was designed to be extremely safe, and was based around a three-layer, steel 'Tridion' safety cage capped with removable composite body panels. Potential transmission-intrusion into the cabin during a head-on crash was solved by placing it under the floor at the rear, from where it could power the wheels.

Inside, the interior design was modern and bright, with plenty of post-modernist detailing such as brightly coloured knobs on the heater controls and the customized mini-Grundig stereo.

Just before the launch, a quiet disaster struck. The infamous 'Elk test' (a sudden swerve at speed to simulate avoiding an elk) that caught out the A-class also hit the Smart. The rear suspension was redesigned, and it was rumoured to have cost Mercedes (who by now owned 80 percent of the Micro Car Company) £100m, putting the planned annual 200,000 output on the edge of profitability.

The Smart got off to a slow start in Europe and the project was losing money. However, sales began to pick-up after the turn of the century and Mercedes announced it would expand the Smart line-up with a conventional supermini and a new roadster based on the City coupe.

Cougar

1967–1970

ENGINE: V8, 3311-7016cc

POWER: 210-335bhp

CHASSIS: Monocoque

BRAKES (F/R): Disc/drum

TRANSMISSION: Three-four-speed manual/Three-speed auto

SUSPENSION: Independent front, live axle rear

TOP SPEED: 130mph (208km/h)

ACCELERATION: 0–60mph (96km/h) in 10 seconds

The Cougar was just the lift Ford's unexciting mid-market Mercury division needed in 1967. Essentially it was another variation on the pony car theme, a stretched Ford Mustang Hardtop with some extra luxury touches to give it a more sophisticated image.

Buyers flocked to Mercury showrooms to buy Cougars. More than 150,000 were sold in the first year of production and Mercury's image was revived with positive knock-on effects on the rest of the range.

Hide-away headlights and full width sequential tail lights gave the car an air of power but the lines were clean and well balanced.

Mechanically there was nothing new. The Cougar came with a range of V8s that grew from a mild 3.3 litre to a huge 7 litre GT-E developing 335bhp. You could have 3 or 4 speed manuals or a 3 speed automatic, the latter being the most usual fitment. Top of the line was the XR-7 model with more chrome and flashier wheel trims than its sister cars, and a fancier interior that included a walnut instrument panel.

Inevitably after a few seasons the clean looking Cougar degenerated into just another grotesque outsize 'personal luxury' car.

KR 200

1955–1964

ENGINE: 200cc, four-cylinder OHC

POWER: 10bhp

CHASSIS: Tubular space frame

BRAKES (F/R): Drum

TRANSMISSION: Four-speed manual

SUSPENSION: Transverse arms front, swinging arm rear

TOP SPEED: 62mph (99km/h)

ACCELERATION: 0-50mph (0-80km/h) in 49 seconds

After the Second World War a German aircraft engineer called Fritz Fend found himself out of work. He turned to making invalid carriages for injured pilots and developed a three-wheeler, constructed on a tubular space frame with such unorthodox features as handlebar steering, compressed rubber suspension and cable-operated brakes. It also had just one seat. Fend wanted to enlarge it to take two seats in tandem, and he managed to persuade that other great German warplane manufacturer Messerschmitt to use their dormant factory to build it.

The result was the Kabinenroller, a two-seater, three-wheeler with handlebar steering and a meagre 173cc engine driving the back wheel. For access it had a Plexiglass roof which lifted up to the side to allow you to climb in.

In 1955 a larger 200cc engine was fitted and the KR200 was born, capable of 62mph, fairly impressive for its size. The engine was reversible, meaning, in essence, that you could select one of four reverse gears if you really wanted to. The ride was slightly improved by the introduction of torsional rubber bushes and the shape became more sleek with a curved-glass windscreen.

A convertible was introduced in 1956 and production of the KR200 continued until 1964, when falling interest in microcars brought about Messerschmitt's demise.

1949–1955

ENGINE: In-line four, 1250cc

POWER: 54 bhp

CHASSIS: Separate steel chassis

BRAKES (F/R): Disc

TRANSMISSION: Four-speed manual

SUSPENSION: Beam axles (TC)

TOP SPEED: 78mph (124km/h)

ACCELERATION: 0–60mph (96km/h) in 19 seconds (TC)

The MG TC gave the Americans a taste for nippy European Sportscars that they never lost. However, after WWII the cheap and cheerful TC, a revised pre-war model, spearheaded the British export drive to the States – and that's where most of the 10,000 car production run ended-up.

Charming as it was, the out-dated TC couldn't go on for ever so for 1949 MG introduced the TD – same chassis, same 1250cc four-cylinder engine but with the new independent front suspension and the rack and pinion steering of the YA saloon. Bumpers front and rear and smaller disc wheels didn't do much for the looks but the TD was roomier and slightly faster, especially in higher compression MkII form from 1952. The TD was a big seller racking-up 29,664 units in its four year production run.

The final flowering of the 'traditional' MG was the TF of 1953. By moulding the headlamps into the front wings, sloping the grille and fuel tank, Abingdon had gently modernised the shape. Inside there were individual front seats for the first time and a restyled dashboard. Early cars had the 1250cc engine, but from 1954 a 1500cc unit giving 63bhp was added to restore some of the performance.

The TF was really a holding operation while Abingdon prepared its first modern post-war model, the MGA of 1955.

MG

MGA

1955–1962

ENGINE: In-line four-cylinder, 1489/1588/1622cc

POWER: 72–108bhp

CHASSIS: Separate steel chassis

BRAKES(F/R): Drum/disc-drum/all-disc

TRANSMISSION: Four-speed manual

SUSPENSION: Beam axles

TOP SPEED: 95–110mph (152–176km/h)

ACCELERATION: 0–60mph (96km/h) in 13 seconds (1600)

The MGA is probably the best-looking MG of them all. Its pretty, pinched-waist body was derived from a special TD raced at Le Mans, and was based on an enormously strong box-section chassis. The 'A' was the first truly modern post-war MG, and, as the first new MG produced after the merger of Nuffield and Austin, it was also the first to use components from the corporate parts bin – much of the drive-train being derived from the Austin A50 saloon.

There was nothing ground-breaking about the suspension, with its front wishbones and leaf-sprung rear beam axle, yet the handling of the A was more than a match for many of its illustrious contemporaries. A top speed of 95mph (152km/h) was deemed fairly respectable, as was the potential 30mpg (9.5litres/100km) fuel consumption from the workman-like B-series engine.

The roadster was joined by a handsome coupe version in 1956,

and in 1958 by the exciting 110mph (176km/h) twin-cam, producing 108bhp. It was available in coupe and roadster forms, and could be spotted by its handsome Dunlop, centre-lock, lightweight steel wheels. Dunlop disc brakes on all four wheels were standard. High prices and its reputation for poor reliability kept sales low, and the British Motor Corporation (BMC) killed off this most exotic of MGs in 1960.

By that time the standard MGA had become the 1600, with 80bhp, front disc brakes and genuine 100mph (160km/h) ability. The only outward difference, aside from badging, was the separate rear indicators. The final Mk II 1600 of 1961 had a slightly bigger-bore 1622cc engine, pushing the power output to 86bhp. You can spot one by its recessed front grille and horizontal rear lights. Production finished in 1962, giving way to the MGB.

MGB

1962–1980

ENGINE: Four-cylinder, 1798cc

POWER: 95bhp

CHASSIS: Monocoque

BRAKES (F/R): Disc/drum

TRANSMISSION: Four-speed manual with overdrive

SUSPENSION: Independent front, live axle rear

TOP SPEED: 106mph (170km/h)

ACCELERATION: 0–60mph (96km/h) in 12 seconds

The main difference between the 1962 MGB and its forebear, the 'A', was in construction – gone was the rugged and heavy separate chassis, replaced by a lighter, unitary-construction shell.

The car appeared originally as an open roadster, with a 95bhp version of the B-Series 1798cc four-cylinder engine. Suspension, steering and rear axle came straight from the British Motor Corporation (BMC) parts bin, but the 'B' was a genuine 100mph (160km/h) car with safe handling. It was joined by the Pininfarina-inspired BGT in 1965, with its tailgate rear door and occasional rear seat.

Mk II models from 1967 had the improved rear axle, as well as an all-synchromesh gearbox and the option of automatic transmission. Fashion dictated some minor styling tweaks in 1969, in the form of a recessed matt-black grille and trendy Rostyle wheels.

There was much worse to come, however... In 1974, MG announced the 'black-bumper' cars, with grotesque plastic bumpers and an increased ride height designed to keep the ageing model legal in the USA, where most of the production still went. Performance was inferior and the handling was ruined by its new taller stance, but the car continued to sell, as it was one of the few open cars still available.

In fact the B, one of the best-selling sports cars ever, was to survive until 1980 with few changes, and it seemed likely it would be the last proper MG sports car when British Leyland announced its decision to abandon the famous Abingdon factory.

MG | MGF

1995–

ENGINE: In-line four-cylinder, variable valve timed, 1791cc

POWER: 143bhp

CHASSIS: Steel monocoque, convertible

BRAKES (F/R): Disc

TRANSMISSION: Five-speed manual

SUSPENSION: Interconnected gas spheres and lower wishbones

TOP SPEED: 126mph (201km/h)

ACCELERATION: 0–62 mph (100km/h) in 7.9 seconds

When the loss-making MG factory was closed by British Leyland (BL) bosses in 1980, there was a huge outcry from enthusiasts. The closure even led to at least one failed attempt to stage a rescue. However, the sad reality was that the MGB that was then being made at the time was an ancient car. It was a dinosaur and it should have been replaced with something more suited to the time several years before.

Although sporty MG-badged versions of BL's mainstream saloons and hatchbacks started appearing three years later, there was a real desire in the industry to see the marque revived with a real sports car. This desire eventually found expression as the appearance of the MG E-XE concept car demonstrated.

In the early 1990s, the cash-strapped Rover board gave the go-ahead for a small, mid-engined two-seater, making clever use of existing components and based substantially on the Rover Metro. It also used the Metro's excellent inter-connected gas suspension and front-wheel-drive powertrain mounted behind the cabin. The styling was in keeping with the MGB – pretty, but conservative.

The MGF proved to be a very capable sports car indeed. The 1.8-litre K-series engine was responsive and punchy, and the mid-engine chassis made it easy to drive the car hard. With the clever and powerful VVC K-series, it was even better. The small-scale nature of the project meant that the MGF would never be sold in the USA, traditionally the biggest market for MGs.

Minor

1959–2000

ENGINE: Transverse four-cylinder, 848/970/997/998/1071/1098/ 1275cc

POWER: 33–76bhp

CHASSIS: Monocoque

BRAKES (F/R): Drum and disc/drum

TRANSMISSION: Four-speed manual, four-speed automatic

SUSPENSION: Independent

TOP SPEED: 74–96mph (118–154km/h)

ACCELERATION: 0–60mph (96km/h) in 27 seconds (850), 0–60mph (96km/h) in 10 seconds (Cooper S)

The BMC Mini defined a new genre of small cars. Other cars may have used front-wheel drive and transverse engines before, but none had done so in such a small space as the Mini. Packaging was perhaps its greatest strength, and every square inch was used: there were big door-bins, tiny 10in. (25cm) wheels that didn't intrude on passenger space, and a boot-lid you could fold down to double up as a luggage platform.

Designer Alec Issigonis sketched his ideas – literally – on the back of envelopes, envisaging the most compact possible 'cube' in which the four passengers would sit, pulled along by a space-saving front-wheel-drive system. The gearbox was mounted under the engine, instead of behind it, saving further valuable inches. Another major innovation was a new rubber-cone suspension system designed by Dr Alex Moulton.

It took BMC just two years to develop the Mini and put it into production, and it was available in basic or De Luxe trim, with prices starting at £496 – costs had been pared down by fitting sliding windows, cable-pull door releases and leaving exposed external welded body seams.

On the road, it handled better than any rival. It was nippy and easy to park, and it quickly became fashionable to own one. The Mini's use of subframes allowed a huge variety of derivatives too – van, pick-up, estate, long-boot Riley Elf and Wolseley Hornet, and the Mini Moke.

On the track, BMC fielded works Mini Coopers with incredible success. 'Normal' Coopers won the Tulip Rally in 1962–63, whilst the 'S' was all-conquering in British saloon-car racing and the legendary Monte Carlo Rally, which it won three times in 1964, 1965 and 1967.

Four decades on, the Mini has seen many technical changes, but the basic concept remains the same. This is probably at the root of its continuing popularity with the car-buying public.

Spacewagon

1984–1991

ENGINE: Balancer-shaft-equipped
16v in-line four, 1755cc

POWER: 88bhp

CHASSIS: Steel monocoque, five-door

BRAKES: (F/R) Disc

TRANSMISSION: Five-speed manual

SUSPENSION: Struts front,
independent U-shape trailing arms
rear

TOP SPEED: 97mph (155km/h)

ACCELERATION: 0–62.5mph
(100km/h) in 12.9 seconds

"The ocean nibbles at established cliffs, but the landslide can be a long time coming," was how Ian Fraser (then editor of *CAR* magazine) summed up his report on the ItalDesign Megagamma. It was an amazingly prescient comment, as the Megagamma could probably be regarded as the original 'people carrier'. It wasn't until the 1996 launch of the similarly cast and exceptionally successful Renault Mégane Scenic that the concept of the Euro-compact MPV suddenly captured the imagination of the buying public.

Six years after the Megagamma's unveiling at the 1978 Turin Motor Show, one manufacturer did have the bravery to try and make a success of a 'tall' family car. Mitsubishi launched the Spacewagon in a much more conservative package than the high-rise Megagamma, but even so it was a real break from the norm – it

was only a year earlier that Ford's mainstream family car had switched from being a saloon-bodied Cortina to the hatchback Sierra.

The Spacewagon wasn't tall, but it had a long-roofed body and plenty of glazing. Inside it was fitted with three rows of seats, allowing six to seven passengers. Ahead of the Espace-style MPVs to come, the Mitsubishi's middle row could be slid backwards and forwards and be folded flat – along with the rear seats – to create a very long load area.

Around the same time both Nissan and Honda launched similar cars (the Nissan Prairie looked like the Megagamma, but had a van-style sliding door), but neither looked into the real possibilities surrounding the interior flexibility of the tall family car. Sadly, Mitsubishi was too far ahead of the market, and never really benefited from the Spacewagon.

Lancer Evolution V

1996–2002

ENGINE: Turbocharged 16-valve, in-line four, 1997cc

POWER: 280bhp

CHASSIS: Steel monocoque

BRAKES (F/R): Disc with ABS

TRANSMISSION: 5-speed manual

SUSPENSION: Struts front, multi-link rear

TOP SPEED: 112mph (179km/h), limited

ACCELERATION: 0–62.5mph (100km/h) in 5.3 seconds

On ordinary roads, there is little that can catch a rally-derived, compact four-wheel-drive car with a turbocharged engine. European makers dominated the genre with the fast and relatively simple Audi Quattro, Ford Sierra Cosworth and the Lancia Delta Integrale. But they all eventually abandoned the road-car scene, however.

Japanese makers kept up the assault on the World Rally Championship, and kept on building road-car spin-offs. The result was a breed of increasingly complex super-high-performance street machines, which proved to be huge showroom hits in the home market. The ultimate realization of this rally-bred 'techno-fest' was probably the Mitsubishi Lancer Evolution Five. The standard four-door family saloon was transformed with the most outrageous body addenda of any street-legal car ever built. The

massive front air dam housed the turbocharger's intercooler behind a mesh grille and two giant spot lamps.

The front wings were specially pressed to clear the wide wheels, and the bonnet was pierced by two huge meshed grilles. Even more extreme was the four-position – for increasing or decreasing aerodynamic downforce – alloy-bladed spoiler mounted on the boot-lid. The brakes were by specialist manufacturer Brembo, and the interior was race-trim inspired. The Evolution was just as fast as it looked. The 2.0-litre turbocharged engine produced a remarkable 280bhp (perhaps a conservative measurement) and a whopping 274lb/ft of torque. It could sprint from 0–60mph (96km/h) in just 5.1 seconds. Few Ferraris have ever been faster than this extreme saloon.

Monteverdi Hai

1970–1977

ENGINE: V8, 6974cc

POWER: 450bhp

CHASSIS: Tubular steel

BRAKES (F/R): Disc

TRANSMISSION: Five-speed manual

SUSPENSION: Independent

TOP SPEED: 169mph (272km/h)

ACCELERATION: No figures available

The Monteverdi Hai is a kind of mythical supercar. Few people have ever seen one. Members of the press have rarely tested one, and the car had a reputation for being a little unruly.

Peter Monteverdi had been building his own Chrysler engined GT cars in Switzerland since 1967, handsome coupes cast in the mould of England's Jensen and Bristol models. The Hai of 1970 was Monteverdi's bid for the mid-engined supercar market whose only player at that point was the Lamborghini Miura.

The Hai was a far more crude machine, with its Chrysler 'Hemi' engine protruding into the passenger compartment and

deDion rear suspension based on the type found on his 375 Series front engined cars. Space generally was tight in the Hai which had no room for a spare wheel or much in the way of luggage. It was well equipped though, and even had air conditioning as standard.

The styling had a certain brutal charm and was the work of Monteverdi himself with help from Fissore, who also built the light alloy body shell. Top speed was said to be 169mph but this never seems to have been verified. The few who did try the car reported unruly handling, particularly in the wet. It remained on the Monteverdi price lists until 1977, but only two are believed to have been sold.

Morgan 4/4

1955–

ENGINE: Four-cylinder, 1172–1599cc

POWER: 36–96bhp

CHASSIS: Separate ladder-frame

BRAKES: Disc/drum

TRANSMISSION: Three-/four-/five-speed

SUSPENSION: Independent front, live axle rear

TOP SPEED: 75–110mph (120–176km/h)

ACCELERATION: 0–60mph (96km/h) in 14.1 seconds

Morgan didn't make its first four-wheeled sports car until 1936. That was the original 4/4, which disappeared in favour of the more powerful Vanguard-engined Plus Four in 1950. However, by the mid-1950s Morgan had perceived a need for a more basic car priced below the Plus Four, and the Series II 4/4 was thus reborn after a five-year break.

Like all Morgans, it used a simple but effective ladder-frame chassis, sliding pillar front suspension and ash framing for the traditional-looking steel or light-alloy bodies with the new-style cowled water fall. Right up until 1960, power came from Ford side-valve Anglia 100E engines. In Series III form, there were 997cc overhead-valve engines from the 105E Anglia

and a four-speed gearbox – something drivers had wanted for a while.

Series IV cars from 1961 to 1963 gained larger 1340cc engines, pushing the top speed to over 80mph (128km/h), and there were now front disc brakes for the first time. In 1963 it got the latest Cortina engines in standard 1498cc and GT forms, and then in 1968 the crossflow Kent engine. From 1969 a four-seater body was offered.

Since the early 1980s, various powerplants have been offered, including the Fiat 1600 twin-cam and the 1600cc CVH Ford Escort engine. A five-speed gearbox was offered from 1982, and the car continues in the late-1990s with the Rover twin-cam engine.

Morgan Plus Eight

1968–

ENGINE: V8, 3528cc

POWER: 160–190bhp

CHASSIS: Separate ladder-frame

BRAKES(F/R): Disc/drum

TRANSMISSION: Four- and five-speed

SUSPENSION: Independent front, live axle rear

TOP SPEED: 125mph (200km/h)

ACCELERATION: 0–60mph (96km/h) in 6.7 seconds

Introduced in 1968, there has been a waiting list for the much-loved Morgan Plus Eight ever since. Its story really began when supplies of the 2138cc Triumph four-cylinder engine dried up in the late-1960s. Suddenly Morgan was left without a high-performance engine for its flagship Plus Four model.

Enter Rover's all-alloy 3.5-litre V8, derived from a discarded Buick design from the early 1960s and then recently introduced in the big 3.5-litre saloon and coupe. Light, compact and powerful (165bhp), it was ideal for the job and transformed the Morgan into a real road-burner – top speed leaped to over 120mph (192km/h), with stunningly rapid acceleration matched by very few road cars.

Renamed the Plus Eight, at first glance it looked identical to its predecessor. This was misleading as in fact it had a slightly longer wheelbase and wider track, and subtly different body contours. The most obvious change was the light-alloy wheels, but the sliding pillar front suspension and leaf-sprung live rear axle remained.

More than 4,000 have been built to date, never at a rate of more than 15 per week. Steel bodywork was standard – with ash framing, of course – but there was an optional sports lightweight version from 1975. Early cars used the noisy, old-fashioned Moss gearbox familiar on Jaguar saloons, but from 1972 onwards the Rover four-speed transmission was used. The five-speed unit from the Rover SD1 hatchback was used from 1977.

Fuel injection came along in 1984, and rack-and-pinion steering from 1986. The latest cars in this long-lived line have a 3.9-litre version of the Rover engine, giving 190bhp.

Morris Minor

1948–1971

ENGINE: In-line four-cylinder, 918/803/943/1098cc

POWER: 27–48bhp

CHASSIS: Monocoque

BRAKES (F/R) Drum

TRANSMISSION: Four-speed manual

SUSPENSION: Independent front, live axle rear

TOP SPEED: 60–78mph (96–125km/h)

ACCELERATION: 0–60mph (96km/h) in 31 seconds (MM)

The Morris Minor, designed by Alec Issigonis, was the outstanding economy car of the post-war era. It is a design classic and rightfully so.

With its rack-and-pinion steering and torsion-bar independent suspension, it had superb handling, whilst unitary construction and the smooth styling made the Minor seem ultra-modern after the warmed-up pre-war cars that British motorists had been used to up until the welcome point that the Morris made its entrance onto the scene.

Powered by the elderly E-Series flat-head in-line engine, early Minors were known as MM-series cars. They featured low-mounted headlights until 1950. The two-door and open tourer were joined by the four-door at about the same time, but the most important change came in 1952 when the overhead-valve Austin A30 engine was fitted.

This engine was the first fruits of the British Motor Corporation (BMC) merger. The classic half-timbered Traveller – a much-loved addition to the range – estate was announced in 1953.

The next landmark in the development of the Minor was the introduction of the 948cc engine in 1956. It was at this point that the cars were badged Minor 1000.

Combined with a higher final drive, this put the top speed up to a respectable 70mph (112km/h). This was a performance that Morris drivers could take some genuine delight in.

The last major update was the introduction of the 48bhp 1098cc engine in 1962. The open tourers and four-door saloons died out in the late-1960s, but the two-door and the Traveller continued until 1971.

1100/1300

1962–1973

ENGINE: Four-cylinder, 1098/1275cc

POWER: 48bhp

CHASSIS: Monocoque

BRAKES (F/R): Drum

TRANSMISSION: Four-speed manual

SUSPENSION: Independent Hydrolastic

TOP SPEED: 78mph (125km/h)

ACCELERATION: 0–60mph (96km/h) in 20 seconds

By the time the Issigonis-designed Morris 1100/1300 was replaced by the Allegro in 1973, over two million examples had been sold. In fact, it was consistently Britain's best-selling car, beating even the ever popular Ford Cortina to the top spot throughout the 1960s.

Following the acclaim the Mini received, the British Motor Corporation (BMC) had total faith in Alec Issigonis's abilities to do the same with a new saloon. Indeed the 1100 was even more sophisticated and, for 1962, very advanced. In addition to front disc brakes, transverse front-wheel drive, subframe construction and an extremely spacious interior, the new car boasted interconnected fluid suspension called Hydrolastic, designed by Dr Alex Moulton, which gave a remarkably smooth ride. Styling was by Pininfarina.

The Morris was the first of a whole raft of badge-engineered 1100s – Austin, Morris, Riley, Wolseley, MG and Vanden Plas versions quickly followed. Each had its own unique grille and trim, whilst the sporty models had twin carburettors for an extra 7bhp. There were two- or four-door saloons and, from 1966, Austin Countryman or Morris Traveller three-door estates. Automatic transmission was also offered on many models.

New 58bhp 1300cc models arrived in 1967, then a four-door 1300GT in 1969. Badged Austin or Morris, it boasted a 70bhp twin-carburettor engine, good enough to hit 96mph (154km/h). Today the BMC 1100/1300's most avid following is in Japan, where the chrome, leather and walnut-trimmed Vanden Plas 1100 – complete with picnic tables – is a genuine cult machine.

Sunny GTi-R

1991–1995

ENGINE: In-line turbocharged twin-cam four-cylinder, 1998cc

POWER: 220bhp

CHASSIS: Steel monocoque, three-door

BRAKES (F/R): Disc with ABS

TRANSMISSION: Five-speed manual

SUSPENSION: Struts

TOP SPEED: 134mph (214km/h)

ACCELERATION: 0–62.5mph (100km/h) in 6.4 seconds

Like its contemporaries, the Ford Escort Cosworth and Lancia Delta Integrale, the Sunny GTi-R was a road-going version of a serious rally machine. Despite this it is important to remember it was essentially based on a humble family car. Given the Japanese love of high technology, it was also a very reasonable commercial bet on the internal domestic market.

In status-conscious Europe, however, a small Japanese hatchback – especially one wearing the Nissan badge – could never be considered any real rival to rallying icons. This was, of course a completely unfair assessment, although the Nissan's peculiar styling wasn't any help in delivering street-credibility. Minimal changes to the homely three-door shell, the 'peaked-cap' aerofoil on the trailing edge of the roof and the large vented hump on the bonnet – actually the air intake for the turbocharger's intercooler, which lay flat on top of the engine – gave the GTi-R an uncomfortable profile. The interior, which was typically Japanese, in that it was dull and plasticky, was enlivened only by a sporty steering wheel and bucket seats.

Yet underneath was a fine car. The excellence of the engine, fine steering, the swift gearchange and progressive power delivery meant that contemporary road tests judged it swifter in real-world driving than the Cosworth. It was the chassis – somewhat unsophisticated – which prevented the GTi-R from developing real cult-car status.

Skyline

1991–

ENGINE: Twin-turbocharged 24-valve straight-six, 2568cc

POWER: 300bhp

CHASSIS: Steel monocoque

BRAKES (F/R): Disc with ABS

TRANSMISSION: five-speed manual

SUSPENSION: Multi-link double-wishbone front, double-wishbone rear

TOP SPEED: 155mph (248km/h), limited

ACCELERATION: 0–62.5mph (100km/h) in 5.4 seconds

When it was launched it was called the 'world's most advanced car' by the Press. Rumours have it that the Skyline's engineers had been told to 'out-Porsche' Porsche. The car was launched in Europe at the extremely challenging Nürburgring circuit in Germany. It was soon clear that Nissan had succeeded in producing the world's most able road car, for the machine was proving capable of running Porsche 928s ragged on the circuit.

Like many other great road cars, the Skyline's technical recipe was simple enough. It had a powerful turbo-charged engine connected to a four-wheel-drive transmission. With typical Japanese thoroughness, however, Nissan had improved on the basics. The straight-six engine, though old, gained a new 24-valve head and a pair of ceramic turbochargers. Power, claimed to be 280bhp, was actually more like 300bhp.

Even more complex was the electronically controlled four-wheel-drive, which used numerous sensors to work out how to split the engine's torque between the front and rear wheels to deliver the maximum amount of horsepower to the road in all conditions. Based on clever multi-link suspension front and rear, the Skyline chassis also used an intelligent four-wheel-steering system, which operated according to the car's cornering state.

The car also looked great in a menacing way, the two-door body livened up with massive blistered wings, a deep air-dam and large boot spoiler. The remarkable Skyline became the choice car for those in the know about the fastest way to travel across-country.

Nissan **200SX**

1994–2001

ENGINE: Turbocharged 16-valve in-line four-cylinder, 1998cc

POWER: 200bhp

CHASSIS: Steel monocoque, two-door

BRAKES (F/R): Disc with ABS

TRANSMISSION: Five-speed manual

SUSPENSION: Struts front, semi-trailing arms rear

TOP SPEED: 143mph (229km/h)

ACCELERATION: 0–62.5mph (100km/h) in 7.7 seconds

Datsun (as Nissan was then called) established a fine reputation for its 1968 240Z coupe, especially in the USA. Its fine styling, exemplary reliability and punchy performance from the straight-six engine meant it outsold the then-dominant sports-car rivals from Europe. Sadly, the subsequent 280 and 300Z replacements just got fatter and less sporting.

In 1989 Nissan got back to the roots of the Z concept with the 200SX coupe, a svelte rear-wheel-drive three-door powered by a turbocharged engine which gave it serious pace. In 1994 the 200SX was replaced by a new, more thoroughly developed model.

The new 200SX was a two-door notchback with styling too subtly drawn for most tastes – especially as it arrived around the same time as the dramatic Fiat Coupe. But it was a very finely crafted fast car, with very few, if any, glaring faults.

Nissan's new linear-charge turbocharging system meant that the 200SX delivered a very even spread of power and torque throughout the rev range. In tandem with the security of the beautifully balanced chassis, this gave the car tremendous pace – especially on winding secondary roads.

The 2.0-litre engine had enormous mid-range thrust, which made the 200SX a very relaxing car to drive quickly. This was a trait amplified by the superb driving position, unobtrusive dashboard – giving a fine view forward – and sweet gearchange.

Slow sales led to a mid-life facelift to give the 200SX a more aggressive appearance, but it made little difference. It was a change too late in the day. Buyers turned towards the vehicle's charismatic opposition, but nothing could match the Nissan's sensationally sweet progression.

NSU **Ro80**

1967–1977

ENGINE: Twin-rotor Wankel, 2000cc

POWER: 115bhp

CHASSIS: Monocoque

BRAKES: (F/R) Disc

TRANSMISSION: Three-speed semi-automatic

SUSPENSION: Independent

TOP SPEED: 115mph (184km/h)

ACCELERATION: 0–60mph (96km/h) in 13 seconds

The NSU Ro80 was the world's first purpose-built, twin-rotor, Wankel-engined saloon. Not only was it fast (with a top speed of 115mph (184km/h) and super-smooth, but it was beautiful too, with a futuristic and aerodynamic five-seater body that pointed the way to styling in the 1980s and 1990s. Front-wheel drive, superb power steering and four-wheel disc brakes gave it excellent handling, whilst long-travel strut suspension provided a comfortable, absorbent ride.

To mask the Wankel's poor low-down torque, NSU specified a three-speed semi-automatic transmission – there was no clutch pedal, but instead an electric switch located in the top of the gear-lever operated a vacuum system when pressed.

The car was a minor masterpiece, but it had one fatal flaw – its rotary engine. Inadequately developed, it suffered from acute wear of its rotor-tip seals, and after 15,000 miles (or less) owners began to notice a lack of power and increased fuel consumption. Engines became difficult to start and smoked heavily. NSU was generous with warranty claims, and some cars had as many as nine new engines.

The costs sent NSU into the arms of Volkswagen in 1969, and as word got round about the Wankel engine problems, sales plummeted. Production lasted at a lower rate until 1977, when the NSU name eventually had to die with this beautiful, innovative saloon.

Oldsmobile Toronado

1965–1970

ENGINE: V8, 6965cc

POWER; 385bhp

CHASSIS: Perimeter frame

BRAKES (F/R): Drum

TRANSMISSION: Three-speed automatic

SUSPENSION: Independent front, dead axle rear

TOP SPEED: 135mph (216km/h)

ACCELERATION: 0–60mph (96km/h) in 8.5 seconds

Front wheel drive had not held much interest for American manufacturers. Cord had been the only manufacturer to try it before the war and they hadn't met with much success. It also presented technical problems when combined with large V8 engines and automatic transmissions. Some even said it couldn't be done.

The Oldsmobile Toronado proved the sceptics wrong. Here was a full-sized American car with unique chain and sprocket drive between its automatic transmission – mounted under the left cylinder bank – and the torque converter on the back of the engine. Power came from Oldsmobile's 7 litre V8 delivering 385bhp which could take this futuristically styled two door coupe up to 135mph. For its size and weight the Toronado had

exemplary handling and could be tossed into curves at speeds that would leave its rear-drive American contemporaries floundering. Only its drum brakes let it down, suffering from severe fade if used hard repeatedly at speed.

Although the Toronado sold respectably it was always out-shone by the conventional Buick Riviera with which it shared some under-pinning. When Cadillac adopted front-wheel drive for its Eldorado in 1967 it too out-sold the Toronado.

Gradually Oldsmobile took the car further down the luxury Coupe route and by 1969 had spoilt its once sharp styling. By the turn of the decade the Toronado had become just another slobmobile on the freeway. At this point, its death was probably something of a kindness.

Kadett

1962–1973

ENGINE: One-litre/1.9-litre, 4-cylinder OHV

POWER; 385bhp

CHASSIS: Perimeter frame

BRAKES (F/R): Drum

TRANSMISSION: Three-speed automatic

SUSPENSION: Independent front, dead axle rear

TOP SPEED: 135mph (216km/h)

ACCELERATION: 0–60mph (96km/h) in 8.5 seconds

Just before World War II Opel had produced a cheap saloon called the Kadett. The name had died off in the war but in 1962 Opel revived it for the car to take on the VW Beetle. Built at Bochum, the new Kadett had a new one-litre engine, synchromesh gearbox and rack-and-pinion steering. The initial two-door saloon and estate versions were soon joined by a coupe with a high-compression engine producing 48bhp.

In 1965 the Kadett received a makeover, the most obvious alteration being squared-off headlight surrounds, but the major evolution took place in 1967 when Opel expanded the engine range from one to four. At base level was a bored-out 1.1 litre unit, with 1.5, 1.7 and 1.9 also available. In this guise the Kadett sold in vast numbers until 1973, by which time well over 3 million had rolled off the production line.

The most exciting addition to the family was a Rallye Coupe, with aggressive styling and power output of 90bhp. It was capable of 102mph and is now a favourite among collectors.

After 1973 the Kadett went through several changes, major and minor, and continued to sell into the 1980s.

Opel GT

1968–1973

ENGINE: In-line four-cylinder, 1897cc

POWER: 90bhp

CHASSIS: Steel monocoque, two-door

BRAKES (F/R): Disc/drum

TRANSMISSION: Four-speed manual

SUSPENSION: Transverse leaf-spring front, beam axle and Panhard rod rear

TOP SPEED: 109mph (174km/h)

ACCELERATION: 0–62.5mph (100km/h) in 11.2 seconds

In the late-1960s, few people would have expected the conservative Opel combine to take an interest in producing a sleek, two-seater sports car. Which is why when the Opel GT was previewed in 1966 as the XVR concept car, the idea was not expected to go any further.

Opel shocked the market when it unveiled the Kadett-based GT in 1968, with shark-nose lines that were very close to those of the show car. It was immediately dubbed the 'baby Corvette', and the General Motors American influence was certainly strong.

The retractable headlamps and engine set well back in the engine bay allowed the GT a very low nose. At the back, the tail was abruptly sawn-off – known as a Kamm tail – and fitted with four Ferrari-look circular tail-lights. All this work had serious aerodynamic intent behind it.

The cleverest and most advanced part of the GT body was the window frames, which were part of the door skin and wrapped smoothly into the curvaceous roof panel. Perhaps because of the Corvette connection, the GT was often thought to be of fibreglass. In fact, it was built of very thin-gauge steel by coachbuilder Chausson in France.

The underpinnings were as aged as the body was up-to-date. The Kadett floorpan meant a narrow cabin, and crude front suspension based on a transverse leaf spring. Despite this, the GT was praised for its chassis performance, and Opel's tough 1.9-litre engine gave it respectable performance.

The majority of the 103,000 GTs made over five years went to the sports-car-hungry US market, but 1974 model-year demands for impact-resistant bumpers and tighter exhaust emissions forced it out of production.

Ironically, 16 years later Opel pulled exactly the same trick. It based the attractively curvaceous and aerodynamic Calibra on the Opel Ascona/Vauxhall Cavalier family car model.

Manta

1970–1988

ENGINE: 1.6/1.9-litre 4-cylinder OHV/2.4-litre, four-cylinder DOHC

POWER; 60-105bhp (144bhp on Cosworth)

CHASSIS: Monocoque

BRAKES (F/R): Disc

TRANSMISSION: Four-speed manual

SUSPENSION: Coils all round, rigid axle rear

TOP SPEED: 90-117mph (144-187km/h)

ACCELERATION: 0-60mph (0-96km/h) in 10.5-12.5 seconds

In 1970 Opel launched the Ascona to replace the prosaic Olympia. Preceding it into the market by a matter of weeks was a stylish coupe version, the Manta, which would prove a strong rival to the Ford Capri.

Sharing the Ascona's floorplan, with coil springs and a rigid rear axle, the Manta was larger than the Capri but slower. In 1.2 litre form it was somewhat underpowered, but there were 1.6 and 1.9 litre engines available which provided the sort of performance buyers were looking for, if not exactly hair-raising. The SR version produced 90bhp.

Build quality and handling were excellent, though, and for those seeking a bit more oomph, a Bosch-injected GT/E version was unveiled in 1973, capable of 117mph. As the decade wore on Opel looked towards rallying success to boost the Manta's cachet. A rally homologation Manta 400 became available in 1981, powered by a Cosworth twin-cam, 16V 2.4 litre engine that was good for 144bhp and capable of 125mph.

Applying the lessons learnt from the rallying experience, Opel gave the Manta a new lease of life with the Family II 1.8 litre engines and improved suspension, prolonging its appeal into the late-1980s, by which time over one million Manta's had been made.

Opel **Monza**

1980–1986

ENGINE: In-line straight-six, 2969cc

POWER: 180bhp

CHASSIS: Steel monocoque, three-door

BRAKES (F/R): Disc

TRANSMISSION: Five-speed manual

SUSPENSION: Struts front, semi-trailing arms rear

TOP SPEED: 132mph (211km/h)

ACCELERATION: 0–62.5mph (100km/h) in 8.9 seconds

After some fine coupe launches in the lower reaches of the market (the GT and Manta), Opel decided to go right upmarket with the Monza. Based on the Senator executive saloon, the Monza was a large car – spacious enough for four adults and benefiting from a huge boot, which was hidden away under a massive tailgate.

It was an audacious proposition, taking the sporty coupe layout and launching it as an expensive businessman's car. It arrived on the market just behind the similarly laid-out Porsche 928, demonstrating how far-sighted stylist Henry Haga had been with his confidently chunky creation. Indeed, Opel didn't modify the Monza – aside from the grille, headlights and dashboard – during the car's nine-year production run.

Looks weren't everything with the Monza. It had a very fine chassis. It was described at the time as well balanced, combining fine

roadholding and handling with a superb ride. The straight-six engine also endowed the Monza with surprising performance for such a heavy car. The car's German origins were obvious with each slam of its hefty doors – the build quality was excellent.

Yet it was not a great success at first, despite clearly being a quality car and massively undercutting the established Porsche, BMW and Mercedes-badged competition. Revisions in 1982 rid the car of its down-market dashboard and instruments, and did much to refine all aspects of the running gear.

It remained something of a small-production cult car until it was phased out after the Senator was replaced by the Carlton saloon. Opel didn't care to repeat the exercise at this level, which was a pity. The company had proven that it was more than capable of knocking on BMW's door.

Hawk

1958

ENGINE: V8, 4737cc

POWER: 275bhp at 4800rpm

CHASSIS: Separate chassis

BRAKES (F/R): Disc

TRANSMISSION: Three-speed auto

SUSPENSION: Independent front, live axle rear

TOP SPEED: 125mph (200km/h)

ACCELERATION: 0-60mph (96km/h) in 8 seconds

Before World War II, Packard had been one of America's finest cars, fit to be compared with the likes of Rolls Royce on the world stage. They intended to keep that reputation after hostilities by building quality cars that were impervious to the yearly changes wrought by the big manufacturers. As an independent Packard couldn't afford to play that game and didn't believe that was what its buyers wanted. They were wrong – buyers, even in the upper end of the market, wanted excitingly new cars typified by V8 engined glitzy Cadillacs.

It wasn't until 1951 that Packard responded with truly modern alternatives, although there would be no V8s until 1955. In an expanding market Packard sales were stable but showing no growth, failing to compete effectively with

the 'Big three' who could afford to make major changes year on year.

It was in a bid to expand that Packard bought Studebaker in 1956. It turned out to be a misguided purchase, as it was Studebaker who dragged Packard to an early grave, but one consequence of the alliance was the Packard Hawk, a two-door sports Coupe based on an existing Studebaker body. There was an attempt to give the car a European flavour with leather trim, full white-on-black instrumentation, wing vents and a fake hood scoop. Best of all there was a McCulloch belt-driven supercharger under the bonnet, increasing the output of the 4.7 litre V8 to 275bhp. Swift, well equipped and restrained compared to its contemporaries, the Hawk failed to save the marque from extinction and only 588 were built.

24 CT

1963–1967

ENGINE: Flat-twin, 848cc

POWER: 60bhp

CHASSIS: Monocoque

BRAKES (F/R): Drum

TRANSMISSION: Four-speed manual

SUSPENSION: Independent front, rear beam axle

TOP SPEED: 100mph (160km/h)

ACCELERATION: 0–60mph (96km/h) in 17 seconds

Panhard, one of the oldest names in motoring, made one of the best economy cars of the 1950s – the twin-cylinder, front-wheel-drive Dyna. The PL17 that followed was a futuristic family six-seater, still with a mere 845bhp air-cooled flat-twin, yet capable of 90mph (144km/h) in Tigre form.

Even more desirable was the glamorous little 24 Series, introduced in 1963. It was the best and the last Panhard of all. Here was a modern-looking 2+2 coupe with a stylish, aerodynamic shape distinguished by large window areas and cowled-in lights behind glass.

It used the same drive-train as the PL17, with front-wheel drive, a four-speed gearbox and two engine options – the most powerful being the Tigre unit, giving 60bhp with a twin-choke carburettor (24CT). Top speed was an amazing 100mph (160km/h), yet still with the potential for 40mpg (7.1 litres/100km) if driven normally. The flat-twin smoothed out beautifully at higher speeds, which was where the CT excelled.

The 24C had the lower-powered 50bhp unit, and the range was broadened by the 24B, BT and BA, with a longer-wheelbase, full four-seater body. All cars had a four-speed, floor-mounted gear-change and, from 1965, four-wheel disc brakes.

By then Citroën had taken over the ailing Panhard, and it was struggling to make the 24 Series profitable. Sales were slow and Citroën gave up the unequal struggle in 1967, killing the marque and using Panhard's Paris factory to increase its own production capacity.

Panther Deville

1974–1985

ENGINE: Straight 6 and V12, 4235/5343cc

POWER: 190-266bhp

CHASSIS: Separate tubular frame

BRAKES (F/R): Disc

TRANSMISSION: Three-speed auto

SUSPENSION: Independent

TOP SPEED: 127mph (203km/h)

ACCELERATION: No figures available

Robert Jankel built the first Panther, the J72, in 1972. It was a Jaguar-powered copy of the 1930s SS 100 Jaguar sports car.

Jankel originally created the beast for his own use, but he was eventually persuaded to put it into production at his Byfleet factory. Many thought it vulgar, but in comparison with Jankel's next project, the Deville, the J72 looked tasteful.

Sitting on a giant 142in wheelbase, the tubular-framed Deville used Jaguar six and 12-cylinder engines. With its flowing wing lines and big headlights the vehicle was styled to have the same feel as the massive straight-eight engined 1930 Bugatti Royale, of which just six were built.

Underneath there was Jaguar suspension, power steering and automatic transmission. This made it an easy car to drive and quite quick. The one thing that held it back was the poor aerodynamic performance which tended to keep the top speeds relatively unimpressive.

Interiors were lavish and often featured TV sets and drinks bars. Somehow, these extras made the car seem more like a luxury American car than a typical British sports car. About 60 of these handbuilt machines were made until 1985, including two-door convertibles and one pink and gold six-door limousine – it was probably the most vulgar model of them all.

Z102/Z103

1951–1958

ENGINE: V8, 2816/3178/3988/4450cc

POWER: 175–360bhp

CHASSIS: Steel platform

BRAKES (F/R): Drum

TRANSMISSION: Five-speed manual

SUSPENSION: Independent

TOP SPEED: 120–160mph (192–256km/h)

ACCELERATION: Not quoted

Although the name Pegaso has always been more famous for commercial vehicles, for a brief period in the 1950s this Spanish company produced the fastest and the most glamorous road cars of the day. Combining racing-car design and engineering with exotic Italian styling, Pegaso production totalled only 100 cars.

First of the line was the Z102 of 1951. Here was a super sports car with a specification of the highest order. It featured four-cam, 2.8-litre V8 engine, dry-sump lubrication, five-speed gearbox located in unit with the differential – all mounted in a state-of-the art pressed platform chassis. Everything was produced in-house at the Barcelona factory, including the rather dumpy coupe and convertible prototype steel bodies.

Most production Z102s had 2.8-litre engines and a much lighter and more-elegant Touring Coupe body, crafted in alloy. This would become the definitive Pegaso style. The performance was fantastic, with up to 160mph (256km/h) in its most powerful, 3.2-litre supercharged form, and an amazing noise generated by its gear-driven camshafts.

They were heavy, brutish cars to drive but, despite the good handling and power, they never found much competition success. The Z103 was a last-ditch effort to make the cars – which were always built on a 'cost-no-object' basis – more commercially successful, with a simpler single-overhead-camshaft V8.

Pegaso built its last sports cars in 1958. They never made any money for the company, but at least it proved it could do a fine job and compete with the best in the world.

Peugeot 504 Estate

1968–1982

ENGINE: Four-cylinder, 1971cc

POWER: 93bhp

CHASSIS: Monocoque

BRAKES: Disc/drum

TRANSMISSION: Four-speed manual

SUSPENSION: Independent

TOP SPEED: 100mph (162km/h)

ACCELERATION: 0-60mph (96km/h) in 13.7secs

Family load carriers didn't come more practical or spacious than Peugeot's big 504 Estate. It came in two versions – a five seater with a fold-down rear seat and the seven-seat Family Estate with an extra row of seats which came at the expense of a much smaller luggage area.

Both had a longer wheelbase than the saloon but were mechanically the same apart from the rear suspension. On the Estate this was a coil sprung beam axle which was chosen in favour of the saloon's independent set-up.

Exciting these cars weren't. Their 1971cc four cylinder engines produced 93bhp – which gave just about 100mph – and if you went for the diesel version the performance was even more plodding.

No, these cars sold to sensible people who wanted dependability, refinement and practicality – with more than six feet of load space even in the seven seater version with the rearmost seat folded. When they bought a 504 Estate, they got exactly what they wanted.

The 504 showed how tough it was on events like the East African Safari, and the model was a best seller in all the really tough motoring territories of the world. The 504 Estate was an important and big selling car for Peugeot – as is demostrated by the lenth of its production life – and one that came at the right time for the company.

Peugeot **304**

1969–1975

ENGINE: Four-cylinder, 1288cc

POWER: 66-75bhp

CHASSIS: Monocoque

BRAKES (F/R): Disc/drum

TRANSMISSION: Four-speed

SUSPENSION: Independent

TOP SPEED: 90-100mph (145-152km/h)

ACCELERATION: 0-60mph (96km/h) in 14.5 seconds

The 1965 204 was Peugeot's first front-wheel-drive model, and as well as the saloon a stylish short wheelbase coupe and convertible were offered – designed, like the saloon, by Pininfarina with whom Peugeot had close relations. They weren't fast but they did have style and more than 40,000 of them were built.

The 304 saloon of 1969 had new front end styling which added seven inches to the length of the 204, which continued in saloon form alongside. From this point it seemed an obvious decision to build the more sporty Cabriolet and Coupe models on the basis of this more powerful version.

The 304 Coupe and Cabriolet kept the same shell (from the screen backwards) as before, but used the new 304 wings, front grille and headlights. The all-alloy engine was stroked to give 1288cc which upped the power to 65bhp, for a top speed figure of around 90mph.

Performance, however, wasn't the point – these were sophisticated little cars with good ride comfort and safe front-wheel-drive handling. They also made excellent long-distance machines. An 'S' version was introduced in 1972, its twin-choke carb increasing the output to 75bhp.

The last 304 Cabriolets were produced in 1975 and had no equivalent in the modern Peugeot range for many years.

504 V6 Cabriolet

1974–1982

ENGINE: V6, 2664cc

POWER: 136bhp

CHASSIS: Monocoque

BRAKES (F/R): Disc

TRANSMISSION: Five-speed manual

SUSPENSION: Independent

TOP SPEED: 115mph (184 km/h)

ACCELERATION: 0-60mph (96km/h) in 10 seconds

The 504 Cabriolet and Coupe were the first cars to use the jointly produced PRV (Peugeot-Renault-Volvo) 2.6 litre V6 engine. This was the moment which transformed it from a plodding if refined car into quite a briskly performing one.

As with the 504 saloon, Pininfarina did the Coupe and Cabriolet shape and built the steel bodywork in their Turin factory. The shells were then sent over-land to Peugeot, who fitted the drive train. The process was a success. The 504 Cabriolets had been built in 1969 with the four cylinder injection engine and this model was reintroduced to run alongside the V6 when it failed to sell in the numbers expected.

Early 2 litre cars had four headlights but the V6 was distinguishable by long one-piece headlights, flush door handles, new bumper over-riders and one-piece back lights. From 1978 there were colour-coded bumpers and on the last cars a veneer dashboard.

Otherwise these cars, only built in left-hand drive, changed little in a long production run. Given the nature of the vehicle that they had first produced, Peugeot didnt really have that much room for improvement anyway. Refined and very comfortable, the 504 V6 Cabriolet and Coupe are among the most stylish four-seater convertibles around, and much coveted.

Peugeot 205 GTi

1984–1994

ENGINE: In-line four-cylinder, 1580cc

POWER: 115bhp

CHASSIS: Steel monocoque, three-door

BRAKES (F/R): Disc/drum

TRANSMISSION: Five-speed manual

SUSPENSION: Struts front, trailing arms rear

TOP SPEED: 122mph (195km/h)

ACCELERATION: 0–62.5mph (100km/h) in 8.8 seconds

When the 205 was launched in 1983, it caught everyone's attention as the very model of a modern supermini. It was compact, but decently roomy inside, and had a good-sized boot. Sensible in practical areas, the 205 was also exceptionally pretty. Over the car's lengthy production run – more than 14 years, as the new models designed to replace it failed to kill it off completely – the exterior hardly changed: the real measure of a classic design.

The key to the appeal of the 205's success was driving pleasure. All versions, including the base 1.1-litre and the 1.9-litre diesel, were enjoyable to pilot. There are precious few mass-manufactured super-minis that appeal to millions on looks and driving ability – rival small cars were stodgier, less fun to run around in and less aspirational.

The 205's dominance of the super-mini brief – which even stretched to a cabriolet version – included the hot hatch. It was launched first as a 1.6-litre, 115bhp 'rocket shopper' with a punchy single-camshaft injected engine. The GTi was widely praised for the excellence of its chassis, which was rated as incredibly nimble and capable of providing tremendous grip.

Other hot-hatch makers had upped the power battle, so Peugeot responded with a 130bhp, 1.9-litre GTi. The 205's sheer verve and manoeuvrability had also been upped, and the razor-sharp throttle response was often described as addictive. However, by the early 1990s, the 205's flimsy interior, raucous nature and transmission shunt meant it was becoming much less competitive.

Even so, more than one publication declared it to be the 'car of the decade,' and drivers who became intoxicated by the 205 couldn't give it up. Peugeot tried to replace it with the bigger 306 and smaller 106, but it didn't work, and in 1998 it announced the all-new 206 as a direct replacement.

106 Rallye

1994–1999

ENGINE: In-line four-cylinder, 1294cc

POWER: 100bhp

CHASSIS: Steel monocoque, three-door

BRAKES (F/R): Disc/drum

TRANSMISSION: Five-speed manual

SUSPENSION: Struts front, semi-trailing arms rear

TOP SPEED: 118mph (189km/h)

ACCELERATION: 0–62.5mph (100km/h) in 9.7 seconds

Popularity meant the 205 GTi wasn't yet dead in 1993, but Peugeot's plan to replace the city-car facet of the 205's personality with the 106 and the family-car facet with the bigger 306 was in place. The stripped-out 106 Rallye was aimed at young motoring enthusiasts with an appetite for a pure driving experience.

Like many of the great road-cars before it, the 106 Rallye was developed to a motor-sport brief, Group N rallying – a class that requires a lithe 1300cc car. Peugeot's engineers managed to push the unit's output up to 100bhp by using a fast road camshaft and a higher compression ratio. The upshot was an engine that required full use of the revs – the engine was redlined at 7200rpm – and it had a close-ratio gearbox to encourage the driver to do just that.

The rest of the Rallye was as uncompromisingly hard-core as the transmission system. The suspension came from the higher-specification XSi combined with anti-roll bars. There was a simple, stripped-out interior, painted steel wheels and some aesthetic highlights including body graphics and bright-red seat-belts and carpets.

There was only one way to drive the Rallye, and that was flat-out, in order to exploit the incredibly direct handling and manic progress which marked the car out. It was not an ideal day-to-day car, though, as it was very noisy and a little uncomfortable on the motorway or any other long-haul journey. But a small market of dedicated hard-drivers was only too pleased to find a mass-maker turning out a machine with supercar-inspired rawness.

406 Coupe

1997–

ENGINE: 24-valve four-camshaft V6, 2956cc

POWER: 194bhp

CHASSIS: Steel monocoque, two-door

BRAKES (F/R): Disc with ABS

TRANSMISSION: Five-speed manual

SUSPENSION: Struts front, double wishbone rear

TOP SPEED: 146mph (234km/h)

ACCELERATION: 0–62.5mph (100km/h) in 7.9 seconds

Peugeot didn't indulge in platform-sharing diversification when it became popular the first time round. Rivals General Motors had spun the Calibra coupe off the Cavalier running-gear and the Tigra off the Corsa platform. When it became time to plan the product strategy for the 406 (the replacement for the 405), the French added a coupe to the standard saloon- and estate-car line-up.

Again, the 406 coupe was a co-production between Peugeot and Pininfarina. It looked like the Italian styling house had possessed a substantial input, as the Coupe's lines had a distinctly languid, Italianate appeal. It was an influence that was only highlighted further by the fact that Peugeot's own home-grown designs were increasingly becoming more aesthetically aggressive.

Like the Calibra – but unlike the opposition – the 406 Coupe didn't get its own unique design of dashboard, instead relying on the well-sculpted (but rather level-headed) dash of the saloon. Aside from some unique door trims and seats, the 406 coupe's interior was very similar to that of the saloon. This also meant room for four adults in the cabin, something of a prerequisite in this market sector. Only something unashamedly style-driven, such as the Alfa Romeo GTV, could have got away with accommodation for two.

The 406 was built by Pininfarina in Italy, like the 205 cabriolet before it, and was available with either a lacklustre 2.0-litre four-cylinder engine or a powerful 3.0-litre V6. The 406 handled as smoothly and suavely as the exterior lines suggested. Indeed, it wasn't uncommon for the uninformed to confuse it with a Ferrari.

Plymouth Fury

1958–1960

ENGINE: V8, 5196-5914cc

POWER: 230-305bhp

CHASSIS: Separate chassis

BRAKES (F/R): Drum

TRANSMISSION: Three-speed manual

SUSPENSION: Independent front, live axle rear

TOP SPEED: 110mph (178km/h)

ACCELERATION: 0-60mph (96km/h) in 11 seconds

The Plymouth Fury represented one of the finest examples of stylist Virgil Exner's 'Forward look' period at Chrysler. The process had begun, quietly, with the 1955 Plymouths, seemingly marked by a gradual increase in fin size in the fight to 'out-glam' its mid-priced rivals.

There was a certain flair and sense of proportion to Exner's designs though, and none was better balanced than the Fury, which for 1959 was Plymouth's premium offering, marketed as a separate series rather than a version of the Belvedere. It came only as a two door coupe or convertible and only with V8 power, from a 230bhp 5.2 litre to a 6.0 litre Golden Commando unit delivering a claimed 305bhp in the top-of-the line Sport Fury.

Sales were strong and Plymouth were riding high, placed 4th in the industry that year, but 1960 would be the last year of the tail fin for Plymouths – the 1961 model year would usher in radical new styling completely bereft of tail fins as buyers began to tire of the excess of the previous decade.

Nostalgic images of the Fury have been kept in the public consciousness with the aid of the classic horror film *Christine*. Based on the best-selling book by Stephen King, evil takes the form of a self-repairing 58 Fury possessed by dark forces. The car – the Christine of the title – terrorises and kills those who harm her fanatical enthusiast owner.

Barracuda

1964–1966

ENGINE: Six-cylinder/V8 2786-4475cc

POWER: 101-235bhp

CHASSIS: Monocoque

BRAKES (F/R): Drum

TRANSMISSION: Three-/four- speed manual, three-speed auto

SUSPENSION: Independent

TOP SPEED: 110mph (178km/h)

ACCELERATION: 0–60mph (96km/h) in 8-13 seconds

With the Barracuda, Plymouth actually beat Ford to the market with a youthful coupe – it was in the showrooms two weeks before the Mustang. It was really just a tidied-up Valiant saloon (Plymouth's 'compact') with a dramatic fastback roofline that incorporated a large wrap-around rear window.

It was fast (with the V8), handled really well and came with a huge range of options, but somehow failed to steal a march on the Mustang. Its styling was too obviously based on the bargain basement Valiant – the front end was clumsy and the wrap-around rear window dated rapidly. Few were surprised when the Mustang out-sold the Barracuda by a ratio of ten-to-one.

Later versions became less tied-in with the Valiant. They also featured smoother styling and ever more powerful engine options as Plymouth began to pursue a performance image.

By the end of 1960s, Plymouth had decided that the 383-S was the top of the Barracuda range. It came with 235bhp V8 allied to heavy-duty suspension and brakes. The car was totally restyled for 1970, with the Muscular 'Cuda 340 as the most powerful model in the range.

Emission regulations eroded the car's performance gradually in the early '70s, and as the Plymouth name became increasing associated with utilitarian transport, the model name was dropped. In many ways this was a kindness and it has certainly helped ensure that the name is best remembered for the startling vehicles of the 1960s as opposed to the dull ones of the 1970s.

Road-Runner/ Superbird

1968–1970

ENGINE: V8, 7213cc

POWER: 375bhp

CHASSIS: Monocoque

BRAKES (F/R): Disc/drum

TRANSMISSION: Four-speed manual/ three-speed auto

SUSPENSION: Independent, live rear axle

TOP SPEED: 130mph (208km/h)

ACCELERATION: 0-60mph (96km/h) in 5.8 secondss

When Ford began fitting air-cleaving droop-snoots to its Talladega NASCAR racers Chrysler realised it had to fight back with something even wilder. Their first attempt was the '68 Charger 500 - based on the Dodge Charger – but the aerodynamic add-ons caused tail lift and it soon became clear the shape would need more dramatic changes if it was to gain any advantage. An 18 inch droop-snoot was added which dramatically reduced front-end lift so dramatically that a giant rear spoiler had to be added to redress the balance. Combined with the 650bhp full race tune these cars could lap the NASCAR circuits at something in excess of 200mph.

The good news was Joe Public could buy a road version of this car – called the Charger Daytona – with up to 390bhp, because manufacturers were required by NASCAR to build 500 road car versions so as to homologate the model for racing.

Plymouth did their own version, the Road Runner Superbird (based on the Belvedere) in 1970, with slightly different additions. NASCAR rules now required that one had to be built for every two Plymouth dealers, which meant a total number of 1,900 were built to homologate the car for competition. In the hands of star drivers like Richard Petty, the Daytona and Superbird cleaned up on the tracks in 1970, winning a total of 38 races to Ford's 10.

The time in the spotlight for the Charger Daytona and Superbird was a short one. The rules changed in 1971 in favour of smaller capacity engines, leaving these wild Plymouths and Dodges as a potent reminder of one of American racing's most exciting periods.

Bonneville

1959

ENGINE: V8, 6377cc

POWER: 260-345bhp

CHASSIS: Monocoque

BRAKES (F/R): Drum

TRANSMISSION: Four-speed auto, three-speed manual

SUSPENSION: Independent front, live axle rear

TOP SPEED: 125mph (200km/h)

ACCELERATION: 0-60mph (96km/h) in 9-11 secs

Pontiac, one of General Motors' most successful post-war Divisions. It achieved this by pitching its models at the middle-class buyer who wanted a car with all the luxury of the expensive marques but at not much more than mid-range prices.

This was the winning formula that led to the creation of the 1959 Bonneville. As soon as it was launched it became one of Pontiac's most critically acclaimed models yet, a full-size machine with new wide-track styling and lower, longer bodywork than the 1958 models.

At the front there was an aggressive split-grille look, at the rear twin-fin rear fenders. An increased glass area across the range gave the car an expensive look that set it apart from mid-priced rivals.

The pillarless four door Vista hardtop had a rear overhang on its roof, while the beautiful two door coupes had a certain affinity with the Cadillac Coupe DeVille models of that year. Naturally, there was a convertible version too.

The Bonneville was Pontiac's top-line offering and all models had V8 engines, the most powerful delivering 345bhp through either a syncromesh manual box or, as usually, an automatic. Thus equipped, the Bonneville was quick and the wide track handling gave the car better cornering ability than the average Detroit product of 1959.

It is always the car with character, the car with something extra that wins people's hearts and this was definitely the case with the Bonneville. It not only looked great externally, it had great interior trim and mechanics that made it a comfortable, reliable and even enjoyable drive. It was a little taste of luxury for those with small pockets.

Pontiac GTO

1966-1971

ENGINE: V8,6556cc

POWER: 365bhp

CHASSIS: Monocoque

BRAKES (F/R): disc/drum

TRANSMISSION: Three-speed automatic

SUSPENSION: Independent front, live axle rear

TOP SPEED: 125mph (200km/h)

ACCELERATION: 0-60 (96km/h) in 6.6 seconds

The muscle car was a very basic idea. Put your biggest, most powerful engine in one of your lightest bodies. Like most strokes of genius, it was breathtaking in its simplicity.

The Pontiac GTO of 1964 created the genre and when sales took off rival American marques could only fall into line behind it. Initially the GTO was only an option package on the Tempest LeMans models, a ruse by Pontiac's chief engineer of the time – John Z DeLorean – to by-pass a GM corporate performance car ban.

However, it was so successful that by 1966 the Tempest GTO had become a separate series in its own right with special wheels, trim and badging – not to mention a sportier interior – to let other

drivers know this one was really hot. Big-block engines gave up to 360bhp in these relatively lightweight bodies – a sports hardtop, a sports coupe and a convertible – and with the suitably heavy duty suspension and brakes the performance was reasonably usable too.

Sales peaked in 1966 at 100,000 cars and as the '60s rolled on the concept was watered down. The cars gained weight and lost power until the original thought behind their conception was diluted. It got to the point where the later vehicles were struggling for their muscle car class rating as well as failing to capture the magic of the original GTOs. There were no more GTOs after 1971 – which may not have been such a bad thing.

Pontiac

Firebird Trans Am

1973–1976

ENGINE: V8, 7459cc

POWER: 310bhp

CHASSIS: Monocoque

BRAKES (F/R): Disc/drum

TRANSMISSION: 4 speed manual, 3 speed auto

SUSPENSION: Independent front, live axle rear

TOP SPEED: 132mph (176km/h)

ACCELERATION: 0–60mph (96km/h) in 5.4 seconds

The original Firebird had appeared in 1967, based on Chevrolet Camaro's 'F' body, but interest in the car didn't really begin to pick up until the restyled 1970 versions were introduced.

These were muscular looking cars, with fat arches, curvy hips and huge implied machismo in their stance. Only one variant had the power to under-pin the looks though – the Trans Am.

The first Trans Ams had appeared in the old shape body and had proved difficult to sell at first as high insurance premiums and a rising nervousness about high performance began to militate against ownership of something really quick. Interest picked-up again in 1973 when the famous Phoenix bonnet decals were first used, but buyers couldn't have known that this would be the last year of the really powerful big-block 455 cars.

Delivering 310bhp, this was the biggest capacity engine ever offered in a pony car, a fact that made Pontiac nervous in the killjoy atmosphere that was all pervading in the American motor industry in the early 70s. In any case, before the end of the year emission controls were already eating into its power. The 455 was a pale shadow of its former self by the time the last big-block Trans Ams were built in 1976.

Another reason why the Firebird Trans Am lives on in so many people's memories is because it was the vehicle chosen to be the invulnerable star of the cult television series *Knight Rider* – in which the car as well as its driver fought crime.

Fiero

1984–1989

ENGINE: In-line four-cylinder, 2495cc

POWER: 90bhp

CHASSIS: Steel space-frame chassis, unstressed composite body panels

BRAKES: Disc all round

TRANSMISSION: Four-speed manual

SUSPENSION: Independent front, struts rear

TOP SPEED: 110mph (176km/h)

ACCELERATION: 0–62.5mph (100km/h) in 11.5 seconds

Pontiac's decision to build a small, inexpensive, mid-engined sports car was not revolutionary. Fiat and Lancia had already marketed similar cars. But two things about the Fiero were unusual – it was commissioned as much as an economical commuting car as a sportster, and the vehicle was constructed in a radically new way.

Under the Fiero's very pretty skin was a tough steel understructure – it was an exceptionally strong little car – providing the majority of the car's strength. The external panels were made from a variety of plastics, including special RRIM for the doors and front wings that could spring back into shape after minor impacts. The skin was attached to the Fiero's chassis by a new 'mill and drill' technique. Pontiac reckoned this system allowed the inexpensive development of Targa and convertible versions, as well as inexpensive re-styling.

Sadly, the drivetrain on the first Fieros was as old-fashioned as the styling and engineering were advanced. The Fiero's reputation also suffered in the early years with a catalogue of quality problems.

Later developments, though, made the Fiero into a fine car – especially the installation of a V6 engine and a re-style that wasn't as crisp as the original, but looked more upmarket. Sadly, despite the symmetrical dash layout – or easy right-hand-drive conversion – and early interest from General Motors in Europe, the Fiero never made it across the Atlantic. The innovative construction technique was also used on GM's MPV (multi-purpose vehicle) line and, much more significantly, the all-new Saturn marque.

Ironically, the easily detachable exterior panels made the Fiero a favourite base for kit-car enthusiasts, who re-clad it as a surprisingly convincing Ferrari look-a-like.

Porsche 356

1946–1965

ENGINE: Flat-four, 1086–1966cc

POWER: 40–155bhp

CHASSIS: Monocoque

BRAKES (F/R): Drum and disc

TRANSMISSION: Four-speed

SUSPENSION: Independent

**TOP SPEED: 87–130mph
(139–208km/h)**

**ACCELERATION: 0–60mph (96km/h)
in 17 seconds (early car),
10 seconds (Carrera)**

Dr Ferdinand Porsche set up his design consultancy in 1931, but the first car to bear his name, the 356, was not built until 1946. Closely related to the Volkswagen Beetle – another famous Porsche design – the 356 had an air-cooled, flat-four, 40bhp pushrod engine, and trailing-link front suspension with swing axles at the rear. There were coupe, cabriolet and shallow-screened sportster versions.

The original styling was changed on the 1955 365A to a crisper shape with a curved, one-piece windscreen, improved front suspension and steering and a bigger 1600cc engine. Top of the standard range was the 110mph (176km/h) Super 90, but even the standard 60bhp car could now achieve 100mph (160km/h). The last of the line 365C had ZF steering and four-wheel disc brakes for extra driving safety.

For advanced students there were the 120mph-plus (192km/h) Carrera versions of the 365 from 1955 onwards. Engines were still flat-fours, but totally different in detail – the crank was a roller-bearing type and, instead of pushrods, there were four overhead camshafts with twin-plug-per-cylinder ignition changing the driving characteristics.

The 365 improved dramatically over the years, growing more and more specialized and increasingly distant from its VW Beetle roots. Compact, beautifully built and – in some cases – very fast, it was the car on which Porsche built its reputation in the 1950s.

Porsche 911S

1966–1973

ENGINE: Flat-six, 1991cc

POWER: 160bhp

CHASSIS: Monocoque

BRAKES (F/R): Disc

TRANSMISSION: Five-speed

SUSPENSION: Independent

TOP SPEED: 140mph (224km/h)

ACCELERATION: 0-60mph (96km/h) in 3.7 seconds (Turbo)

The development potential of the Porsche 911S flat-six, which has one of the most instantly recognisable growling engine notes on the road, has seemed limitless. Power has leapt from 130bhp of the original 2 litre of 1963 to the 360bhp of the turbo – and that's not counting the 450bhp of the 911-based 959, a technological powerhouse which was basically designed to meet the likes of the Ferrari 288GTO and F40 head on.

One of the nicest all-rounders was the original 911S of 1967, the first of the up-rated 911s. With its higher compression ratio, bigger valves, forged pistons and two triple-choke Webers this car produced a sparkling 160bhp, increasing later on to 170bhp with fuel injection — an astonishing output for a 2 litre

unit. The only way of spotting a 140mph S was by its starfish alloys.

This was in 1967, when the 911s shape was still pure and unadorned, based on the shorter wheelbase chassis that forged the car's reputation for tricky, tail-heavy handling.

There are a lot of enthusiasts for the Porsche marque who became fans due to this car. It's an understandable state of affairs. The 911S has a little of everything that makes a great car. It has power enough for anyone who dreams of feeling the urge for speed and it has tremendous style. Some might point to its tricky handling as a drawback, but there are a lot of people who only see that as a welcome challenge.

Porsche 914

1969–1975

ENGINE: Flat-four, 1679/1991cc

POWER: 100bhp

CHASSIS: Monocoque

BRAKES (F/R): Disc

TRANSMISSION: Five-speed

SUSPENSION: Independent

TOP SPEED: 107mph (171km/h)

ACCELERATION: 0–60mph (96km/h) in 10.3 seconds

Unloved, and now almost forgotten, the Porsche 914 was a hybrid, conceived to give Porsche a foothold in the mass-market sports-car sector, which it later achieved with the Boxster. For collaborator Volkswagen – worried by poor sales of its mainstay Beetle – it meant some much-needed showroom glamour to draw in the customers.

Launched in 1969, the Karmann-built targa-top – which always seemed to look as if it was going both ways at once – was powered by an injected VW411, air-cooled, mid-mounted flat-four. This produced a modest 85bhp for a disappointing top speed of little more than 107mph (171km/h).

Later versions had a much superior and much needed 2-litre unit specially developed by Porsche, although the top-of-the range 914/6 – with the 2-litre 911 flat-six – proved short-lived due to its ridiculously high production cost.

The 914 had considerable appeal as a superior entry-level sports car, particularly in the USA. There was road-holding aplenty, decent luggage space in its nose and tail, and, importantly, it was built as well as any 911.

Historians tend to view the Porsche-VW 914 as a commercial flop, but in reality this wasn't the case – 119,000 examples of all types were built before Porsche pulled the plug in 1975. In terms of sales figures, the car was a success. Of these, 84,000 went to North America, the main intended market for the 914. However, there is a lot more to a good car than sales, as the 914 very aptly demonstrates.

911 Carrera RS 2.7

1975

ENGINE: Flat-six, 2687cc

POWER: 210bhp

CHASSIS: Monocoque

BRAKES (F/R): Doisc

TRANSMISSION: Five-speed manual

SUSPENSION: Torsion bar front, trailing arms rear

TOP SPEED: 149mph (238km/h)

ACCELERATION: 0–60mph (96km/h) in 5.7 seconds

After sales of the Porsche 911 started to fade in the early 1970s, the company decided to develop a range-topping version that would capture the imagination until the planned turbocharged 911 was unveiled in 1975.

Above everything else, the 911 Carrera had to be very quick. The first move was to take the capacity of the flat-six engine up to 2.7-litres, which required new cylinder barrels so the bore could be increased by 6mm to 90mm, though the stroke remained the same. Porsche used the advanced Nikasil coating process inside the barrels to reduce friction and wear. With Bosch mechanical fuel injection, the engine produced 210bhp.

The effectiveness of the new engine was increased by making the rest of the car much lighter than a standard-issue 911. The RS's body was made of thinner gauge steel and the windows were also thinner than normal. Other weight-saving measures included the deletion of soundproofing, and the replacement of the steel bumpers with one-piece plastic units.

The resulting 911 Carrera RS – with some 150kg knocked off the kerb weight and a much more powerful engine – was capable of hitting 60mph in just 5.5 seconds and could get up tp 149mph. Most of the cars were produced in white with the now-classic Carrera livery running across above the sill and the small 'duck tail' spoiler mounted on the engine lid. Despite the go-faster looks, this spoiler massively reduced rear axle lift at high speeds. Porsche also produced a slightly more civilised and self-effacing version without the spoiler called the RS Touring.

The rare RS is still regarded as one of the greatest 911s – and, indeed one of the greatest sportscars ever, with a rawness and aggression that was rarely equalled in the production motor world.

Porsche 924

1975–1985

ENGINE: Four-cylinder, 1984cc

POWER: 125bhp

CHASSIS: Monocoque

BRAKES (F/R): Disc/drum

TRANSMISSION: Four and five-speed manual, three-speed automatic

SUSPENSION: Independent

TOP SPEED: 125mph (200km/h)

ACCELERATION: 0–60mph (96km/h) in 9.5 seconds

The Porsche 924 was conceived in the early 1970s as a joint project with Volkswagen/Audi. It was to be designed by Porsche, but produced and marketed by Volkswagen using as many stock VW parts as possible. The engine was an injected 2-litre unit from the Audi 100 – also found in the VW LT van – and whilst the rear transaxle was new, the gears inside were from Audi too.

It was only when the fuel crisis began to bite hard, and sales of the ugly-duckling 914 began to flag, that Porsche realized it was faced with the prospect of having no cheap sports car to sell in the second half of the 1970s. With the 911's future also looking somewhat uncertain, Porsche decided to take over the project as a purely Porsche model, with production sub-contracted out to VW.

Launched in 1975, the 924 was an instant success, and the rest is history. It was no 911, though – the van-derived engine could be raucous, even if it endowed the 924 with brisk acceleration in the very long-legged fifth gear and a 125mph (200km/h) top speed in fifth gear. More impressive was the handling, 50/50 weight distribution giving the 924 good, well-balanced poise.

The 924 Turbo hardened the model's performance image in the late-1970s with 170bhp, thanks to a KKK turbocharger. Top speed surged from 125mph (200km/h) to 141mph (226km/h), and acceleration was almost in the super-car class, with 0–60mph (96km/h) coming up in 6.9 seconds.

In the 1980s the 944, using the basic 924 shell with a proper Porsche 2.5-litre four-cylinder engine, finally shook off any associations with the VW LT van, although the 924 itself lingered on until 1985.

Porsche 928

1977–1996

ENGINE: 90 degree V8, 4474cc

POWER: 240bhp

CHASSIS: Steel monocoque, three-door

BRAKES (F/R): Disc/disc

TRANSMISSION: Five-speed manual transaxle

SUSPENSION: Double wishbone front, trailing arm rear

TOP SPEED: 150mph (244km/h)

ACCELERATION: 0-62mph (100km/h) in 7.4 seconds

Although marked by continued perseverance with the ancient 911 concept, the launch of the Porsche 928 in 1977 blew away any doubts about the company's capabilities in innovation and whole-car development. A V8-engined grand-touring sports coupe, the 928 was a huge leap into the future of the motorcar, from the aerodynamic styling to the details of the sun visor design.

Porsche's future-shock styling for the 928 was actually started before work began on shaping the 924. It must have been a revelation in 1977. Its all-in-one shape managed without separate bumpers, there were no external flanges or drip rails and the door skin was a masterpiece of integrated styling.

This shape was certainly a suitable shell for the equally advanced under-skin engineering. The biggest single step-forward was the so-called 'Weissach Axle' – named after the company's development centre – which used flexible rubber brushes to allow the rear suspension to slighty 'self-steer' improving cornering power and stability under braking.

The rest of the car was thoroughly and ruggedly engineered. An all-new V8 engine drove a five-speed gearbox which was sitting on the rear axle – the engineers also placed the (plastic) fuel tank and battery behind the rear axle line in order to achieve an ideal 50/50 front-to-rear weight distribution.

Other details – like the pantograph wiper for the rear window and illuminated sun visor – were very new at the time and demonstrated Porsche's ability to think laterally about all aspects of car design. The 928 was an exceptional grand tourer and survived until 1996 without massive changes, but even so, the model was never a huge commerical success. Enthusiasts seemed unable and unwilling to view the company as anything but the maker of the legendary 911.

Porsche 944 Turbo

1985–1991

ENGINE: 90 degree V8, 4474cc

POWER: 240bhp

CHASSIS: Steel monocoque, three-door

BRAKES (F/R): Disc

TRANSMISSION: Five-speed manual transaxle

SUSPENSION:Steel monocoque

TOP SPEED: 150mph (240km/h)

ACCELERATION: 0–62mph (100km/h) in 7.4 seconds

There was much disquiet amoung die-hard Porsche fans when the company launched the 924 coupe in 1976. Porsche may have needed this inexpensive 2+2 sportster, but it went down badly with informed enthusiasts who knew it started life as a VW/Audi car, had a VW van-derived engine under the bonnet and also incorporated plenty of bits from a range of other VW cars, including the Beetle.

In 1979, Porsche launched the much-improved 924 Turbo which had the chassis and the pace to make it count as a real Porsche, or so they thought. The model still wasn't selling, so Porsche re-invented the 924 with a very clever re-styling – effectively just flaring the front and rear wings – and a new four-cylinder engine which was half of the 928's V8. Finally, with the 944, Porsche made a success out of the project, which was still built by Audi.

The powerful 944 Turbo arrived in late 1984, with both the horsepower and the price tag to match the 22-year-old but classic 911 Carrera. Despite the subtle changes to the 944's fine styling, the Turbo was much changed, particularly under the skin.

The suspension was heavily modified and the engine's electronic management system much more sophisticated than the non-Turbo. Inside, Porsche's chief stylist Tony Lapine had finally expunged the remaining 924 genes by designing a completely new dashboard and interior for the car.

In the final judgement, the 944 Turbo was a better car than the then-current 911. It required less effort to drive hard and was a much better day-to-day supercar. It would take the 911 another five years to catch up, but if you had a 944 turbo you weren't going to be worried by the wait.

959

1987–1988

ENGINE: Twin-turbocharged 24 valve flat-six, 4474cc

POWER: 450bhp

CHASSIS: Steel monocoque, composite body panels

BRAKES (F/R): Disc

TRANSMISSION: Five-speed manual

SUSPENSION: Spring struts front, semi-trailing arms rear

TOP SPEED: 197mph (316km/h)

ACCELERATION: 0-62mph (100km/h) in 3.7 seconds

Porsche's new-found determination to re-invent the 911, after coming close to giving it the axe in 1981, managed to scale new heights of automotive technology. The 959 was so far ahead of the opposition when it was first driven in 1987 that it re-defined the term.

Although based on central section of a standard 911, the 959 bore little resemblance to it. The familiar 911 lines had been swollen, with new nose and a radically-different tail. Under the new lines was a 4x4 drivetrain and a high-tech twin-turbo version of the flat-six engine. Even the damping and the ride height were electronically adjustable.

One German publication managed to clock the 959 at a maximum speed of 197mph, but then the 959 was small for a 'supercar' and had 450bhp to push it through the air. The 959 smashed

other performance benchmarks too, achieving the 0-100mph dash in just 8.3 seconds. What really surprised the first drivers of the 959, was the ease with which this performance could be accessed. Up until the 959 arrived, seriously fast cars were generally large, heavy and extremely difficult to drive flat-out.

The traditional supercar was more closely related to out-and-out race cars. Porsche moved the goalposts in a very significant way with the 959. It deployed complex but reliable technology to allow the averagely-skilled driver to pilot a car at a tremendous speed. Experts brought up on the pleasure gained from driving a challenging car quickly were astounded by the outright performance of the 959, but less impressed by what some critics and drivers thought a characterless road-rocket.

911 Carrera 4

1989–1993

ENGINE: Flat-six, 3600cc

POWER: 250bhp

CHASSIS: Steel monocoque, two-door

BRAKES (F/R): Disc

TRANSMISSION: Five-speed manual

SUSPENSION: Spring struts and wishbones front, semi-trailing arms rear

TOP SPEED: 161mph (257km/h)

ACCELERATION: 0-62mph (100km/h) in 5.7 seconds

Even though the Porsche 911 was saved from extinction in 1981, it was the best part of seven years before the heavily-revised 911 – codenamed 964 – was launched. Despite looking like a more modern and slightly more aerodynamic version of the old car, the 964 was actually 85 percent new. The roof section, doors and bonnet were retained from the old car, but the whole floorpan had been redesigned, as had the rear section of the car and the newly-sculpted aerodynamic nose and tail sections, in place of conventional bumpers. Inside, the 964 was also newly re-designed, although it remained true to the classic 911 styling heritage.

The re-designed floorpan was a major expense but necessary to accept the new coil-sprung suspension and to accommodate the productionised version of the 959's four wheel-drive

transmission. The first of the 964 series to be announced was the Carrera 4, a sort of down-to-earth 959. Although it lacked turbochargers the engine was bigger (3.6-litres, up from 3.2) and it developed 250bhp.

The Carrera 4's new-found stability and all-weather confidence transformed the 911's reputation. The previous model was little changed from the original 911 launched in 1962, and was a tricky car to drive. The Carrera 4 offered thrills without overwhelming risk. In pure performance terms, the car also offered some truly fabulous pace.

Project 964 proved the expertise of Porsche's engineers and showed that a 25 year-old concept could still become the basis of the best supercar on the market at the time.

Porsche 911

1997–

ENGINE: 24 valve flat-six, 3387cc

POWER: 300bhp

CHASSIS: Steel monocoque, two door

BRAKES (F/R): Disc with ABS

TRANSMISSION: Five-speed manual

SUSPENSION: Struts front, independent multi-link rear

TOP SPEED: 175mph (280km/h)

ACCELERATION: 0-62mph (100km/h) in 5.3 seconds

This visionary release was the most radical interpretation of the world's most enduring sports car. Until the new car, known as project 996, all the various versions of the 911 had been based on the previous model. That gave the 911 a unique genetic link back to the original 1962 launch model.

There were just two things that connected the 996 with the previous 911, the superb 993 – that the engine was rear-mounted and the rear suspension (originally developed for the five-door 989) was carried over. Otherwise, the 996 was a completely new project design.

To save development costs, the 996 shared its whole structure with the Boxster, from the dashboard forward. Even the distinctive headlamps were the same. The 911 had a bigger version of the new water-cooled flat-six developing 300bhp, although it didn't make it feel dramatically quicker than the Boxster. Perhaps that was because the 911 was now a wider, longer car, feeling more like a grand tourer than a compact supercar. Even so its handling was still exemplary and the engine still dominated the tactile thrills delivered to the driver.

Other commentators raised questions about the quality of the interior and the switchgear and asked whether a car of nearly twice the price of the Boxster should be sharing its interior fittings. However, considering the comprehensiveness of the reworking, the new 911 was accepted with an enthusiasm that, for Porsche, was encouraging.

Sales were strong at the outset and Porsche revealed that it was to develop a 'SUV' with VW. Its mantra of continuous development saw the 996 project spawn 4x4 versions, a convertible and the searing Turbo.

Boxster

1997–

ENGINE: 24 valve flat-six, 2490cc

POWER: 205bhp

CHASSIS: Steel monocoque, convertible

BRAKES: disc with ABS

TRANSMISSION: Five-speed manual

SUSPENSION: Struts front, independent multi-link rear

TOP SPEED: 149mph (238km/h)

ACCELERATION: 0-62mph (100km/h) in 7.2 seconds

Although the new-generation Porsche 911 arrived just in time to catch the end of the 1980s economic boom, Porsche was in deep financial trouble by early 1990s. Although the stalwart 911 had been re-developed, the 944 and 928 were very old designs, and sales were sliding all round the world, especially in the crucial US market.

Ironically, Porsche had been spending huge amounts of money on a secret project called the 959, which was basically a five-door 911 look-a-like powered by a nose-mounted V8 engine purloined from the 928. Porsche's thinking was that it would replace both the 911 and 928 with a car that merged the crucial aspects of both, and offer a car that was useful to the executive driver on a genuinely everyday life basis.

The world economic state though indicated that this was the wrong time for a super-expensive executive sports car, a peculiar niche that Ferrari had tried to establish with 400i and failed.

To boost faith in Porsche's ability to launch a second, successful model line, it unveiled the Boxster concept car at the 1993 Detroit show. It was designed to demonstrate that the company had fresh ideas and boost confidence in the beleaguered US dealer network. What wasn't known at the time was the Boxster was one half of a future product plan that relied on two models based on the same basic parts. These were an all-new 911 and a cheaper mid-engined roadster.

The real Boxster arrived in 1997 to a slightly muted response, as the extraordinary styling of the show car had been toned down, especially inside. The excellence of the new water-cooled flat-six engine and superb chassis, soon changed minds, however. And although the Boxster wasn't as cheap as some hoped, the car was an instant success, delivering the feel of a mini-911 for just over half the price.

Cayenne

2002–

ENGINE: 4511cc, turbocharged V8

POWER: 450bhp

CHASSIS: Steel monocoque

BRAKES: 18in and 17in discs with aluminium monobloc callipers

TRANSMISSION: five-speed auto with manual override

SUSPENSION: Struts front, multi-link axle rear, air-springs

TOP SPEED: 165mph (264km/h)

ACCELERATION: 0-62mph (100km/h) in 5.2 seconds

Porsche's plans for a family car were hatched in the late 1980s. It was called the 989 and looked like a big four-door 911. Unlike the 911, the engine was in the nose and the sloping tailgate formed a hatchback. Rumour had it that there was to have been under the skin the aluminium spaceframe and four-wheel drive transmission that also made up the 1994 Audi A8. Porsche's engineers got some way through the 989's development programme before the global recession and heavy losses forced the project to be canned.

But Porsche wanted another stab at the family car market. It reckoned that it had hardly any buyers in their 40's - those drivers with children. So in the mid 1990s it decided to enter the booming SUV market. SUVs were becoming the de facto upmarket family car and Porsche tied up with Volkswagen to produce its own upmarket off-roader.

Porsche's version was called the Cayenne and, initially came in two versions V8 and turbocharged V8. Although the styling of the five-door machine attracted much criticism, there's little doubt that car's engineering was top-flight. It had permanent four-wheel drive (unlike many SUVs) and the option of air-suspension so the car could jack itself up off-road. Buyers could also choose a special off-road chassis specification which allowed the car to perform in the worst conditions. Porsche claimed 'supreme onroad and equally outstanding off-road qualities'.

But it was the Cayenne Turbo that shocked the market. Despite its size, the turbocharged 4.5-litre V8 delivered a 0-62mph time of just 5.2secs–a peppery performance to live up to its name.

Reliant Scimitar

1968–1985

ENGINE: V6, 2994cc

POWER: 138bhp

CHASSIS: Steel ladder chassis with fibreglass bodyshell

BRAKES (F/R): Disc

TRANSMISSION: Four-speed manual

SUSPENSION: Independent

TOP SPEED: 120mph (192km/h)

ACCELERATION: 0–62mph (100km/h) in 8.7 seconds

Who could have expected one of the most influential new car-body styles to have emerged from a small firm in the Midlands region of the UK with a history of building plastic-bodied three-wheeler cars? Unexpected it may have been, but the Reliant Scimitar GTE had a huge influence on the car industry, with manufacturers such as Lancia, Volvo and BMW unashamedly rushing to copy the vehicle's unique sporting-estate styling.

The GTE grew out of the more conventional – and booted – Scimitar GT coupe, which was launched in 1964. The basic ingredients were the same, a substantial separate chassis, fibreglass body shell and rugged Ford V6 power.

Like the GT, the GTE was styled by the noted industrial-design company, Ogle. The recipe was quite simple, but clever and versatile – a futuristic long-roof two-door body, with tapering side windows and a handy glass hatchback. Inside, the Scimitar had room for four adults, and the decent boot space could be extended by folding the rear seats.

Despite Reliant's tiny operation, the Scimitar was extremely well thought out and finished up to mass-market standards of the time. The rugged Ford V6 gave the car excellent performance, and the optional switchable overdrive helped deliver good economy and relaxed motorway cruising.

The Scimitar was a fine car. It was many years ahead of its time, and it is still influential more than 20 years later.

Renault Dauphine

1956–1968

ENGINE: Four-cylinder, 845cc

POWER: 30bhp

CHASSIS: Monocoque

BRAKES (F/R): Drums (disc from 1964)

TRANSMISSION: Four-speed manual

SUSPENSION: Independent

TOP SPEED: 74mph (118km/h)

ACCELERATION: 0-60mph (96km/h) in 25secs

Renault committed itself to rear engined cars after the war, beginning with the 4CV in 1947. That car was a willing little saloon which went quite well on 760cc and boasted refinements like rack and pinion steering and hydraulic brakes.

The Dauphine of 1956 was simply an up-rated, restyled 4CV but with enough power to bring the shortcomings of its tail-heavy engine configuration and into focus. Not that buyers seemed to care – they liked it for its economy and comfort and bought 2 million of them over a 12 year production run. More interesting was the Dauphine Gordini which, on a tuned 38bhp, was good for 75mph. Both versions are remembered for their propensity for alarming corrosion.

In search of a more glamorous image Renault developed a Dauphine Coupe and convertible called the Floride, a pretty Frau design cast in the mould of VWs Karmann Ghia. It was followed up in 1962 by the more powerful, all disc braked Caravelle which had a different, squarer roof line and, on most models, a bigger 1108cc engine giving the potential for 90mph.

Renault remained faithful to rear engines until 1972 with the 8 and 10, but its new generation of small cars for the '70s – the 5, 6 and 12 – were all front driven. The Dauphine is a name that brings a flush of nostalgia to many fans of Renault and their high sales mean that it is a car that is also very fondly remembered by the company itself.

Alpine A110

1962–1977

ENGINE: Four cylinder, 968 to 1600cc

POWER: 127bhp (1600cc)

CHASSIS: Tubular backbone

BRAKES (F/R): Disc

TRANSMISSION: Four- or five-speed manual

SUSPENSION: Independent

TOP SPEED: 129mph (206km/h)

ACCELERATION: 0-60mph (96km/h) in 6.3 seconds

With two Monte Carlo Rally victories and a world rally championship to its credit, the rear engined, polyester bodied Alpine A110 is France's most thoroughly decorated sportscar.

Father of the Alpine was Jean Adele, once the youngest Renault dealer in France, who built his first complete sports car – based on the humble Renault 4CV – in 1954. The definitive, back-bone chassised A110 Berlinette appeared in 1962, and was to stay in production until 1977.

Competition victories came quickly as drivers learned to make the best of its agility, despite primitive Volkswagen style swing-axle suspension, and amazing speed – on just 1300cc, the lightweight A110 could nudge 120 mph. Sales were slow until Adele finally managed to persuade Renault to market his cars in 1967. Soon A110s were emerging from the small Dieppe factory at twice the rate, and were being built under licence in Renault satellite factories all over the world. Spain, Brazil, Mexico and even Bulgaria all built versions of the A110. With Jean Adele now heading Renault's competition department, rallying of the A110 continued full steam ahead, and it was a top level winner until the mid-'70s, causing much consternation to big names like Porsche and Ford.

The A110's days should have been numbered when the up-market chisel-edged 310 Coupe appeared in 1971, but enthusiasts prefered the old car. Renault kept it in production until 1977.

Renault 16

1964–1979

ENGINE: In-line four-cylinder, 1470/1565/1647cc

POWER: 55–93bhp

CHASSIS: Monocoque

BRAKES (F/R): Disc/drum

TRANSMISSION: Four- and five-speed manual, three-speed automatic

SUSPENSION: Independent

TOP SPEED: 90–105mph (144–168km/h)

ACCELERATION: 0–60mph (96km/h) in 12 seconds (TX)

The 1964 Renault 16 was a milestone in the development of the family car. It has the honour of being the first four-door hatchback with fold-down rear seats. Surely, such an achievement will guarantee it a place forever in the annals of motoring history.

Just as important as the breakthrough in space-saving interior design was the fact that the Renault 16 was comfortable and practical. Not surprisingly, it went on to become a favourite not only in France but across the rest of Europe as well.

Front-wheel drive gave the 16 excellent road-holding, whilst long-travel all-independent suspension ensured a soft, absorbent ride on even the roughest of French roads. Front disc brakes were also to its credit, and even on a modest

1470cc the original 55bhp 16 could touch 90mph (144km/h). It offered both a degree of performance and a high level of comfort and handling that were not standard in other cars in its class.

The 16TS of 1968 was a higher-performance 1565cc, 88bhp version of the car giving 100mph (160km/h), although the ultimate 16 was the TX of 1973. The power went up to 93bhp, and you could spot a TX by its four-headlamp nose and sports wheels. A five-speed gearbox made it an ideal motorway cruiser, while electric front windows were a rare luxury on a family car in the mid-1970s.

Despite its well-deserved high popularity, the Renault 16 eventually had to give way to the Renault 20 in 1979.

Renault 4

1961–1992

ENGINE: 750cc/780cc/850cc /950cc/1.1 litre four cylinder

POWER: 27-34bhp

CHASSIS: Monocoque

BRAKES: (F/R): Drum (later disc/drum)

TRANSMISSION: Four-speed manual

SUSPENSION: Torsion bar

TOP SPEED: 66-76mph (105-122km/h)

ACCELERATION: 0-62mph (0-100km/h) in 40.5 seconds

The Renault 4CV had been a successful model for Renault after the war but by the late-1950s it was no longer practical. Work began on a replacement with a brief very much on the same lines as the Citroen 2CV. It was to be sold all round the world so it needed to be suitable for all climates and road surfaces. In meeting this brief, practicality took precedence over design and the result was something of an ugly duckling, the R4.

With its unique fifth door in the rear, it was the first hatchback and it had removable seats. The gearshift was a push-pull column extending from the dashboard and torsion bar springing made for a very bouncy ride and rather haphazard handling. And yet the public fell in love with it, farmers especially, then the young and then families in need of a second car. As time progressed, its looks became an asset, with regular design tweaks keeping pace with the times. Practicality and economy were enough to make it beautiful.

The launch model ran off a water-cooled 750cc engine from the 4CV, driving the front wheels, but 850, 780, 1.1 litre and 950 engines were to come in the Renault 4's 30 odd years of production.

Still popular when it gave way to the Twingo, over 8 million Renault 4s were sold around the world.

1984–1996

ENGINE: V6, 2500–3000cc

POWER: 200–250bhp (Turbo models)

CHASSIS: Fibreglass body, steel backbone chassis

BRAKES: Disc all round

TRANSMISSION: Five-speed manual

SUSPENSION: Independent

TOP SPEED: 150–160mph (240–256km/h)

ACCELERATION: 0–60mph (96km/h) in 6 seconds

Alpine GTA/A610

Launched in 1984, the Renault Alpine GTA was the last of these rear-engined French sports cars, using Renault V6 power in a steel back-bone chassis. Gunning for the Porsche 911 market, it offered superb driver involvement and high levels of grip – despite the tail-happy layout – but never managed to tempt many buyers away from their Porsches.

Alpines were quick – particularly in Turbo form – topping 150mph (240km/h) and turning in 0–60mph (96km/h) times in the six-second bracket. Drivers loved the GTA for its feel and responsiveness, yet it was a comfortable, quiet, long-distance machine.

Despite its exotic looks the GTA was surprisingly practical, too, with usable rear seats and rust-free plastic bodywork. The Douvrin V6 – straight out of the big Renault 25 – offered no reliability problems either. Another major plus was the

fact that the overall quality of the cars was good, even if they were not strictly in the 911's league.

In 1992 the GTA became the A610, with a few styling tweaks that somehow robbed the crisp-edged shape of its character, but gave it broader showroom appeal – pop-up headlights are the quickest way of telling the cars apart. The power of the Turbo model was hiked up to 3 litres and 250bhp, top speed to 160mph (with no turbo-lag), and the double-wishbone suspension was tuned to cure any hint of 'twitchiness' suffered by the older model. With power steering, parking the A610 wasn't such a muscle-building exercise either.

The GTA and A610 Alpines were hailed as classics while still in production, but always lived in the shadow of the Porsche 911. Production ended in 1995, with no successor being offered.

Renault **Espace**

1985–1991

ENGINE: In-line four-cylinder, 1995cc

POWER: 110bhp

CHASSIS: Galvanized steel chassis, composite body panels

BRAKES (F/R): Disc

TRANSMISSION: Five-speed manual/automatic

SUSPENSION: Struts front, semi-rigid rear

TOP SPEED: 109mph (174km/h)

ACCELERATION: 0–62.5mph (100km/h) in 10.2 seconds

When a really good idea is born, plenty of people want to claim it as their own. Although French engineering company Matra did claim that the Espace concept – a car which it also builds – came from its drawing boards, British stylist Geoff Matthews reckoned the idea originated with his period at the old Peugeot-Talbot studios in the UK.

Despite Matthews' fine conceptual efforts, the 'tall car' concept had been around since Giugiaro's 1978 Megagamma concept, and three Japanese makers had tried to take advantage of the idea – none with much success. The Espace concept, though, was a rather cleverer attempt and took the Megagamma idea a crucial stage further.

Despite not being longer than an ordinary family car, the Espace could carry a total of up to seven passengers by creating three rows of seats. But the key difference was the articulation of the seats – rows two and three could be swivelled around, the backs folded to create a table-top, or they could be removed altogether for van-like carrying capacity.

But it was the Espace's ability to, in the words of one Renault engineer at the launch in 1984, "combine the carrying capacity of a van with the spaciousness of a minibus and the road manners of an estate," that really set it apart from lesser vehicles.

The popularity of the Espace grew steadily throughout the rest of the 1980s, but it remained a niche product until the early 1990s. Like the Range Rover before it, the Espace defined a new genre and then dominated it. The term eventually coined to describe the concept – Multi Purpose Vehicle (MPV) – summed the car up well.

Renault continued to develop the car through another three generations, improving the build quality enormously along the way.

Renault **Clio Williams**

1993–1996

ENGINE: 16-valve in-line four-cylinder, 1998cc

POWER: 150bhp

CHASSIS: Steel monocoque, three-door

BRAKES (F/R, Disc with ABS

TRANSMISSION: Five-speed manual

SUSPENSION: Struts front, transverse torsion bars rear

TOP SPEED: 134mph (214km/h)

ACCELERATION: 0–62.5mph (100km/h) in 7.9 seconds

Renault carried through the inspiration behind the 5 Turbo 2 and created the 5 Turbo in 1986, two years after the introduction of the second-generation 5 supermini. Although only rated at 115bhp, the 5 was probably the hottest of the 1980s hot-hatch brigade, thanks to the tremendous torque of the 1.4-litre engine in such a light body shell. It was a frustrating car in many ways, being flimsily built and suffering from hot-starting problems. The chassis, though, was well-liked and highly rated.

When the 5 was superseded by the all-new 1991 Clio supermini, the Turbo died with it. Renault, after some huge success with turbocharged engines, decided to switch to a four-valve-per-cylinder arrangement for extra power. The replacement for the 5 was the 137bhp Clio 16V, which was another Renault success in the hot-hatch sector.

Renault's decision to compete in Group N of the 1993 French Rally Championship meant it was allowed to stretch the 1.8-litre engine to 2.0 litres. The result was the Clio Williams, a 150bhp volcanic hatch. Modifications to the engine were extensive, and a stronger gearbox (from the Renault 19 TD) was fitted. The 19 16v also donated longer lower front wishbones – which widened the front track – and uprated springs and dampers.

Only 3,800 Clio Williams were built initially, with distinctive blistered front wings and gold wheels. But the car's success meant a Clio Williams 2 and 3 – upsetting the owners of the original model, who thought they had a low-run future classic in their garages. The Williams was rated as one of the most enjoyable hard-driving cars on sale when it was launched.

Twingo

1993–

ENGINE: In-line four-cylinder, 1239cc

POWER: 55bhp

CHASSIS: Steel monocoque, three-door

BRAKES (F/R): Disc/drum

TRANSMISSION: Five-speed manual

SUSPENSION: Struts front, independent torsion beam rear

TOP SPEED: 91mph (146km/h)

ACCELERATION: 0–62.5mph (100km/h) in 15.0 seconds

French car designer Patrick Le Quement's career was marked by involvement in the radical – he was part of the Ford team that produced the Sierra and 'aero'-Granada – and the rejection of the staid. After two years as VW's design boss, he left for a job with the greater possibility of making design statements. In 1988 Le Quement took over as the head of Renault's design department.

Not surprisingly, his first production car was one of the most radical to come out of Europe in over a decade. The Twingo city car was a serious jolt for rival car makers, the majority of whom had become very complacent about the importance of design and the need to produce fresh and exciting ideas.

Le Quement revived a previous city project that had been shelved, and saw his opportunity to break away from the conventional. However, he did have to plead directly with Renault's chairman to get the go-ahead – Le Quement claimed that he was put under pressure to 'normalize' the Twingo, by removing details such as the semi-circular headlamps.

Early in the project, when the design was being rated at 'customer clinics', over 40 percent of those questioned actively disliked the car – Le Quement's now-famous reply was that, "the greatest risk was to take no risk at all." The 'one-box' Twingo went on sale replete with wacky design details, including the unusual dashboard with a centrally mounted digital instrument binnacle, and efficient pantograph wiper arm.

The Twingo was a massive sales success, and laid the foundations for more radical designs from Le Quement's studio.

Mégane Scenic

1996–2003

ENGINE: In-line four-cylinder, 1995cc

POWER: 115bhp

CHASSIS: Steel monocoque

BRAKES (F/R): Disc with ABS

TRANSMISSION: Five-speed manual

SUSPENSION: Struts front, trailing arms with torsion bars rear

TOP SPEED: 114mph (182km/h)

ACCELERATION: 0–62.5mph (100km/h) in 10.7 seconds

In 1992 Renault's portfolio of 'one-box' utility cars spanned the Twingo city car at one extreme and the much larger seven-seater Espace at the other. It might seem logical to plug the gap with another one-box car, but the decision to build a VW Golf-sized people carrier was a much more significant risk for Renault.

It was risky, but a supremely perceptive move. MPVs in the American mould were almost too big for European in-town use, as well as being too expensive for young families. A smaller, cheaper version of the Espace could potentially attract a very wide audience. Renault gave a clue to its plans in 1991 with a concept car called the Scenic. It was a move the company was later publicly to regret.

Renault merged plans for the Scenic with a bigger overall strategy of replacing the 19 range with a new single model line-up of cars encompassing six different bodystyles. Called Mégane, all the vehicles were based on the same basic running gear, and used the same dashboard and switchgear. Ahead of the mainstream, Renault produced the Mégane hatch, saloon, cabriolet, coupe, estate and Scenic.

The Scenic was a huge sales success. It offered five individual seats – which could be removed and folded – in a taller-than-normal body, which heightened the sense of space. Superb design detailing included storage cubby-holes in the floor, and a structural parcel shelf in the tall boot which could take the weight of shopping.

Other manufacturers raced to launch their own interpretation of the mini-MPV. It's quite possible that the Scenic heralds the beginning of the end for the conventional family car.

Sport Spider

1996–1998

ENGINE: 16-valve in-line four-cylinder, 1998cc

POWER: 150bhp

CHASSIS: Welded aluminium extrusions, composite body panels

BRAKES (F/R): Disc

TRANSMISSION: Five-speed manual

SUSPENSION: Double-wishbone with horizontal dampers front, double-wishbone rear

TOP SPEED: 132mph (211km/h)

ACCELERATION: 0–62.5mph (100km/h) in 6.7 seconds

Perhaps worried that it would become stereotyped as the manufacturer of clever family transport, Renault branched out in an unexpected way in 1996. The Sport Spider was an attempt to update the Lotus 7/Caterham Seven format with a more modern, raw, two-seater roadster built from hi-tech materials.

The Sport Spider arrived on the market just ahead of the very similar Lotus Elise, using the same method of chassis construction. Clad in lightweight fibreglass panels, the Spider chassis was made up of a network of extruded aluminium beams and tubes, which were welded together. The central section of the chassis was constructed as a separate unit. The front sub-frame was constructed in the same way, but the 6000-series aluminium was given a different heat treatment to optimize its ability to absorb energy in an impact.

Behind the driver, the transmission and suspension were attached to the main tub as a self-contained 'pack'. Essentially, the Spider was based around the Clio Williams' engine and gearbox, although the front and rear suspension was specially designed, very sophisticated and bore a resemblance to race car designs.

All this did little to help the Spider become as highly regarded as the Lotus and Caterham it sought to emulate. The arrival of the lighter, faster and much sharper-handling Lotus Elise rendered the Spider overweight, and it was felt that the Spider's handling was much duller than that of the Elise.

More importantly, the car developed by the mass-manufacturer had no heater and no weather gear, while the car from the small bespoke maker had a very capable heating system and a proper removable roof. Sadly, the more usable Elise was also cheaper than the Renault, knocking the final nail into the Spider's coffin in terms of its opportunity of becoming a real cult classic.

Riley **RM Series**

1946–1955

ENGINE: In-line four-cylinder, 1496/2443cc

POWER: 54–100bhp

CHASSIS: Separate chassis

BRAKES: Drum all round

TRANSMISSION: Four-speed manual

SUSPENSION: Independent

TOP SPEED: 75–100mph (120–160km/h)

ACCELERATION: 0–60mph (96km/h) in 15.2 seconds (2.5-litre)

Founded in 1898, Riley made its reputation in the 1920s and 1930s with a series of well-built saloons and thoroughbred small sports cars. It forged a fine racing record too, but by the late-1930s the company's finances were in poor shape, and the Nuffield organization took control in 1938.

Even so, immediate post-war cars – the famous RM Series – managed to retain their individuality. The RMA and RMB saloons featured a classic, high-cam, four-cylinder engine, torsion-bar independent front suspension and elegant, fabric-topped, timber-framed steel bodies.

The 1.5-litre RMB could manage 75mph (120 km/h) and the 90bhp (later 100bhp) 2.5-litre RMB a nice and highly respectable 95mph (152km/h), with long-legged cruising at over 80mph (130km/h). With the longest stroke of any post-war British production car, the RMB had lots of torque, too.

The ultimate RM variant was the RMC, an open three-seater roadster with sweeping, rakish lines built to capture American sales. A fold-flat screen and lowered bonnet line were other recognition points.

Last of the RM line were the 1952 RME (1496cc) and RMF (2443cc) with full hydraulic brakes, a hypoid back axle and bigger rear windows. For the run-out 1954 model year, the styling of the RME was subtly changed with no running boards, streamlined headlights and rear wheel-spats.

By that time the flagship RMF had been replaced by the unfortunate Gerald Palmer-designed Pathfinder, which had nothing but the traditional four-cylinder Riley engine to recommend it. There were no more thoroughbred Rileys produced after the death of the RME in 1955.

Rolls-Royce **Silver Cloud**

1955–1965

ENGINE: Straight-six and V8, 4887/6230cc

POWER: Not quoted

CHASSIS: Separate chassis

BRAKES (F/R) Disc

TRANSMISSION: Four-speed automatic

SUSPENSION: Independent

TOP SPEED: 106–116mph (170–186km/h)

ACCELERATION: 0–60mph (96km/h) in 13 seconds (Series I), 11 seconds for Series II and Series III)

The Rolls-Royce Silver Cloud of 1955 (and the virtually identical Bentley S-Type) were Crewe's second 'standard steel' cars after the post-war Dawn and R-Type. They rode on a box-section chassis with independent front suspension, and had rear dampers that could impressively be altered from the driving seat for extra control.

Beautifully proportioned, exquisitely constructed and very refined, it isn't surprising that they remained in production until 1965. They were absolutely everything that a Rolls-Royce should be. The interior was luxurious, of course, with superbly crafted leather seats and a magnificent walnut dashboard. Power steering and air conditioning were soon available as options, and automatic transmission was fitted as standard.

The engine in the Cloud and Series I was the same 4.9-litre power unit carried over from the previous R-Type (and Silver Dawn), except that it had a new aluminium cylinder head and twin SU carburettors. It could propel the Cloud up to 106mph (170km/h), but was replaced in 1958 with a new all-alloy 6.2-litre V8. In this form the Silver Cloud became the Silver Cloud II, and suddenly the car was in a new high-performance bracket.

These all-alloy V8s were far more powerful – good for nearly 120mph (192km/h) with a likely 200bhp and far more torque on tap – but not as refined and quiet. The later V8-powered Series III cars had a lower bonnet-line and quad headlamps.

Rolls-Royce Silver Shadow

1965–1980

ENGINE: V8, 6230/6750cc

POWER: Not quoted

CHASSIS: Monocoque

BRAKES (F/R): Disc

TRANSMISSION: Three- or four-speed automatic

SUSPENSION: Independent

TOP SPEED: 117mph (187km/h)

ACCELERATION: 0–60mph (96km/h) in 10 seconds

Rolls-Royce Silver Shadow and Bentley T-series cars were made in much larger numbers than any previous models – by the time they were replaced by the Silver Spirit in 1980, a total of well over 30,000 units of all types had been built. The all-independent self-levelling suspension, disc brakes and monocoque structure of the 1965 Silver Shadow came as a powerful retort to critics who had accused Rolls-Royce of falling behind the times.

Built by Pressed Steel at Oxford, the main bodyshell was of steel, while the doors, bonnet and boot-lid were of aluminium. The all-round independent suspension had hydraulic height control at both ends – a system supplied by Citroën. Disc brakes were used all round.

The 6.2-litre V8 engine and GM Hydramatic four-speed automatic gearbox were standard, and with a 117mph (187km/h) maximum speed, a 0–60mph (96km/h) time of 10.9 seconds, and a standing quarter-mile covered in 17.6 seconds, the Shadow was a fast car. You could expect between 12–15mpg (19–24litres/100km) on a long run, but probably half that in town driving. As usual, there was a Bentley version of the new car, called the T-series. However, the differences were limited to a 'B'-winged radiator grille, badges, and small items of trim.

Changes came slowly until the engine was enlarged to 6.75-litres in 1970. The Shadow II models of the mid-1970s had rack-and-pinion steering to tighten up the soggy handling, rubber bumpers and an air-dam, plus an impressive split-level air-conditioning system. Production of the Shadow ended in 1980, but much of the engineering was carried over into its replacement, the Silver Spirit.

Phantom VI

1968–1992

ENGINE: V8, 6750cc

POWER: Not disclosed

CHASSIS: Separate box section

BRAKES (F/R): Drum

TRANSMISSION: Four- / three-speed automatic

SUSPENSION: Independent front, live axle rear

TOP SPEED: 110mph (178km/h)

ACCELERATION: 0–60mph (96km/h) in 13 seconds

The Phantom VI was the last Rolls-Royce to have a separate chassis and non-independent rear suspension. Right to the end of production in 1992 it still had drum brakes. It was built specifically to be fitted with coachbuilt seven-passenger limousine bodywork of the most formal kind and all but a handful came with a H.J. Mulliner, Park Ward design, built in alloy at their factory in North West London.

The first Phantom VI limousines were built in 1968 but the model was only a derivative of the Phantom V, announced in 1959. Mechanically and structurally this car was merely a stretched Silver Cloud II with the latest 6.2 litre V8 engine fitted, allowing a top speed of well over 100mph. It gained twin headlights in the mid-'60s and when the change over to Phantom VI came the only real difference was the use

of a Silver Shadow type V8 engine with the latest cylinder heads. Conventional front-hinged rear doors were fitted from 1972 to comply with European safety legislation and in 1978 the Phantom gained the new, bigger 6750cc V8 and three- speed automatic gearbox, as fitted to the latest Silver Shadows.

Many Phantom VIs were supplied to Royalty and heads of state and passengers enjoyed the best of everything in the rear compartment. This was often trimmed in West of England Cloth, although it was possible to order almost any deviation from the standard specification – if you could pay for it. Enormously expensive, the Phantom VI was the last car of its type and was finally ousted from production by modern legislation.

Corniche Convertible

1971–1975

ENGINE: V8, 6750cc

POWER: Not disclosed

CHASSIS: Monocoque

BRAKES (F/R): Disc

TRANSMISSION: Three-speed automatic

SUSPENSION: Independent

TOP SPEED: 115mph (184km/h)

ACCELERATION: 0–60mph (96km/h) in 10 seconds

Big convertibles don't come any more opulent than the Rolls-Royce Corniche. Elegant and beautifully built, it out-lived the Silver Shadow on which it was based by many years, such was its popularity as the ultimate in open-topped glamour.

The body shape goes back several years before the Corniche label was first used in 1971. In fact the first two-door open-topped Silver Shadows appeared in 1967, entirely different to the four-door models behind the front pillar with an elegant, curving waistline above the rear wheels. This bodywork was built by H.J. Mulliner Park Ward and featured an electric hood. The Corniche was merely an updated version of this car with a bolder radiator shell, different wheel trims and a new dashboard that incorporated a rev-counter. As before there was a (rare) Bentley version of the vehicle available.

Technically the Corniche followed – or sometimes anticipated – the specification of Crewe's mainstream saloons, receiving the Silver Spirit's improved suspension and, later, fuel-injected engines. It became the Corniche II after 1987, while the Continental name was revived for the Bentley version. Increasingly the Corniche was becoming much tighter and more modern to drive, especially after 1992 when the automatic ride control was fitted. The cars finally bowed out of production in 1995 with the introduction of the Continental R-based Bentley Azure, although for once there was no Rolls-Royce equivalent of this car.

Camargue

1976–1987

ENGINE: V8, 6750cc

POWER: Not disclosed

CHASSIS: Monocoque

BRAKES: Disc all round

TRANSMISSION: Three-speed automatic

SUSPENSION: Independent

TOP SPEED: 120mph (192km/h)

ACCELERATION: 0–60mph (96km/h) in 11 seconds

The Pininfarina-styled Camargue, Crewe's flamboyant 1970s Rolls-Royce super-coupe, was a car for kings, princes, diplomats and superstars – a hedonistic two-door with no true rival. There was little to match it for size in the coupe stakes, and nothing for price – the Rolls-Royce Camargue was the most expensive car on sale in America at its US launch in 1976, 50 percent more expensive than even a Corniche convertible. In Britain it even out-shone the massive Phantom VI, then a mere £21,000.

The Camargue was in production for 11 years with a total of 534 being built, and even then never at a rate of more than one a week. Each car was six months in the making and finishing.

Unsurprisingly, the Camargue's best market was the USA (390 cars); 75 went to Saudi Arabia, whilst Europe's best market was its native Britain – with 136 being sold over its lifespan.

The 120mph Camargue was the first ever Rolls-Royce to have curved window glass, and the first to be designed to metric dimensions. It used a slightly more powerful 6.7-litre alloy Rolls pushrod V8 allied to the GM three-speed automatic gearbox, with the usual independent suspension.

The star technical attraction of the £29,000 Camargue – apart from its Pininfarina styling – was its superb split-level air-conditioning system, which on its own cost as much as a Mini, and had the cooling capacity of 30 domestic refrigerators.

A brave attempt to do a Rolls Continental for the '70s, the Camargue's effective replacement – the Continental R – has already outsold it in three years of production, which proves that the idea was right.

Rolls-Royce Silver Spirit

1980–1998

ENGINE: V8, 6750cc

POWER: Not disclosed

CHASSIS: Monocoque

BRAKES (F/R): Disc

TRANSMISSION: Three/four-speed automatic

SUSPENSION: Independent

TOP SPEED: 130mph (208km/h)

ACCELERATION: 0–60mph (96km/h) in 9.3-10.4 seconds

By 1980 the Silver Shadow had been in production 15 years and was Crewe's most successful model ever. With the Silver Spirit, Rolls-Royce were looking to update the successful concept of a not-too-big monocoque-bodied luxury saloon built to traditional standards but with the power and convience expected of the latest luxury cars. In fact, the Spirit was a Shadow under its new, squared-up styling.

The base unit was the same as before, as was much of the running gear, and it adopted the revised rear suspension found on the lower volume Camargue and Corniche models the year before. It was a quieter, better handling car than its predecessor but no faster, as the 6.7 litre V8 and automatic transmission were basically unchanged. Other models in this revised range were the long wheelbase Silver Spur – replacing the Silver Wraith II – and the Bentley

Mulsanne, which took over from the T2.

The increasing popularity of the Bentley marque during the '80s tended to eclipse the less popular Silver Spirit, but its story has been one of constant development. Fuel injection and anti-lock brakes arrived in 1987, followed by a computer activated ride system in 1989 on the Spirit II, which improved the ride and handling considerably. The Silver Spirit III models featured a dramatically revised engine which was both quieter and more powerful.

By the end of the '90s the Spirits body was beginning to look dated and the introduction of its replacement, the all-new Seraph of 1998, hadn't come a moment too soon. Sadly, the difficulties of being a tiny car maker in a global market meant that Rolls-Royce's days as independent British manufacturer were numbered.

Rover P5/3-litre

1958–1973

ENGINE: V8, 3528cc

POWER: 151bhp

CHASSIS: Monocoque

BRAKES (F/R): Disc/drum

TRANSMISSION: Three-speed automatic

SUSPENSION: Independent front, live axle rear

TOP SPEED: 110mph (176km/h)

ACCELERATION: 0–60mph (96km/h) in 11 seconds

Dispensing at last with the separate chassis of the P4, the P5 – standing for Post-war design number 5 – 3-litre of 1958 was Rover's new flagship. It featured modern but dignified styling, and a traditional interior with African cherry wood on the dashboard, thick Wilton carpet under foot, and leather upholstery almost everywhere else.

At first nobody really minded that the 3-litre, joined by a hunch-roofed Coupe version in 1962, was a bit slow – its soothing refinement was more or less all that was asked of it by most owners. By the mid-1960s, however, mere gravitas was not enough.

Enter the Buick V8 engine – a left-over from General Motors' brief flirtation with 'compacts' in the early-1960s – acquired by Rover as an end-of-line bargain engine package in 1966.

Packing 151bhp – the last 3-litre power-plants gave 134bhp – it was a perfect fit under the P5's bonnet and gave this hefty car – renamed 3-litre in 1967 – a whole new lease of life, pushing the top speed up to 110mph (176km/h).

Suddenly the P5 was the car it always should have been. Best of all, it was available at a shade under £2,000. Rover found that they could barely keep pace with demand, which remained strong until its death in 1973.

In a sense, there was nothing to replace the P5 as a ministerial limousine. No other British car being built in the 1970s had the same air of solid worth and self-effacing dignity.

Rover P6

1968–1976

ENGINE: V8, 3528cc

POWER: 144bhp

CHASSIS: Steel 'base unit' with bolt-on exterior steel panels

BRAKES (F/R): Disc/drum

TRANSMISSION: Three-speed automatic

SUSPENSION: Horizontally mounted springs and struts, de Dion rear

TOP SPEED: 115mph (184km/h)

ACCELERATION: 0–62.5mph (100km/h) in 10.3 seconds

The Rover P6 saloon was a perfect product for the 1960s. It reflected the period of modernization, especially in its home market of Britain, but also had enough in the way of traditional styling cues to satisfy Rover's more traditional customer base.

Chief stylist David Bache was said to be an admirer of Citroën's incredible DS. He was also fascinated by the aerodynamic work of Jaguar, and the possibility of gas-turbine engines. So convinced were Rover's engineers by the possibility of the latter, that the P6's engine bay was made very wide to accommodate a turbine unit. This meant that Rover had to develop a new front suspension system that could operate in a very narrow space.

Like the DS, the car was built around a strong 'base unit.' The non-structural exterior panels, including the roof, were bolted on. Aside from easier accident repair, this system should have also made

it much easier and cheaper to facelift the car.

Rover's management would only go so far, in deference to the marque's well-established middle-class clientele. Bache's original P6 sported a long, pointed nose, but Rover wasn't ready for a grille-less car, and the nose was simply chopped off to create a flat front. The gas turbine plans were dropped.

Inside the P6 was refreshing, using Bache's trademark low tray-like dash and separate instrument binnacle. The P6 was also highly regarded for its safety features, including the superb forward visibility and panoramic rear-view mirror. Even the front seats received a safety award. The P6 was a great success, although it failed in the US market. It lasted 10 years practically unchanged, and was the beginning of a period of forward-thinking development for Rover and Land Rover, before it eventually lapsed into marketing-led styling.

Rover SD1

1976–1986

ENGINE: V8, 3528cc

POWER: 155bhp

CHASSIS: Steel monocoque, five-door

BRAKES: Disc/drum

TRANSMISSION: Five-speed manual

SUSPENSION: Struts front, live axle and coils rear

TOP SPEED: 123mph (197km/h)

ACCELERATION: 0–62.5mph (100km/h) in 8.9 seconds

Years of decline, poor models and being saved from bankruptcy by the government meant that any good news about the British motor industry was eagerly received by the British public. When the shape of the SD1 was revealed, the media excitement was marked. The replacement for the P6 saloon turned out to be an ultra-modern five-door hatchback, with more than a passing resemblance to Ferrari's Daytona.

The smoothly sculpted machine was credited to David Bache, probably Britain's greatest-ever stylist, but bore the hallmarks of a late-1960s Pininfarina aerodynamic study which also influenced the Citroën CX. Bache admitted the Daytona was a great influence, and pictures exist of the SD1 (Solihull Developments One) styling model being viewed alongside a Maserati Khamsin.

Inside, Bache went in for more ground-breaking modernism. Out went wood and chrome and in came logical and blocky industrial design. The instrument pack was all contained in a simple box which sat on the flat dashboard top. This made conversion to left-hand drive as simple as attaching the pack to the other side of the dashboard. But, as clever and functional as the SD1's interior undoubtedly was, buyer reaction was rather muted.

Despite the advanced design, the SD1 was quite ordinary under the skin, the biggest demerit being the live rear axle. Rover engineers, though, managed a decent job with the simple rear-drive chassis. It was launched with the excellent V8, before being supplemented by six-cylinder engines.

It was a popular, perhaps much-loved car in the UK, but suffered from poor quality early on. Rover used it to re-launch into the USA, but the plan failed dismally. It was ground-breaking in its design, but born into a family that prevented it from really flourishing.

Mini Cooper

1991–2000

ENGINE: In-line pushrod four-cylinder, 1275cc

POWER: 61bhp

CHASSIS: Steel monocoque, two-door

BRAKES (F/R): Disc/drum

TRANSMISSION: Five-speed manual

SUSPENSION: Hydragas interconnected suspension

TOP SPEED: 89mph (142km/h)

ACCELERATION: 0–62.5mph (100km/h) in 11.6 seconds

With the process of 'Roverization' in the late-1980s, the company realized that its rich heritage could be the biggest selling point it had. Modernism was out and overtly 'retro' nostalgia was in. Rover had already released the chrome-grilled 800, and plans were well advanced for a short-production run of an updated MGB V8. Most easily realized of all the retro-relaunches was that of the Mini Cooper in late-1990 – easy, because the Mini was still in production and had barely changed since 1959. The famous Cooper version required little more effort than some handsome period graphics, alloy wheels and a power tweak. Rover added a white roof, chrome-rimmed driving lights and bonnet stripes marked with John Cooper's signature. There's no doubt that in a period of particularly bland styling, the Cooper stood out as a fabulous-looking car.

The 1275cc engine delivered 61bhp through a single carburettor, up from the standard 50bhp. It was

enough to give the car a genuine spring in its step which, combined with the kart-like steering and roll-free handling, offered the average driver the sort of tactile thrills unavailable in anything less than a full-blown sports car. By late-1991 a catalytic converter-equipped engine was needed, but Rover engineers managed to get the ancient A-series over the eco-hurdle by fitting single-point injection.

After BMW bought the Rover Group in 1994, the re-development of the Mini continued apace, with an even more striking Cooper and the re-introduction of some superb period colours and trims.

The original Mini was due to go out of production at Longbridge in mid-2000. However, BMW's sell-off of Rover (in March 2002) occurred just as development of the new Mini was being wrapped up and the new Mini factory at Longbridge was being installed. The new car was hastily pulled out.

Production of the original Mini finally ended in autumn 2000.

Saab 95

1959–1979

ENGINE: In-line three-cylinder, 841cc

POWER: 38bhp

CHASSIS: Steel monocoque, three- and five-door

BRAKES (F/R): Disc/drum

TRANSMISSION: Four-speed manual

SUSPENSION: Springs and wishbones front, beam axle rear

TOP SPEED: 75mph (120km/h)

ACCELERATION: 0–62mph (100km/h) in 47 seconds

In 1946 Saab, then a small aircraft manufacturer, launched the remarkable 92001. A wide, radically shaped, teardrop-bodied car, it featured some far-sighted technical innovations – including a transversely mounted engine driving the front wheels, and a one-piece welded-steel monocoque body. It was powered by a 20bhp two-cylinder two-stroke engine.

This unusual little car was put into production as the 92, with a restyled, less aircraft-like body. The body styling stayed in production, with only relatively slight modifications, for 35 years. Thus Saab established, right from its beginnings as a car maker, that it would play with aircraft-inspired solutions and be as innovative as possible.

In 1959 it launched the 95 estate car, a year ahead of the 96 saloon equivalent. In many ways Saab saw the way ahead for the versatile multi-purpose vehicle that would accelerate in popularity over the next 40 years. A three-door version also anticipated the 'sports hatch'.

The cleverest innovation was a third row of rearward-facing seats in the luggage compartment, intended mainly for carrying children. The 95 also wore a small spoiler on the trailing edge of the roof above the tailgate window. Aerodynamic forces meant the upright rear window was prone to being excessively plastered with road dirt, and the aerofoil attempted to minimise that. It was a solution that would not re-emerge until the arrival of the hot hatchback in the 1970s.

99 Turbo

1977–1980

ENGINE: In-line four-cylinder, 1985cc

POWER: 145bhp

CHASSIS: Steel monocoque, two/three/four-door

BRAKES (F/R): Disc/disc

TRANSMISSION: Five-speed manual

SUSPENSION: Wishbone front, 'dead' axle rear

TOP SPEED: 123mph (197km/h)

ACCELERATION: 0–60mph (96km/h) in 9.4 seconds

By the late 1960s Saab had developed its philosophy further to include safety at all costs. The result was the distinctive 99 model of 1967, the central section of which would prove durable enough to remain in production (as the 900) until 1994. The 99's appearance was guided by Saab's principles of aircraft design. It was known as the 'Little Draken' – a Saab jet fighter – within the company. It placed great emphasis upon occupant protection. The upright, narrow windscreen pillars were immensely strong tubular structures.

However, the 99's weak link was its slant-four engine, a design originally borrowed from Triumph in the UK – but so flawed that it had to be totally redesigned by Saab's own engineers. Even so, performance was felt to be the 99's weakest area.

Saab started to look at turbocharging in the late 1960s, and Per Gillibrand became Saab's turbo expert, introducing the concept of a 'wastegate' to help reduce what became known as 'turbo lag' – the delay between the point where the driver starts accelerating and the engine delivering full power.

The 99 became Saab's first turbocharged car in 1977. It became an icon, partly thanks to the restrained styling changes which made it stand out, including subtle airdams front and rear and – most celebrated – the 'Aztec' alloy wheels. The Saab 99 predicted the 1980s performance car boom, with a range of similarly fast and similarly adorned cars appearing on the scene.

Saab 900 Turbo 16S

1984–1993

ENGINE: In-line four-cylinder, 1985cc

POWER: 175bhp

CHASSIS: Steel monocoque, two- and three-door

BRAKES (F/R): Disc

TRANSMISSION: Five-speed manual

SUSPENSION: Double-wishbone front, 'dead' axle rear

TOP SPEED: 130mph (208km/h)

ACCELERATION: 0–62mph (100km/h) in 8.9 seconds

In 1980 Saab launched the 900. A development of the 99, it used the 99's central body section, but added a longer nose and a more stylishly shaped rear. Inside, the car got a new interior, said to be based on the principles of cockpit design. The dash was not very deep and was set high in the car. The instruments were a lesson in clarity. All the essential controls were set within the driver's eyeline, including the heater controls, auxiliary switches, headlamp switch and radio.

In 1984 Saab took the Turbo concept another great leap forward by launching the 900 Turbo 16S. Saab's 2.0-litre engine was matched with a new, and still relatively novel, 16-valve head, a modern Garrett turbocharger and an intercooler to improve the effect of the turbocharger. The resultant 175bhp and huge 201lb ft of pulling power was a revelation for the performance-oriented enthusiast. Not only did the car offer the performance of much bigger-engined cars, it was safe and – in three-door form – it was also very spacious.

Saab didn't leave it there. The stylists came up with the Aero body kit, which clad the lower half of the body in grey plastic, integrating neatly with the bumpers. Combined with a 'ducktail' spoiler and three-spoke alloy wheels, the effect managed to look astonishingly futuristic.

With the 900 Turbo, Saab had once again managed to combine giant leaps in technology with cars that also looked stunning.

Saab 9-5

1997–

ENGINE: In-line four-cylinder, turbocharged, 2290cc

POWER: 170bhp

CHASSIS: Steel monocoque, four-door

BRAKES (F/R): Disc with ABS

TRANSMISSION: Five-speed manual

SUSPENSION: Struts front, independent three-link rear

TOP SPEED: 139mph (222km/h)

ACCELERATION: 0–62mph (100km/h) in 8.6 seconds

Despite the 1980s economic boom and the increasing success of the 900 and 9000 in many markets, Saab was in deep trouble by the end of the decade. Remaining independent when total unit production was only just in six figures was no longer an option.

Failed discussions with Ford and Mazda led to plans for an alliance with Lancia in 1989, which only failed at the last minute when GM swept in and bought Saab. The first new product of the alliance was the Calibra-based 900 replacement in 1993. It looked like a Saab, had a world-beating interior and huge luggage space, but the GM-supplied chassis was heavily criticised. Saab continued to lose money in the marketplace.

Salvation surfaced in 1997 with the 9000's replacement, badged 9-5. Although it utilised some of the GM Vectra's floor

pressings, it was uniquely and distinctively a Saab – from the handsome nose and 'clamshell' bonnet to the cockpit-style dashboard. With a fine reception from the press and a very fine range of engines, particularly the light-pressure turbos, the 9-5 got off to an excellent start.

An estate derivative, essential in this market segment, was unveiled in 1998 and also proved very popular. Moves in the European market towards 'prestige' badges were also working very much in Saab's favour.

A vastly improved 900 (badged 9-3) in the same year provided some much-needed icing on the late-1990s cake. Saab at last had the overall success that its commitment to advanced engineering and style so richly deserved.

Saturn

1990–2002

ENGINE: 16-valve, in-line four-cylinder, 1901cc

POWER: 123bhp

CHASSIS: Steel space-frame, composite body panels

BRAKES (F/R): Disc

TRANSMISSION: Five-speed manual

SUSPENSION: Struts front and rear

TOP SPEED: 112mph (179km/h)

ACCELERATION: 0–62.5mph (100km/h) in 8.8 seconds

General Motors, like other US manufacturers, was becoming extremely worried by the rise and rise of inexpensive imported cars from Far Eastern manufacturers. So in the mid-1980s it committed $3.5 billion to the creation of a completely new brand, with an all-new product line which would be built at a greenfield site. It was christened Saturn.

Saturn's products would be aimed at re-capturing the younger generation of Americans who had grown up with Eastern cars and were unlikely to be won back by conventional domestic products. Indeed, the image of the home-grown product built by one of the 'big-three' US car manufacturers was clearly so off-putting that GM felt it needed a clean sheet.

GM bosses took the need for a completely new approach to making and selling cars, and applied it to everything – from the way in which factory workers build a car, to the latest in Toyota-inspired just-in-time product delivery and on-site manufacturing.

The first Saturn cars, a saloon and a coupe, used the same basic construction as the Pontiac Fiero – a steel space-frame chassis clad in non-structural composite panels. The 1.9-litre engines (8- or 16-valve) were an all-new, very lightweight design, and the Saturn rode on all-round strut suspension to deliver a Germanic ride quality. Saturn's advertising blitz in the American press couldn't have been more forthright about the clean-break approach of the new company. Unfortunately, the early cars were a little rough around the edges, and the situation didn't get any better. The new brand failed to take off, and by 1998 it had cancelled plans for expansion at Spring Hill, and was still manufacturing the original (albeit facelifted) and very aged car.

There would be no more Saturn-designed cars, and its new model – an Opel Vectra with a nose job – was to be built at an old GM factory elsewhere. The Saturn adventure can be judged as a failure.

Ibiza GTi

1994–2002

ENGINE: In-line four-cylinder, 1984cc

POWER: 115bhp

CHASSIS: Steel monocoque, three-door

BRAKES (F/R): Disc/disc

TRANSMISSION: Five-speed manual

SUSPENSION: Struts front, torsion beam rear

TOP SPEED: 122mph (195km/h)

ACCELERATION: 0–62mph (100km/h) in 10.0 seconds

Spanish car-maker SEAT was known for building Fiats under licence when it made a serious attempt to join the premier league by developing its own supermini in the early 1980s. Despite nice Porsche-engineered engines and some impressive styling by Italian maestro Giugiaro, the Ibiza was a flawed – but brave – attempt.

Volkswagen bought the troubled spanish maker in 1990, and laid plans for an all-new Ibiza that would share components with the new-generation Polo. It was a very sound strategy.

The new Ibiza was launched in 1993 to some very enthusiastic reviews. Under the chunky, high-waisted shell – another Giugiaro design – were the floorpan and suspension of the 1994 Polo. The cars' interiors were also near-identical. However, the SEAT had an important difference – the nose was longer and could accommodate larger-capacity engines than the Polo.

The upshot was the GTi, powered by the Golf GTI's torquey 2.0-litre injection engine. This was combined with stiffer suspension and smart styling tweaks, it emerged as one of the finest cars to wear the emotive badge. Its compact dimensions and constant stream of pulling power made it a delight to drive quickly on winding lanes. This combination of a large engine in a small car also meant the GTi was refined and economical over long distances. It remained a vastly underrated car with the general public, but it was pivotal in VW's decision to re-craft the SEAT of the 1990s as the sporting brand in the group.

Octavia 1.8 20V

1995–

ENGINE: In-line 20V, four-cylinder, 1781cc

POWER: 125bhp

CHASSIS: Steel monocoque, four- and five-door

BRAKES (F/R): Disc/disc with ABS

TRANSMISSION: Five-speed manual

SUSPENSION: Struts front, torsion beam rear

TOP SPEED: 121mph (194km/h)

ACCELERATION: 0–62mph (100km/h) in 10.0 seconds

When Volkswagen bought Skoda out in the early 1990s, the company had just switched from building the final development of its long-running rear-engine coupes and saloons to an all-new, Euro-style family hatchback, the Favorit. Of all the Eastern-bloc makers, Skoda was the most able, but the new car couldn't really compete with Western European cars. This was in spite of the fact that the Favorit's admirably roomy body and neat styling were drawn up by Bertone in Italy.

VW drew up plans to bring Skoda straight into the first division. The Favorit was completely made over as the Felicia, and the Skoda Octavia was launched in 1995. It looked like – and was built like – a VW because it was part of VW's platform project, which took the basic structure of the Mk4 VW Golf

and utilised it for various Skoda, Audi and Seat models. It was a successful plan

The Octavia's resemblance to other VW group cars was no surprise – it was designed by an ex-Audi stylist. At a stroke Skoda leaped ahead of Japanese and Korean-made models with a very solid and beautifully built car. A handsome estate version was launched in 1998. It proved to be an absolutely huge success. VW had cleverly aimed the Octavia at 'Volvo and Rover' drivers – those sensible middle-market customers who might have been left behind in the move upmarket that those two marques had made. VW had seen its strategy over the acquisition of Skoda pay off very effectively and very quickly. Neither it nor Skoda were going to be the butt of any jokes over the Octavia.

Simca | Aronde

1951–1960

ENGINE: 1.2/1.3-litre, four-cylinder OHV

POWER: 45-57bhp

CHASSIS: Monocoque

BRAKES (F/R): Drum/drum

TRANSMISSION: Four-speed manual

SUSPENSION: Coil spring/wishbone/
anti-roll bar front

TOP SPEED: 75-90mph
(120-144km/h)

ACCELERATION: 0-60mph
(0-96km/h) in 27.9 seconds

Simca began making Fiats under licence in 1934 and the association was to give them a springboard to becoming one of the leading independent manufacturers in the whole of France.

The Aronde was developed as a replacement for the Simca 6 and used the same Fiat 1.2 litre engine from the 8 and 9, but apart from that there was not an element of Fiat in the car. The Aronde (meaning 'swallow') marked Simca's flight to independence, with modern lines and spirited performance, capable of 81mph. Coil spring/wishbone/anti-roll bar front suspension gave it very sure-footed handling, backed up by robust build quality and a range of colours and upholstery that increased sales. It proved an instant hit, annual production quickly reaching the 100,000 mark.

The initial four-door saloon was joined by an estate called Chatelaine, with a Grand Large coupe following in 1952. Engine size increased to 1.3 litre in 1955 and the following year a restyle saw fins added to the back end with hooded headlamps at the front.

Having sealed Simca a prominent place in the French motor manufacturing hierarchy, the Aronde remained in production until 1960 when it was replaced by the P60, having reached the magic one million mark.

Spyker

1903–1925

ENGINE: 1.9-litre, 2-cylinder/7.9-litre, four-cylinder

POWER: Not available

CHASSIS: Separate box section

BRAKES (F/R): Drum/drum

TRANSMISSION: Manual

SUSPENSION: Independent springs

TOP SPEED: 68mph (109km/h) for 3.4-litre model

ACCELERATION: Not available

Due to a certain degree of ill fortune, the Spijker family business does not take up a big space in the annals of motoring history. But they did leave one indelible mark at the start of the 20th Century that was to inspire immense popularity 90 years later. We're talking about four-wheel drive.

The family firm, run by Hendrik and Jacobus Spijker of Holland, began in motoring as coach builders, working on chassis and engines from Benz. By 1900, however, they were ready to go ahead with their own fully developed car. They changed the spelling of the company name to Spyker to make life easier for the English market and unveiled their

revolutionary product at the Paris Motor Show in December 1903.

Engines ranged from a 1.9-litre twin to a 7.9-litre, in-line four, driving all four wheels through a clever swivel-housing with universal joints. It also had brakes on all four wheels, where other cars of the time had rear-wheel braking only.

The four-wheel drive gave the Spyker a unique performance advantage and it was a strong contender at hillclimbs, but the complexity of the mechanism made it heavy and expensive to build. When Hendrik Spijker was killed in a ferry accident, Jacobus found it hard to run the business. By the time it folded in 1925, only around 1,500 cars had been made.

Avanti

1963–1984

ENGINE: V8, 4737-4983cc

POWER: 210-335bhp

CHASSIS: Separate chassis, GRP body

BRAKES (F/R): Disc/drum

TRANSMISSION: Three-speed manual/ three-speed auto

SUSPENSION: Independent front, live axle rear

TOP SPEED: 130mph (210km/h)

ACCELERATION: 0-60mph (96km/h) in 7.5 secs (supercharged)

The Avanti was the last car created by the self-styled 'father' of industrial design Raymond Loewy, the man responsible for such immortal greats as the Gestetner duplicating machine, the classic Coca-Cola bottle, the Lucky Strike cigarette pack and the NASA Skylab interior.

Lowey created the car in just 13 months, taking up market European marques as his inspiration for the design which was aerodynamically sound as well as being nicely handsome.

The interior had a posh European look too and the Avanti came in three states of tune – 240bhp (R1) and Supercharged models (R2 and R3), giving 290 and 335bhp respectively. Fast and taughtly sprung, the Avanti could hold its head – not to mention its pace – up in any company.

Its modern futuristic lines were instantly recognised as classic and would have made this glassfibre-bodied Avanti a success if Studebaker hadn't gone bankrupt the following year.

All was not lost for the Avanti, however. Two Studebaker dealers, Nate Altman and Leo Newman, bought the old South Bend, Indiana Studebaker factory and continued to make 100 'Avanti IIs' each year. They ensured that the model remained available well into the '80s.

Of the original Avanti only 4650 were ever made, but this hasn't stopped its relentless push towards its current status as a much-loved classic. As you would expect, it has a strong, numerous and enthusiastic following which is partly generated by nostalgia and partly by a love of great design.

Subaru SVX

1992–1996

ENGINE: 24-valve flat-six, 3319cc

POWER: 226bhp

CHASSIS: Steel monocoque

BRAKES (F/R): Disc with ABS

TRANSMISSION: Four-speed automatic

SUSPENSION: Struts front, independent struts rear

TOP SPEED: 146mph (234km/h)

ACCELERATION: 0–62.5mph (100km/h) in 8.9 seconds

Subaru has always been committed to producing cars that reflect its own highly individual and recognizable approach to engineering. The 1980s' XT coupe wasn't really a success – from the brutal 'big wedge of cheese' styling to the turbocharged engine and four-wheel drive, the whole thing just failed to hang together.

However, this failure didn't put Subaru off investing in another coupe as it would have done many other manufactuers. No, Subaru's next attempt was to be even more complex and even more unusual than their first bash.

The SVX could be described as a combination of the Porsche 911 Carrera 4 and Jaguar XJS, as the SVX had the mechanical cleverness of the former and the refinement of the latter.

The 2+2 coupe was styled by Giugiaro, and it looked as if a jet fighter's one-piece glass cockpit had been lowered on to a fairly normal coupe body. This effect was secured by using half-size side windows, which allowed the doors to close completely flush against the roof.

Under the skin was a superb 3.3-litre, flat-six engine driving an advanced and effective automatic gearbox. The 4x4 drivetrain came with a computer-controlled torque-split system.

The SVX was a remarkably refined and surefooted car to drive, delivering the level of comfort that made very long journeys swift, safe and enjoyable. There was, perhaps, too much technology under too odd a skin, capped with too obscure a badge. It wasn't a success, but the SVX was an excellent car anyway.

Subaru Impreza Turbo

1994–

ENGINE: Turbocharged, flat-four, 1994cc

POWER: 208bhp

CHASSIS: Steel monocoque, four- and five-door

BRAKES (F/R): Disc with ABS

TRANSMISSION: Five-speed manual

SUSPENSION: Struts front, independent struts rear

TOP SPEED: 141mph (226km/h)

ACCELERATION: 0–62.5mph (100km/h) in 6.8 seconds

Subaru replaced its dull and rapidly ageing 1.6/1.8 series with the all-new Impreza in 1993. Like the outgoing car, the Impreza came in four and five-door guises and had – like nearly all Subarus – permanent four-wheel drive installed.

The first Imprezas were quickly praised, but with just 101bhp under the bonnet, they couldn't help but be regarded as somewhat sluggish. It was a fair criticism, and Subaru had to some degree already anticipated this problem.

Subaru was known for its keenness for turbocharging, so few people were surprised when the company released the 208bhp Impreza Turbo, complete with bonnet scoop, deep front bumper, rear spoiler and wide wheels.

What few expected, however, was that the Impreza would turn into a modern-day 'junior super-car' classic, following in the tyre treads of the Audi Quattro and Lancia Delta Integrale.

Unlike the other contemporary 4x4 turbocharged sports hatches – the Ford Escort Cosworth, for example – the Impreza was smaller, more wieldy and less intimidating to drive. The simple, Audi-like four-wheel-drive layout and low centre of gravity afforded by the flat-four engine helped give the Impreza a fabulous 'roadability' and the Impreza's sheer performance was breathtaking.

Subaru used the car for the World Rally Championships, and chassis improvements figured out by Prodrive made it even better and helped the vehicle's impressive performance. The Impreza became a cult classic. Very few cars could beat it from A to B across country, but it cost little more than a high-specification family car.

Forester

1997–

ENGINE: Flat-four, 1994cc

POWER: 122bhp

CHASSIS: Steel monocoque, five-door

BRAKES (F/R): Disc with ABS

TRANSMISSION: Five-speed manual

SUSPENSION: Struts front, independent struts rear

TOP SPEED: 110mph (176km/h)

ACCELERATION: 0–60mph (96km/h) in 11.6 seconds

Subaru had a long history of producing rugged four-wheel-drive road cars that became popular with farmers and country-bound drivers. But the rise and rise in the popularity of the off-roader as a leisure and recreational vehicle – often called the SUV (sport utility vehicle) – did not encourage Subaru to follow the trend, despite having the right kind of transmission sitting in their parts bin.

After some consideration, Subaru launched the Streega concept car in late 1995, which gave heavy hints as to what Subaru thought an SUV should look like. The result was the Forester, best described as an amalgam of SUV and estate car.

Despite the substantial looks, the Forester was based on the chassis and running gear of the Impreza. Careful attention to space utilization meant the Forester was surprisingly roomy. The upright driving position and fine seats made the Forester an exceptionally comfortable car over long distances, especially as it was capable of very refined running at motorway speeds – something that most conventional truck-based SUVs were not really known for.

Although nowhere near as heavy as an ordinary SUV, the Forester was quite a weighty machine, and the basic 122bhp engine had to work hard, although at high revs the performance was remarkably good. Later, more powerful 160bhp and 250bhp versions were launched.

The Forester marked the beginning of the end for the truck-based SUVs that were so enormously popular in the USA at the time. Lighter, safer and more ecologically sound solutions like the Forester pointed the way forward.

Alpine

1959–1967

ENGINE: 1494-1725cc

POWER: 78-93bhp

CHASSIS: Monocoque

BRAKES (F/R): Disc/drum

TRANSMISSION: Four-speed manual/ three-speed auto

SUSPENSION: Independent front

TOP SPEED: 100mph (162km/h)

ACCELERATION: 0-60mph (96km/h) in 13-14seconds

The Sunbeam Alpine always had a more civilised flavour than its MG and Triumph contemporaries, something its owners were never afraid to point out in the most polite of fashions. An open-topped 2+2 sports car based on the floorpan of the Hillman Husky/Commer Cob van, it was always a bit too heavy to have a really stirring, inspiring and dramatic performance, but it attempted to make up for this shortcoming with comforting features like wind-up windows, better trim and a really good hardtop for maximized stability.

Where its rivals were ruggedly handsome, the Alpine, announced in 1959, was stylish and urbane, though many felt its styling was too feminine.

Early versions had prominent tail fins, but these were thought of by many as too American and too gawdy. They were duly trimmed back fairly early on in the vehicle's life-time.

The Alpine was far from out-classed technically – it had a 78bhp 1.5-litre engine from the Sunbeam Rapier, front disc brakes and was good for nearly 100mph – though it never quite made it all the way to that Holy Grail of the 100mph (162km/h) mark.

Suitably tuned the car acquitted itself well in competition too. The Alpine became gradually more powerful during the '60s culminating in the MkV which had a 92bhp 1725cc engine for a genuine 100mph for the first time. It died in 1967 with no successor and, unlike some of its contemporaries, is still missed by many a devoted fan.

Tiger

1964–1967

ENGINE: V8, 4260–4727cc

POWER: 164–200bhp

CHASSIS: Monocoque

BRAKES (F/R): Disc/drum

TRANSMISSION: Four-speed manual

SUSPENSION: Independent front, live axle rear

TOP SPEED: 120–125mph (192–200km/h)

ACCELERATION: 0–60mph (96km/h) in 9.5 secs (Mk I), 7.2 seconds (Mk II)

The Sunbeam Tiger was a V8-engined version of the four-cylinder Alpine. As with the AC Cobra, the initial engineering was carried out by the American Carroll Shelby, but all subsequent work was by the parent company, Rootes. Out came the four-cylinder 1592cc engine, and in went a Ford V8 engine of 4.2 litres, along with a new 'top loader' four-speed gearbox to help transmit the power.

Extensive re-engineering was required under the bonnet, so rather than clog up the higher-volume Alpine production lines with the new car, Rootes subcontracted the job out to Jensen. With a leap in power from 97bhp to 164bhp, the Tiger was a very different kind of car from the modest little Alpine, although they looked identical apart from discreet badging. Top speed was 117mph (187km/h), with 0–60mph (96km/h) coming up in 9.5 seconds. The Tiger was no car

for the novice, however. The rack-and-pinion steering – somewhat hastily conceived – wasn't of the best quality, and the Hillman-derived suspension was never really up to coping with the power now going through the rear wheels.

However, despite these problems it was still good value for money, and sold well in the USA, although it wasn't offered in the UK until 1965.

The Tiger's life was cut short when Chrysler took a controlling interest in Rootes – the new regime didn't like the idea of a car using an engine from its Detroit arch-rival. Thus, the axe came down on the Tiger, although not before Rootes had produced 571 Mk II models in 1967–68 with a bigger 4.7-litre engine from the Ford Mustang. This version had wider gear ratios, and was easily spotted by its bold body stripes and 'egg-crate' grille.

Tatra 603

1957–1975

ENGINE: V8, 2500cc

POWER: 105bhp

CHASSIS: Monocoque

BRAKES (F/R): Drum

TRANSMISSION: Four-speed manual

SUSPENSION: Independent

TOP SPEED: 100mph (162km/h)

ACCELERATION: Not available

First sight of the wild Czechoslovakian Tatra 603 came in 1957. There had been no Tatra passenger cars since the demise of the flat-four Tatraplan in 1954, but the new 603 maintained the tradition of an air-cooled V8 rear-mounted in a six-seater saloon – the last in a noble line of streamlined Tatras that started with Ledwinka's T77 in the 1930s.

The 603 took its name from its hemi-head V8, a 2.5-litre unit with pushrods and twin down-draught carburettors. Twin belt-driven scavenge-blowers did the cooling with vents let into the rear wings, plus a cunning thermostatically opening grille in the bumper. Alloy construction meant a low engine weight of 373lb (169kg), but with a low 6.5:1 compression ratio it packed just 100bhp, denying the 3240lb (1472kg) 603 sparkling acceleration.

Top speed was a 106mph (170km/h), though – testimony to the car's slippery shape. The floorpan was virtually flat, with no exhaust or propshaft to impede clean airflow. Drive went through a four-speed transaxle with column gear-shift, and early 603s used big hydraulic drums with advanced twin circuits. At the back, trailing arms with coil springs were no surprise, but a new front suspension system was schemed for the front of the 603, a form of Macpherson strut with trailing swinging arms saving space in the big front luggage compartment.

Throughout the 1960s, Tatra made gradual changes to the car, toning down the styling first with a new split, four-light nose and then for the 603-2 of 1967 a wider grille, with the lights spaced further apart in a fibreglass panel. Accidents or factory refits meant many earlier 603s gained this later front-end look. Production ended in 1975, as the 603 began to give way to the four-cam, Vignale-styled 613.

Tatra 613

1975–2000

ENGINE: V8, 3495cc

POWER: 165bhp at 5200rpm

CHASSIS: Monocoque

BRAKES (F/R): Disc

TRANSMISSION: Four-speed manual

SUSPENSION: All independent

TOP SPEED: 115mph (184 km/h)

ACCELERATION: 0-60mph (96km/h) in 12 seconds

Rear-engined cars were few and far between by the mid-'70s, yet Tatra, cut off from the rest of the world in communist Czechoslovakia, were committed to the layout. So when the new 613 saloon appeared nobody was shocked to find that its engine was in the tail.

Aware of the handling problems associated with tail-heavy cars, this new four-cam air-cooled unit was moved much further forward in the chassis than in the old 603, ahead of the rear axle line. Thus, the 613 behaved far more predictably than its forerunner – which, in reality, had handled much better than it looked. However, all notions of aerodynamic styling had been abandoned in the new car for a crisp, modern looking body by Vignale of Italy. There had been talk

of a two-door coupe version but in reality all 613s had four-door bodywork and were intended for use by Government officials who enjoyed lots of legroom in the rear.

These were swift, quiet cars built in small numbers as a sideline to Tatra's truck business. After the fall of communism, their future looked under threat from the influx of prestige European marques, but they remain in very limited production in 1998, in modernised form.

Since the opening up of Czechoslovakia, the older versions of the Tatra have started to surface in western Europe, where there is a small band of enthusiasts committed to this example of engineering from the Cold War.

Toyota MR2

1985–1990

ENGINE: In-line 16-valve four-cylinder, 1587cc

POWER: 122bhp

CHASSIS: Steel monocoque, fixed and targa-roof two-door

BRAKES (F/R): Disc

TRANSMISSION: Five-speed manual

SUSPENSION: Struts front and rear

TOP SPEED: 121mph (194km/h)

ACCELERATION: 0–62.5mph (100km/h) in 7.9 seconds

Toyota has long been known as a conservative car maker, particularly where its mainstream cars are concerned. But as one of only two manufacturers to be in profit every year for nearly four decades, it would be difficult to argue that Toyota's business sense was flawed in any important way.

The mid-engined MR2 project had started as far back as 1976, but Toyota seemed to have been easily distracted by the energy crisis, and put a swift stop to it. The idea for a compact and inexpensive mid-engined sports car was revived in 1979. However, it took some convincing of the management that the US market was awaiting such a car, especially as the British Triumph and MG sports cars were close to death.

The engineering plan called for a car in the exact mould of the Fiat X1/9 – a small two-seater based on the running gear of a conventional front-wheel-drive hatch – in this case, the Corolla. The product planners weren't wrong. Pontiac had come to the same conclusion, and were about to launch their own inexpensive, mid-engined two-seater. MR2 stood for 'Mid-engined Recreational with 2 seats.'

The great advantage of the MR2, though, was its inherent reliability and fine build quality, something Pontiac – and certainly not Fiat – could not match at the time. The MR2 was also an easy car to drive quickly, and it was always a pleasurable experience.

The styling of the original was also very well executed in a taut and razor-sharp manner. It was a great success, because it offered the looks and cachet of a serious sports car with the reliability and build of a family car. It also proved there would be a ready market for inexpensive convertibles.

Toyota Supra Turbo

1993–1997

ENGINE: Twin sequentially turbocharged 24-valve in-line six-cylinder, 2997cc

POWER: 330bhp

CHASSIS: Steel monocoque, three-door

BRAKES (F/R) Disc

TRANSMISSION: Six-speed manual

SUSPENSION: Wishbones front and rear

TOP SPEED: 155mph (248km/h), restricted

ACCELERATION: 0–62.5mph (100km/h) in 5.7 seconds

Toyota was feeling adventurous when it planned the replacement for the Supra coupe. In the late-1980s, Toyota produced the exceptionally avant garde 4500 GT super-coupe for research purposes. Serious passion went into its conception at every level.

The 4500 GT's influence was clear when the twin-turbo Supra was launched in 1993. Project manager Isao Tsuzuki described it as "a race car that could be driven with confidence on American streets and highways."

The 1993 Supra was one of the best-looking cars ever produced in Japan, a dramatic three-door bodyshell with a giant frontal air intake and huge headlamps. Under the bonnet was a 3.0-litre, 24-valve straight-six engine

bolstered by twin sequential superchargers. With 320bhp and a massive 300lb/ft of torque available, the Supra was an exceptionally fast car. Tsuzuki put huge effort into making the new 1993 Supra 300lb (136kg) lighter than the old car had been.

The upshot was a better power-to-weight ratio than a Ferrari 348. Inside, lessons had been learned

from the 4500 GT. The dashboard swept up and around from the centre console, housing brilliantly situated heating and audio controls.

On the road, the Supra was not only devastatingly fast – overtaking in third with full turbo boost was a mind-bending experience – but exceptionally stable and secure, despite such massive power being directed to the rear wheels.

Toyota RAV-4

1994–

ENGINE: In-line 16-valve four-cylinder, 1998cc

POWER: 129bhp

CHASSIS: Steel monocoque, three- and five-door

BRAKES (F/R): Disc with ABS

TRANSMISSION: Five-speed manual

SUSPENSION: Struts front, trailing arms rear

TOP SPEED: 105mph (168km/h)

ACCELERATION: 0–62.5mph (100km/h) in 11.6 seconds

Like the 'Mid-engined Recreational 2-seater' (MR2) of a decade earlier, Toyota's product planners had spotted yet another new US market niche in the early 1990s. The 'Recreational Active Vehicle with four-wheel drive' – RAV-4, as it became known – was a simple proposition.

The Recreational Active Vehicle simply combined the snappy acceleration and nippy handling of a sporty hatchback with the looks and high driving position of an off-roader. It was a formula that other manufacturers eventually rushed to follow.

It was obvious by the turn of the decade that, with the market share of off-roaders increasing every year especially in the USA there was something integral to the 4x4 character that was attracting buyers, despite the inherent disadvantages. The vast majority of 4x4s tended to be derivations of genuine off-roaders, which meant they had heavy separate chassis and long-travel suspension.

Used as road cars, these off-roaders handled poorly, were noisy, overweight, oversized and uneconomical. Even Suzuki's small 4x4s were basically just flashy farm vehicles.

Toyota correctly figured that it was the looks and driving position that was attracting buyers (particularly women) who would not previously have considered a 4x4. So they used the running gear of an ordinary Toyota road car as the basis of a 4x4 that would be an ideal urban runaround.

The RAV-4 was very swift (thanks to a 129bhp engine from the Carina), handled very well and was surprisingly refined. Such was the RAV-4's success that manufacturers such as Honda and Land Rover were forced to follow suit.

Trabant 601

1964–91

ENGINE: Two-cylinder, 595cc

POWER: 26bhp

CHASSIS: Tubular frame, Duroplast body

BRAKES (F/R): Drum

TRANSMISSION: Four-speed manual

SUSPENSION: Independent

TOP SPEED: 65mph (106km/h)

ACCELERATION: No figures available

The Trabant has only ever once been in the spotlight and even then it was for all of the wrong reasons. Its brief moment of fame came in the late 1980s when it became a symbol of the final crumbling of the communist bloc. Thousands of these boxy, smoky little saloons were to be seen crossing the border into west with the reunification of Germany and the collapse of the Berlin Wall in 1989. Their impact on popular consciousness was so large at the time that they even ended up being featured heavily in a U2 pop video.

The roots of the model can be traced back to the late-'40s as the Zwickau and then as the restyled Trabant P50 from 1956. Its air-cooled, two-stroke, front-wheel-drive running gear was topped by a Duraplast body built on a tubular frame and owners had to put up with poor performance – no more than 65mph – and a clumsy crash gearbox.

The most familiar of the breed is the 601 which came as a saloon, estate and a military style open-topped 'utility'. When the 'dirty' two-stroke engine was outlawed in reunified Germany the last Trabants were built with Volkswagen Polo engines in 1990-91, but by then the car had become unsaleable in the commercial marketplace in any form and the Trabant name died. Most cars have a band of enthusiasts somewhere that try desperately to keep the car alive and running and that is even true for the Trabant – a car that no one could claim was popular when it was actually being produced.

Triumph

1800/2000 Roadster

1946–1949

ENGINE: Four-cylinder, 1776-2088cc

POWER: 65-68bhp

CHASSIS: Separate box section

BRAKES (F/R): Drums

TRANSMISSION: Three- or four-speed

SUSPENSION: Beam axles

TOP SPEED: 77mph (123km/h)

ACCELERATION: 0-60mph (96km/h) in 25 seconds

After the Second World War, The boss of the Standard motoring company, Sir John Black, was looking to use his newly acquired Triumph company as an upper-crust sister marque to Standard. He wanted to build a sportscar for the all important export market, and take on mighty sportscar builders Jaguar at the same time. It was obvious that he was still irritated by Jag boss William Lyons' rejection of his take-over proposal.

The result was the 1800 Roadster of 1946. Styled to evoke the low-slung SS 100 Jaguars of pre-war years the new Triumph was a rather over-weight, under-powered device that struggled along on 65bhp. Its saving grace

was the versatility of its three-plus-two accommodation – three on the front bench seat and two in the dickey that doubled as a roomy boot.

As an open tourer with sporting overtones the Roadster had a certain charm (it also had a touch or two of character) but this wasn't enough to convince the market to buy it in quantity.

Even the introduction of a more powerful 2 litre version that was introduced in 1948 couldn't do anything to boost sales of the Roadster. Production finally finished in 1949 with a whimper, no more than 4,500 examples having been built.

TR2/TR3

1953–1962

ENGINE: In-line four-cylinder, 1991/2138cc

POWER: 90–100bhp

CHASSIS: Separate

BRAKES (F/R): Drum

TRANSMISSION: Four-speed manual

SUSPENSION: Independent front, live axle rear

TOP SPEED: 103–110mph (165–176km/h)

ACCELERATION: 0–60mph (96km/h) in 12 seconds

With his bid to take over Morgan and Jaguar having been rejected, Standard/Triumph boss Sir John Black needed a Triumph sports car to Challenge MG in the all-important export market after the war. By fitting a Standard Vanguard 2-litre engine in a shortened Standard 8 chassis, clothed in a two-seater roadster body, the TS20 was created. However, it was greeted with muted applause when it was revealed at the 1952 London Motor Show.

The TR2, which was revealed a year later, overcame its predecessor's problems – it featured a simple ladder-type chassis, and a longer body with a much bigger boot. A 90bhp, 1991cc version of the Vanguard engine with twin carburettors was mated to a four-speed gearbox, whilst suspension was coil-spring and wishbone at the front, and a live rear axle on semi-elliptic springs. It could reach 60mph (96km/h) in under 12 seconds, return fuel consumption of 25mpg (11.4litres/ 100km) in daily use, yet still do 100mph (160km/h) – or 108mph (173km/h) with the optional overdrive. A simple, enjoyable small sports car, American buyers lapped it up, and the TR2 quickly became the company's top dollar-earner.

The TR2 sired the similar 1955 TR3, which featured a power increase and new front grille. In 1956 it became the first mass-produced car with front disc brakes, while triple overdrive and a token rear seat became available at the same time. The 1957 TR3A was the last of the cut-away-door TRs, with a full-width grille, outside door handles and a 2138cc engine. The TR3B was a US-only version, with a full synchromesh gearbox.

Although the TR4 that followed had smoother Italian styling, mechanically it followed the same principle. Indeed, the basic TR chassis survived until the demise of the TR6 in 1976.

Triumph TR4-5-6

1962–1976

ENGINE: Four- /six-cylinder 2138-2498cc

POWER; 100-150bhp

CHASSIS: Separate box section

BRAKES (F/R): Disc/drum

TRANSMISSION: Four-speed

SUSPENSION: Independent front, live axle rear (TR4) / All independent (TR 4a, 5 & 6)

TOP SPEED: 119mph (190km/h)

ACCELERATION: 0-60mph (96km/h) in 8.2 seconds

By the beginning of the '60s, Triumph's enduring TR 3 needed a facelift if the needed sales and interest were to be maintained. Triumph decided on a European look and went shopping for Italian styling. They ended up hiring Michelotti to re-skin the car in a more shapely body that also had to be both roomier and a little more comfortable than the TR3

Launched as the TR4 in 1962 it retained all the rugged qualities of its predecessor. Chief among these were a torquey 2.2 litre four-cylinder engine and a separate chassis. However, an all-syncromesh box was an innovation.

Complaints about the poor road holding and the bumpy ride were answered by the TR4a of 1965, which came with a new form of semi trailing arm rear suspension shared with the highly-praised Triumph 2000 saloon.

More power was the next obvious step, so Triumph fitted their new 2.5 litre straight six in the TR5 of 1967. Injected and producing 150bhp, this gave the TR a much smoother delivery and the potential for up to 120mph. This was a short-lived variant, however, and it was supplanted in 1969 by the TR6, with new, crisper – if less characterful – styling from the German firm of Karmann.

Mechanically little changed, and the TR6 continued to sell in large numbers – mostly to the North American market – until 1976 when it was no longer able to meet the increasingly strict challenge of the Federal safety requirements.

2000 Mk 1

1963–1969

ENGINE: Straight-six, 1998/2498cc

POWER: 90–132bhp

CHASSIS: Monocoque

BRAKES (F/R): Disc/drum

TRANSMISSION: Four-speed manual, three-speed automatic

SUSPENSION: Independent

TOP SPEED: 100mph (160km/h), Triumph 2000; 106mph (170km/h), Triumph 2.5PI

ACCELERATION: 0–60mph (96km/h) in 14.1 seconds (Triumph 2000); 10.4 seconds, (2.5PI)

With the introduction of the Michelotti-styled Triumph 2000 of 1963, a new kind of executive car was born. A luxurious 2-litre, six-cylinder, four-door saloon with compact dimensions and youthful driver appeal, it clashed head-on with the Rover 2000 – a technically more sophisticated car than the Triumph. However, the Rover was bereft of the refinement of the Triumph's six-cylinder engine.

Making 90bhp, the old Standard Vanguard-derived twin-carburettor straight-six could haul the 2000 up to just on 100mph (160km/h) in manual overdrive form. With all-independent suspension (struts up front, semi-trailing arms at the back) and servo front discs, the 2000 was a comfortable, nicely finished, well-mannered car – just right for the new breed of young executives who didn't want big, lumbering cars of the old school.

Leather seats, with a wooden dashboard and door cappings, increased its up-market image and sales were strong. The car's appeal was broadened in 1965 by variants such as the 2000 Estate, one of the most handsome load-carriers of its generation, which wasn't bettered at the time.

Best of the bunch however was the 2.5 PI of 1968, with the Lucas-injected 2.5-litre engine from the Triumph TR5 – detuned to 132bhp by virtue of a single outlet exhaust manifold, tamer valve timing, and the milder camshaft from the GT6 Mk II.

Top speed leaped to 106mph (170km/h), with 0–60mph (96km/h) in 10.6 seconds. Production of the classic original 2000/2500 saloons and estates ended in 1969. It was a landmark car for Triumph and opened up a new niche market that it very capably filled during its six-year lifetime.

Triumph Stag

1970–1977

ENGINE: V8, 2998cc

POWER: 145bhp

CHASSIS: Monocoque

BRAKES (F/R): Disc/drum

TRANSMISSION: Four–speed manual/ three-speed auto

SUSPENSION: Independent

TOP SPEED: 116mph (185km/h)

ACCELERATION: 0-60mph (96km/h) in 9.3 sec

The Stag looked like a potential world beater when it first appeared in 1970. Triumph had high hopes that it was going to mark a real change in the company's fortune, but expectations of its success were set to be cruelly dashed.

Here was a stylish four-seater V8 convertible that could drastically undercut the foreign opposition. With a hard top to convert it into a cosy Coupe the only Grand Tourer that got anywhere near the Stag's versatility was the Mercedes SL – at twice the price. Available with manual or automatic transmission it sounded wonderful and went very well, with a top speed of 120mph.

Launched to excellent reviews it quickly acquired a reputation for poor reliability in the field. Under-developed, the overhead-cam 3 litre engine had a tendency to overheat and blow its headgaskets, damage its crank and eventually break its timing chains if neglected.

These problems led to its withdrawal from the all-important American market and from that point on its fate was sealed. It struggled on, in mildly improved MkII form, until 1977, never receiving the Rover V8 conversion it had been crying out for right from the very beginning.

That transplant was left to outside specialists, although the original V8 has long since been made reliable. It is not surprising that today good Stags are much sought after as their sheer driving pleasure remains a solid attraction.

Triumph TR7

1975–1981

ENGINE: 4 cylinder, 1998cc

POWER: 105bhp

CHASSIS: Monocoque

BRAKES: Disc/drum

TRANSMISSION: Four/five-speed manual. Three-speed auto

SUSPENSION: Independent front, live axle rear

TOP SPEED: 110mph (178km/h)

ACCELERATION: 0-60mph (96km/h) in 9.1 seconds

The TR7 was a completely new kind of Triumph sportscar for the '70s. It was a wedge-shaped Coupe with a four cylinder engine built to satisfy a new and more demanding clientele. It was only available in closed form for most of its life. Unfortunately, it was never a particularly pretty sight and it was also highly controversial.

Powered by a 105bhp 1998cc version of Triumph's slant-four, the car's top speed was only 110mph, well down on the meaty straight-six TR6. The promised and anticipated Dolomite Sprint engined version never materialised, although some prototypes were built.

A five-speed gearbox made the car a nicer drive from 1976 and the TR7 did handle and ride better than its forebears but, somehow, lacked the one thing it should have had in abundance – a strong personality. A

convertible didn't appear until 1979, by which time the car was already on death row, beset most of its life with build-quality problems typical of the kind that dogged Triumph throughout this period of its history.

One uplifting last-ditch development was the V8 engined TR8 which gave the car the kind of power it should have had from the beginning. But by then (1980) it was too late, and British Leyland closed down the TR7 production lines in 1981.

Unloved as it was, it would be a mistake to dismiss the TR7 as a complete and utter flop. 112,000 were built in just six years – which, by the standards of the company and the British motory industry of the time, was a fairly respectable amount.

Torpedo

1948

ENGINE: Flat-six, 5491cc

POWER: 166bhp

CHASSIS: Separate steel chassis

BRAKES (F/R): Drum

TRANSMISSION: Four-speed manual

SUSPENSION: independent

TOP SPEED: 120mph (195km/h)

ACCELERATION: 0-60mph (96km/h) in 10 seconds

The Tucker Torpedo was the most exciting car of 1948. While every other American manufacturer simply dished out big, unimaginatively engineered machinery to the same old Formula, Preston Tucker conceived a rear engined saloon that was both fast and futuristic, with safety features ahead of its time such as a crushable passenger compartment and a pop-out windscreen. Its wide-track stance and low slung fast-back styling were completely original and, under the skin, features such as all-independent suspension put it years ahead of the competition.

Tucker assembled a talented design team and raised millions on the stock market to fund development. A massive former Chicago aircraft factory was leased with which to build the car.

Inspired by its specification 300,000 people placed orders for the Torpedo but, behind the scenes, the massive 9.7 litre former Helicopter engine and over ambitious Tuckermatic transmission were giving trouble. At the eleventh hour a much smaller Air Cooled Motors flat-six and ex-Cord transmission were substituted but by then it was too late – Tucker had run out of money and hit trouble with the Wall Street power brokers because the production cars didn't include all the features he'd promised his investors.

Tucker was indicted for fraud and, although his name was cleared, it came to late for the Torpedo, of which just 37 examples had been built when the plant closed down. A further 14 were built up from remaining parts. If Preston Tucker had been a little less ambitious and a little more patient, his car could have changed the face of the American industry. It remains the greatest 'nearly' car of all.

Vixen

1967–1973

ENGINE: Four–cylinder, 1588cc

POWER: 88bhp

CHASSIS: Tubular backbone

BRAKES (F/R): Disc/drum

TRANSMISSION: Four-speed manual

SUSPENSION: Independent

TOP SPEED: 106mph (170km/H)

**ACCELERATION: 0-60mph (96km/h)
in 11 seconds**

Under new ownership of Arthur and Martin Lilley, TVR, sportscar builders of Blackpool, Lancashire, became a more professional company. The 1967 Vixen, son of the earlier Grantura, was one of the first products of this new approach.

Outwardly the entry-level TVR looked much like its predecessor with the usual 'sausage bonnet' front end. A closer inspection revealed new 'Manx-tail' styling with a bigger rear window and MkI Cortina lights behind, at the rear.

Although the first few cars had an MGB engine, TVR policy was now to offer just one unit, the 88bhp 1599cc Ford Cortina GT lump, matched to the excellent Ford four-speed gearbox. The

optional brake servo became standard on the S2 of 1968, which also had a longer wheelbase chassis developed for the Tuscan SE, bolt-on (not bonded on) body panels, twin bonnet vents and Cortina MkII rear lights. The S3 of 1970 had a 92bhp engine, and vents in the front wings.

It was still available as a kit but the new Lilley management no longer encouraged do-it-yourselfers and, in any case, by the turn of the decade new British purchase tax rules wiped out the kit market. The 1600M carried on the tradition of a small-engined TVR after 1973, but by then the majority of buyers were opting for the much faster 3 litre models.

Tuscan V6

1969–1971

ENGINE: V6, 2994cc

POWER: 128bhp

CHASSIS: Tubular frame

BRAKES (F/R): Disc/drum

TRANSMISSION: Four-speed manual

SUSPENSION: Independent

TOP SPEED: 125mph (200km/h)

ACCELERATION: 0–60mph (96km/h) in 8.3 seconds

TVR began building fibreglass sports cars with tubular-chassis frames in the 1950s, and they sold most of them as kits to be built at home. The first cars had four-cylinder engines but, in the 1960s, TVR offered the Griffith with Ford V8 power and the Tuscan V6, the first of a long line of cars using the 3-litre Ford 'Essex' engine.

In concept the Tuscan V6, launched in 1969 at £1,500 for the do-it-yourself kit, was a niche-filler between the four-cylinder Vixen and the slow-selling Tuscan V8. The chassis and demountable body was a Series Two Manx-tail Vixen with Tuscan V8 alloy wheels and brakes, and Ford's 3-litre V6 engine (giving 128bhp) and four-speed gearbox – optionally over-driven on third and top – it also had the strengthened Salisbury Power-lock differential of the V8. The only way you could spot one from the outside was by the badging and twin exhaust pipes. The delicate corner bumpers, big tapering rear window and Mk II-Cortina rear lights were pure Vixen.

In fact, only 101 V6 Tuscans were built between 1969 and 1971. Its engine, the unit from the Ford Zodiac 3-litre, didn't meet North American emission regulations, and TVR couldn't sell the Tuscan there with 'dirty' power. It was this scenario that gave rise to the TVR 2500 with a 'clean' Triumph straight-six engine, but the V6 would live in the improved M-series models.

TVR 350I

1982–1990

ENGINE: V8, 3528

POWER: 190bhp

CHASSIS: Tubular backbone

BRAKES (F/R): Disc

TRANSMISSION: Five-speed manual

SUSPENSION: Independent

TOP SPEED: 138mph (220km/h)

ACCELERATION: 0-60mph (96km/h) in 6.0 seconds

The 1980 Tasmin was a new breed of plush and pricey TVR in the mould of the Lotus Elite. Fashionably angular, it appeared first with the German 2.8 Ford V6. The problem was that things didn't get really interesting until the V8 350i was announced to the market in 1982.

These 138mph machines were initially built for the Arab market. However, they soon banished the V6 Tasmin from the TVR order books. You could understand why buyers loved their beefy exhaust notes and muscular performance. Most of them were convertibles using Rover's injected Vitesse V8, good for 190bhp.

The 350i spawned a whole raft of ever more aggressive derivatives throughout the 1980s, increasing TVR's stature as a maker of credible performance cars. The shape seeemed to date quickly but exhibitionists were attracted to the car's extrovert character.

If the shape didn't have much class, then the chassis of the 350i certainly did, offering composure, poise and instant oversteer if necessary. Production of the 350i held out until 1990, with no slackening of demand, as TVR began to prepare their new range of Griffith and Tuscan sportscars that really took the company into the big league.

Cerbera

1995–

ENGINE: V8, 4185cc

POWER: 350bhp

CHASSIS: Tubular space frame

BRAKES (F/R): Disc

TRANSMISSION: Five-speed manual

SUSPENSION: Independent

TOP SPEED: 180mph (288km/h)

ACCELERATION: 0-60mph (96km/h) in 4.0 seconds

Other TVRs had looked good and performed strongly but the Cerbera was different. For the first time here was a TVR with its own bespoke engine.

This was in the form of a 4.2 litre V8 packing a 350bhp punch, the promise of 185mph and scorching acceleration. Best of all, this came for the price of an ordinary executive saloon.

Engine apart, the Cerbera was mostly traditional TVR, the GRP body covering tubular space frame. It was a fixed head only though, with an imaginative 2+2 interior that showed little evidence of the parts-bin plundering so typical of this type of low-volume car.

The engine had flat plane crank that gave it a much busier, less brutal engine note than the Rover-engined cars. Low down it wasn't as torquey either, but a light flywheel allowed pin-sharp pick-up for devastating through-the-gears acceleration. The Cerbera was renowned for the way it could demonstrate its power. It could accelerate up to 100mph (162km/h) in 9 seconds – supercar-beating speed.

However, the Cerbera was a supercar in all but price. It was the car that put TVR on the map at last as maker of sportscars that were more than fit to be compared with the best offered by marques with more established pedigrees and higher prices.

4-Litre R

1964–1968

ENGINE: Straight-six, 3909cc

POWER: 175bhp

CHASSIS: Monocoque

BRAKES (F/R): Disc/drum

TRANSMISSION: Three-speed automatic

SUSPENSION: Independent front, live axle rear

TOP SPEED: 112mph (179km/h)

ACCELERATION: 0–60mph (96km/h) in 12.7 seconds

Launched in 1964, the Vanden Plas 4-litre R was the only fruit of a liaison between Rolls-Royce and the British Motor Corporation (BMC). It was a high-specification, wood-and-leather luxury saloon based on the 3-litre A110 Westminster shell, but using a 4-litre Rolls-Royce straight-six engine.

Externally, it sported clipped tail fins and horizontal tail-lights, and more upright front and rear windscreens to increase the headroom inside. The shell was stiffened to improve the handling, and featured smaller 13in. (33cm) wheels.

Inside, the 4-litre R had the full Vanden Plas treatment, with Connolly leather on the seats and lavish use of walnut veneer on the dashboard, door cappings and picnic tables. With a claimed 175bhp, the smooth, all-alloy,

seven-bearing, Rolls-Royce straight-six gave the 4-litre R an impressive turn of speed. It accelerated cleanly up to 100mph (160km/h), and road testers attained up to 112mph (179km/h) flat-out.

With the standard Borg-Warner Model 8 automatic gearbox – there was no manual option – the car would whisk up to 60mph (96km/h) in an effortless 12.7 seconds. The pay-off was a dismal 14mpg (20litres/100km) thirst, and the critics were underwhelmed by the 4-litre's overlight power steering, which lacked feel and precision.

A projected output of 100 cars a week from the Vanden Plas Kingsbury works never actually rose above 60. Even at that rate there was a big stockpile of 4-litre Rs. BMC ended the unequal struggle in 1968, with sales totalling just 6,555 cars.

Cresta PA

1957–1962

ENGINE: Straight-six, 2262/2651cc

POWER: 83–95bhp

CHASSIS: Monocoque

BRAKES (F/R): Drum

TRANSMISSION: Three-speed, overdrive and automatic

SUSPENSION: Independent front, live axle rear

TOP SPEED: 90–97mph (144–155km/h)

ACCELERATION: 0–60mph (96km/h) in 15.2 seconds

The PA Cresta was Vauxhall's answer to the Ford Zodiac. It was inspired by the products of its American parent, General Motors of Detroit.

Small fins sprouted from the rear wings, whilst the front and rear windscreens had a heavy 'dog leg' wrap-around. Optional whitewall tyres and two-tone paint only served to further emphasize the heavy American influence.

Launched in 1957, the PA Cresta – and its cheaper, less-well-equipped sister, the Velox – leaned heavily on the E-series, although they were physically bigger cars. The smooth, understressed 2262cc pushrod six-cylinder powerplant remained, now producing 75bhp for a reasonably impressive top speed of well over 90mph (144km/h).

The three-speed, column-shift gearbox was all-synchromesh now, but the PA retained the leaf-sprung rear axle and soft wishbone-and-coil-spring suspension of its predecessor. For 1959, the wrap-around rear screen became one-piece. There was also the addition of a new grille, along with the option of an estate model.

The best of the bunch was the 1960 model, with a bigger 2.6-litre, 95bhp engine. Other recognition points were bigger wheels and fins. Two-pedal Hydramatic control or dual overdrive for the manual gearbox broadened the car's appeal. Servo-assisted front disc brakes were a welcome improvement, too. Sales remained strong right up to the model's demise in 1962.

Chevette HS

1978–1979

ENGINE: Four-cylinder, 2279cc

POWER: 135bhp

CHASSIS: Monocoque

BRAKES (F/R): Disc/drum

TRANSMISSION: Five-speed

SUSPENSION: Independent

TOP SPEED: 115mph (184km/h)

ACCELERATION: 0-60mph (96km/h) in 8.5 seconds

Exciting '70s Vauxhalls are few and far between. However, in anyone's book, the HS Chevette definitely has to be one of them.

Dealer Team Vauxhall built the first HS Chevettes in 1976 for use in the RAC rally, but it would be another two years before production cars were available. These were built in order to homologate the rally car for high-level competition. This meant they were available to be offered to an interested section of the public.

Although quite crude in many ways these HS Chevettes – based on the innocuous three-door Chevette hatch – made exciting road machines. They were powered by a 135bhp, twin-cam versions of

Vauxhall's 2300cc slant-four engine. The 240bhp rally cars had used a Lotus cylinder head and a ZF gearbox but for the road car a Vauxhall designed 16-valve head and a Getrag box were fitted.

All of the HSs were painted silver and had front and rear spoilers. They also came with very chunky alloys. Despite this, the HS Chevettes managed to look an awful lot less vulgar than many of their hot-hatch contemporaries.

Quick and capable the 2300HS was probably a bit too exotic and expensive to appeal to your average 'boy racer' – it was £1,000 more than an RS 2000 Escort – which was why it remained exclusive. Only 400 of them were built.

Astra 16V

1988–1991

ENGINE: In-line 16-valve four-cylinder, 1998cc

POWER: 156bhp

CHASSIS: Steel monocoque, three-door

BRAKES (F/R): Disc

TRANSMISSION: Five-speed manual

SUSPENSION: Struts front, trailing arms rear

TOP SPEED: 131mph (210km/h)

ACCELERATION: 0–62.5mph (100km/h) in 7.8 seconds

The press's disappointment when it first saw the boxy lines of the Mk 2 Golf was turned into delight when General Motors launched the new Astra a year later, in 1984. Here was a car that looked like it was fit for the 1980s, with a low, rounded nose, rising window line and high tail. The body details, such as the wing mirrors and bumpers, were carefully smoothed and integrated into the futuristic shape.

Vauxhall had already built up a decent reputation for its SRi- and GTE-badged sports models, and few were disappointed by the unveiling of the smartly dressed 1.8-litre GTE in the late summer. The interior was as well considered as the outside, getting heavily bolstered sports seats and an LED-display dashboard.

The feeling was that the Golf GTI was just too civilized and refined to be a hot hatch; the

Vauxhall was rather more brutal and torquey in its delivery.

The Astra, though, trumped the hot-hatch pack in 1988 with the launch of a new 2.0-litre 16-valve engine for the GTE. An advanced mass-market design for the era, the engine produced 154bhp which, mounted in the relatively light shell of the GTE, allowed near-supercar in-gear performance. Unlike the vast majority of the new 16-valve engines, the General Motors unit was very torquey – even at low revs.

The Astra GTE 16V was about as hot as the hot hatch got in its heyday, but that didn't guarantee sales success. It was quick, but had a rather ragged ride, a propensity to torque-steer and was difficult to drive flat-out. Ultimately, the Golf's suave image and more mature road behaviour proved a more popular driving blend with buyers.

Lotus Carlton

1990–1992

ENGINE: Twin-turbocharged 24-valve in-line six-cylinder

POWER: 377bhp

CHASSIS: Steel monocoque, four-door

BRAKES (F/R): Disc with ABS

TRANSMISSION: Six-speed manual

SUSPENSION: Twin-tube struts front, multi-link rear

TOP SPEED: 176mph (282km/h)

ACCELERATION: 0–62.5mph (100km/h) in 5.4 seconds

To open a motoring magazine of the late-1980s was to be confronted by an extraordinary number of super-high-performance road cars. The most extreme road-car-based super-car was the Lotus Carlton, which was launched in a blizzard of bad publicity. The company had to suffer police chiefs in the UK sounding off about the irresponsibility of producing a car capable of 176mph (282km/h). GM gave the respected mid-sized Carlton/ Omega saloon to Lotus (its then subsidiary) to be transformed into a car that could carry four people, and frighten the average Ferrari at the same time.

Most of the modification centred on the straight-six 24-valve engine. The block was strengthened, then Lotus increased the capacity and made some modifications to the head design. Manifolds that could resist 750-degree temperatures were fitted, along with twin Garrett turbochargers. A new electronic management unit was sourced, and a charge cooler was also fitted, to massively increase the effectiveness of the turbos.

Other GM companies around the world were roped in, with Holden in Australia donating the rear differential and Chevrolet the Corvette ZR-1's six-speed manual gearbox. One of the finest body styling kits ever seen – designed by Lotus's Julian Thomson – completed the Lotus Carlton project. A four-wheel-drive conversion was mooted, but GM decided against the investment.

The result was a staggeringly fast car – 0–100mph (160km/h) in 11.8 seconds – that was also very refined. The Lotus Carlton was well-capable of crossing continents faster than anything else on four wheels, but needed the kind of road space to exploit its performance that's rarely on offer in Europe.

Calibra

1990–1997

ENGINE: In-line 16-valve four-cylinder, 1998cc

POWER: 150bhp

CHASSIS: Steel monocoque, three-door

BRAKES (F/R): Disc with ABS

TRANSMISSION: Five-speed manual

SUSPENSION: Struts front, semi-trailing arms rear

TOP SPEED: 139mph (222km/h)

ACCELERATION: 0–62.5mph (100km/h) in 7.9 seconds

During the second half of the 1980s, the work of the German-based General Motors styling studio was some of the best in the world. After the advanced Astra and slickly aerodynamic Carlton, the Cavalier range arrived in 1988 to widespread praise. This was as much for the excellent detailed industrial design as for its efficient and extremely tidy overall shape.

Even so, few expected the next big surprise – a two-door coupe based on the Cavalier chassis. The stunning Calibra was a serious wake-up call for the mass-market motor industry.

In base-model, 2.0-litre, 8-valve form, the Calibra recorded a Cd figure of just 0.26, making it the most aerodynamic car on sale – an extraordinary achievement, when it was based on the running gear of an ordinary family hatchback – and one that was exemplary in its space-utilization.

Overseen by design boss Wayne Cherry, the Calibra project was completed quickly. According to GM designers who worked on the car, the speed at which it went into production was the real reason why those in the design department managed to preserve the radical styling, which was rarely the case with mainstream car design of the late-1980s.

The Calibra range included two four-wheel-drive models. One was powered by the well regarded 16-valve engine and another by a turbocharged engine, good for over 200bhp.

The Calibra was never a great car to drive, even if was very quick in Turbo form. Try as it did, it was never convincing in any of the departments that make for a pleasurable drive. It was, though, probably one of the best-styled mass-produced cars ever seen.

Beetle

1945–1978

ENGINE: Flat-four, 1131–1584cc

POWER: 25–78bhp

CHASSIS: Separate platform

BRAKES (F/R): Drum and disc/drum

TRANSMISSION: Four-speed

SUSPENSION: Independent

**TOP SPEED: 50–84mph
(80–134km/h)**

**ACCELERATION: 0–60mph (96km/h)
in 47.6 seconds (1131cc), 18
seconds (1500cc)**

The Volkswagen Beetle was borne out of Adolf Hitler's desire to provide low-cost motoring for the masses in Nazi Germany. Ferdinand Porsche created the original rear-engined, air-cooled saloon in the 1930s, although very few were actually built before the Second World War. Production started again in 1945 with a very basically specified 1100cc model. In the USA, the model started a small-car revolution as millions of Americans, looking for a cheap second car, fell in love with the Beetle's good engineering, practicality and economy. The size of the flat-four pushrod engine grew from 1131cc to 1200cc in the 1950s, and the range expanded with the pretty Karmann Ghia sports models and a cabriolet version.

Calls for a faster, more modern-driving Beetle were answered in the mid-1960s with 1300 and 1500 models – they gained an all-synchromesh gearbox, and could be

had with disc brakes, and even a semi-automatic transmission – but ultimately VW's reliance on one basic model had serious effects on sales in the latter part of the decade.

VW tried to woo buyers with dressed-up Beetles. The 1961 1500cc version amounted to nothing more than a rebodied version of the original car, and even the big four-door 411 with its fuel injection didn't fool many buyers. Salvation eventually arrived in the form of the water-cooled, front-engined Golf in 1974, which became a benchmark for front-wheel-drive hatchbacks.

The last German-built Beetles came out of the Wolfsburg factory in 1978, but the model was still in production under licence in the late-1990s in South America. Total sales stand at 21 million – it overtook the Ford Model T's 15 million in the early 1970s – a figure that is unlikely ever to be beaten.

Karmann Ghia

1955–1974

ENGINE: Flat-four, 1192-1584cc

POWER: 30-50bhp at 3400rpm

CHASSIS: Platform chassis

BRAKES (F/R): Drum (later disc/drum)

TRANSMISSION: Four-speed manual

SUSPENSION: Independent

TOP SPEED: 87mph (139km/h)

ACCELERATION: 0-60mph (96km/h) in 25 seconds

The exotic Italian looks of the VW Karmann Ghia hid annoyingly uncharismatic VW Beetle power, but for some that very deceit has always been part of the car's charm – and the looks of the Karmann Ghia are more than enough to make you forgive it almost anything – even its reliance on Beetle power.

Designed by Ghia of Italy and built by Karmann in Germany – on a slightly widened Beetle platform – the car made an instant hit when it was revealed to the general pubic in 1955 and sales lasted strongly for almost 20 years.

A Cabriolet followed the Coupe into production in 1957 and in America they sold by the boatload – nobody seemed to mind that

these rather expensive machines drove just like a humble VW Beetle. In fact, some enthusiasts almost seemed to relish the fact of this limitation.

There was an attempt to update the concept in 1961 when a bigger more modern version with a 1500 engine was offered, based on the Type 3 VW. It was plusher and faster but never really caught on like the original – although 42,000 sales in eight years is hardly disastrous.

The power went up gradually over the years, but the Beetle's trusty backbone platform, air-cooled, rear-mounted engine and rattling exhaust note remained the same. As did, of course, the well-known reliability.

Golf GTI Mk1

1976–1983

ENGINE: In-line four-cylinder, 1595cc

POWER: 110bhp

CHASSIS: Steel monocoque, three- and five-door

BRAKES (F/R): Disc

TRANSMISSION: Four- and five-speed manual

SUSPENSION: Front struts, torsion bar rear

TOP SPEED: 112mph (179km/h)

ACCELERATION: 0–62mph (100km/h) in 9.3 seconds

In the early 1970s Volkswagen desperately needed to replace the venerable Beetle. A lot of people – especially in the motoring press – thought that the company might fail to meet the challenge. It didn't and it replaced the old stalwart with a car that was destined for amazing success.

The Mk1 Golf was an utterly conventional interpretation of what was becoming the Euro-small-car norm – a hatchback body powered by a transversely mounted front engine. Because it was a Volkswagen, the Golf was sensibly and ruggedly engineered and, perhaps best of all, it came wrapped in a shell crisply styled by the Italian designer Giugiaro.

However, the Mk1 Golf will be remembered for more than those admirable traits. It was the basis for one of the most enduring automotive trends ever – the hot hatch. It is this fact that makes it a true landmark car and has forever ensured it a place in the history of the automobile.

Early in the model's life, enthusiast VW engineers tried fitting the Golf with the 110bhp fuel-injected 1.6-litre engine destined for the Audi 80 GTE, and the resulting prototypes had a magic that made production – and eventual popularity with the car buying public – a certainty. The winning formula for the original GTI was simple: a punchy engine, stiffish suspension and some sporty additions and trim.

The unobtrusive chin spoiler, restrained striping and alloy wheels made for a subtle, but effective formula that was still being copied more than two decades later.

The combination of reliability, strong performance and razor-sharp handling meant the GTI became the common man's sports car.

Golf GTI Mk2

1983–1991

ENGINE: In-line four-cylinder, 1781cc

POWER: 112bhp

CHASSIS: Steel monocoque, three- and five-door

BRAKES (F/R): Disc

TRANSMISSION: Five-speed manual

SUSPENSION: Front struts, torsion bar rear

TOP SPEED: 114mph (182km/h)

ACCELERATION: 0–62mph (100km/h) in 9.8 seconds

With the success of the Mk1 Golf, VW wasn't going to stray too far from a winning format with its replacement model. Even so, there was initial widespread disappointment that the Mk2 Golf wasn't a bigger step away from the original.

However, VW must have been very satisfied when early scepticism was replaced by near-universal rapture for a simply, but very robustly, engineered car, whose styling matured superbly.

The Mk2 GTI was launched shortly after the more humdrum models, and stuck to the subtle GTI badging, red-lined bumpers, striped upholstery and Pirelli 'P-slot' alloy wheels. The 113bhp 1.8-litre engine also remained, but the new car was more refined and stable – as well as benefiting from improved braking for right-hand-drive markets.

Despite competition from faster, if more ragged, GTis – like the Peugeot 205 and Ford Escort XR3i – the Golf achieved a near-impregnable up-market image. This was entirely in keeping with the car's engineering and build quality.

Two years after the launch, VW offered the 1.8-litre engine with a twin-cam 16-valve head. This pushed the power up to 136bhp and offered higher performance – although it was at the apparent cost of peaky torque delivery.

Demand accelerated through the 1980s, and in the UK it fitted perfectly the 'yuppie' image that had pervaded the nation. The overweight Mk3 replacement arrived in 1992, and disappointed with its lack of sparkle and wallowy handling. The Mk2 is yet to be properly replaced by VW.

Corrado

1992–1996

ENGINE: Narrow-angle V6, 2861cc

POWER: 190bhp

CHASSIS: Steel monocoque, three-door

BRAKES (F/R): Disc

TRANSMISSION: Five-speed manual

SUSPENSION: Struts front, torsion beam rear

TOP SPEED: 145mph (232km/h)

ACCELERATION: 0–62mph (100km/h) in 6.7 seconds

Although it appeared to be a replacement for the Mk1-Golf-based Scirocco coupe, VW was aiming the Mk2-based Corrado at higher targets. They were gunning for the wave of sophisticated Japanese coupes that arrived during the late 1980s, and the entry level Porsches that were proving so popular.

The styling was something of a surprise after VW's previously conservative approach, but the bluntly-drawn front and rear were a great success with critics and car buyers alike.

The car also benefited from reasonable space for four passengers and good boot space. Some commentators, however, were not impressed by the Passat-derived dashboard and switchgear.

Despite the humble underpinnings, the Corrado's handling was superb, although the performance on offer from the entry-level 1.8-litre 16v engine wasn't startling. VW also offered an innovative 160bhp supercharged version of the 8-valve GTI engine in the car for those wanting more power.

However, the engineering involved in the G60's supercharger was both difficult and expensive, and it was destined to never capture the promise that it had once seemed to offer.

Once VW had fitted its new, narrow-angle 190bhp VR6 engine into the Corrado's nose, a modern classic was born. The languid power delivery and fail-safe handling blended to create an uncommonly satisfying car that could switch between long-legged grand tourer and frenzied sports car in an instant. Production was halted in 1996 with the special-edition VR6 Storm model.

Golf VR6

1992–1997

ENGINE: Narrow-angle 2.8-litre V6, 2792cc

POWER: 174bhp

CHASSIS: Steel monocoque, three- and five-door

BRAKES (F/R): Disc with ABS

TRANSMISSION: Five-speed manual

SUSPENSION: Struts front, torsion beam rear

TOP SPEED: 138mph (221km/h)

ACCELERATION: 0–62mph (100km/h) in 7.5 seconds

Initial press reception for the Mk3 Golf was somewhat muted – a fact that must have greatly stung Volkswagen on its release. For a start it suffered from dumpy styling, the lower-end models handled poorly and the 2.0-litre GTI was much less of a sporting car than its well-liked forerunner.

All eyes were on the powerful VR6, which promised to invent a whole new market niche – the red-hot hatch. VW had struggled for many years and overcome several complex problems to make their innovative compact narrow-angle V6 engine production-ready. The two banks of the engine were so close together that the engine could be fitted with a single cylinder head.

Although this saved a great deal of money over a conventional V6, the main reason for creating the VR6's compact dimensions was to enable it to fit sideways into the nose of what was a family hatchback. It was certainly a ground-breaking idea.

Enthusiasts who expected some kind of super-GTI were disappointed to find that VW saw the Golf VR6 as a kind of mini executive express, and tuned the car's chassis for long-distance comfort rather than sporting prowess.

Where the Golf VR6 was bad – poorly damped rear suspension, and poor attention to detail, especially in such areas as build quality on earlier models – it was abysmal, but where it was good, as in the extraordinary character of the engine, the turbine-smooth power delivery and liquid gearchange, it was quite exceptional.

Thanks to the unique engine, no rival manufacturer has been able to offer the same blend of six-cylinder refinement and six-cylinder muscle in a compact car. That is why it has proved so addictive to its many enthusiasts.

Volkswagen Passat

1996–

ENGINE: In-line 20V turbocharged four-cylinder, 1781cc

POWER: 150bhp

CHASSIS: Galvanised steel monocoque, four- and five-door

BRAKES (F/R): Disc/disc with ABS

TRANSMISSION: Five-speed manual, or five-speed Tiptronic

SUSPENSION: Four-link front, torsion beam rear

TOP SPEED: 135mph (216km/h)

ACCELERATION: 0–62mph (100km/h) in 8.9 seconds

By the mid-1990s Volkswagen had developed a solid and well-deserved reputation for building fine small and medium-sized hatchbacks. This wasn't too surprising as they had pioneered the market way back in 1976. More importantly, they had always managed to keep themselves and their cars one step ahead of the opposition in this now crowded section of the market.

However, the company had greater ambitions: "We build good small cars, but we need to build good big ones as well," said an executive prior to the launch of the fourth-generation Passat.

The Passat marked VW's determination to grab the middle-market initiative and nothing – either in styling or engineering terms – was left to chance. This showed when the Passat was launched.

Under the bold skin the Passat is effectively an Audi – marked out by the characteristic longitudinally mounted engine – and sized to sit between the Audi A4 and the Audi A6. The Passat, however, was cheaper than both, and offered the family car driver more space, better build quality and a more prestigious badge than Ford, Vauxhall/Opel or even Peugeot/Citroën could possibly manage. A capacious estate was also offered, as was the option of Audi's quattro drivetrain.

VW boss Ferdinand Piech's manic devotion to engineering excellence meant the Passat featured a fully galvanised rust-proof body, and an exemplary standard of fit and finish inside and out.

The Passat was also the first of the new VWs to feature the company's revised styling theme of prominent wheel arches, large wheels and a hooped roofline, all drawn from the Concept One styling model – a post-modern interpretation of the classic Beetle profile.

New Beetle

1998–

ENGINE: In-line 8V four-cylinder, 1984cc

POWER: 115bhp

CHASSIS: Galvanised steel monocoque, three-door

BRAKES (F/R): Disc

TRANSMISSION: Five-speed manual

SUSPENSION: Struts front, torsion beam rear

TOP SPEED: 110mph (176km/h)

ACCELERATION: 0–62mph (100km/h) in 11.6 seconds

Concept One – an ultra-modern interpretation of the Beetle's classic form – was going to be nothing more than a little light relief for the then troubled Volkswagen Group. It was styled under the leadership of J.C. Mays in VW's Californian design studio Concept One, made its debut at the Detroit Motor Show in 1994, and became the one vehicle that grabbed the headlines from the premier event.

The car touched off something deep in the collective American psyche – perhaps because five million original Beetles had been sold there – and the project took on a life of its own. Soon VW had included it in breathtakingly audacious plans to build seven completely different model ranges on one set of common under-skin components.

Despite having to be built on the floorpan of the Mk4 Golf, VW engineers and designers managed to retain the simple, even child-like, geometry of the original styling model, even if practicality was sacrificed.

Although headroom for front passengers was massive, those in the back were rather more cramped. The sloping tail enclosed a small boot, although the hatchback and folding seats increased the potential carrying capacity.

Inside, the Beetle's dashboard design was just as radical, featuring a single instrument pod and beautifully detailed fittings. The new Beetle was even equipped with a dash-mounted vase, just like the original car. The Mexican-built Beetle was launched in the USA in late-1997, to an ecstatic response and vast waiting lists.

Volvo

120 Series (Amazon)

1956–1970

ENGINE: Four-cylinder, 1583-1985cc

POWER: 60-115bhp

CHASSIS: Monocoque

BRAKES (F/R): Drum (later disc/drum)

TRANSMISSION: Four-speed manual

SUSPENSION: Independent front, live axle rear

TOP SPEED: 108mph (174km/h)

ACCELERATION: 0–60mph (96km/h) in 13 seconds

Probably the most famous Volvo of all the 120 Series, like the PV, had American-inspired styling, with the same taught bull-nosed look as the Chryslers did in their mid-1950s period. It also gained a reputation for durability, with an amazing resistance to corrosion because of the high quality steel used in its construction.

Mechanically it was pure PV444 at first with three speeds on the early 121s, but the range began to look quite a lot more interesting after 1958, with the introduction of the twin-carb 122S, which had four speeds as standard.

As the 1960s unfolded so did the successful Amazon range – it was only sold under that name in Sweden, though. It grew ever more complex. With the bigger 1.8 litre B18 engine of 1961 came optional two-door bodywork (131) and again you could have single carb or twin-carb (S) variants.

The five-door Estate was known as the 221 and later, with twin carbs, the 222. Overdrive was a commonly specified option on the Amazon, and front disc brakes were standard from 1965 onwards. Rarest and most desirable of the breed was the 123 GT with its stronger 115bhp, coming in the much better looking two-door shell.

To some of its enthusiasts, the Amazon has become known as 'The car that cannot die.' The durability of the Volvo 120 series is certainly without doubt, as the surprisingly high number of roadworthy – and rust free – Amazons still attest to.

PV444

1958–1965

ENGINE: Four-cylinder, 1414-1583cc

POWER: 40-85bhp

CHASSIS: Monocoque

BRAKES (F/R): Drum

TRANSMISSION: Three and four-speed

SUSPENSION: Independent front, live axle rear

TOP SPEED: 95mph (156km/h)

ACCELERATION: 0–60mph (96km/h) in 14 secs

Before World War II Volvo built its reputation on solid, boring, middle class saloons but realised it would have to broaden its appeal post-war to encompass smaller, more mass market cars. The PV 444 emerged in 1947, a new fashionably styled two-door that looked suspiciously like a downscaled 1942 American Ford.

Its lively performance soon gained it a good reputation and before long Volvo were making sales in-roads into the American market where it was appreciated for its quality, reliability and sporty handling. The first ones had a 1414cc engine, the last 1583cc, twin carbs and 85bhp.

The 444 became the 544 in 1958 with five seats, a one-piece screen and a new-style dashboard. You could have 3 or 4 speeds and a single or twin-carb (Sport) engine.

From 1961 onwards, the cars gained the up-rated five-bearing engine of the more modern 'Amazon' models, which in 85bhp form took the top speed up to the magic 100mph.

There was only one body style variant on the 'PV' theme, the Duett estate first seen in 1953. It was a dual-purpose vehicle that could be used as either a van or a passenger carrier.

Durable and fun to drive – not something that could really be said of certain later Volvos – these no-nonsense vehicles are now very fashionable classics, appreciated for their durability and wonderful period styling.

P1800
1800S, 1800E and 1800ES

1960–1972

ENGINE: Four-cylinder, 1778/1986cc

POWER: 100–125bhp

CHASSIS: Monocoque

BRAKES (F/R): Disc/drum

TRANSMISSION: Four-speed manual, three-speed automatic

SUSPENSION: Independent front, live axle rear

TOP SPEED: 102–115mph (163–184km/h)

ACCELERATION: 0–60mph (96km/h) in 11 seconds

Although not a sports car in the true sense of the word, the Ghia-styled Volvo P1800 was a good long-legged cruiser. It featured an overdrive gearbox and had a respectable top speed of over 100mph (160km/h). The 107bhp engine was a twin-carburettor, in-line four-cylinder unit with a four-speed transmission sending the drive to a coil-sprung live rear axle. Servo-assisted front disc brakes were standard, giving safe but uninspiring handling.

Handsome and practical, the P1800 quickly gained popularity – despite a high price tag – and its profile was further raised by weekly appearances in the TV series 'The Saint', in which it was driven by the show's star Roger Moore (who also owned one in real life). The initial production of Volvo's stylish P1800 coupe was somewhat convoluted. The steel bodies were built in Britain by Pressed Steel in Scotland, and

then sent to Jensen of West Bromwich who, with chassis parts supplied from Sweden, assembled the complete cars.

But Volvo was never very happy with the quality of the Jensen-built cars, and in 1964 it shifted production to Sweden. With more power and detail trim differences, the car became known as the 1800S. The engine developed into a full two-litre unit, with 115bhp in 1968; from 1969, it gained fuel injection, increasing the power output to 125bhp.

The final evolution of the design was the 1800ES, Volvo's answer to the Reliant Scimitar GTE 'Sporting Estate'. With its extended roof-line and rear hatchback, it was a useful small load carrier with a good turn of speed. However, by the early 1970s Volvo was beginning to lose interest in its old sports car, and stopped production in 1973.

Volvo 240

1974–1993

ENGINE: 590cc two-cylinder OHV

POWER: 82-155bhp

CHASSIS: Monocoque

BRAKES (F/R): Drum/drum (later disc front)

TRANSMISSION: Four-speed manual and automatic

SUSPENSION: MacPherson struts front, live axle rear

TOP SPEED: 90-120mph (144-192km/h)

ACCELERATION: Not available

From the late 1960s Volvo had been working on an experimental safety car (VESC), developing features such as airbags, anti-lock brakes and telescopic bumpers. Now it was time to introduce these features to the public. Volvo took the old 144 and stuck a new nose on it. They fitted a new range of overhead-cam engines, improved the front suspension with MacPherson struts and grafted on the safety features from the VESC.

Offered as a two-door, four-door and five-door estate, the 240 was the archetypal safe 'brick' with which Volvo became synonymous. It was used as the benchmark for safety standards in the United States was renowned for its build quality

and handling.

A diesel unit was added in 1979 and then, in the 1980s, came greater performance. First came the 240 GLT producing 140bhp, and then the 240 Turbo producing 155bhp. For those wanting power and space, 1983 saw the introduction of the Turbo Wagon, offering the performance and handling of the Turbo in an estate car.

Volvo kept the changes to a minimum from then on, but commemorated the end of the run in 1993 by producing around 2,000 special-edition 240 Classics, with some nice trim touches and an edition number. By the time the 240 line came to a halt, it had produced close to three million cars.

V70 XC

1997–

ENGINE: In-line, light-pressure turbocharged five-cylinder, 2435cc

POWER: 193bhp

CHASSIS: Steel monocoque, five-door

BRAKES (F/R): Disc with ABS

TRANSMISSION: Five-speed manual

SUSPENSION: Struts front, trailing arms with transverse spring rear

TOP SPEED: 132mph (211km/h)

ACCELERATION: 0–62mph (100km/h) in 8.5 seconds

With its newly acquired nous for marketing-led niche models, Volvo excelled itself by managing to tie together the areas in which it was strongest with the latest cutting edge technology that had been developed by its engineers. The V70 XC was a clever niche-market car that straddled the off-road and estate-car markets – not easy in anyone's books.

The problem of harnessing high power outputs in the 850's front-wheel-drive chassis was solved by the introduction of an effective and friendly four-wheel-drive system. Volvo then added some fashionable off-roader styling cues such as raised ground clearance, more chunky and solid bumper styling and double-sided interior carpeting.

It wasn't quite the first to the market though. Subaru had applied a similar treatment to its 'Outback'

4x4 Legacy and Impreza estates, which sold in huge numbers. Volvo also found success in the USA, the XC taking a significant chunk of all Volvo's US sales. Unlike the more rugged Subaru, the XC was a luxurious, leather-lined cruiser. It had macho appeal but it didn't stint on the creature comforts that modern drivers yearn for.

It had more than power, style and character to slot in beside the conventional truck-based luxury Sport Utility Vehicles (SUVs) so popular in the USA in the late 1990s. The XC marks the beginning of the end for that lumbering SUV – a gas-guzzling, polluting and dangerous (to other road-users) strain that was starting to attract the attention of an increasingly unsympathetic US government. If nothing else, we should all be grateful to Volvo for that fact.

Wartburg **311**

1956–1962

ENGINE: 900cc, three-cylinder

POWER: 37bhp

CHASSIS: Monocoque

BRAKES (F/R): Drum

TRANSMISSION: Four-speed manual

SUSPENSION: Independent

TOP SPEED: 62-72mph (99-115km/h)

ACCELERATION: Not available

After the war BMW's former factory in Eisenach, East Germany, continued to build BMW-badged cars until stopped by legal action. Even so, EMW (Eisenacher Motoren-Werke) as the company was forced to call itself, continued to produce cars bearing an uncanny resemblance to BMW models.

In 1955, however, work began on the manufacture of the Wartburg 311. This wasn't a wholly original model, taking as its basis the IFA F9, which had developed from a pre-war DKW project using a three-cylinder two-stroke engine. The Wartburg had a longer wheelbase and a full-width, four-door body, giving a more spacious interior. It was more refined all round, and

looked prettier too.

Heavy-guage steel was used for the chassis with aluminium castings adding to excellent build quality. Independent double wishbones in the rear suspension and coil springs at the front provided a ride to match.

Initially the Wartburg came with a two-speed manual gear box, but this was replaced with a four-speed crash gearbox, and in 1958 the engine was upgraded to give 40bhp, making a top speed of 72mph achievable.

The 311 gave rise to a variety of off shoots, includng an extraordinary-looking dormobile, the Camping, and it continued in production until 1962.

Willys-Overland Jeep

1945–

ENGINE: L4, 2260cc

POWER: Not available

CHASSIS: Monocoque

BRAKES (F/R): Drum

TRANSMISSION: Three-speed manual

SUSPENSION: Independent

TOP SPEED: 87mph (139km/h)

ACCELERATION: 0–60mph (96km/h) in 25 seconds

The idea of a universal military vehicle surfaced in 1939. The Jeep (from the initials GP, General Purpose) soon surfaced. US military wanted a replacement for the aging motorcycles with side cars used in World War I, and the Model T Ford had proved itself too fragile for the job.

The Willys Military Model MB Jeep – or, as the army called it, "Truck, quarter-ton, four by four, and command reconnaisance" – was mechanically simple. The 4-cylinder engine could run at 4000 rpm for 100 hours without a break, and without challenging the three-speed manual transmission. Oil and air filters were easily accessible, as was the simple fold-back cloth roof. The headlamps were on swinging levers, so that they could be pointed at the engine for repair work at night. It could tilt 50 degrees left or right, drive up a 40-degree slope, and pull other vehicles through mud. Jeeps even served as ambulances, card tables and altars on occasion.

The sheer numbers of Jeeps in production – there were 40 being made every hour – made sure that they became forever linked with the US army. After the war, there was a lot of demand. Servicemen all wanted Jeeps of their own, and the US Department of Agriculture wanted them for hundreds of different purposes. Willys responded with the CJ-2A, CJ standing for Civilian Jeep, and you could find them everywhere, particularly where other vehicles could not get to. It really could do everything except bake a cake.

Willys continued the Jeep up to 1970, although from 1955 they were part of the Kaiser corporation. They sold the line to American Motors in 1970, and it passed to Chrysler, the current owners, in 1987.

Wolseley 6/80

1948–1954

ENGINE: In-line six-cylinder, 2215cc

POWER: 72bhp

CHASSIS: Monocoque

BRAKES: Drum all round

TRANSMISSION: Four-speed manual

SUSPENSION: Independent

TOP SPEED: 85mph (136km/h)

ACCELERATION: 0–60mph in 27 seconds

The 1948 Wolseley 6/80 became the classic British police car of the 1950s. When it was phased out of service, many of the cars were snapped up by members of the public keen to get their hands on one of the cars that the forces of law and order had been using. This wasn't to do with macho appeal, it was simply the recognition of good, solid engineering.

Based on the M/O Series Morris saloons, the basic monocoque body looked very like an overgrown Morris Minor – which was effectively what it was – although in 6/80 form it shared the 13in. (33cm) longer wheelbase of the Morris Six. At the front were the bold Wolseley grille and twin spotlights to give it a more upmarket image. The 6/80 shared its straight-six overhead-cam engine with the Morris Six, too – at 72bhp, it wasa a heady 6bhp more powerful than the Morris.

Its best feature was its interior, with leather seats, a wooden dashboard and the rare luxury of a heater as standard equipment. Less impressive was the steering, a bishop-cam system which was both vague and heavy – and no doubt somewhat off-putting in a car that was quite powerful for its day. The 6/80 could easily manage 85mph (136km/h). The last 6/80s were built in 1954 but, amazingly, some remained in use with police forces until 1961.

Xedos 6

1992–1998

ENGINE: 24-valve V6, 1995cc

POWER: 146bhp

CHASSIS: Steel monocoque, four-door

BRAKES (F/R): Disc with ABS

TRANSMISSION: Five-speed manual

SUSPENSION: Struts front, struts and transverse links rear

TOP SPEED: 131mph (210km/h)

ACCELERATION: 0–62.5mph (100km/h) in 9.3 seconds

The increasing confidence and ability of Japanese manufacturers towards the end of the 1980s saw them trying to expand into new markets and directly challenge some of the most prestigious car makers in the world. In the USA and Europe, the Japanese makers realized that their image was suffering because of buyers' memories of their early cars, which were always reliable but rarely pretty and usually unfashionable.

A number of Japanese makers decided that all-new branding was the way to conquer the elusive prestige markets dominated by the German brands. In the USA, Nissan had invented Infinity and Toyota created Lexus – which proved to be a massive success. Mazda decided to invent the Xedos – supposedly pronounced 'K-see-dos' – marque for the European market. The US equivalent, which would use the same two-model range, was to be called Amati. But Amati was cancelled

at the eleventh hour, at a huge cost to the company.

Xedos went ahead in Europe from mid-1992, and started with the BMW 3-series-sized Xedos 6 saloon. Mazda could hardly have started with a more eye-catching car. The Xedos 6 was exceptionally distinctive for a saloon of the time, and was especially noted for the small heart-shaped grille – even if this hinted at a heritage the brand clearly didn't have.

Many observers thought it looked like a small, modern Jaguar – a thought that is hard to dispute, especially around the pert tail and very steeply raked rear window.

Mazda said the car was styled

after a satellite-linked styling competition between Japan, Germany and the USA. Others suggested the car started life at Ford and was then worked up by various teams of Mazda stylists.

Under the skin was the running gear of the ordinary Mazda 626 family car, although the Xedos's 2.0-litre V6 was a real gem and the dashboard design and heater controls genuinely innovative.

Despite the mechanical slickness and beautiful lines, neither the Xedos 6 – nor its rather duller bigger brother, the Xedos 9 – was a great success. The project proved that brand creation was impossible without genuine technical innovation.

Hyena

1993–1994

ENGINE: Turbocharged 16-valve in-line four-cylinder, 1995cc

POWER: 210bhp

CHASSIS: Steel floorpan and structure, aluminium body panels

BRAKES (F/R): Disc with ABS

TRANSMISSION: Five-speed manual

SUSPENSION: Struts front and rear

TOP SPEED: 143mph (229km/h)

ACCELERATION: 0–62.5mph (100km/h) in 5.4 seconds

Italian coachbuilder Zagato has a long history of turning out the dramatic, the bizarre and the plain ugly. After the madcap Alfa SZ coupe, many commentators wondered where the tiny Italian design house would go to next.

Typically, Zagato managed the unexpected – Dutchman Paul Koot, who owned a restoration business, commissioned 75 Lancia Delta Integrale-based coupes, which would cost £75,000 when they were launched in 1993. The result was tagged the Hyena, and was easily Zagato's best contemporary work.

The small, tight, muscular body lacked any extraneous fittings – the bumperless bodywork helped give the car great overall tension. In fact, a sketch shown by Zagato had the outline of a pouncing hyena contained within the car's shape. The bespoke interior was made entirely of carbon-fibre, and helped make the Hyena a much lighter car than the Integrale on which it was based, helping to boost the performance.

Comparison with a mad dog seemed to be borne out by road-test reports on the Hyena. The four-wheel-drive chassis and turbocharged engine were made even more effective by a car that had phenomenal direction-changing abilities – partly because it didn't roll at all – and massive amounts of grip.

The Hyena's precise steering and powerful brakes were also praised. It was also said to be more refined than the Delta, and the Hyena's ride – while not exactly soft – was described as remarkably pliant considering that this was designed as an out-and-out performance machine.

ZIL 114

1956–1987

ENGINE: V8, 5980-6962cc

POWER: 220-300bhp

CHASSIS: Separate ladder type

BRAKES (F/R): Drum, later Disc/drum

TRANSMISSION: Two-speed automatic

SUSPENSION: Independent front, live axle rear

TOP SPEED: 118mph (188km/h)

ACCELERATION: No figures

The ZIL was a large limousine built for high-ranking communist party officials in Russia. It was targeted as a replacement for the ZIS, which had been nothing more than a 1941 Packhard under a different badge. The tooling had been bought off the Americans after the war.

Though heavily influenced by contemporary American design, the ZIL was more its own car. It has a 220bhp V8 engine – with light alloy cylinder heads – and a push-button two-speed automatic gearbox. ZIL drivers enjoyed luxury unknown to the average Lada or Moskvitch owner, including power steering and electric windows.

The earlier 111 G limousine had a 5 litre engine and could manage 105 mph, but from 1967 there was a longer wheelbase 114 model with a 7 litre V8 and a claimed 300bhp. These cars had squarer, more modern styling, and came with disc front brakes and air conditioning as standard. No one has been able to come up with too much information on what type of options were available.

As Communism crumbled and Russia began to open up there was less need for a special state party-officials-only limousine and ZIL production finally finished in 1987.

The ZIL was one of the luxuries of life that high-ranking members of the party enjoyed and there was never any problem with other traffic. No one driving a Lada or Moskvitch was foolish enough to halt the progress of a person in a ZIL.

Index of Models